THE WORD OF GOD
AND THEOLOGY

THE WORD OF GOD
AND THEOLOGY

KARL BARTH

translated by

AMY MARGA

t&t clark

Published by T&T Clark International
A Continuum Imprint
The Tower Building, 11 York Road, London SE1 7NX
80 Maiden Lane, Suite 704, New York, NY 10038

www.continuumbooks.com

British Library Cataloguing-in-Publication Data
A catalogue record for this book is available from the British Library

ISBN: 978-0-567-63500-6 (hardback)
978-0-567-08227-5 (paperback)

Typeset by Pindar NZ, Auckland, New Zealand
Printed and bound in Great Britain

CONTENTS

LIST OF ABBREVIATIONS

Anfänge I + II	*Die Anfänge der dialektischen Theologie*, Vol. I, 2nd ed., Jürgen Moltmann, ed. (Munich, 1962).
BC	*The Book of Concord. The Confessions of the Evangelical Lutheran Church*, Robert Kolb and Timothy J. Wengert, eds. (Minneapolis: Fortress Press, 2000).
BDT	*The Beginnings of Dialectical Theology*, James M. Robinson, ed. (Richmond: John Knox Press, 1968).
BRC	*Book of Reformed Confessions* (Louisville: The Office of the General Assembly, 1999).
BSLK	*Die Bekenntnisschriften der evangelisch-lutherischen Kirche*, Deutscher evangelischer Kirchenausschuß [The German Evangelical-Church Committee], ed. (Göttingen: Vandenhoeck & Ruprecht, 1930, 1979).
BSRK	*Die Bekenntnisschriften der reformierten Kirche*, E. Fr. Müller, ed. (Leipzig, 1903).
Busch	Eberhard Busch, *Karl Barth: His Life from Letters and Autobiographical Texts.* John Bowden, trans. Philadelphia: Fortress, 1976. ET of *Karl Barths Lebenslauf, Nach seinen Briefen und autobiographischen Texten* (Munich: Christian Kaiser Verlag, 1975).
Bw.R.	Karl Barth and Martin Rade, *Ein Briefwechsel*, Christoph Schwöbel, ed. (Gütersloh: Mohn, 1981).
Bw.Th. I + II	Karl Barth and Eduard Thurneysen, *Briefwechsel Band I, 1913–1921*, in Eduard Thurneysen, ed., *Karl Barth Gesamtausgabe, V Briefe* (Zürich: Theologischer Verlag Zürich, 1973); and *Briefwechsel Band II, 1921–1930* (Zürich, 1974).
CD	Karl Barth, *Church Dogmatics*, G.W. Bromiley and T.F. Torrence, eds. and trans, (Edinburgh: T&T Clark, 1936ff.).

Chr. Dogm.	Karl Barth, *Die christliche Dogmatik im Entwurf: Die Lehre vom Worte Gottes. Prolegomena zur christliche Dogmatik, 1927*, Gerhard Sauter, ed. (Zürich: Theologischer Verlag Zürich, 1982).
CR	*Corpus Reformatorum*, Vol. 71 (*Calvini Opera*, Vol. 43) (Berlin, 1834ff.).
CSEL	*Corpus Scriptorum Ecclesiasticorum Latinorum* (Vienna/Leipzig/Prague, 1866ff.).
CW	*Die Christliche Welt. Evangelisch-Lutherisches* (later: *Evangelisches*). *Gemeindeblatt für Gebildete aller Stände* (in 1920–1921 it carried the subtitle *Wochenschrift für Gegenwartchristentum*; from 1922 on it had no subtitle) (Leipzig/Marburg i.H.; Stuttgart/Gotha; Gotha).
EKG	*Evangelisches Kirchengesangbuch* (introduced in 1950).
GA	*Karl Barth Gesamtausgabe, I–V* (Zürich: Theologischer Verlag Zürich, 1973ff.).
GD	*The Göttingen Dogmatics, Instruction in the Christian Religion*, Vol. 1, Geoffrey W. Bromiley, ed. (Grand Rapids, MI: William B. Eerdmans Publishing Company, 1990).
GERS	*Gesangbuch für die evangelisch-reformierte Kirche der deutschen Schweiz* (introduced 1891).
HpB	*Die Dogmatik der evangelisch-reformierten Kirche, dargestellt und aus den Quellen belegt*, Hermann Heppe, ed. (Elberfeld, 1861). Newly edited by Ernst Bizer (Neukirchen, 1958); ET *Reformed Dogmatics*, repr. (Grand Rapids, MI: Baker Book House, 1978).
KBA	Karl Barth Archive; unpublished materials by item number.
KD	Karl Barth, *Die Kirchliche Dogmatik* (Munich: Christian Kaiser Verlag, 1932; Zürich: Zollikon, 1938–1959, 1967).
KGB	*Gesangbuch für die evangelisch-reformierten Kirchen der deutschsprachigen Schweiz* (introduced 1952).
LBW	*Lutheran Book of Worship* (Minneapolis: Augsburg Publishing House, 1978).
LW	*Luther's Works*, J. Pelikan and H. Lehmann, eds. (St. Louis and Philadelphia: Concordia and Fortress Press, 1955).
MPL	J.-P. Migne, *Patrologiae cursus completes, Series latina, accurante* (Paris, 1844–1845).

p.	Parallel positions to the cited Biblical quotation in the Synoptics.
PhB	*Philosophische Bibliothek* (Hamburg : Meiner).
RG	*Reformierte Gesangbuch* (introduced in 1998).
RGG	*Die Religion in Geschichte und Gegenwart*, 3rd ed. (Tübingen, 1956–1965).
Romans 1919	Karl Barth, *Der Römerbrief (Erste Fassung) 1919*, H. Schmidt, ed., *Karl Barth Gesamtausgabe, II: Akademische Werke* (Zürich: Theologischer Verlag Zürich, 1985).
Romans 1922	Karl Barth, *Der Römerbrief* (Munich: Chr.Kaiser Verlag, 1921 [the first printing of the new ed.]); ET *The Epistle to the Romans*, translated from the 6th ed. by Edwyn C. Hoskyns (London: Oxford University Press, 1933).
Schaff I, II, III	*The Creeds of Christendom*, Philip Schaff, ed. (Grand Rapids, MI: Baker Book House, 1985).
SchmP	Hermann Schmid, *Die Dogmatik der evangelisch-lutherischen Kirche, dargestellt und aus den Quellen belegt* (1843). Newly edited by Horst G. Pöhlmann (Gütersloh, 1979–1983).
SgV	*Sammlung gemeinverständlicher Vorträge und Schriften aus dem Gebiet der Theologie und Religionsgeschichte.*
T.u.C.	Karl Barth, *Theology and Church: Shorter Writings 1920–1928*, Louise Pettibone Smith, trans. (New York: Harper and Row, 1962).
Th.u.K.	Karl Barth, *Die Theologie und die Kirche.* Volume 2 of *Gesammelte Vorträge* (Munich: Chr. Kaiser Verlag, 1928); ET *Theology and Church: Shorter Writings (1920-1928),* translated by Louise Pettibone Smith, (New York: Harper & Row, 1962).
TVZ	Theologischer Verlag Zürich
Unterricht	*Unterricht in der christlichen Religion, Erster Band:Prolegomena 1924*, Hannelotte Reiffen, ed., *Karl Barth Gesamtausgabe, II: Akademische Werke* (Zürich: Theologischer Verlag Zürich, 1985); ET *The Göttingen Dogmatics, Instruction in the Christian Religion*, Vol. 1, Geoffrey W. Bromiley, ed. (Grand Rapids, MI: William B. Eerdmans Publishing Company, 1990).
V.u.kl.A. 1905–1909	Karl Barth, *Vorträge und kleinere Arbeiten 1905–1909*, Hans-Anton Drewes and Heinrich Stovesandt with

	H. Helms, eds., *Karl Barth Gesamtausgabe, III/1* (Zürich: Theologischer Verlag Zürich, 1992).
V.u.kl.A. 1909–1914	Karl Barth, *Vorträge und kleinere Arbeiten 1909–1914*, Hans-Anton Drewes and Heinrich Stovesandt with H. Helms and Friedrich-Wilhelm Marquardt, eds., *Karl Barth Gesamtausgabe, III/2* (Zürich: Theologischer Verlag Zürich, 1993).
V.u.kl.A. 1922–1925	Karl.Barth, *Vorträge und kleinere Arbeiten 1922–1925*, Holger Finze, ed., *Karl Barth Gesamtausgabe, III/3* (Zürich: Theologischer Verlag Zürich, 1992).
WA	Martin Luther, *Luthers Werke. Kritische Gesamtausgabe*, J.F.K. Knaake, *et al.* (Weimar: Hermann Böhlau, 1883ff.).
WA.B.	Martin Luther, *Luthers Werke. Kritische Gesamtausgabe. Briefwechsel*, G. Bebermeyer and O. Clemen, eds. (Weimar: Hermann Böhlau, 1930–1970).
WA.TR	Martin Luther, *Luthers Werke. Kritische Gesamtausgabe. Tischreden*, Karl Drescher, ed. (Weimar: Hermann Böhlau, 1912–1921).
W.G.Th	Karl Barth, *Das Wort Gottes und die Theologie* (*Gesammelte Vorträge I*) (Munich, 1924; Zürich: Zollikon [probably between 1936–1940]).
ZThK	*Zeitschrift für Theologie und Kirche*, Tübingen.
ZZ	*Zwischen den Zeiten*, Munich.

TRANSLATOR'S PREFACE

In the Foreword of the 1957 edition of *The Word of God and the Word of Man*, the original translator of Karl Barth's 1924 collection of essays, Douglas Horton — who was astute and humble enough to comprehend the theological revolution that is outlined between these pages — wrote that Barth's "mighty *Dogmatik* has grown out of the soil which is to be found in *The Word of God and the Word of Man*." It is in this spirit that this new translation should be read. The core commitments of Barth's theology and the trajectory of his later thought can all be found here. While the title has been changed to more closely reflect Barth's own original title, *Das Wort Gottes und die Theologie*, the material that Horton discovered so many decades ago remains as riveting and moving today. The goal of this new translation is to bring Barth's "passionate intensity and penetrating faith," as Horton describes it, to a new generation of English readers, and introduce them to a theology that has profoundly shaped Christian thought in both the German-speaking and English-speaking worlds to this day.

Several of the essays that originally appeared in the 1924 edition of *Die Wort Gottes und die Theologie* have been brought into the *Karl Barth Gesamtausgabe* (*GA*), the German critical edition of Barth's works, sermons, letters, and conversations, which are published in connection with the Karl Barth Archive in Basel, Switzerland by the Theologischer Verlag Zürich. The following essays, including the critical apparatus that appears as footnotes, have been translated from *GA, III: Vorträge und kleinere Arbeiten 1922–1925*, edited by Holger Finze and published by Theologischer Verlag Zürich in 1990: "The Need and Promise of Christian Proclamation"; "The Problem of Ethics Today"; "The Word of God as the Task of Theology"; "The Substance and Task of Reformed Doctrine." The page numbers that appear in square brackets throughout this translation refer to the German edition of the *GA* for these particular essays.

The remaining essays have been translated directly from the original edition, with the exception of "The Christian in Society" and "Biblical Questions, Insights, and Vistas," reprinted (in German) on pages 3–37 and 49–76 respectively of *Anfänge der dialektischen Theologie*, Teil I, edited by Jürgen Moltmann and published by Christian Kaiser Verlag in 1962. However, the reader will note that the page references in square brackets in these two essays refer to the pagination of the original *Das Wort Gottes und die Theologie* from 1924. The archivist of the Karl Barth Archive, Dr. Hans-Anton Drewes, graciously and thoroughly researched and provided the footnote apparatus for the essays that do not yet appear in the *GA*. He also wrote the introductions to these essays and provided the Scriptural references that appear throughout. These essays and the critical apparatus will appear in volume 48 of the *GA: Vorträge und kleinere Arbeiten 1914–1921,* which is forthcoming.

When it comes to rendering the German into English, I have striven to remain as close to Barth's own rhetorical style as possible while taking into consideration the universal nature of the German term, *der Mensch*. Therefore, I have translated *der Mensch* and *man* as "the human," "the individual" or "humanity." Where gendered pronouns in reference to humanity could not be avoided, I have used masculine pronouns to reflect the language style of Barth's time. Regarding language about God, I use masculine pronouns and imagery according to Barth's own usage. I have used "church" or "Church" for Barth's *Kirche*, leaving it up to the context to determine whether he is speaking of the universal Church or denominational bodies. The term "community" is used wherever possible as a translation of "*Gemeinde*," except where it is quite clear that he is most likely referring to a "congregation." The New Revised Standard Version of the Bible is the main source for many of the Scriptural quotations.

Horton noted in his 1957 edition of *The Word of God and the Word of Man* that he changed the original ordering of Barth's lectures out of reasons of "logic." For the sake of remaining true to Barth's own words in the Preface about the "*inner* line" that runs through these lectures, given across a span of several years, I have restored the essays to their original ordering, which is also chronological.

My deepest thanks and respect goes to Hans-Anton Drewes, who tirelessly and swiftly produced the introductions, Scriptural references and the footnote apparatus for the three essays which have not yet appeared in the *GA*. Without his friendship and intellect, this volume could not have appeared as it is. I would also like to thank Dr. Darrell Guder, along with Clifford Anderson, of Princeton Theological Seminary, who invited me to participate in the annual Karl Barth Translators' group. My work with this group has helped me better understand the joys, challenges, and technical knowledge that accompany the important work of translating and transmitting German theology into English, especially that of Barth. Thanks goes as well to the Rev. Dr. Tom Trapp for his assistance with the translation of the introduction to "The New World in the Bible," and my research assistants at Luther Seminary, Saint Paul, Minnesota, Joshua Miller and the Rev. Justin Nickel, who helped copy edit and proofread the manuscript and to John Burgess for his invaluable suggestions for "The Problem of Ethics Today." I am grateful to Bruce McCormack, who invited me into this translation project several years ago, and who translated the first part of "The Christian in Society." Thanks to Victoria Smith at Luther Seminary for all her assistance and I am also grateful to Thomas Kraft at Continuum and his colleague Anna Turton, and Graeme Holbrook at Pindar, for their patience and willingness to see this project to its conclusion. Finally, I owe my deepest gratitude to my husband, Uwe, and I would also like to thank my young son, Leo, for giving me the gift of time to bring this volume to fruition.

My hope is that Barth's theology in this volume will give English-speaking readers access to his early thought, and inspire them to take the time to learn the original language so as to explore Barth's life and work in his native tongue.

Saint Paul,
Minnesota, 2010

PREFACE

The suggestion of a new, unified edition of these lectures came first from my publisher (as is the rule in such cases). I heartily agree with it because it is always good to formulate anew the things that have already been said, and further, all those things that I have expressed on different kinds of occasions will now be altogether in one place.

On the way from the first of these lectures to the last, the reader may remain the same but the landscape changes. This is true not only of the *style* (as a Swiss country pastor I employ a somewhat different language from that which I use as a Reformed professor in Göttingen), and not only true of the *concepts* (naturally, I would no longer characterize the voice of the preacher in the wilderness as "the voice of conscience" as I have done here in the first lecture!!), it is also true of the *content*. Many things which stood in the foreground of my mind at one time have had to recede and vice versa. And there is no lack of places where over the course of the years I have had to very consciously revise and make excisions in my thought. But all this does not deny my earlier work. For even in all its one-sidedness, it still remains my own. Sympathetic readers will keep this in mind and read the entire work — as a whole.

I would just like to note that the themes of these lectures were set, and even partly formulated, by the organizers of the various gatherings at which they were delivered. If, in spite of this, I may still call this collection a complete whole, then its unity must be sought along an *inner* line.

Göttingen,
February 1924

CHAPTER 1

THE RIGHTEOUSNESS OF GOD, 1916

Barth delivered this lecture in the city church of Aarau in January 16, 1916, at the invitation of Pastor Rudolf Wernly.[1] The congregation at Aarau had "for decades made good use of four Sunday evening lecture-hours during the winter: November, December, January, and February," To which sometimes even "two external speakers at a time" were invited. For the occasion of January 1916 ("when possible on the sixteenth of January"), Wernly requested that Barth give a lecture "on a theme from the field of history or from Christian, church or social life that you deem appropriate." What may have played a role in this particular request by Wernly is the sermon that he heard Barth deliver in the Bern Cathedral on October 17, 1915.[2] After two audacious moves, which in hindsight Barth could not rightly claim to be breakthroughs,[3] he was uncertain how to interpret Wernly's inquiry. "Is this a burning coal upon my head or a 'triumph of the good' or both?" In any case, he "of course" agreed to do a lecture on "the righteousness of God"[4] — an "interesting and highly relevant theme" for which Wernly thanked Barth and requested that he submit his "choice of chorals"[5] because "the evening lecture begins promptly at eight o'clock in the evening, accompanied by an organ prelude and a hymn sing by the congregation."[6]

Barth wrote the lecture amidst the recent excitement around the "great debauchery" by the Safenwil industrialist, Hochuli, "at the celebration of his daughter's marriage . . . which he threw for his five hundred employees and workers."[7] Barth reacted to this local event in worship on the morning he was to deliver his lecture in a sermon which spoke "against the dominating power of mammon, to which

---

1   Letter from R. Wernly to Barth, December 12, 1915 (KBA 9315.170).
2   Karl Barth, *Predigen 1915*, Hermann Schmidt, ed., *GA I* (Zürich: TVZ, 1996), 399–410.
3   One occasion was the petition to cancel the synod worship service on November 11, 1915 in Aarau (see *Bw. Th.* I, 100f.). The other occasion was the lecture, "Kriegszeit und Gottesreich," which Barth delivered on November 15, 1915 in Basel (see *Bw. Th.* I, 101–104, esp. 102).
4   Letter from Barth to Thurneysen, December 20, 1915 (*Bw. Th.* I, 118).
5   Postcard from R. Wernly to Barth, December 12, 1915 (KBA 9315.174).
6   As stated in the postcard (KBA 9315.174).
7   Letter from Barth to Thurneysen, January 10, 1916 (*Bw. Th.* I, 123f.).

everything is subject."[8] The same gravity can be perceived in the lecture that he gave in Aarau that same evening.

The only reactions to Barth's lecture that evening came from an audience member who remarked that he had "never heard such a lecture in our national church," "which came so directly from the heart, but which also penetrated all the hearts that are not completely shut."[9] The other was from Wernly himself from January 17, 1916, who wrote,

> I want to shake your hand in deep gratitude for the powerful wake-up call to the conscience . . . and for the fine development of the motif of the building of the tower of Babel as well as the clear reference in your conclusion to Jesus Christ, who is the atoning finale to the foregoing difference between the will of humans and the will of God.[10]

Both men asked about a possible publication of the lecture; Wernly suggested the journal, *Neue Wege*.

Barth ended up sending his text to Leonhard Ragaz in February of that same year, to whom he promised in December 1915 to "once again" send a sermon for the *Neue Wege*.[11] Ragaz thanked Barth for the lecture, which "had all the fundamental characteristics of a sermon." He claimed that he was "in agreement" with the "main point" of Barth's lecture — with "the whole piece actually, since the rest of it is so precisely bound up with the main point." The lecture would "appear in the April issue, where it would act as a kind of response to an article by R. Liechtenhan that will have appeared in the March issue."[12]

Upon the printing of Barth's lecture, Ragaz added a reference to Liechtenhan in the journal notes which stated: "See the article 'Können wir an eine sittliche Weltordnung glauben?' von R. Liechtenhan in issue No. 3."[13] Barth, who was aware of the intent of this reference, appeared concerned when he contacted Liechtenhan about it (who incidentally was his cousin), but the answer he received reassured him: "I did not notice in that particular footnote any digs at my article from your side," remarked Liechtenhan, who claimed to see "no opposition of the positions whatsoever, but rather a mediating between the two articles."[14]

At first glance, it does appear that there are parallels in the content of the two articles. In his lecture, Barth calls the righteousness of God "the deepest, innermost,

8   Karl Barth, *Predigen 1916*, Hermann Schmidt, ed., *GA I* (Zürich: TVZ, 1998), 20–28, esp. 23.
9   Letter from G. Wild to Barth, January 17, 1916 (KBA 9316.10).
10   Letter from R. Wernly to Barth, January 17, 1916 (KBA 9316.9).
11   Letter from Barth to Ragaz, December 10, 1915 (KBA 9215.33).
12   Letter from Ragaz to Barth, February 26, 1916 (KBA 9316.30).
13   *Neue Wege. Blätter für religiöse Arbeit*, 10 (1916): 143–154, esp. 143, n. 1. The reference here was to the article by R. Liechtenhan, "Können wir an eine sittliche Weltordnung glauben?" *Neue Wege*, 10 (1916): 93–109.
14   Letter from R. Leichtenhan to Karl Barth, May 10, 1916 (KBA 9316.60).

surest fact of our lives. There is nothing more certain than that which the conscience gives for our sake."[15] This statement appears to be related to statements made by Liechtenhan, who argues that the "Yes" does not become the sense and goal of our existence as "knowledge out of experience." Rather "it is a voice out of the deepest depths of our soul, something in us that answers the call of Jesus," a call which "speaks to our conscience." But this thing in us "is not therefore less certain, but in fact, much more certain."[16] Methodologically speaking, however, Liechtenhans's dialectical argument is clearly quite different from Barth's thetical argument. Liechtenhan tries to guide the listener to faith by way of an "apologetic," as he noted in his letter to Barth. As he states at the conclusion of his article, "in one's faith," The believer has "the key to the revelation of the living God who greets him everywhere in nature and history, who, through his ethical ordering of the world, guides it for the sake of the salvation of his children."[17] This train of thought could indeed, as Leichtenhan foresaw,[18] be understood by some readers as precisely that attempt "to approach the fact with critical reason" which Barth rejected.[19] Even Ragaz tended to agree with this view.

Despite the explicit appeal to read the collection as "a complete whole," which appears in Barth's 1924 Preface to this volume, Barth placed this text at the forefront of his first essay collection — perhaps a sign that he really did see in this particular lecture the *beginning* of an "*inner*" unity.

[5] It is a voice of the preacher in the wilderness, "Prepare the way of the Lord! Make his paths straight. Every valley shall be filled and every mountain and hill shall be made low. The crooked shall be made straight, and the rough ways made smooth, and all flesh shall see the salvation of God." [Isa. 40.3-5; cf. Lk. 3.4-6f.]. This is the voice of our conscience, telling us that God is righteous. The righteousness of God is not a question, not a riddle, not a problem. It is a fact — the deepest, innermost, surest fact of our lives. There is nothing more certain than that which the conscience gives for our sake. The simple question is what kind of attitude we want to *take* toward this fact.

You do not need to approach this fact with critical reason. Reason sees the small and the great, but not "the great thing." It sees the temporal but not the final, the derived but not the original, the complicated but not the simple. It sees what is human but not what is divine [Mt. 16.23f.].

You will not be taught about this fact by your fellow human. Indeed,

15   Barth, *W. G. Th.*, 5.
16   Liechtenhan, "Können wir an eine sittliche Weltordnung glauben?" (108).
17   Ibid., 109.
18   Barth, *W. G. Th.*, 5.
19   Barth, *W. G. Th.*, 3.

a person can tell another about the righteousness of God. A person can perhaps provoke another to reflect upon the righteousness of God. But no human being can bring another to the particular, immediate, resounding certainty that stands behind such a phrase. We human beings must once again learn to speak to one another with authority and not like the scribes [Mt. 7.29f]. For now, we are all much too artificial and jaded to be able to really help one another.

You must let the conscience speak, for it already speaks of God's righteousness in such a way that that righteousness becomes a certainty to you. The conscience can be practically reduced to silence and crushed to oblivion. It can be led astray to the point of folly and [6] wrongdoing, but it will always remain the place — the only place — between heaven and earth where God's righteousness is revealed to us. Like a blast of trumpets from another world, it interrupts your reflections about yourself and your life, about the fulfillment of your obligations to your family, your vocation, and your nation — it even interrupts the nurturing of your religious thoughts and feelings.

Its message comes to you here as a bitter and urgent accusation, and there as a quiet, steadfast assertion, here as an imperious task set for your will, there as an obstacle, an inexorable "No" placed before you, here as a curse and condemnation which knocks you to the floor, and there as a saving joy that lifts you out of yourself and out of everything which exists. In every case it is always waking you and calming you in the most profound way and by equal measure. It is always pointing you in the same direction. In every change and transformation of your life experience it attests that your living and learning have a goal. In the up and down of every joy and sorrow it speaks to you of an existence which is higher than any joy and deeper than any sorrow. In the rise and fall of all sincerity, strength, and purity of our will, the conscience speaks to us from a will which remains true to itself. This is the righteousness of God.

We are delighted whenever we discover a will that seems to be clear and constant in itself, free from arbitrariness and fickleness, a will which orders itself, which is directed toward something and cannot be bent. The conscience tells us that the final and most profound essence of all things is just such a will — that God is righteous. We live by knowing this. But too often we forget it, we overlook it, we trample on it. And yet we could not keep on living if we did not know in the most profound way that God is righteous!

This is so because we suffer from unrighteousness. We are horrified by it. Everything in us revolts against it. We know more of it than we do of righteousness. We constantly have before us, in the great and small activities of our lives, in our own conduct and in that of others, another kind of will before us. And the more closely we look, the clearer this will becomes — a will which does not know any fixed and unbending order, but is founded, rather, on arbitrariness, fickleness, and egoism, a will without faithfulness that is divided and torn, a will with no logic or coherence. [7] This is how we are. This is life. This is the world. Human critical reason wants to come and prove to us that it has always been like this and thus must always stay like this. But we also see the consequences of this unrighteous will. Its name is distress, disorder, disaster of the refined and raw kind, as well as the private and public kind. We have before us compassion and crime, the demons of commercial competition and the war of peoples, the battle of the social classes, and the run-down within every class. We have the economically driven sovereignty above and the spirit of slavery below.

We could certainly explain these things away and prove to ourselves and others quite cleverly that all of it has its necessary reasons. We could imagine that we are inwardly free from these things. But then we will never come to terms with the fact that we are suffering under these things. All of this lies upon us like a heavy burden that cannot be borne. Life bedevils us, whether we admit it or not. We live in its shadow. The unrighteous will pervades our life, dominates it, turns our lives upside-down. We may hide from it for a while, or resign ourselves to it for a while. But obviously, it will never do so with us. The unrighteous will of the world is by nature unbearable. Impossible. We live by knowing that there is actually something else out there besides unrighteousness — and precisely this is the most frightful anxiety that seizes us from time to time. What if unrighteousness has the last word? We are haunted by the thought that the unjust will which now persecutes and tortures us may be the most profound — the only — will in life. And the impossible decision looms: Make your peace with unrighteousness! Surrender yourself to the fact that the world is hell, and conform! That is the way it is.

In this need and fear in the middle of it all comes the assurance of the conscience, unflinching and consistent like the theme of a Bach fugue — no, it is not true! Above all of our warped and weakened wills, above the absurd and lunatic will of the world, there is another will, one which is straight and pure. If *it* is to prevail, it must have another, completely different outcome than that which we see now. When *it* is recognized, another life must come forth. If *it* breaks through, a new world will emerge. [8] Our homeland is where this will prevails. We have lost this home but we can find it again. There is a will of God which is righteous. As a drowning person grasps at a straw, all that lives within us reaches out toward this assurance that our consciences give us. If only we could stand in the shining presence of this other will, not in doubt, but with assurance!

We do not want to only imagine this will as hopeful and wishful thinkers, but as those who can quietly see it and rejoice in it. If only we were no longer strangers to it, but had it for our own! The deepest longing in us is born out of our deepest need: Oh that you would tear open the heavens and descend out of them [Isa. 64.1]! And this is the most overwhelming thing about humanity: oppressed and afflicted by his or her own unright-eousness and the unrighteousness of others, every human being cries out for righteousness, the righteousness God. Whoever understands human-ity on *this point* understands it completely. Whoever reaches out one's hand to another at *this point* can help. This is why the figures of Moses, Jeremiah, and John the Baptist are seared into human memory. They have exposed humanity in our deepest need. They have brought the human conscience to speech. They have awakened in humanity the desire for the righteousness of God, and have kept it awake. They have prepared the way of the Lord [Isa. 40.3].

But now comes a remarkable turn in our experience with the righteous-ness of God. The trumpet of the conscience has sounded, startling us; we feel touched by the sacred but at first it does not occur to us to let ourselves be helped out of our need and anxiety. Quite the opposite. "They said to one another, 'Come, let us make bricks, and burn them thoroughly . . . Let us build ourselves a city and a tower with its top in the heavens, and let us make a name for ourselves; otherwise we shall be scattered abroad upon the face of the whole earth." [Gen. 11.3-4]. So we come to our own rescue and build the Tower of Babel. We lose no time in satisfying the stormy desire for the righteousness of God. And unfortunately, satisfaction means to cover up, to reduce to silence. It is as if we could no longer bear our own perfervid cry. It is as if we were [9] afraid of an all too real and complete fulfillment of our longing. The conscience speaks, we listen: Something must be done! But we do not listen to the end. We are alarmed, but then drowsily stumble away from it before we notice *what* it is actually about and *what* must happen so that something can *really* happen.

We stand here before the most fundamental and tragic error of human-ity. We yearn for the righteousness of God, but we do not let it into our lives and our world — we cannot let it in because the entryway has long been blocked. We know what we actually need, and yet we will not be helped because long ago we pushed aside the one thing we need [Lk. 10.42]. We have postponed it until later, until "better times,"[20] mak-ing ourselves sicker and sicker with substitutes in the meantime. We go off and build the pitiful tower at the Babel of our human righteousness,

---

20   See David Lloyd George, *Better Times: Speeches* (London, 1910). Translated into German by Helene Simon as *Bessere Zeiten*, in *Politische Bibliothek*, E. Bernstein, ed. (Jena: Diedrichs, 1911). Cf. *V.u.kl.A 1909–1914*, 734–738.

our human self-importance, our human earnestness! Our answer to the call of the conscience is *one* great substitute extending over the whole of life, a singular gigantic "as if."[21] So long as we are willing to think, speak, and act according to this "as if" — as if it were serious, as if something were happening, as if we acted in obedience to our consciences — the reality of the righteousness after which we so hunger and thirst eludes us [Mt. 5.6].

Should we call this pride on our part? There is something like pride in it. We are inwardly resentful that the righteousness after which we pant is solely God's affair and can only come to us from God. We would like to take this mighty thing into our own hands and under our own management, as we have done with so many other things. It seems highly desirable that righteousness, without which we could not exist, is simply put into the program by our will. We do not take into account what kind of will it actually is. Without being asked, we seize the right to pose the tumultuous question, "What shall we *do*?" [Acts 2.37] as if it were the first and most pressing question. Let's just get to work as quickly as possible to reform, sanitation, methods, cultural, and religious endeavors of all sorts! Let's just do the "real work"!

Then, before we know it, the trumpet blast of the conscience no longer holds a disconcerting tone. The anxiety in which we found ourselves in the face of the overpowering will of the world gently transforms [10] itself into that pleasant feeling of normality once we have landed again at our activities of reflecting, criticizing, constructing, and organizing. The longing for a new world has lost all its bitterness, sharpness, and agitation; it has become the joy of progress, and now unloads itself gently and securely in commemorative speeches, honorary donor plaques, committee meetings, reviews, annual reports, twenty-five-year anniversaries, and countless mutual bows. The righteousness of God itself has been leisurely transformed from the most secure fact into the highest of a variety of high ideals, and has now become entirely and completely our own affair. This is already evident in our ability to happily hang it out the window as an ideal and then roll it up again like a flag. "You will be like God!" [*Eritis sicut Deus!* Gen. 3.5]. You can act "as if" you were God, you could put God's righteousness to your own use without any effort. This is certainly pride.

It could just as well be called despondency. And it is curious how both of these opposites actually stand by one another in our relation to

---

21   See Hans Vaihinger, *Die Philosophie des Als ob. System der theoretischen, praktischen und religiösen Fiktionen der Menschheit auf Grund eines idealistischen Positivismus. Mit einem Anhang über Kant und Nietzsche* (Berlin: Reuther & Reichard, 1911); ET *The Philosophy of "As if": A System of the Theoretical, Practical and Religious Fictions of Mankind*, C.K. Ogden, trans. (London: 1924; repr. London, 2001).

God. We have a fundamental fear of the flowing of God's righteousness [cf. Amos 5.24] that seeks entrance into our life and our world. The secure citizen is startled when he hears of tuberculosis, general strikes, and war. But it is far more painful for him to think about the radical reversal of life that comes from God, bringing an end to not only the consequences of unrighteousness but to unrighteousness itself. The same cheerful, cultured person, who today so pluckily drives up in his little car of progress and who cheerfully waves the pennants of his various ideals, will anxiously remind you tomorrow, if it comes down to it, that humans are small and imperfect, and that one indeed cannot demand or expect too much of them — cannot be too partial about it, anyway. This will happen as soon as he has finally understood that compared to the righteousness of God there is nothing to reflect upon, to reform or to gain; that, compared to the righteousness of God, every intelligent newspaper article and well-attended convention is completely irrelevant; that it is about a very unilateral "Yes" or "No" toward an entirely new world. We are afraid of the righteousness of God because we hold ourselves to be too small and too human for anything different and new to really be born in ourselves and among us. This is our despair. [11]

And because we are so prideful and so despondent, we build ourselves a Tower of Babel. Therefore the righteousness of God, which we have already seen and touched, has been transformed in our clumsy hands into a whole variety of human righteousness.

I have in mind the righteousness of our morals, the good will that hopefully we all develop and exercise in certain principles and virtues. Indeed the world is full of morality but where have we actually gotten with it? Our morality is always an emergency measure; I would have almost said an artificial dislocation of our will. But it is not a new will. You lift yourself up through your morals, through, let us say, thriftiness, dedication to family, hard work, patriotism, and incidentally or on purpose rise to a level above your own or that of your neighbor. You can tear yourself from the general unrighteousness and build yourself a pleasant garden hut of morals beyond it all — seemingly beyond!

But what has really happened? Will the unjust, self-absorbed, arbitrary will of the world actually be influenced, much less overcome, by your slight movement on the side in your seeming morality? Don't your morals keep you from the insight that you are only all the more strongly chained to them on a hundred other points? Do they not make you blind and hardened against the deep and actual needs of existence? Isn't it remarkable that the greatest atrocities of life — here I think of the capitalistic order of society and the War — can justify themselves on purely moral principles? The devil can also use morals, and he laughs about the Tower of Babel that we erect for him.

The righteousness of the State and of the judges and lawyers — what a wonderful tower! A most necessary and useful substitute to protect us in some measure from certain unpleasant outcomes of our unrighteous will! Very appropriate for quieting the conscience! But what does the State really do for us? It can order and organize the fickleness, arbitrariness, and egoism of the human will. It can place certain inhibitions upon it through regulation and threat. It can set up certain institutions, for example, schools, for the refining and ennobling of it. An enormous amount of respectable work is put into all this. Millions of valuable lives were and will be used internally, unified as one and sacrificed for the construction of this tower of the State. [12] But for what purpose? Even the righteousness of the State in all of its forms does not touch the inner nature of the world's will. Indeed, it is governed by the world's will. War again provides a striking illustration: If it were ever possible that the State tried at one time to make a human out of the wild animal, it must now, in reverse and by a thousand means, make wild animals out of men. The devil will laugh about this Tower of Babel too.

Religious righteousness! Unfortunately there is no other more certain means of rescuing us from the alarm cry of the conscience than religion and Christianity. A wonderful feeling of security and safety sets in against unrighteousness. We get a whiff of its power whenever religion gives us the chance — despite irritating interactions with our professional or political neighbor — to celebrate hallowed hours of devotional worship, to flee to Christianity as to an eternally green island in the gray sea of everyday life. It is a wonderful illusion when we can comfort ourselves with the fact that in our Europe the "religious life" runs its inexorable course — next to capitalism, prostitution, land speculation, alcoholism, tax evasion, and militarism, even church proclamation and ethics. And we are Christians! Our nation is a Christian nation! It is a wonderful illusion, but still an illusion, a self-deception!

At this point we should above all be honest with ourselves in a way that is completely different from how we usually are. We must honestly ask ourselves what we really gain from religion. Who benefits? [*Cui bono?*]. What is all the preaching, baptizing, confirming, bell-ringing, and organ-playing supposed to mean! All the religious feeling and edification, all the "ethical religious" advice "which shall accompany the couple,"[22] the congregation halls with or without film-projector equipment, the

---

22 See *"Mein Haus meine Burg!" Den Eheleuten zum Geleite!*, edited by the Protestant-Reformed Synodical Council [Evangelisch-reformierte Synodalrat] in connection with the Medical Society of the Canton of Bern [Ärztegesellschaft des Kantons Bern] (Bern, 1914). The first section of the "little book on marriage" [*Ehebüchlein*] contains "ethical-religious advice," and the second section contains "medical advice for married couples."

efforts to enliven church hymns, our untold, tame church newslet-
ters which do not say anything, and whatever else that belongs to the
machinery of modern churchliness! Will something different happen in
our relationship to the righteousness of God through all this! Are we
even *expecting* that something different will come of all this? Do we *want*
something to happen through all this, or do we actually want to conceal
in the most subtle way the fact that the decisive thing which must happen
has *not* yet happened, and probably never will? Do we not also act, with
our religious righteousness, "*as if*" precisely in order to *not* have to do
the real thing? [13] Isn't our religious righteousness, too, a product of our
pride and our despair, a Tower of Babel, which the devil laughs about,
louder than about anything else!?

We are deeply, deeply stuck in human righteousness. We are alarmed
by the call of the conscience but we have gone no further than to play
drowsily with the silhouette of the divine righteousness. In, itself, is too
great and too high for us. Therefore, the need and anxiety we suffer under
unrighteousness remain with us. Our consciences continue to cry out.
Our deepest longing goes unfulfilled.

This is now the internal situation in which we come to the quite pointless
question of whether God is righteous, in which the righteousness of God
absurdly becomes a problem and topic for discussion. In the War, it has
once again become a "real question." There is now hardly a congregation
anywhere in the surrounding area in which this question is not muttered,
loudly or softly, clumsily or delicately. It is running through the mind of
basically every one of us: If God were righteous, could he then simply
"allow" all that is now happening in the world?

"A pointless question?" you ask. Yes, it is pointless when God, the
living God is meant by it. For the living God never reveals himself at
any moment in our consciences in any other way than as a righteous
God. And it is pointless to ask God: "Are you righteous?" when we can
see him as he is and when he asks *us* whether we recognize him and want
to have him as he is. However, it is quite a meaningful, proper and weighty
question when we direct it to the god to whom we have constructed
the Tower of Babel in our pride and our despair, to the great personal
or impersonal, mystical, philosophical or naïve background and patron
saint of our human justice, our morals, our State, our culture, our religion.
Indeed, if we mean *this god*, then we have the full right to ask: Is "God"
righteous? The answer is quickly given. This is our misery, a misery
without an exit or deliverance: That we have made a god for ourselves,
after our image, through a thousand different ways [cf. Gen. 1.26f.], and
that we must now keep this god, a god to whom such comfortless questions can and must be posed, [14] and to which there are only the same

comfortless answers. With the question, "Is God righteous?" our entire
Tower of Babel collapses.

With this question, which now burns in us again, it becomes apparent
that we want righteousness without God, that we want to have God
without God and against God — and that none of this will work. It
becomes evident that *this* god is *not* God. He is not righteous. He can not
even prevent his believers — all the excellent European and American
people of culture and pilgrimage and progress, all the valiantly assiduous
citizens and pious Christians — from falling upon one another with
fire and sword to the amazement and derision of the poor heathens in
India and Africa. *This* god is really an unrighteous god. It is high time to
become right now doubters, skeptics, deriders, and finally atheists in the
face of *this* god. It is high time to openly confess and gladly admit with
relief that *this* god, to whom we have built the Tower of Babel, is not a
god. He is an idol. He is dead.

The solution is this: God himself, the real, living God and his love
which comes in glory. We have indeed not yet even begun to listen
quietly to that which our consciences want from us when it reminds us in
our need and anxiety of the righteousness of God. We have been much
too eager to do something ourselves. We became too comfortable too
quickly in our emergency shelters. We have confused the tent with our
homeland, the moratorium with the normal course of things. We have
prayed: "Your will be done!" [Mt. 6.10] but we meant by it "Your will be
done, just *not* now!" We have believed in eternal life, but what we took
for eternal life, and what we became satisfied with was only temporary. Amidst all this, we have remained the same unrighteous people that
we always have been. The unrighteousness has remained as well. And the
righteousness of God has once again disappeared from view. God himself
has become problematic to us because in his place have stood the dubious
figments of our own imagination.

There is a fundamentally *different* way to enter into a relationship with
the righteousness of God. We enter this other way not by speaking,
reflecting, or reasoning but by being still, and by not silencing the
conscience before we have barely even heard its voice. [15] If we let
our conscience speak till the end, it will not only tell us that there is
something different, righteousness beyond unrighteousness, but also, and
more importantly, that this something else for which we long and which
we need is God. *God* is right, not us! *God's* righteousness is an eternal
righteousness! This is what we so easily miss. Something needs to happen
for us to get far enough away for us to hear it again. We make a veritable
uproar with our morals and culture and religion. But it can come so far
that we will be brought to silence, and then our real salvation will begin.

It will then be, above all, finally, about recognizing God as God once again. It is easy to say "recognize," but recognizing is a matter which is only fought for and gained in a fierce inner-personal conflict. Next to this task, all the other cultural, social, and patriotic tasks, all the "ethical religious" efforts, are only child's play. For, it is about giving ourselves up in order to give ourselves over to God and to do his will. However, to do God's will means to begin anew with God. God's will is not an improved continuation of *our* will. God's will stands against our own as something completely different. Against God there is nothing but a radical "becoming new" of our will. No reforming; only a new growth and a becoming new. For the will that is revealed to us in the conscience is purity, goodness, truth, and community as the perfect will of God. It is a will that does not know any excuses or reservations or any temporary compromises. It is a thoroughly unilateral will, a will that is inwardly and fundamentally holy and blessed. This is the righteousness of God. In its presence, humility must be the first priority. Haven't we had enough of humility already? Can we somehow take humility as an obvious presupposition and move on to all kinds of tower building! Aren't we already on our way by establishing this presupposition?

And then a second consideration: In the place of despair a childlike joy will step in, a joy that God is so much greater than we ever thought. Joy that God's righteousness has far more depth and meaning than we have ever allowed ourselves to dream. Joy that there is much more to expect from God for our poor, confused, and burdened lives than [16] we, with our foundations, with our idealism, with our Christendom, have ever allowed ourselves to dream. There is simply more to *expect*! We ought not to scatter our emotions everywhere. We ought not to let our hearts always be so foolishly confused again and again by the constant building of new towers of Babel. We should not let our faith be wasted on convincing ourselves and others about our unbelief. We ought not to let the fruitful moments continually slip away while we are stuck in the belief that it is more pious and wiser to think humanly than divinely [cf. Mt. 16.23]. We should, therefore, use all of our power to expect more from God, to let grow within us that which he will in fact cause to grow. We should use all our power to accept what God is constantly offering us [cf. Mt. 26.41], to wakefully and prayerfully follow what God does. Like children, we ought to rejoice about the great God and his righteousness, and to trust everything to him. Have we already done enough in *this* direction? Do the fountains then flow as abundantly as they could? Don't we also stand in the true, creative joy that is just beginning as we stand in God's presence?

In the Bible this humility and joy is called faith. Faith means refraining from all kinds of murmuring, becoming quiet and letting God, the righteous God, speak with us, for there is no other. When this happens, God will work in us. Then a radically new thing will begin in us, as from a seed — a growing seed — which overcomes unrighteousness. Where there is belief, there — in the middle of the old world of war and money and death — the new spirit is born, out of which grows a new world, the world of God's righteousness. The need and anxiety in which we now stand will be broken where this new beginning is. The old chains will be ripped off; the false idols will begin to topple over. For something real has happened now — the only real thing which can happen: God himself has taken things into his own hands. "I saw Satan fall from heaven like a flash of lightening" [Lk. 10.18]. Life, the life of the individual and the life of all things, regains its sense. The lights of God brighten up the darkness and the powers of God become effective in weakness [2 Kgs 12.9]. Real love, real truth, real progress become possible for the first time, indeed morality and culture, State and Fatherland, even religion and Church become possible now, but only now! A bright outlook is found for the future, for a life, indeed for a world here on earth, in which [17] the righteous will of God breaks through and is true, and happens like it happens in heaven [cf. Mt. 6.10]. In this way, the righteousness of God, far, strange, high, becomes our possession and our great hope.

This inner way, the way of simple faith, is the way of Christ. Here there is more than Moses and more than John the Baptist [Mt. 12.41f.]. Here the love of God, original and new, stands with honor. One cannot say that humanity has already exhausted the possibilities of this way. We have made many things out of Jesus. But we have not yet comprehended the simplest thing, that he was the Son of God and that we may go with him on the way. It is a way upon which one does nothing but believe that the truth is the Father's will, and that it must happen. One can object that this method of squaring the circle is immature and inadequate. I hear these objections. But in this immature and inadequate solution there is *also* a plan! It remains to be seen whether the quaking of the Tower of Babel which we are now experiencing is strong enough to bring us a little bit closer to the way of *faith*. An opportunity to do so has now arrived. It may or may not happen. But sooner or later it will happen. There is no other way.

CHAPTER 2

THE NEW WORLD IN THE BIBLE, 1917

There is unfortunately only minimal documentation available about what precipitated the lecture, "The New World in the Bible" (and its subsequent history), which Barth gave in the church of Leutwil on February 6, 1917[1] as part of a series of presentations that Eduard Thurneysen arranged for his congregation in Leutwil between February 4–6, 1917. Emil Brunner and Gottlob Wieser gave the two lectures before Barth. Brunner spoke on February 4 about "The Development of the Bible" — a topic explained by Thurneysen in his letter to Barth from January 17, 1917 as "God's Word in the Bible that still awaits explanation."[2] Wieser's topic, presented on February 5, treated "Hope in the Bible." The order of presentations was adjusted after Brunner's and Barth's topics were switched. Brunner was not completely comfortable with the purely thetic treatment of the topic as it was initially proposed. He preferred some sort of analysis or advancement of thought."[3] This is how Barth happened to "take up the topic of 'the new world in the Bible' set for the sixth of February."[4]

As Thurneysen wrote to Barth on February 20, 1917, the "response" To this "Bible Week amongst the people" was "most gratifying." Barth's lecture in particular had been "really heard and understood. [. . .] It shows that what we have to say did not fall on deaf ears. And the like-mindedness shared by you and I was also seen by some more perceptive individuals."[5] When it was proposed that this like-mindedness should lead to the publication of a volume of their sermons, Barth proposed to Thurneysen regarding the volume: "your presentation at Safenwil concerning the church and mine from Leutwil concerning the Bible should be appended at the conclusion of the volume, as the main way in which these points that are so important to us might be brought to light."[6] But Turneysen's presentation

---

1   *W.G. Th.* locates this lecture in the Fall of 1916, but according to *Bw. Th.* I, 170, n. 1 (January 17, 1917), it was actually given in February 1917.

2   See *Bw. Th.* I for a different formulation of this remark.

3   Letter from Thurneysen to Barth, January 17, 1917. See *Bw. Th.* I for a different formulation of this remark.

4   *Bw. Th.* I, 173 (January 26, 1917).

5   *Bw. Th.* I, 175.

6   Letter from Barth to Thurneysen, June 25, 1917 (*Bw. Th.* I, 207, cf. 228, 230).

was left out of the first edition of *Suchet Gott, so werdet ihr leben!*[7] Barth's presentation from Leutwil provided a striking conclusion to that volume.[8] Since the same presentation reappeared in Barth's first volume of "collected essays" in 1924 in *The Word of God and Theology*, of which our present essay is a translation,[9] it was removed from the second edition of *Suchet Gott, so werdet ihr leben!* and replaced by Blumhardt's *Hausandachten* ["Home Devotions"], written in 1916. The original plan was followed, however, to the extent that Thurneysen's Safenwil presentation was reproduced in the second edition under the title "Our Hope and the Church" ["Unsere Hoffnung und die Kirche"].[10]

[18] We are trying to find an answer to the question: What is in the Bible? What sort of house is it that the Bible is a door to? What sort of land spreads out before our eyes when we open up the Bible?

We are with Abraham in Haran, and we hear a call that commands him: "Go from your country and your kindred and your father's house to the land that I will show you!" Then we hear a promise: "I will make of you a great nation!" [Gen. 12.1-2]. "And Abraham believed the Lord; and the Lord reckoned it to him as righteousness" [Gen 15.6]. What is the meaning of all this? We can feel that there is something behind these words and events. But what? Let's find out.

We are now with Moses in the desert. For forty years he has been living among the sheep, doing penance for a rash act [Exod. 2.11ff.]. What comes next for him? We are not told. Apparently, it is not our concern. Suddenly he, too, is called: "Moses! Moses!" [Exod. 3.4]. Then a great command: "Come I will send you to Pharaoh to bring my people, the Israelites, out of Egypt!" [Exod. 3.10]. Then only a simple assurance: "I will be with you" [Exod. 3.12]. Here again are words and events that appear at first to be nothing but pure riddles. We read no such thing in the newspaper or in other books. What is behind all this?

The land of Canaan is suffering under enemy occupation. We see Gideon, son of a farmer, under the oaks at Ophrah [Jud. 6.11-14]. The "angel of the Lord" appears to him and says: "The Lord is with you, you mighty warrior!" Gideon sees nothing amiss in retorting: "If the Lord is with us, then why has all this happened to us?" But "the Lord" knew better how to silence Gideon: "Go in this might of yours and *you* deliver Israel from the hand of the Midianites! *I* hereby commission you."

7   See *Bw. Th.* I, 240.
8   Karl Barth, Eduard Thurneysen, *Suchet Gott, so werdet ihr leben!* (Bern: Stählin, 1917), 154–174.
9   Karl Barth, *W.G. Th.*, 18–32.
10   Karl Barth, Eduard Thurneysen, *Suchet Gott, so werdet ihr leben!*, 2nd ed. (Munich: Chr. Kaiser Verlagn, 1928), 160–174.

In the temple of Shiloh there is the young Samuel, and again a call: "Samuel, Samuel!" and the old pious priest, Eli, [19] wisely advises Samuel: "Go lie down again." Samuel obeys, and sleeps until he could no longer sleep because the call keeps coming and coming, and now it even occurs to the pious Eli that it might be . . .! Even Samuel has to listen and obey [1 Sam. 3.4-14]. We read all of this, but what are we actually reading here? We feel it. We have felt something like the tremors of an earthquake, or the unceasing rumble of ocean waves crashing upon the embankments. But what is it that is actually pounding there, which obviously wants to come in?

We remember how Elijah defies the entire authority of the king in the name of the "Lord," but then how he himself had to first get to know this "Lord," not in the storm and lightning, but in a "the sound of sheer silence" [1 Kgs 19.12]! How Isaiah and Jeremiah did not want to speak [cf. Isa. 6.5; Jer. 1.6], but then indeed had to speak the mysteries of the divine judgment and blessing upon the sinful people. How, in the middle of the deepest humiliation of these people, a small group of unlikely and solitary "servants of God" wrestled ever more fiercely with the question of "Where is your God now?" and its answer, "But in God Israel has a comfort!" [Pss. 42.2,11; 79.10; 115.2] Finally, in the midst of all the misery and unrighteousness of the people [Ps. 73.1], they could not help but blare out the proclamation, "Expose yourself! Become light! [Isa. 60.1] For your light comes and the glory of the Lord goes out upon you!" What is all this? Why do these individuals speak in such a manner? Where does the fire of all the fury, mercy, joy, hope, unconditional confidence come from, which we still see today in every part of the books of the prophets and the Psalms, blazing like a fire?

Then come the unbelievable, incomparable days where time, history, and every event up until then appeared to stand still — like the sun at Gibeon [Josh. 10.12] — around a man who was no prophet, no poet, no hero and no philosopher, and yet who was all of these and more. His words horrify and agitate, for he speaks with authority and not like us theologians. With compelling force he calls to the individual, "Follow me!" He makes an irresistible impression of "eternal life" on those who distrust him and who are his adversaries. "The blind see, the lame walk, the unclean will become clean, the deaf will hear, the devil will be driven out, the dead will rise up, and the good news will be proclaimed to the poor!" "Blessed is the womb that gave you birth!" is the cry of the people. The quieter and lonelier [20] he becomes, and the less he finds real "faith" in the world around him, all the more strongly *one* triumphant tone sounds through his entire existence: "I am the resurrection and the life! [Jn 11.25]. I live and you will also live!" [Jn 14.19]

And then comes the echo, feeble as it is in comparison to the ringing of Easter morning, but still strong, much too strong for our ears which are used to weaker, mercifully weaker, tones. This is the echo which this man's existence finds in a little flock of those who were paying attention, who were awake, who were waiting. It is the echo of the first courageous messengers who felt the necessity to go out into all the world to proclaim the Gospel to every creature. It is the echo of Paul: "Now the righteousness of God has been revealed! [Rom. 3.21f.] If someone is in Christ, then he is a new creature! [2 Cor. 5.17] And the one who has begun a good work in you will also complete it!" [Phil. 1.6]. It is the silent, deep echo of John: "Life has appeared [1 Jn 1.2]. We have seen his glory. We are now children of God [Jn 1.14; 1 Jn 3.2]. And our faith is the victory that overcomes the world" [1 Jn 5.4].

Then even this echo falls silent. The Bible is finished. Who is this man who has spoken and acted in such a way, who touched off this echo! Again we ask, what is in the Bible? What does this deep, remarkable course from Abraham to Christ mean? What does the choir of the prophets and apostles want and call for? What is *the one thing* that all these voices apparently want to announce, each in its own tone and key? What lies between the strange statement, "In the beginning God created the heavens and the earth" [Gen. 1.1] and then the equally strange cry of longing, "Amen, come Lord Jesus!" [Rev. 22.20]. What stands behind this and what wants to appear?

It is a dangerous question. We might do better not to come too near to this burning bush [cf. Exod. 3.2-5], for we are sure to betray what stands behind *us*! The Bible answers these questions for every person and in every era as they deserve. We will find in it only as much as we are looking for: Great things and divine things if we look for great and divine things, or inane and "historical" things if we look for inane and "historical" things — or nothing at all if we do not look for anything at all [cf. Lk. 1.53]. The hungry will be satisfied with it, and to those who are satisfied, the Bible is already spoiled before they even crack it open. The question: "What is in the Bible?" has a mortifying way of turning into the opposing question: [21] "Well, what do you want?" and "Who do you think you are anyway, daring to ask in this way?"

But in spite of all this, we *must* trust ourselves enough to ask our questions — even at the risk of making quite shameful discoveries about ourselves. At the same time, we must trust ourselves enough to reach boldly for an answer, an answer which is too great for us and for which we actually are not ready at all — even if we feel quite unworthy to pluck the fruit, which *we* most certainly did not plant with our yearning, striving, wrestling, and inner work. This fruit, this answer, is suggested by the title of my lecture today, namely, that in the Bible there is *a new world*, the world of God. This overwhelming answer is the same as that

which came to the first martyr, Stephen: "Look, I see the heavens opened
and the Son of Man standing at the right hand of God!" [Acts 7.55].
Neither the seriousness of our faith nor the depth and the riches of our
experiences have earned us the right to give such an answer. Therefore
I will only say something scant and unsatisfying about it, and you too,
will only be able to understand and comprehend bits of it, and it will be
unsatisfying to you.

We must openly admit that we are reaching way beyond ourselves
with this answer. But that is precisely the point. If we are to focus more
closely to the content of the Bible at all, then we must risk overreaching
ourselves. The Bible permits nothing less. It gives to each one what fits
him and what he rightly deserves — to one much and to the other only a
little, and to the third nothing. And if we would only be *honest*, we would
admit that it will not leave us in peace either, if we, with our feeble eyes
and fat fingers, pull out an answer that fits *us*. We then quickly notice that
the Bible's answer is something, but it is not everything. It may satisfy me
for a few years, but I cannot stick with it.

The Bible says quickly, very clearly, and in a very friendly manner
about the certain "versions" we make of it: "So this is *you*, but not *me*!
Now this is what perhaps in fact fits you very well, your emotional
needs, and your views, your schedules and your 'circles,' your religious
or philosophical theories! See, you wanted to mirror yourself in me, and
sure enough you have rediscovered your own image in me! But now
[22] go and search for *me*! Look for what is there!" The Bible itself, the
certain implacable logic of its connection that drives us beyond ourselves,
regardless of our worthiness or unworthiness, is what invites us to reach
toward the final, highest answer, in which everything that can be said is
said. And even if we barely comprehend it and can only stammer it out,
that answer is: There is a new world in the Bible, the world of God. There
is a spirit in the Bible that allows us to linger among secondary things
for a while and play with them — as is our habit — but then it begins
to urge us on. Despite our objection that we are only weak, imperfect,
simple folk, it still urges us on toward the main point, whether we want
to or not. There is a stream in the Bible that carries us away once we
have entrusted ourselves to it; it carries us from ourselves to the seas! The
Holy Scripture interprets itself[11] despite all of our human limitations.

We need only dare to follow this drive, this spirit, this stream in the
Bible, to grow beyond ourselves and to reach for the highest answer. This
daring is *faith*; and we read the Bible properly not when we read it with

---

11 See Luther's "the Scripture interprets itself" (*scriptura sui ipsius interpres*), in the "Assertio omnium
articulorum" (1520) (WA 7: 97, 23). Cf. his sermon on the day of St. Jacob, July 25, 1522 (WA 10/
III: 238, 10f.).

a false humility, reserve, or other alleged sobriety but when we read it
in faith, as those who travel along on the way which they are led. This
invitation to dare to reach for the highest, even though we do not deserve
it, is precisely the expression of *grace* in the Bible. Where the grace of
God encounters us, where we are led, pulled and made to grow, there,
the Bible becomes clear.

What is in the Bible? *History!* It is the history of a remarkable, even
peculiar people; the history of mighty, spirit-filled personalities; the history of Christianity in its nascency. It is a history about great men and
ideas in which anyone who considers themselves to be educated must be
interested, if for no other reason than because of its effects on the eons that
have followed, including our time. This answer can be satisfying for quite
a while, and one can find in it many things that are beautiful and true.
It simply is so that the Bible is entirely history. It is a history of religion,
history of literature, culture, the world, and with it a human history of
every sort. An image of living action and color unfolds itself if one looks
closely. But the joy is short-lived. Upon a closer inspection, the image
is absolutely incomprehensible [23] and unenjoyable if it is only meant
to be history. Whoever is looking for history or for stories will be glad
to quickly turn away from the Bible to the newspaper or other books.

For, when we study history or entertain ourselves with history, we
always like to know, how did this all come about? How does one event
relate to the other? What are the natural, concrete origins for things? *Why*
have humans spoken and acted in such a way? But precisely at these
decisive points in its account of history, the Bible does not give us
answers to our "Why?" This is so not only about the Bible but about all
the truly decisive figures and events in history. The greater an event, the
fewer answers we receive to our inquisitive "Why?" And vice versa: The
less significant a time or an individual, the more the "historians" find
to explain and establish. But on this point the Bible presents an unpar-
alleled difficulty to history lovers. Why did the people of Israel not
completely perish in Egyptian bondage but remain together as a people,
and in fact, become one in the depths of their greatest need? Why? Just
because! Why was Moses able to produce a table of laws that still today
brings us to shame with its purity and humanity? Just because! Why
does someone like Jeremiah simply stand there during the occupation
of Jerusalem with his message of doom as an enemy of the people
and a bloke without a fatherland?[12] Why Jesus' healing of the sick, his

---

12 With the expression, "a bloke without a fatherland," the German Kaiser, Wilhelm II, voiced
    his displeasure about the rejection of a bill by a majority of the German Parliament that
    would have increased the fleet of battleships. See E. Eyck, *Das persönliche Regiment Wilhelms II*
    (Erlenbach-Zurich: Rentsch, 1948), 161.

messianic consciousness, his resurrection from the dead? Why does a Saul become a Paul? Why is there the supernatural image of Christ in the Fourth Gospel? Why does John retreat to the island of Patmos, which is the new Jerusalem [Rev. 21.2], the city of God, coming from heaven to earth like a bride dressed up for her groom — right in the middle of the glory of the reign of the Roman Empire, as if it were all nothing? Just because!

The poor, poor history scholars! What a major project the Bible gives them! "Just because!" is by no means a proper answer in the study of history, and if we explain the historical moments of the Bible with a "Just because" and with an "!" then its history is indeed pure nonsense. Some are compelled to search for reasons and explanations where there are none, with the result that the search becomes a history for itself, namely, a terrible history, with which I do not want to engage right now. [24] The Bible itself, however, does not answer our inquiring "Why?" with a "Just because!" as the Sphinx does, or like a lawyer with a thousand arguments, deductions and parallels. It tells us "*God* is the decisive reason. Because *God* lives, speaks, and acts, there is a reason . . .!" Of course, when we hear "God" it might at first mean the same thing to us as "Just because!" But this is precisely where history temporarily stops, where there is nothing more to ask, where there is something completely different, where something new now begins. It is a history with its own unique ground, possibilities, and presuppositions. In the headlines of our newspapers or the stories of the Aargau school books, there is never an event explained by "God created; God spoke!"

The main question now is whether we can have any understanding for this other, new thing, or even a good enough will toward it to think it over and give an internal response to it. Do we want to get involved with "God?" Do we dare go where we apparently are being led? That would be "faith"! A new world projects itself into our old, ordinary world. We could reject it. We could say, "God is nothing, it is just illusion, lunacy." But we may deny or prevent our being led by the biblical "history" into a *new* world, into the world of God — far beyond what is elsewhere called "history."

It is true as well to start out by saying, "There is *morality* in the Bible! It is a collection of examples and teachings of human virtue and human greatness." To this day, no one has ever seriously disputed that the people of the Bible were good, exemplary individuals in their own way, from whom we have an endless amount to learn. Whether we seek practical wisdom for life or lofty models of a certain type of heathenism, we always find what we are looking for. Then again, in the long run, we do not. Large parts of the Bible, with their lack of practical wisdom and "good role models," are virtually unusable in schools, for example, which in the best case have moral goals. Indeed, the heroes of the Bible are to a certain degree all completely respectable in their own way. But as models of the kind, efficient, hard-working, State-educated average Swiss citizen, a Sampson, a David, an Amos, or a Peter is hardly appropriate. Models such as Rosa [25] of Tannenburg[13] or the figure of Amici's "Heart,"[14] or the magnificent figures of modern Swiss history are fundamentally different people! The Bible is an embarrassment and is foreign to schools. How should we find in the life and teachings of Jesus something to "do" in "practical life?" Doesn't it seem to us that he wishes to say to us at every step: "What does your "practical life" have to do with me? I have nothing to do with it. Follow *me* [Mt. 4.19 etc.] or let me go my own way!"

Indeed, precisely at certain high points, the Bible surprises us with its display of a peculiar disregard for our concepts of good and evil. It shows Abraham, who wants to sacrifice his son to God as the highest test of his faith [Genesis 22]; Jacob who took for himself the rights of a first-born through a refined cheating of his blind father [Genesis 27]; Elijah who slaughtered the four-hundred-and-fifty priests of Baal on the river of Kishon [1 Kgs 18.19, 40]. None of these are exactly what we would call praiseworthy models. And how much moral substance is the Bible painfully lacking! How little instruction it offers about the difficult questions of business, life, marriage, culture, politics, with which we must wrestle! One need only think of the greatest moral and fatal issue of today, namely, how blithely and persistently war is conducted in the Bible. Again and again it becomes necessary for the teacher or the pastor to reach for all kinds of extra-biblical materials when this kind of question comes up in class, because the New Testament as well as the Old virtually breaks down on this topic. Time and again, even earnest Christians — who are seeking "comfort" and "inspiration" in the personal difficulties of their lives — very quietly close their Bibles and reach for the conventional hurdy-gurdy of a Christian Fürchtegott Gellert or for the books by Hilty,[15] if not psychoanalysis, where everything becomes so much more practical, clear, and comprehensible. Time and again, the Bible makes the impression on us that there is no wisdom, advice or models for a good

13   *Rosa von Tannenburg: Geschichte des Althertums für Ältern und Kinder* by Christoph Schmid (1768–1854), published in Augsburg, 1823.

14   *Cuore* (Milan, 1886) by Edmondo de Amicis (1846–1908) was rendered into German as *Herz. Ein Buch für die Knaben* (first published in Basel, 1889). It tells stories of the experiences of an Italian elementary school pupil during the school year.

15   Carl Hilty (1833–1909) was a Swiss lawyer and author of religious books. With his writings, he reached many who were searching, especially with his Christian, lay-theological instruction on being happy [*Glücklichsein*], entitled *Glück* (3 Vols., Frauenfeld, 1890–1899; Zürich: Oesch, 1987).

and proper life, neither for the individual person nor for the nations and governments. At first, it offers us nothing that we are looking for in it!

Once again, we stand precisely before this "other," before this new thing which arises in the Bible. In fact, the chief consideration of the Bible is not the activities of humans but the activity of God — not the various paths that we could take if we had the good will to do so, but the powers from which a good will is first created. [26] Its chief concern is not the way in which love unfolds and proves itself as we understand it, but with the existence and outpouring of an eternal love, love as God understands it. Its chief interest is not our capability to function in our ordinary old world, hard-working, honest, and helpful, but in the establishment and growth of a new world, the world in which God rules, and in which *his* morality rules.

In light of this coming world, someone like David is a great man despite his adultery and blood-spilling sword: "Blessed is the man whose sins God does not reckon to him!" [Ps. 32.2; cf. Rom. 4.8] "The tax collectors and the prostitutes will enter this new world rather than their ten-times finer and more ethical members of the good society!" [Mt. 21.31]. In this new world the true hero is the lost son, who amounts to nothing when he is lost and among the pigs — and not his moral, older brother! [Lk. 15.11-32]. See? What lies behind Abraham and Moses, behind Christ and his apostles, is the world of the Father, in which morality is a settled matter because it is self-evident. This is the blood of the New Testament that wants to run through our veins [Mt. 6.10]. It is the will of the Father that wants to be done on earth as it is in heaven.

Even once we have understood this as the meaning of the Bible, as *its* answer to our great and small questions, we still say: "I do not need this, I did not ask for this! This says nothing to me! I cannot get anywhere with it!" It could very well be that we cannot get anywhere with it on our present highways and byways along which we have been traveling with such perseverance in the churches and schools of today, for instance, or in our individual, personal lives. There are a thousand dead ends from which the way to heaven can at first only lead backwards. Yet it is certain that the Bible, if we read it with careful attention, leads us exactly to the point at which we must decide to accept or disavow the royal sovereignty of God.

This is precisely the *new* world of the Bible. What it offers us is the glorious, driving, hopeful life of the seed [cf. Mk 4.26-29], a new beginning out of which everything shall become new. This new world, this life of the divine seed, cannot be learned or imitated. We can only live with it, grow with it, mature with it. We can only believe and set our faces toward the place to where we are being led. Or we can not believe. There is no third way.

Let us continue our search from yet another side. We could also assume that in the Bible true *religion* is revealed to us: [27] what we think of God, how we find the proper way to him, and how we are to relate to him in community. Thus, it reveals something that we now gladly call "piety." So much has been said and written in the last twenty years about the Bible as the "charter document of piety" — and it is completely true. How could we not take all sorts of lessons about piety from the Bible, about the proper relationship of humans to the eternal, to the divine? But the same law holds here too: We have only to search the Bible with honesty, and we will most certainly find something greater in it than merely religion and "piety." These are only a crust which we must break through. We are all concerned about the tremendous variety of Christianity in the world: Catholic, Protestant, and the like, all kinds of communities and "trends" both old-fashioned as well as modern — all, all of these permutations have invoked the Bible with the same earnestness and zeal. They all claim that *they* have the proper piety like it is revealed in the Bible, or at least its legitimate continuation.

How do we want to respond to that! A strong dose of impertinence is required to simply answer them by saying, "Now we Protestants, or we members of this or that group are right precisely for this or that reason, and everyone else is wrong." Once we understand how easy it is to find "reasons," we would no longer take pleasure in this unending game. But then would we come to the conclusion that everyone has the right to invoke the Bible for their piety? If we say this, then we are reaching toward that which the spirit of the Bible turns a deaf ear, namely, the general brew of tolerance that is being proclaimed as the highest good, especially in our national church! Or could we all simply be wrong with our "piety"? We must seek out our answer in this direction: "It therefore remains rather, that God is true and all humans are liars" [Rom. 3.4]. Every religion can be found in the Bible if one wants it to be. But when we look closely, there are none at all. Instead, there is again only the "other," the new, the greater thing.

When we come to the Bible with our questions of, "How should I think of God and the world? How do I get to the divine? What kind of attitude shall I take?" it answers us with something like, "My dear friend, that is *your* affair, [28] which you must not ask *me* about! You can and must work with yourself as to whether it would be better to hear the Mass or the sermon; whether the Salvation Army or 'Christian science' has the correct Christianity; or whether the old man Pastor Müller or the young Pastor Meyer has the correct faith; or whether your religion should be more a religion of the intellect, of the will, or of the feeling! If you do not want to get involved in *my* questions, you can find all sorts of great and small reasons for one viewpoint or another, but you will not glean from it what actually stands there." The final result will always be the great human game of I'm-right-you're-wrong — far, far away from what is actually true and what would like to become true in our lives. Can you guess what is coming next? It is precisely not the right human thoughts about God that form the content of the Bible, but rather the right thoughts of God about humans.

The Bible does not tell us how we are supposed to talk with God, but rather what God says to us. It does not say how we are to find our way to him, but how God has sought and found the way to us. It does not show the right relationship into which we must place ourselves with him, but the covenant which God has made with all those who are the children of Abraham in faith, and which God has sealed in Jesus Christ once and for all. This is what stands in the Bible. The Word of God stands in the Bible.

Our grandfathers were certainly right when they fought so fiercely for the Bible as revelation and not just religion, particularly when they did not let this truth be turned upside-down, even by so pious and astute a man as Schleiermacher. Our fathers were right to protect themselves with healthy skepticism from stepping on to the wobbly floor of the religious cult of personality. The more attentively we look for piety in Scriptures, all the more surely will we receive an answer, sooner or later. "What kind of piety is there?" [Jn 5.39]. It is the "piety which testifies to *me*!" In seeking ourselves, we find God. Then we stand there with all of our religions, our Christianities, our viewpoints, each one of us, like blundering pupils of the ABCs. Yet we cannot be sad about it but rejoice in it, for amidst all the secondary issues, we have indeed come upon the chief concern, without which even the most profound piety is only a delusion and deception. Again, this chief concern contains the living seed out of which a proper relationship to God, a service of God "in the spirit and in truth" [Jn 4.24], must necessarily emerge, whether [29] we stress this detail more or that detail less. The Word of God! The viewpoint of God!

Once more, we have the freedom of choice. We could certainly declare: "I cannot get anywhere with this. The concept 'Word of God' is not a part of my world view. I will stand by that old 'pious' Christianity that I am used to, with its particular viewpoints of this or that stripe." Or, we could open our ears to what "passes all understanding." We can request in the power of God and the saints to grow with it and become mature in it throughout the great processes of life set forth in the Bible. We can obey the spirit of this book and for once admit that God is right instead of trying to prove ourselves right. We could dare to *believe*. Indeed here we stand again precisely before the question of faith. Yet we must be able to agree upon the fact, without anticipating the answer, that in the Bible, in the Old and New Testaments, the piety of God — so to speak — is the theme, and never and nowhere is the piety of Jews or Christians or heathens the theme. We must agree that even in this relationship, the Bible leads us out of the stale atmosphere of humanity and into the open doors of a *new* world, the world of God.

But we are not quite done yet. Therefore *a new world* stands in the Bible. God! God's lordship! God's honor! God's inconceivable love! Not the history of humanity but the history of God. Not the virtues of humanity but the virtues of God, who has called us out of the darkness to his wonderful light! Not human standpoints but the standpoint of God.

Now, however, a final set of questions can arise: "Who is this God? What is God's will? What are God's thoughts? What is the mysterious 'Other,' the New, the Greater One who is present in the Bible, who is behind and above every human being, who surfaces and commands us to come to the decision to believe or not to believe? Who did Abraham believe in? For whom did the heroes fight and reach victory? For whom have the prophets spoken their wisdom? In whose power did Christ die and was raised from the dead? Whose name have the apostles proclaimed? 'God' is the content of the Bible! But what is the content of this content! A 'new' thing breaks in! But what is this new thing?"

There is a series of rash, ready-made answers to this question, which we can hardly wait to hear, for they are all serious, well-grounded answers taken from the Bible itself. [30] For example, God is the Lord and the Redeemer, the Salvation and the Comforter of every soul who turns to him. The new world is the kingdom of blessedness, which is being prepared for the small flock that flees perdition. Isn't it stated like this in the Bible? Or, God is the source of life that begins to rush in when we finally turn ourselves from the external things of the world and for once become still before him. And the new world is precisely the unforgettable peace of this hidden life with Christ in God [cf. Col. 3.3]. Does this not also stand in the Bible? Or, God is the Lord of the heavens, who is waiting for us and in whom we have our citizenship [cf. Phil. 3.20], and which we will enjoy after we have completed our pilgrimage through the suffering and imperfection of these present times. The new world is precisely this blessed "other side," the "silent eternity,"[16] that will eventually take in the believers. Indeed, even these are truths taken purely from the Bible.

Why shouldn't they be true? But are they *the* truth? Is that all? Can we read or listen to the Bible or even only a few chapters from it, and then with a good conscience say: "For this, God's Word has gone out to humanity; this is why God made his miraculous way through the history of humanity from Abraham to Christ. This is why the Holy Spirit had

---

16   In 1915 Barth had become particularly suspicious of this expression through Paul Wernle's use of it. See *Bw. Th.* I, 46 (May 25, 1915).

to come down on Pentecost to the apostles in fiery tongues; this is why a Saul turned to a Paul, and traveled land and sea? Therefore, here and there or even in many places, a person like you or me 'converts' and finds inner 'peace.' And, after a redeeming death, we will arrive eventually 'in heaven!'" Is *that* all? Is *that* all of God and his new world? Is this the sense of the Bible, the content of the contents! All the mighty resources that come to be displayed in the Bible — the movement of peoples, the battles and commotion that play out before us, the miracles and revelations that constantly take place, the immeasurable promises of the future which always make us into something new — don't all these things stand in a rather strange relation to so small a result — if precisely these few things are everything? Is God not greater than this?!

In the answers given above, as serious and pious as they might be, haven't we just measured God with *our* standards, conceived God with *our* conceptions, wished for a God according to *our* wishes? If we want to begin reading the Bible properly, don't we have to also grow beyond the answers? [31] For precisely this reason, we must also grow beyond the peculiar question, "Who is God?" As if we could even pose such a question at all once we have truly, willingly, let ourselves by led to the gates of the new world, to the threshold of the kingdom of God. Here, the questioning ceases. Here, we see. We hear. We have something. We know. Here, we no longer give a petty, curt, and narrow answer. The question, "Who is God?" and our inadequate answers to it arise only where we have become stuck somewhere along the way toward the open gates of the new world, where somewhere along the line we have not let the Bible honestly speak to us, where we have not really wanted to . . . believe. At this point, once again, the truth becomes unclear, confused, problematic — or even narrow, airless, "churchly," dwarfish like a chapel,[17] boring, meaningless. "Whoever sees me sees the Father!" This is precisely it: When we let ourselves be driven to the highest answer, when we have found God in the Bible, when we have risked it with Paul to obey the heavenly voice, then God stands before us as the one who he *is*. "If you believe, you *have*!"[18] God is God.

But who may say, "I believe!"? "I believe, dear Lord, help my unbelief!" [Mk 9.24]. We are all still embarrassed by the question, "Who is God?" We feel small and ashamed next to the fullness of the divinity that the men and women of the Bible have looked upon and proclaimed. Therefore I can now only stammer something out and make

---

17 In Swiss-German, the word "chapel" also has the particular connotation of being a place where inter-denominational Pietist societies could gather.

18 See Martin Luther, "Freedom of a Christian" (1520): "glaubst, so hastu" ("whoever has faith will have everything") (WA 7: 24, 13; *LW* 31: 349).

hints at a couple of words that are promised by that which would be revealed to us, if the Bible could speak with us, unhindered and in the full power of its revelation.

Who is God? He is the heavenly Father! Indeed. But he is the heavenly Father on *earth* and on earth really the *heavenly* Father! The One who does not want to split life into "this side" and "that side." The One who does not want to leave it up to death to set us free from sin and suffering. The One who wants to bless us with the powers of life not with the powers of the Church. The One who has let his Word become flesh in Christ. The One who let eternity break into *time* here and now and who truly let it break *in* to time [cf. Jn 1.14] — for what kind of eternity would it be if it first came "afterwards?" He is the One who does not have just any old idea in his head but who constructs a new world.

Who is God? He is the Son, the One who has become "Mediator of my soul."[19] Indeed. But more than that: He is the Mediator of the *entire* [32] world, the redeeming Word which was in the beginning of all things and which everything anxiously awaits [cf. Jn 1.1; cf. Rom. 8.19]. Therefore he is even the Redeemer of my brothers and sisters. He is even the Redeemer of confused humanity which is governed by evil spirits and powers. Thus he is even the Redeemer of that sighing creature within us [cf. Rom. 8.22]. The entire Bible powerfully proclaims to us that God must become *all in all* [cf. 1 Cor. 15.28]. What happens in the Bible is already the glorious inception of the beginning of the new world!

Who is God? He is the Spirit in those who believe in him, the "Spirit that is opened up to us from the Son and who flows, crystal clear, from the throne of God and the Lamb into silent hearts."[20] Indeed, indeed! But God is also the One who as Spirit — and that means as love and good will — wants to and must *break out* of silent hearts into the external world so that God becomes evident, visible, and manifest. Look, there is God's tent among humans! [Rev. 21.3] It is the Holy Spirit, the One who creates a new heaven and a new earth [Rev. 21.1], and along with them new people, new families, new relationships, new politics. The Holy Spirit is the One who has no respect for old habits simply because they are traditional. He is the One who has no respect for celebrations simply

---

19   There is no obvious source for this appellation; it is a characteristic formulation of what Barth called "a Christianity of the soul" [*Seelenchristentums*] in the *Romans* 1919 commentary (109, 117). He may have had in mind the closing words from the third verse of the song, "Wo findet die Seele die Heimat, die Ruh?" in *Lieder zur Ehre des Erretters! Vereinslieder des Blauen Kreuzes*, 14th ed. (Bern, 1924), 90, Nr. 80: "Ruh', Ruh', Ruh', Ruh', himmlische Ruh'/Im Schoße des Mittlers; ich eile ihr zu."

20   From the sixth verse of the song "O Gott, O Geist, O Licht des Lebens" by G. Tersteegen (*GERS* 151; *RG* 510; *EKG* 425).

because they are celebratory; no respect for the old powers simply because they are powerful. The Holy Spirit is the One who respects nothing but the truth, nothing but itself! He is the One who sets up the righteousness of heaven in the midst of unrighteousness upon the earth. He will not rest or repose until all those who are dead have become alive and a new *world* has entered into existence.

See, all *this* is in the Bible. This is even in the Bible for *us*. We are baptized into this. If only we would risk it in faith to take what grace offers us! Do I now need to say to you that *this* is necessary for us all? We live in the old, sick world, whose soul cries out of a deep need, "Heal me, Lord, and I will be healed!" [Jer. 17.14]. There is a desire in every person for that which the Bible contains, no matter who, where, what, and how it may want to be. You all know this as well as I do.

Now hear this: "There was a man who prepared a great feast and invited many to it, and sent out his slave onto the streets of the banquet to say to those invited, 'Come, for everything is now ready!'" [Lk. 14.16f.].

CHAPTER 3

THE CHRISTIAN IN SOCIETY,
1919

The invitation which occasioned Barth's "Tambach Lecture" came from a circle gathered around the pastor and lecturer Otto Herpel. While serving as pastor to a garrison in the Great War, Herpel had become a critic of the "organized injustice of the war" and a resolute opponent of the "power-state and capitalism, for the sake of the welfare state and socialism."[1] After the war, having become in the meantime a pastor in Lissberg in Oberhessen, he found a like-minded friend in Georg Flemming, the rector of the school in Schlüchtern. With him, he founded a weekly newspaper whose initial goal, like that of the German Democratic Party (DDP), was to win Christians over to the cause of the new German democracy (hardly a self-evident thing at the time) and "to make them into a power-block"[2] within it. "The Christian Democrat: Weekly Paper for the Evangelical Home" first appeared on June 4, 1919. To support it a "Union of Friends of the Christian Democrat" had been formed earlier, on March 29, 1919.[3] Although the paper aligned itself generally with the "left-leaning parties,"[4] it was not tied to the socialists in particular at the outset. However, Herpel and other coworkers did seek to orient their readership toward Leonhard Ragaz. In this context belongs an appeal published at the end of May 1919 by a friend from Herpel's student years, Pastor Heinrich Schultheis from Glenhaar in Oberhessen. The appeal was addressed to "all those men and women who are convinced of the necessity of religious-socialist beliefs and activities in the Swiss religious socialist sense."[5] As a result of this appeal, a "German Religious Socialist Union" was formed. This was also used to explain the renaming of the newspaper, which from October 1, 1919 on appeared under the title: "The New Work: The Christian in the People's State." Eberhard Arnold, who soon became coeditor, became one of the leading

---

1   See Friedrich-Wilhelm Marquardt, *Der Christ in der Gesellschaft, 1919–1979: Geschichte, Analyse und aktuelle Bedeutung von Karl Barths Vortrag*, Theologische Existenz heute 206 (Munich: Chr. Kaiser Verlag, 1980), 7f.

2   KBA 9319.96.

3   Marquardt, *Der Christ in der Gesellschaft*, 9.

4   Letter from O. Herpel to K. Barth, June 30, 1919.

5   Marquardt, *Der Christ in der Gesellschaft*, 10; cf. the announcement in *CW*, 33 (1919), col. 359.

figures in the "New Work Movement," which developed its own direction.[6] That led to still another name change for the newspaper, which was now called "New Work: A Service for That Which is Becoming."

On behalf of the "German Religious Socialist Union," whose "creation" was being "contemplated" in "these days," Otto Herpel sent out a letter on June 22, 1919 which was apparently sent in carbon copies to a number of recipients, each with the salutation "Most Honored Brother in Ministry." Karl Barth was one of these recipients. The letter asked for support and even for "charitable help" with the "organization" of a "lecture or lecture tour of religious socialist men and women" planned for the winter. But even before that, it asked for help in organizing the "first Religious Socialist Conference in Germany," which was envisioned as taking place in the fall — an undertaking that "would remain but a half-measure if the fathers of Swiss Religious Socialism did not act as godparents in its creation."[7]

Barth answered on June 26:

> Your enquiry has brought me great joy . . . I understand your letter as an invitation to collaboration, not just to help. Your need is truly our need as well, and our hope is your own. There cannot be too much cooperation if our aims are to be realized. I feel myself drawn to Germany in the present moment as to no other place because, for the time being, I do not expect to find fellowship in the real need and the real hope anywhere else.

He proceeded, however, to add three "comments" That "touch upon the event you are planning." The first was:

> You may not, under any circumstances, reckon me among the "fathers" of "religious socialism" — perhaps not even to the children, if you understand by "religious socialism" the presuppositions and methods of the circle gathered around Ragaz. I am grateful to Ragaz for many impulses, but for me, the heart of the matter is no longer to be found in the relation of the fixed magnitudes "religion" and "socialism." It lies rather in posing the Socratic question, the question of God.

After referring Herpel to *Suchet Gott, so wedet ihr leben!*, "a work I edited with my friend Eduard Thurneysen" and the *Römerbrief*, Barth gave expression, in the second place, to "the advice or wish" that "You might not proceed with your strivings too quickly into the great public, but instead devote all of your attention for now to working out the premises of 'what we want' in the circle of those

6   See G. Späth, "Neuwerk," *RGG*, 2nd ed., V, col. 523; idem, "Arnold, Eberhard," *RGG*, 2nd ed., I, col. 562; H. Zumpe, "Arnold, Eberhard," *RGG*, 3rd ed., I, col. 633; U. Schwab, "Neuwerk," *RGG*, 4th ed., 6, cols. 253f.; D. Dunkel, "Arnold, Eberhard," *RGG*, 4th ed., 1, col. 791.
7   Letter from O. Herpel to K. Barth, June 22, 1919 (KBA 9319.95).

who are already awakened to a desire for it." Third, Barth suggested that he be allowed to speak together with Thurneysen, with whom he had stood "for years in the closest fellowship of work and thought."[8]

On the same day, Barth forwarded Herpel's letter and his answer on to Thurneysen who, for his part, answered enthusiastically on the 28th. "Oh Karl, what a hopeful letter this is to receive from Germany."[9] Herpel's answer on June 30[10] made Barth "somewhat nervous" because of its "Religious Socialist cheering, in which something of the "'with God and for the Kaiser and the Fatherland' still resounds."[11] In spite of the critical distancing not only of Thurneysen,[12] but most certainly also of Barth, Herpel sent Barth a copy of the invitation to the conference, dated "end of July," in which the first responsible group named was the "Religious Socialist Union of Germany." The organizers made it clear that it was going out "only to a select number of men and women who were being extended personal invitations" to participate in the meeting in Tannenberg House in Tambach (Thüringia) — and this "in accordance with the wish frequently repeated by the Swiss." In any event, "in accordance with a suggestion coming from Switzerland," plenary addresses devoted to each of the three aspects of the conference theme "The Christian in the Church, in the State, and in Society" by each of the "Swiss gentlemen" was envisioned. In each case, a correlative paper would be offered by one of the Germans. For this purpose, the names of Dr. Hans Hartmann (pastor of Solingen), businessman Kurt Woermann (Hamburg), and Dr. Eberhard Arnold (director of a publishing house in Berlin) had already been decided upon. Herpel was asking each of the Swiss brothers in ministry to whom he had written to "deliver one of the Swiss papers." Once it was clear who could "come and give a paper, then I will tell you the names and ask you, as soon as you possibly can, to tell me how you have divided up the themes."[13]

Barth and Thurneysen, however, cancelled in August, as Barth explained in a letter to Pastor Hans Bader (Zurich), in order "to allow you and Ragaz to go first. You will probably serve the Germans better, in any case, since the questions that come to expression in themes they have chosen fit better with your task than to those we are now discussing."[14] Herpel answered Barth on August 21: "We are all very sorry that you have declined our invitation because it was precisely in your letters that we had read so very much of that which we wanted to hear from you Swiss in Tambach. Why then?" Herpel asked him to come "at least to the

8　　Letter from K. Barth to O. Herpel, June 26, 1919, rough draft (KBA 9219.11).

9　　*Bw. Th.* I, 335.

10　Letter from O. Herpel to K. Barth, June 30, 1919 (KBA 9319.96).

11　*Bw. Th.* I, 336f.

12　See *Bw. Th.* I, 339.

13　Letter from O. Herpel to K. Barth, end of July, 1919 (KBA 9319.116).

14　M. Mattmüller, *Leohard Ragaz und der religiöse Sozialismus: Eine Biographie*, Bd. II (Zürich: EVZ Verlag, 1968), 254.

plenary discussion" and perhaps "open one of them."[15] In the meantime, plans were being made to replace Barth as lecturer with his brother, Peter. Peter wrote to Safenwil on the same day: "Now it is I who am supposed to go to Tambach with Ragaz and Rudi Liechtenhan, to report on 'Christians in Black Ties and Tails.'"[16]

The very next day, Karl Barth spoke very critically about the Tambach venture and the participation of his brother in a letter to his German school-friend, Wilhelm Loew: "I do not expect much from this business." Herpel had left him with

> a very confused impression. The whole situation is strange: as if we had something to say to you which you could not know just as well yourselves. Ragaz will control the proceedings and, if he manages to impress, then the good German religious socialists will be in the same fix the movement here has been led into under his leadership.[17]

He clearly expressed himself in the same way to his brother Peter, who answered him on August 25: "I am grateful for your letter. It underscores all the doubts that I too have about going to Tambach." In addition, Karl Barth had "too little time at his disposal" due to another obligation; he would gladly pass the job on to someone else. "Bader or one of the other Zückers would most certainly fit better with the other two Swiss being sent to speak."[18] But Bader had already taken the place of Ragaz. Ragaz saw himself needed in the political struggle over the decisive question whether the Swiss Social Democracy should enter the Third International; a question that was soon to be voted upon. Moreover, he did not feel well, so he had declined the invitation to Tambach.[19] Gottlob Wieser, who was the backup candidate in such an eventuality, declined. And so it came about "by the strangest turn of events," as Karl Barth wrote to Thurneysen on September 2, 1919, "that in spite of all, I should go to Tambach to speak on 'The Christian in Society.'"[20]

Barth gave several reasons for his change of mind, with the removal of the "burden of Ragaz's presence"[21] weighing heavy in significance. Decisive for his decision was probably the fact that, under these circumstances, he saw an opportunity to present in Germany an outline of an argument that might overcome

15   Letter from O. Herpel to K. Barth, August 21, 1919 (KBA 9319.134).

16   Postcard from P. Barth to K. Barth, August 21, 1919 (KAB 9319.135). It should be noted that Peter's reference to "Christians in Black Ties and Tails" is a joke that had its source in a pun on the German word "Gesellschaft." The title proposed to Karl originally and now to Peter by the planners of the Tambach conference was "Der Christ in der Gesellschaft." The basic meaning of the word "Gesellschaft" is "society." But it can also be used to refer to "high society" or a quite formal reception where formal dress would be required.

17   Letter from Barth to W. Loew, August 8, 1919 (KBA 9219.18).

18   Letter from Peter Barth to Karl Barth, August 25, 1919 (KBA 9319.140).

19   Mattmüller, *Leonhard Ragaz und der religiöse Sozialismus*, 253f.

20   *Bw. Th.* I, 342f.

21   Ibid., 243.

the aporias of the religious socialist position of Ragaz in particular (Barth based this lecture on his Aarburg lecture of June 9, 1919, on "Christian Life"[22] and his sermon series on the great synthesis of the Epistle to the Ephesians.[23]) His lecture to a gathering of the Christlichen Studenten-Vereinigung in Aarburg had placed "the entire problematic of our practical conduct" under "the three great viewpoints" of the three kingdoms: *regnum naturae, regnum gratiae,* and *regnum gloriae,* which would give the Tambach address its outline as well.

[33] The question of the Christian in society is one that fills us with hope but at the same time leaves us strangely unsettled.

The Christian in society! Society is not left completely to itself. Marriage and family life, the economy and culture, art and science, the State, political parties, and international relations are not problem-free or uninhibited. They do not simply run their own courses according to laws that have their own logic and drive without being at least conditioned by another factor that is full of *promise.* We understand better today than we have in the past that the well-worn way is a false way. The catastrophe that we have experienced and in which we still stand has made that shockingly clear to many, but not to all. Wouldn't we prefer to turn away from life and society in deep skepticism and discouragement? But turn to what? One cannot turn away from life, from society. Life surrounds us on all sides [cf. Ps. 149.5]. It evokes questions in us. It places decisions before us. We must stand firmly in life. Today we long for a promise precisely because our eyes have been opened wide to the problematic character of existence. We want *out* of this society. We want a different society. But this is only a *wish.* We are painfully aware that despite all of the changes and all of the revolutions, everything remains as it was before. And so we ask, "Watchman is the night almost gone?" [Isa. 21.11f.].

It is here that the thought of *"the Christian* in society" becomes a promise. It brings a new element in the midst of the old, a new truth in the midst of errors and lies, a new righteousness in a sea of unrighteousness, a spiritual presence among coarse, material tendencies, a formative power of life in all of the weak, unstable spiritual movements, a unity in the complete disintegration of society, even in our [34] own times. We

22   This lecture will appear in the third edition of *GA,* in the forthcoming volume, 48, *Vorträge und kleinere Arbeiten, 1914–1921.* Marquardt offers a summary of its contents in *Der Christ in der Gesellschaft, 1919–1921,* 22f.

23   See Karl Barth, *Predigten 1919,* H. Schmidt, ed., *GA,* I (Zürich: TVZ, 2003), 172–334. Barth speaks in connection with the citation from Col. 1.28 of the "great synthesis of the Epistle to the Colossians," which finds parallels in the Epistle to the Ephesians, as his interpretation shows. See p. 37.

agree that "*the Christian*" cannot mean "*the Christians*" — neither the mass of the baptized nor somehow the elect little company of religious socialists, nor even the most noble and pious Christians of whom we might otherwise think. The Christian is *the Christ*. The Christian is that which dwells within us. It is not us but is, rather, Christ in us [cf. Rom. 8.10; 2 Cor. 13.5, Col. 1.27].

This "Christ in us" must be understood in all of its Pauline depth. It does not refer to a psychic condition, a being grasped or overpowered, or some such thing. Rather, it is a presupposition. "In us" means "above us," "behind us," "beyond us." It must be understood in all of its Pauline breadth as well. We will do well to avoid putting up once again the protective wall that separates Jews from Gentiles, so-called Christians from so-called non-Christians [Eph. 2.14; cf. 2.12], those who are grasped from those who are not. The congregation of Christ is a house that is open on all sides, for Christ is always also for the others, for those who are outside, for those who have died [Heb. 13.12f.; cf. 3.2; 6; 10.21]. In us, above us, behind us, beyond us — there is a reflection upon the meaning of life, a reminder of the Origin of humanity, a turning to the Lord of the world, a critical "No" and a creative "Yes" upon the entire content of our consciences. It is a change from the old to the new eon. The cross is its sign and fulfillment!

That is Christ in us. But *is* Christ in us? Is Christ even in today's society? We hesitate to answer, do we not! And we know why we hesitate. But where would we get the right to deny it? Christ the Savior is *here*[24] — otherwise the question would not be raised, the question that is the secret meaning of all of the movements of our time, the question that has brought us together in these days as those who are unknown and yet well-known [cf. 2 Cor. 6.9]. There are questions that we could not pose at all if an answer were not already there; questions that we could not even take up without the courage of that Augustinian claim: "You would not seek me if you had not already found me!"[25] We *have* this courage. We must now *acknowledge* it. By doing so, we acknowledge Christ; we acknowledge his presence and his future. If Christ is in us, then society is not God-forsaken — despite its folly. To speak of him as the "image of the invisible God," the "firstborn of all creatures" in us [1 Cor. 1.15], means that we

24   "Christ der Ritter ist da" is the concluding line to the second verse of the Christmas hymn "Stille Nacht" ("Silent Night") by Joseph Franz Mohr (*RG* 412; *EG* 46). In English it is "Christ the Savior is born" (*LBW* 65; *The Presbyterian Hymnal* [Louisville, KY: Westminster/John Knox Press, 1990], 60).

25   See Blaise Pascal, *Pensées* (1670), Fragment 553 [L. Brunschvicg], CH.-M. Granges, ed. (Paris, 1961), 212: "Le Mystère de Jésus": "Console-toi, tu ne me chercherais pas, si tu ne m'avais trouvé." For the background of this thought, see Augustine, *Confessions* X, 20, 29.

have a goal and a future. We think of the leaven that a woman took and hid under three bushels of flour until it [35] was completely leavened [Mt. 13.33f.]. "The hope of glory" is what Paul called this "mystery among the Gentiles" [Col. 1.27]. Therefore, we call you to hope.[26]

But our theme has another, painfully remarkable meaning and this is what may have been foremost in the minds of those who selected it. The Christian — in society. How these two things fall apart, how abstractly they stand facing each other! How strange, almost fantastic do the great syntheses of the Epistle to the Colossians appear to us! But why should that be so?

What does 'the Christian' mean for us? What *must* it mean for us? In all likelihood, we think in terms of a holy realm set apart unto itself, irrespective of whether we explain this separation in a more metaphysical way or in a more psychological way. Christians appear to us as special people next to other people, Christianity as a special concern next to other concerns, Christ as a special phenomenon next to other phenomena. The complaints of philosophy about the presumption of religion which is expressed in this separation are not new, nor are the activities of theologians which nourish such suspicions. Instructed by the experiences of our time, many today recognize an emergency situation in that which was truly a theological presumption. But the emergency situation appears almost inescapable. Even philosophy has not yet spoken the word which would overcome it. Indeed, we sense once again that the meaning of so-called religion consists in its relation to life as it is really lived, living in society and not in separation from it. A separated, holy realm is no holy realm. From the secure port of our specifically religious location — once praised often and loudly — we look with longing out at the world because we sense that, as many theologians are once again beginning to sense, that there can be no "inside" so long as there is an "outside."[27] But there is still more a looking-out and a looking-across. For, the basis of the separation of the religious realm is not annulled simply because it dawns on us that it ought not to be. Truly, between the "Christ in us" and the world, it is not simply a matter of opening the floodgates and allowing the waiting water to flow over the thirsty land. Readily available are the combinations like "Christian-Social," [36] "Evangelical-Social," "Religious-Social," but it is well worth considering whether the hyphens we boldly draw are not dangerous short-circuits.

---

26   "Wir heissen euch hoffen" is the concluding line of J.W. Goethe's poem "Symbolum."
27   See J.W. Goethe's poem, "Epirrhema":

> Nothing is inside, nothing is outside:
> For what is inside is outside.

The paradox that the service of God must be or become the service of people is highly spiritual.[28] But whether our zealous service of people — even if it takes place in the name of the purest love[29] — becomes the service of God by way of such inspiration is a topic for another time. The evangelical reminder that the seed is the Word and the world is the field is quite true [Mt. 13.38p.], but what is the Word and which of us has it! And should we not for once *be fearful* when confronted with the task of becoming sowers of the Word on behalf of the world, a task which filled even the likes of Moses, Isaiah, and Jeremiah with dread [c.f. Exod. 2.11f.; Isa. 6.5; Jer. 1.6]? Is the initial refusal of these men to relate the divine to the life of human beings any more inappropriate than our rash readiness to do so? Is the flight of Jonah from the Lord only to be explained by reference to the presumption of religion [Jon. 1.3]? These men did not do what they did on merely a little experience, insight, and good will. The divine is something complete in itself, self-contained, new in kind, different from the world. It does not allow itself to be divided and distributed precisely because it is more than religion. It does not allow itself to be used. It wants to tear down and build up. It is complete in itself or it is nothing at all.

Where, then, does the world of God have open windows to our social life? How do we come to act as if it did? To be sure, we may succeed in *secularizing* Christ for the umpteenth time — today (for example) for the sake of social democracy, pacifism, the Christian Youth Movement [*Wandervogel*], just as it was in the past for the sake of our fatherlands, for being Swiss and German, and for the sake of the liberalism of the educated classes. But are we not horrified by such a prospect? We do not want to betray Christ yet again. But on the other hand, we get ourselves into quite the jam when we try to do that which insight and good will lead us to do, and leave undone those things which they tell us not to do! How difficult it is to take even the smallest steps with Christ in society with a pure heart and reverence for the holy! With what brittleness does the divine — if it is the divine — relate to the human, which we so gladly want to mix together today! How dangerous it is to get involved with God in the midst of the questions, concerns, and agitations of society! Where will we be led if [37] we give up the separation of the religious realm and engage God with *seriousness*? Truly, God is less cheaply to be had today than ever before, and we would do well to take very seriously

---

28   See Leonard Ragaz, *Das Evangelium und der soziale Kampf der Gegenwart*, 2nd ed. (Basel: Lendorff, 1907), 27: "Worship of God is the service of humans. We are not allowed to receive anything from God without letting our brother participate in it."

29   See J.W. Goethe, *Faust I*, V, 2349 (the witches' kitchen scene); ET *Goethe's Faust*, Walter Kaufmann, trans. (New York: Anchor Books, 1963), 235.

the scruple that is raised precisely from this side against our new rallying cry. "Who among you, wanting to building a tower, does not sit down first and consider the costs, to see whether he can complete it?" [Lk. 14.28]. This is the one side.

On the other side, we see *society*. However true it may be that it is inwardly crumbling, it relates to everything outside of itself as a self-contained whole — without windows to the kingdom of heaven. Where is the sense in all of the nonsense, the Origin in all that is degenerate, the wheat among the tares [Mt. 13.24-30, 36-43]? Where is God in all that is human, all too human?[30] You are dust and to dust you will return [Gen. 3.19]! Isn't that the judgment which falls upon humanity and its own confession of faith? We too, suffer today under *this* self-enclosedness because we have become aware of its bitter consequences.

Everything in us bristles at the thought of hearing and repeating any-time soon those statements made ad nauseam before the War concerning the anatomy of culture, the State, and economic life.[31] So much, so very much, would we like to understand today's society in Christ, to renew it in Christ, "to employ the fundamental principles of Jesus' way of being as maxims for any and every public, ethnic, state, and worldly formation of society" — as you put it in your program.[32] If only we had the trans-figuring optimism of a Richard Rothe for such "employment"! There is now no way for us to be led back to him. But won't the way forward lead us to Friedrich Naumann, who also at one time began with such optimism? We are hindered from such "employment" first of all by the brutal fact that the autonomy of social life, having once been acquired and made present, continues inexorably to have its effect even in this age of revolution. It is not overcome simply because we have become thoroughly tired of it. We wanted it to be, so that "roughly jostling, things crowd close in space."[33] And now, for the time being, we have to have it

---

30   See Friedrich Nietzsche, *Menschlisches. Allzumenschliches. Ein Buch für freie Geister* (Chemnitz: Schmeitzner, 1878; ET *Human, All Too Human*, trans. and ed. by R.J. Hollingdale (New York: Cambridge University Press, 1996).

31   As the allusions which follow make clear, Barth is thinking here above all of the programmatic remarks of Friedrich Naumann as stated most impressively in his "Briefe über Religion" in *Werke I: Religiöse Schriften* (Cologne: Westdt.Verlag, 1964), 566–632.

32   See *Der christliche Demokrat (Das Neue Werk)*, 1, cols. 191, 208, 240.

33   ". . . hart im Raume sich die Sachen stoβen . . ." is from Friedrich Schiller, *Wallensteins Tod*, II, 2, in *Schillers sämmtliche Werke 3* (Stüttgart: J.G. Cotta'schen Verlag, 1860), 221–222; ET *The Robbers and Wallenstein*, trans. by F.J. Lamport (London: Penguin Books, 1979), 350.

Schnell fertig ist die Jugend mit dem Wort,

. . .

Gleich heiβt ihr alles schändlich oder würdig,
Bös oder gut — und was die Einbildung

that way. We might wish to strip these spheres once again of the religious radiance by which — with the courage of despair or to the point of aesthetic excess — they were surrounded at the turn of the century by Naumann and his followers. But wishing does not yet set us free from the spirits which have been called up.[34] [38]

If today, and perhaps for the first time in history, the holy is asserting its rights over the profane — much to our chagrin — then the profane is just as aggressively asserting its rights over the holy. Society is now governed by its own logos or, actually, by a whole series of god-like hypostases and powers. We might like to compare ourselves to the most pious and best of the Hellenistic and pre-Reformation ages who came to the realization that the idols are nothing [1 Cor. 8.4]. But even when we know they are nothing, their demonic power over our lives is not yet broken. Critical doubt directed toward the god of this world is one thing; it is an altogether different thing to know the δύναμις, the meaning and power of the living God who is creating a new world. Without this knowledge, "Christian-Social" is probably still nonsense, even today.[35] To be sure, here too, lies the possibility of patching old clothing with cloth cut loose from new clothing [Mt. 9.16p]. I am thinking here of the attempt to add an ecclesiastical superstructure or extension onto worldly society in accordance with the old misunderstanding of the words of Jesus, "give to the Kaiser that which is the Kaiser's and to God that which is God's" [Mt. 22.21p]. The attempt made by the Christian Middle Ages to *clericalize* society will be undertaken once again, perhaps, and once again crowned with the success which can be granted to it, given its nature.

Already the beginnings of such an effort have shown themselves on Protestant soil as well: "Let us build a new church with democratic airs and a Socialist impulse! Let us build parish houses, look after the welfare of young people, host evening discussions and musical services! Let us

Phantastisch schleppt in diesen dunklen Namen,
Das bürdet sie den Sachen auf und Wesen.
Eng ist die Welt, und das Gehirn is die *weit*,
Leicht beieinander wohnen die Gedanken,
Doch hart in Raume stoßen sich die Sachen,
Wo eines Platz nimmt, muß das andere rücken,
Wer nicht vertrieben sein will, muß vertreiben,
Da herrscht der Streit, und nur die Stärke siegt.

34   See the next-to-last stanza of Goethe's poem "Der Zauberlehring."
35   Kaiser Wilhelm II said something similar in a dispatch from February 23, 1896: "Political pastors are nothing [*ein Unding*]. Whoever is Christian is also social. 'Christian-Social' is nonsense and leads to an overestimation of oneself and impatience. Pastors should take care of the souls of their parishioners, practice love of the neighbor and leave politics out of it. Politics is no concern of theirs."

get off our high horses and allow the laity to take our place in the pulpit! Let us go the old way with new enthusiasm which begins with the Inner Mission's pietism of love, and which will end with deadly certainty in the liberalism of Naumann!" Perhaps we can forget, with all the new patches — new *to us* at least — that the old clothes are still the *old* clothes. But surely we will reject precisely this attempt as the most dangerous betrayal of society. If we refuse to learn once again to wait upon God, and instead set out with renewed zeal to build up our churches and chapels, we will deceive society about that which we really intend, namely, God's help. But it is just as certain that when we do not allow ourselves to be lulled to sleep by the siren songs of modern ecclesiasticism, [39] we stand, with our program of "*omnia instaurare in Christo*,"[36] before the naturally developed and steadfast realities of society as those who bite down on granite!

We must bravely resist the new churchly temptation! But the more bravely we resist, the more powerfully the giants we are preparing to conquer stand before us. We cannot, therefore, in accordance with the old admonition, reckon soberly enough with "reality" if we are to confront the task of carrying out our program. If things stay as they are, it is with good reason that there are impossible ideals and unreachable goals. That is the other side of the problem.

This, then, is what I have discovered in our theme: First of all, a great hope, a light from above, falling upon our situation, but with it an evil abstraction, a frightening confrontation of two completely different magnitudes! We must look both squarely in the face. That is our hope, and that is our need in Christ and in society. Do not expect me to present a solution though. None of us may boast of a solution here. There is only *one* solution, which is to be found in God himself. Our task can only be the honest, thorough, and, dare I say, priestly *awakening* of others to our hope and need, for it is through an awareness of both that God's way to us is made more smooth. Obviously, what I can offer you here today is the only the sketch of some *viewpoints* [*Gesichtspunkte*] under which that priestly work must take place. Today, this is all that is necessary [Lk. 10.42]. One can always speak of these viewpoints in different ways. But I am confident that the viewpoints of which I speak now are the essential ones, and that there are no others to be placed next to them.

Let us first identify the *standpoint* [*Standort*] which we are taking with regard to the situation — without consideration at this point for that

---

36   See Eph. 1.10 in the Vulgate. See also the motto of Pius X in his first encyclical from April 10, 1903, and in his *Motu proprio* from March 19, 1904.

which is hopeful and that which is needful about it. I say "in fact" for it is not a matter of [40] first taking it up. We have already taken it up in that this situation has become a problem to us.

"Standpoint," however, is not the right word. Our position in relation to the situation is a moment in a *movement*, comparable to a freeze-frame portrait of a bird in flight. Outside of the context provided by the movement, the picture is meaningless, impossible, incomprehensible. With that image, I am certainly not referring to the socialist movement or the religious socialist movement or the more general, somewhat questionable movement of Christianity. I refer rather to *the* movement, that movement that cuts vertically from above[37] through all of these movements as their hidden, transcendent meaning and engine, the movement that does not have its origin and its goal in space, time, or the contingency of things. It is not one movement among others. I am referring to the movement of the history of God or, alternately expressed, the movement of the knowledge of God, the movement whose power and significance are unveiled in the resurrection of Jesus Christ from the dead. This is what we are connected with when the situation of the Christian in society becomes an issue for us, whether in hope or in need or in both at the same time.

Now prepare yourselves to hear my weakest but most important point. Methodological discussions always have something unfortunate, impossible, and dangerous about them. Almost unavoidably, they lapse into the most laughable desire to try to go ahead and paint the bird in flight anyway, thereby making the movement a theme or an object in its own right, cut off from that which produces the movement. It was not for nothing that Kant anxiously guarded himself against attempts to understand his *Critique of Pure Reason* as a new metaphysic rather than as prolegomena.[38]

That his warnings were so easily ignored shows us how great the danger with which we are dealing really is. The critique of reason must complete itself in critical science; the history of God must take place in deeds and proofs; the knowledge of God must be given in compelling, open-minded, self-authenticating understanding and speech; life must be conducted in a lived existence — otherwise what are all of the words

37   See Friederich Zündel, *Aus der Apostelzeit* (Zürich: Höhr, 1886), 26: "It was certainly a tremendous thing that the Apostles set forth in their proclamation that something new and unheard of had happened, like the shock of a storm that falls down from the heavens, perpendicularly form above."

38   See the Preface to the second edition of Kant's *Critique of Pure Reason*, Paul Guyer, Allen W. Wood, trans. and ed. (New York Cambridge University Press, 1998 [B XXIII], 113: "The critique of pure reason" is a "tractate of method, not a system of science itself." See also the preface to his *Prolegomena to Any Future Metaphysic That Will Present Itself as a Science* (Oxford: Oxford University Press, 2004) [A3], 63: "These Prolegomena . . . are . . . not serviceable for the systematic exposition of a ready-made science, but merely for the discovery of science itself."

about the Word about? The philosopher experiences this unfortunate state of affairs when he proclaims the Origin in which knowing and doing, what ought to be and what is, are one.[39] We experience this unfortunate state of affairs when we testify to the [41] reality of the living God. Make us participants in the power of the Origin! Make us participants in the power of the living God! This is what the listener might long for, if he were allowed to do so! It is at this point that we stand in the presupposition, in the face of our great poverty. That of which we would speak must be present, must be mediated, be effective, or else it is not that of which we want to speak. "The Word of God is living and powerful and sharper than any two-edged sword, and it penetrates . . ." [Heb. 4.12]. It is not in my power to speak this living, powerful, sharp, penetrating Word of God any more than it is in your power to hear it. Of course, we may profess our longing for it with the religious pathos that is appropriate to that longing — such an act is possible for us. For the sake of the object of our interest, however, I would forbid even that much. It is better that we become conscious of our poverty — precisely in the presupposition — and that we surrender to no religious opinion, which, for all its truthfulness, might well serve only to conceal it. Therefore, I *cannot* give you here what I ought to give you. A miracle would have to happen. To testify in positive terms that we are dealing here with a very great thing is something I do not *care* to do. The only option left for me is to describe in dry words what is at stake. Bear in mind, however, that in what I try to say here, I am thinking of the real bird, the bird in flight, and not some enigmatic picture. I invite you to be caught up in its movement just as I am trying to do — to the extent that it is given to any of us to do so.

We are concerned here with God. Not with religion, but with the movement that proceeds *from* God, with our being moved by *him*. Hallowed be *thy* name! *Thy* kingdom come! *Thy* will be done! What we call "religious experience" is a completely derived, secondary, broken form of the divine. Even in the highest and purest instances, it is form and not content. For far too long, the whole of our theology has read the Bible and church history under the guidance of this formal point of view. For far too long, the Church has directed all of its activities toward the cultivation of all kinds of piety. Today, we would like to turn our attention entirely away from this form. The Immediate, the Origin, will never be experienced as such. All "experiencing" is but a *gesture* toward the Origin, toward God. And the [42] movement of life unveiled in Jesus

---

39   It is above all Karl Barth's brother Heinrich who is in view here. Cf. Heinrich's lecture at the Aarau Student Conference of 1919, "Gotteserkenntnis" (reprinted in *Anfänge* I, 221–255, esp. 238f. See also Heinrich Barth, *Das Problem des Ursprungs in der platonsichen Philosophie* (Munich: Chr. Kaiser Verlag, 1921).

is not some kind of new piety. It is for that reason that Paul and John
take no interest in the personal life of the so-called historical Jesus but in
his resurrection only. It is for that reason that the Synoptic reports about
Jesus are completely incomprehensible without Bengel's insight into their
intention: *spirant resurrectionem* ["they breathe of the resurrection"].[40] The
Catholic Middle Ages and the Reformation still understood that to some
extent. It remained for Pietism, Schleiermacher, and modern Christianity
to intentionally read the New Testament kerygma backwards. We must
again acquire the great objectivity [*Sachlichkeit*[41]] out of which Paul
encountered the prophets and Plato. Christ is the unconditionally *new*
thing from *above*; the way, the truth, and the life of *God* in the midst of
men; the Son of Man in whom humanity becomes aware of its *immediacy*
to God. But keep your distance! Not even the finest psychic givenness
of the *form* of this becoming-conscious may replace or conceal the true
transcendence of this *content*. The step from the *experience* of Yahweh to
the experience of Baal is too small. Religious processes are all too closely
related to sexual processes. It is out of concern for the *purity* and *superiority*
of the life-movement in which we stand, and the deepest understanding
of ourselves that I emphasize that this life-movement is not our accidental experience of God, our accidental piety. It is not an experience
next to other experiences. (I am deliberately speaking in as abstract and
theoretical a way as possible, so that all emotional misunderstandings
might be excluded for once.) The life-movement in which we stand is
the perpendicular line which cuts through all of our pieties and experiences, essentially passing them by. It is the breakthrough into profane life
and the appearing of the world of God out of its inaccessible holy place.
It is the bodily resurrection of Christ from the dead. Our sharing in its
significance and power — *that* is the way we are moved.

We must return to that inapproachability we mentioned earlier,
the inapproachability in which the divine stands over and against the
human. Already at that point, we probably had the impression that the
separation of the holy from the profane could not be the end of the

---

40   This phrase has often been cited and constantly attributed to Johann Albrecht Bengel without
     supporting evidence, especially by Barth himself. According to several specialists in the works
     of Bengel, it is not to be found in there. Its origins must remain unknown for now.

41   The word "*Sachlichkeit*," as it is used here is virtually untranslatable. Although the standard definition
     is "objectivity," Barth does not intend his listeners to think in terms of a psychic condition — as
     the whole of this lecture makes amply clear. For us, perhaps, to be "objective" would mean that
     when we think about a problem, we think about it in a way that is "neutral", "cool," "detached,"
     "without a vested interest." For Barth, however, "objectivity" refers to thinking "out of" or "on the
     basis of" the history of God, a history that is nowhere given directly to us for inspection. Thinking
     on a basis of this kind is clearly impossible apart from a wholly gracious divine action, for it is a
     mode of thinking in accordance with an object that is not directly "given" to human cognition.

matter. God could not be God if that were the end of the matter. *In spite of* the inapproachability of God, there *must* be a way from there to here. With this "must" and this "in spite of," we confess [43] the miracle of the *revelation* of God. However much the holy, the divine, may frighten us away by virtue of its unattainable heights, we cannot but take the risk of relating it immediately to our life in its entirety. We need to attend to the voice which says to us: "Come no closer! Remove the shoes from your feet for the place on which you stand is holy ground!" [Exod. 3.5]. Like Moses, we need to be frightened of gazing upon God.

But now we hear the same voice saying something more. "I have seen the suffering of my people in Egypt. I have heard their cry. And I have come down to deliver them from the hands of the Egyptians" [Exod. 3.7f.]. And we recognize that the prohibition is given only for the sake of the fullness and clarity of the message that follows. Even Isaiah, even Jonah, finally had to show some reverence for the holy so that they might take upon themselves the task of relating the divine directly to the profane life of humans [Isa. 6.8f.; Jonah 3]. The time of the *mysterium tremendum*,[42] the time which is nothing more than what it is, has run its course, and with it, the time of dread before the divine, which is and remains only dread. The kernel breaks through the hard outer shell. Our hearing the message, our sharing in the courage of God to direct our attention to the meaning of his "coming down" for us, our sharing in the triumph over all *mere* dread, even as it is carried out with dread — none of these things are the deeds of humans. They are, rather, the act of God in humans. Precisely for this reason, the *knowledge* of God is essentially the *history* of God and no mere event in our consciousness. Something happens from God's side; a miracle takes place before our eyes [cf. Ps. 118.23]. A *new* possibility and reality opens up before humanity.

Once we have become conscious of the Life in life, we can no longer bear living in the land of death, in an existence whose forms cause us most painfully to miss the meaning of life, the relation to the creative Origin. Surely, we recognize the Wholly Other,[43] eternity in the life of the divine. But we cannot get over the fact that only *eternal* life is and can be called "life." It is precisely the wholly otherness of God, that which struggles against all secularizing, against all mere practice and hyphens, which forces us to be on the lookout for a deeply rooted, fundamental,

---

42   This phrase is used to describe one moment in the experience of the Numinous in Rudolf Otto, *Das Heilge. Über das Irrationale in der Idee des Göttlichen und sein Verhältnis zum Rationalen* (Munich: Beck, 1963), 31; ET *The Idea of the Holy: An Inquiry into the Non-rational Factor in the Idea of the Divine and its Relation to the Rational*, 2nd ed., trans. John W. Harvey (Oxford: Oxford University Press, 1950), chapter 4, 12f.

43   Otto, *Das Heilige*, 28–37; ET *The Idea of the Holy*, chapter 5, 25–30.

and original connection of our life to that wholly other life. We want
to live and not die. It is the living *God* who, in his encounter with us,
compels us to believe in *our* life [44] too. It may be that at the end of the
day, this revival of our life, in which God makes us believe, consists in the
absolutely otherworldly reconstruction [*Aufhebung*] of all that is creaturely,
of all that which places us over and against the life of God here and now.
Most fundamentally, that is precisely what we believe. "We await the
redemption of our bodies" [Rom. 8.23]. And yet this reconstruction must
relate to the entirety of our life in this world. And the longer the beam
of light becomes that shines into our souls through a growing knowledge
of God, the less it will allow us to rest content in even a single point of
the character of our existence in this world, which is, ultimately, fatal.

With the insight of this breakthrough of the divine into the human, it
is clear that we also cannot rest content with the isolation of the human
toward the divine. The unrest that God is preparing for us has to bring
us into critical opposition to "life." "Critical" is here to be understood in
the most profound sense, deeper than the meaning that it has acquired
in the history of ideas. The miracle of faith corresponds to the miracle of
revelation. The history of God is on this side as well, as is the *knowledge*
of God. And once again, this is no mere event in our consciousness but
rather a new, necessary thing from above. Indeed, it may be fully clear to
us that the State and the economy, the arts and the sciences, or even more
basically, the brutal presuppositions of society such as the banal necessities
of eating, drinking, sleeping, growing old, follow their own set of laws
of movement and inertia. And indeed, we must seriously reckon with
the fact that we will experience the power of these laws again and again.
But despite the absolute foolishness of biting on stone, there is one thing
that is clearer still, and it is that we can no longer concede an ultimate,
independent validity to these laws.

The reason we cannot do this is *not only* because we have been shamed
into becoming outwardly wise regarding the experiences of our times.
It is *not only* because we have become spiritually tired of the pantheon
of independent deities — tired to the point of exhaustion. It is *not only*
because skepticism and enlightenment have set in vis-à-vis the "cosmic
powers of darkness" [Eph. 6.12] after the euphoria [at the outbreak of
the War] faded — indeed, all this pales in the meaning and the power of
the resurrection. Rather, it *is because* our soul has been awakened to an
awareness of its immediacy to God, awakened to an immediacy of all
things, relationships, orders, and arrangements to God, an immediacy that
has been lost [45] and must be regained. For in that the *soul* is reminded
once again of its origin in God, it locates the origin of *society* therein as
well. In that it comes to itself, it finds the meaning of *life* in its complete
breadth — together with a sense of its own most real participation, guilt,

and responsibility. It places itself under the same judgment that the world faces and takes the world as a burden upon itself. There is no awakening of the soul that could be anything other than "a compassionate bearing of the troubles of its contemporaries."[44]

This awakening of the soul is the movement in which we stand, the movement of the history of God or of the knowledge of God, the movement in life toward Life. In that we are in the process of awakening, we can no longer avoid subjecting all the "validities" of life to a fundamental negation, testing them to see whether they stand in any kind of connection to that which alone can be valid. Everything that lives must allow itself to be measured by Life itself. An independent life *next to* Life is not life but death. Dead are all things that want to be more than matter, which would like to lay claim to being a course lump of materiality in and for themselves. Dead is our personal life, even when it is the noblest, finest, and most pious, if it does not have its beginning in the fear of God [cf. Ps. 11.10; Prov. 1.7; Sir. 1.16]. Dead are all separated parts, no matter how enthusiastically we might like to hold them in our hands. If the spiritual bond that joins them together is missing,[45] then they are missing everything. Dead is "inwardness" for its own sake, just as much as "outwardness" for its own sake. Dead are all "things-in-themselves," all here and there, then and now, this and that which are not at the same time one. Dead are all mere "givens." Dead is every metaphysic. Dead would be God himself, if he only pushed against the world from the outside,[46] if he were a "thing-in-itself" and not the One in All, the Creator of all things visible and invisible, the Beginning and the End. It is the revolution of Life against the powers of death that surround it, the powers in which we ourselves are caught.

We can no longer allow ourselves to be *completely* deceived as to the true character of the powers of death by the ideologies with which they surround themselves and by everything that speaks only relatively for their validity. There is something in us that calls them into question from the ground up. That is, in fact, the meaning of our situation, a meaning that stands out in an uncommonly clear and significant way in the *current circumstances*, even if not in an altogether new [46] way. The Life has risen

---

44   From the fifth verse of the song "Zerstreut und mannigfach geschieden" by S. Preiswerk, in *Evangelischer Liederkranz aus ältere und neuere Zeit* (Basel, 1844), Nr. 124, 155f.

      Lass uns ein Salz der Erde werden
      Und als der Menschheit erste Kraft
      Mitleidend tragen die Beschwerden
      Der ganzen Zeitgenossenschaft

45   See Goethe, *Faust I*,V, 1938f. (the scene in the study); *Goethe's Faust*, 199.
46   See Goethe's poem "Was wär ein Gott, der nur von aussen stiesse."

up against the death that is in life. There can be no question of reading something into the strangely convoluted and ambiguous movements of our time. But it is a question of grasping their deepest meaning with compassion and hope. We do not deceive ourselves with regard to the fact that the shaking of so many "things-in-themselves" that we are experiencing today threatens *here* to remain under the spell of the old ways and *there* to turn into the genesis of new materiality and godlessness in place of the old. Therefore, we will remember to bear in mind what all this is really about: We are speaking of the deadly isolation of the human from the divine which is being called into question with bitter earnestness at more than one point today.

However justified we may be to shake our heads over the fantastic drive for freedom on the part of the youth of today, alienation and opposition should by no means be the final word where our attitude toward them is concerned. It is *authority for its own sake* against which the modern youth movement in all of its variations is directing itself. And whoever would like to be an educator today must place themselves on their side in this battle — no matter what Foerster says.[47] However true it may be that the sanctity of family life is at risk in the dissolution that we see happening in families today, we may not — despite the anger and opposition we are experienceing with this development — miss the fact that what is ultimately at stake is an attack on *the family for the family's sake*. In truth, the family has not been a holy thing at all but the most voracious idol of the bourgeoisie. However strong our aversion to the products of modern expressionistic art may be, it is abundantly clear that these men are concerned with something, with the content, with the relationship of the beautiful to the one thing most necessary in life in contrast to *art for its own sake*, an art that truly may not appeal with certainty to either Raphael or Dürer for its justification. Our response to the new direction in art must be something more than a mere shake of the head. And if we should, in all seriousness (for it concerns the question of existence), join our voices with those who are saying that it is work, work which Europe needs now, we should not be astonished or indignant if the response of the Sparticists is that they would rather perish and see everything else perish than to take up the [47] yoke again of *work for its own sake*. And finally, in our efforts to comprehend the movements of our time, we will be full participants where the Church is called into question. Did you too, think that one of the most surprising things about the German Revolution, and for the near future most discouraging, was the way the

---

47   Friedrich W. Foerster (1869–1966) was among those who came to place a strong emphasis upon the value of authority and the dangers of individualism. See idem, *Authorität und Freiheit: Betrachtungen zum Kulturproblem der Kirche* (Kempten/Munich: Kösel, 1910).

new government quickly came to a halt before the gates of *religion for its own sake*? How easily this abstraction, this power of death in both its Catholic and Protestant forms, could assert its validity without having to contend with a single, noteworthy protest! If anywhere, it is precisely at this point that we should be the first to comprehend this protest if it comes. Indeed, we should raise it ourselves, if it does not come. We should be the first to comprehend that which the pathetic opponents of the Church in our day have clearly not comprehended, namely, that the divine is the thing which least of all can be treated and paid attention to as a "thing-in-itself."

Comprehending! Allow me to summarize the meaning of this unified movement in which we find ourselves, the movement of Life in death and Life out of death, in this one word: comprehending. We want to comprehend the great unsettling of humans by God and, therefore, the great shaking of the foundations of the world. We want to comprehend all that moves and all that is moved, even in its godless rest. We want to comprehend our contemporaries, from Naumann to Blumhardt, from Wilson, to Lenin, in all the various stages of the same movement in which we see them. We want to comprehend our time and its signs, to comprehend ourselves in our strange unrest and turbulence. To comprehend means to see that from God's point of view [*von Gott aus*] everything is as it must be and could not be otherwise. To comprehend means taking the entire situation upon ourselves in the fear of God and in the fear of God entering into the movement of the times. To comprehend means to receive forgiveness in order to forgive ourselves. That is what we are being driven to because it is necessary for us. Let us not be deceived: The unrest that comes from God, the unrest that brings us into critical opposition to life, contains the most positive and fruitful achievement imaginable. The judgment of God upon the world is the establishment of his own righteousness. To allow oneself to be "thrown back" to the beginning is not an empty negation if we [48] are really "thrown back" upon God. For only with God can we truly be positive. The *negation* that proceeds from God and which God intends is positive, whereas all *positions* that are not built on God are negative. To *comprehend* the meaning of our times in God and, therefore, to enter into the critical opposition to life and the unrest that God brings would mean, at the same time, to *give* our times their meaning in God.

In contrast to all ideologies that would like to dress up and transfigure materiality, forgiveness is the power of God on earth that is creating something new. It is precisely by passing through all fear, reluctant skepticism, and polemical resolution vis-à-vis the things of this world to their origin in God that we approach the point where the living Word and the creative deed must appear again. In our falling back upon God, however, let us not be misled about the direction of the movement itself by the negative and degenerative appearances that we experience along the way in ourselves and in the world. The watchmen, who according to the bold intuition of Grünewald and Rembrandt,[48] stagger down from their seat on the closed tomb at the moment of the resurrection, offer merely a negative, an "unpleasant and far from instructive sight."[49] But what does it matter? We also know that this sight is *not* the resurrection. So who is directing our attention to this sideshow? Who hinders us from seeing the resurrection itself, from acquiring knowledge of God, from experiencing the history of God! And who could see the resurrection without *participating* in it, without being made *alive*, without joining in the *victory* of life?

What have we accomplished by describing our situation as a moment in the movement in which we stand? Have we merely placed a new title over the old, unholy conflict? Perhaps so. We have tried to *remind* ourselves of what we have forgotten and what we continually forget about God's revelation and our own faith. But perhaps we have failed. We have tried to direct our attention to the *Life* which triumphs over death in Christ. But perhaps we have seen only one dead thing among others. We have tried to describe the *Archimedean point* on the basis of which our [49] soul is moved — and with it, society. But perhaps we have only spoken and heard once again of a reified metaphysical reality. Perhaps we have spoken only of a false transcendence. In this evil possibility there is to be found the weakness and the danger of what I have been saying. But isn't it actually profane to take this evil possibility — as possibility — much too seriously? In God, it is obviously an impossibility, and it is in God that we live, move, and have our being [Acts 17.28]. How could we appeal to this highest court, to this presupposition of all our examinations without finally coming to an understanding of ourselves in spite of all possibilities to the contrary? How can we not understand that we draw our *Life* from the power of the resurrection regardless of the poverty of our knowledge of it and of our being moved by it; without understanding that the resurrection of Christ from the dead is not a question but the answer which has been given to us and which we have already given, ". . . [the gospel] which you also have received, in which you also stand,

---

48   See, for example, Matthias Grünewald's depiction of the resurrection in his Isenheim Altar in Colmar, France and Rembrandt's portrayals of Mt. 28.3 from the year 1639 in the Alte Pinakothek Museum in Munich.

49   The phrase plays on a line from Goethe's *Italienische Reise*, March 6, 1787, where he considers the "inside of the maw" of Mt. Vesuvius: "The sight was neither instructive nor pleasing . . ."; ET J.W. Goethe, *Selected Works: Including the Sorrows of Young Werther, Elective Affinities, Italian Journey and Faust* (New York: A.A. Knopf, 2000), 573.

by which you are also being saved . . ." First Corinthians 15.1-2? We *are* part of this movement, following along, being carried along — with or without a religious mood. It would be completely profane, given the truth of the facts of our lives, to deny that we are following and being carried along. There is at least something in us that is carried along by this movement, and if there is anything in us at all, then the description of our situation is more than just a description. We are not disinterested observers. We *are* moved by God. We do know God. The history of God is happening in us and toward us.

Therefore, our hope and need have entered into the light of victory. As compared with our need, our hope is the decisive, the superior moment. No longer is there an equilibrium of godly and worldly interests, tendencies, and powers. God is positioning the lever needed to lift the world. The history of God is *a priori* a victorious history. That is the sign under which we stand. That is the presupposition from which we proceed. To say this much is not to obscure the utter seriousness of the situation; it is not to paint over the tragic rift in which we find ourselves. What is established thereby is simply the fact that the last word has already been spoken. The last word is rightly called *the kingdom of God*; creation, redemption, the completion of the world by God and in God. The last word about God is not the "Come no closer!" [Exod. 3.5] but rather "God so loved the world that he gave his only-begotten Son!" [Jn 3.16, 19]. The last word about [50] the world of human beings is not the "You are dust and to dust you will return!" [Gen. 3.19] but rather "I live and you also will live!" [Jn 14.19]. With this *last* word in *open* ears, we would like to set in motion the hope and the need that is within us.

Our "given" is the advancing rule of God. The unholy equilibrum of a static relationship between God and the human is overcome. Our life acquires depth and perspective. We stand in the midst of a series of divine deeds and demonstrations, which is tragic but also certain in its outcome. We stand in the turning of the times, in the reversal of the unrighteousness of humans to righteousness, from death to life, from the old creature to the new. We stand in society as those who have been grasped and, therefore, as those who are reaching in, as those who are moving forward. We are surrounded by the holy but not completely hemmed in, rebuffed by the profane but not completely pushed back. The great syntheses of the Epistle to the Colossians *cannot* be *completely* foreign to us. They are revealed to us. We believe them. They are complete. We ourselves complete them. *Jesus lives.* "In him, all things were created, that which is in heaven and that which is on earth, the visible and the invisible, whether thrones or dominions or authorities — all things have been created through him and for him" [Col. 1.16].

"*Created* through him and for him." This next prospect is surprising enough. It may not suit the mood of the moment, but we cannot avoid it. The situation between God and the world has been altered in such a fundamental and absolute way that our being in Christ radically governs the attitude we take toward life. If we are to go into the particulars of the meaning and power of the kingdom of God, we cannot limit our view to a narrow understanding of revolutionary movements or social criticism. Of course, the protest against a particular social order is an integral moment in the kingdom of God — the times when this moment of protest was suppressed and hidden were dark, lifeless, and godless. Yet it is also lifeless and godless to continually characterize Christ as someone who only appears out of [51] some incomprehensible hiddenness as the Redeemer — the Judge, rather — of our present, earthly disorder [cf. 1 Jn 5.19]. The kingdom of God does not begin with our protest movements. It is a revolution that *precedes* every other, just as it *precedes* everything that exists.

The great negative thing comes before the smaller ones, just as it comes before the small positive things. The synthesis is the original thing. The antithesis — even the thesis itself — arises out of it. This insight into the genuine transcendence of the divine origin of all things permits, no, commands, us to conceive of the existing social order *as such* in connection with God, as being in God. The direct, natural way leads us first to *affirm* the world as it is, not negate it. To find ourselves in God means to affirm him in the world as it is, and not in some transcendental dream world. The genuine and radical denial that we intend in our protest movements can grow only out of this affirmation. The true antithesis can only grow out of the thesis. The true — that is, the original — antithesis grows out of the synthesis.

So we accept the world as it is, however naïvely. We accept it on the terms that it has been given to us and not as we wish it would be. Its relationship to God is our question. If God were not the Creator of this world, he could not be its Redeemer. Only because the world *is* God's possession could it *become* his possession [cf. Jn 1.11]. The light that is cast by a genuine eschatology is thrown not only forward but also backward. We say Jesus Christ *yesterday*, not only for the first time today [Heb. 13.8]. It is God's will to be recognized as Creator, and worshiped in that which simply exists and occurs, and "simply" here does not mean only *plainly*, but *simplemindedly*, in all the bad things, in all the degeneration and disorientation of our present situation. The kingdom of God is also the kingdom of nature [*regnum naturae*],[50] including the veil that

50   Since the theology of Johann Gerhard, Protestant orthodoxy has distinguished between the offices

lies over *this* particular aspect of God's glory and, I am quick to add, in spite of it. Admittedly, this conception of the kingdom does not skirt the notorious Hegelian proposition of the rationality of all that exists.[51] For, in every social relation in which we find ourselves, we recognize something ultimate. We affirm an original grace in them, in the way they are and in the way they came into being. [52] We recognize in them the orders of creation within which we are obliged to live, orders just as natural for us as the nature that surrounds us [cf. Rom. 12.11]. Therefore, we do not submit to the dead and godless things of the universe, but to the living and godly things that continue to move with the universe. Precisely by *submitting* to *God* in the world we have the power *not to submit* to a world *without God.* We are "created *through him* and *for him.*" This "through him" and "for him," through Christ and for Christ, contain our triumph over the false *denial* of the world but also an absolute security against a *false* affirmation of the world.

In this sense, we understand the worldly wisdom of the preacher Solomon, which is Epicurean in appearance only: "Go, enjoy your bread and drink your wine with a merry heart, for God has long ago approved what you do. Let your garments always be white; do not let oil be lacking on your head. Enjoy life with the wife whom you love, all the days of your vain life that are given you under the sun, because that is your portion in life and in your toil at which you toil under the sun. Whatever your hand finds to do, do with all your might, for there is no work or thought or knowledge or wisdom in Sheol, where you are going" (Eccl. 9.7-11). "Whoever has ears to hear, listen!" [Mt. 11.15]. These words need no explanation. Jesus is poorly understood if those who believe in him refuse to speak with Solomon as well, for his wisdom is entirely compatible with the character of Jesus. Whoever has gone through the narrow gate of critically denying life and the world [Mt. 7.13; Lk. 13.24] is compelled to say such things again. "It is all completely vain, all completely vain," the preacher said [Eccl. 1.2, 14; 2.1, 11, 15, etc.]. This recognition of the *absolute vanity* of life under the sun, of existence in light of the life of God above the heavens, gives rise to the knowledge of the *possibility* and *value* of this vain life, a possibility

---

of Christ as the kingdom of nature, [*regnum naturae*], the kingdom of grace [*regnum gratiae*] and the kingdom of glory [*regnum gloriae*]. See SchmP, 240–243.

51 Georg Wilhelm Friedrich Hegel, *Grundlinien der Philosophie des Rechts*, in *Werke in zwanzig Bänden*, Vol. 7 (Frankfurt am Main: Suhrkamp, 1970), 24; ET *Philosophy of Right*, T.M. Knox, trans. (New York: Oxford University Press, 1967), 10: "Whatever is rational is actual; and whatever is actual is rational." Cf. Hegel's remarks in his *Enzyklopädie der philosophischen Wissenschaften, Erster Teil: Die Wissenschaft der Logik*, Vol. 8, par. 6, 47–49; ET *Hegel's Logic: Being Part One of the Encyclopedia*, William Wallace, trans. (Oxford: Clarendon, 1975), 9.

and value that are not completely irrelevant and futile, even if they are *relative.*

With this in mind, we can now understand the peculiar fact that Socrates did not devise his theory about the Ideas such that they are first separated from the world and then, only later, conveyed to unwitting humans as strange and new things. On the contrary! The newness from above is that very ancient of ancients, buried and abandoned. To devise something means to *find* it. And Socrates *finds* a relation between those particular things that he experiences on the streets and squares of Athens and a general, original knowledge about the meaning of life, and surely the Athens of Socrates' day, during the Peloponnesian War, was no *civitas Dei!* [53] This relation is found in the meaningful actions and knowledge of doctors, builders, helmsmen — despite the specialized and fragmentary nature of their professions. Its revelation astonishes us. It illustrates the true worship of God the Creator.

In this regard, we can begin to understand — or misunderstand — the painful step of Friedrich Naumann from Christian Socialism to a distinct national and economic policy. Naumann admires and affirms the "aesthetic" of nature, technology, and humanity on their own terms. Why should such wonderment be anything other than a delight in the original one [Ps. 36.10], in whose lights we see the Light, a Light that shines even in the darkness? If we were to pick up today where Naumann left off, we would see that his tracks have most certainly opened up our eyes onto the Light that shines in the dark. It defies all darkness [cf. Jn 1.5]. The example of Naumann, however, is a reminder of the great danger that lies in this. Our gaze upon the Creator through the lens of an affirmation of the world can become the mere reflection of the creature upon itself. After all, the streets of Athens found not only Plato at the side of Socrates, but even the unruly Alcibiades. The very fact that the actions of Socrates could be interpreted in a Platonic manner should urge us in our criticism of the orders of our age not to stop at ascetics and protest. On the other hand, in our new lives in Christ and the critical attitude toward this life that comes with it, we must not lose him as the meaning of that which occurs in daily life [1 Cor. 2.16]. They are occurrences that must happen and that happen properly in their own right. Regardless of the much overused and misused maxim, "Don't spoil it; it contains a blessing!" [Isa. 65.8], our critical stance toward this life requires a patient gratitude, an outward joy and a good will toward the world, our neighbor, and ourselves. We ought to be better at it than those who know nothing about the critical stance toward life when one is in Christ! We in particular could afford to be more romantic than the Romantics and more humanistic than the Humanists.

Allow me to get more specific. Let us take the attitude toward life evident in the Gospel *parables*. [54] What is the one characteristic of all these stories that sets them apart from the fables of Aesop and Gellert, from the fairy tales of the Grimm brothers and Anderson, from the stories of Christoph Schmid, and from Indian religious myths? The answer is that it is the simple way in which they equate the world with the kingdom of heaven. They begin with, "the kingdom of heaven is like this," followed by a typical image of life in society — and life in society as such has no heavenly qualities at all. There is no moral or "Christian" world described here, only the world as it is, on its own terms, its drives, and its course. Not much afterthought is put into the quite massive, earthly residue that is part and parcel of the relations and situations described. A rascal is welcomed back by his father because that is what fathers do — and this father does it with a goodness that is incomprehensible to all who witness it [Lk. 15.11-32]. A fearless judge is forced to submit to a nagging woman [Lk. 18.2-8]. A king wages a careless war but at the last minute calls a retreat [Lk. 14.31f.]. One single costly pearl causes a speculator to risk his entire fortune [Mt. 13.45f.]. A rogue, a true profiteer, knows how to acquire an accidentally discovered treasure [Mt. 13.44]. A cheat makes shady deals as if there were no such thing as "mine" and "yours" [Lk. 16.1-9]. Children quarrel in the street [Mt. 11.16-19], and a farmer sleeps soundly and wakes up in peace knowing that his land is at work [Mk 4.26-29]. Individuals still fall victim to the hands of criminals [Lk. 10.30-37] and must wait long periods of time for a sympathetic Samaritan soul to come along, even though the world is full of pious people [Lk. 14.16-24]. A lively host wants to entertain a full house under any condition [Lk. 15.18f.]. The loss of a single penny causes a woman to act as if she had just lost everything [Lk. 15.8f.]. In all this, the righteous and the unrighteous stand side by side in worship, each faithful in his own way [Lk. 18.10-14]. It is the banality of it all that strikes us. There is no illusion here, no need for any eschatologically charged climax. This is exactly how earthly life is. Because of this, these stories overflow with eschatology. It is not about some particularly effective story-telling technique or literary form. However, just like every other thing that is shaped by an inner necessity, its content already has meaning, it displays an attitude toward life where the phenomena of daily life are envisioned to be in seamless [55] relation to their inner necessity, authority, and perfection.

This one and the same perception and portrayal of actual life is what distinguishes the novels of Dostoyevsky from those of Tolstoy, whose stories give us the sense of being preached at. Only out of the most radical knowledge of redemption can we place life as it is into its proper context, as Jesus did. Only from the standpoint of the antithesis that has its roots in the synthesis can one accept the validity of the thesis. The position of redemption, and it alone, lends the platform from which we can stand in *absolute* criticism of life. In turn, we can refrain — in a way that Tolstoy did not — from a *relative* criticism of life. We can recognize the *analogy* to the *divine* in the *worldly things* that surround us, and rejoice in it, for we dwell in an abiding peace. Here too, we are dealing with the act of viewing that does not get lost in the object upon which it fixes its gaze. Our viewing penetrates that object and gazes into its original creation, the heavenly kingdom, whose laws cast their shadows upon the events and relations of the present era. "Ever since the creation of the world, his eternal power and divine nature, invisible though they are, have been understood and seen through the things he has made" (Rom. 1.20).

With Jesus the picture is even clearer than with Socrates. That expansive, calm patience moves everything transitory, even their unnatural forms, into the light of the permanent. For the Lord does not only praise the good doctor and the clever helmsman but the corrupt housekeeper as well [Lk. 16.8]. With Jesus it is clear that everything transitory is *only* a parable.[52] The clarity here comes precisely from this peace in relation to its object. The original thing, that being and becoming as such in accordance with creation, is by no means to be sought in the object itself. It is to be sought in its platonic idea, its heavenly analogy. Laid out even more clearly here is that aspect of gazing upon God whereby his invisibility can be seen through the rationality of his works. Paul emphasized, "For what can be known about God is plain to them because God has shown it to them" (Rom. 1.19). But this aspect is in no way rational, self-evident, or obvious. Only a few have been given the knowledge of the mysteries of the heavenly kingdom. They alone can look upon the eternal through the parables of the transitory. To others, no such knowledge is given. The knowledge must be hidden behind the veil of the parables for those who cannot see [56] so that the divine is not comprehended in a godless manner. Seeing *cannot* take place without eyes; forgiveness does not come without the forgiving God. Instead, to those who *have, to them* more will be given. They will have their fill [Mt. 13.12; 25.29]. The so-called Marcion theory of the parables, although often maligned and ridiculed, is in fact the most congenial interpretation of them (Mark 4.10-12; Matthew 13.10-17) no doubt it comes from Jesus himself!

The parables are snapshots of life as it *is lived*. They are images that carry meaning, because, surely, life as it *is lived* does have meaning. Whoever does not recognize life as it *is lived* cannot comprehend its meaning. Those who take the bold and free step of viewing heaven and earth, that which is present and that which is originally-future, have a

---

52   Cf. J.W. Goethe, *Faust II*, V, 12104f. (heaven); *Goethe's Faust*, 503. Cf. also *Selected Works*, 1049.

strong sense of "objectivity" [*Sachlichkeit*]. The one thing the parables are not is superficial, shoddy, or half-baked. The actions of even the good-for-nothing servant boy who buried his coins make him a complete man in his own way [Mt. 25.18, 24f.]. After all, the children of this world are clever: They know how to take care of their business often better than the children of light — and the Lord praises them for this! [Lk. 16.8]. They give hopeful impressions. For, when a person takes care of his own business properly what is revealed is the great possibility that the heavenly kingdom has virtually penetrated into his particular life and consciousness. This is not the heavenly kingdom itself, but its possibility. As far as we know, when Jesus called his apostles into *his* service, he did not call men who were idling around, but men who were working. Fishers of men were made out of those who were already fishermen [cf. Mt. 4.19]. The simple obligation to give to Caesar what is Caesar's gives rise to the knowledge that it is much greater — and completely different — to give to God what is *God's* [cf. Mt. 22.21]. It is the captain of Capernaum who is the classical example of one living in the nexus of earthly relations that are penetrated by the heavenly archetype. Regardless of our approval, the military leader of Capernaum himself becomes a parable for the order of the kingdom of the Messiah. His simple insight was praised by Jesus as being that of faith. In him, Jesus experienced a faith that he had not experienced in an Israel that understood itself in a far too spiritual manner, and that was forever protesting the existing order of the world.

So what are we to make of all this? What becomes evident here is that the simple *objectivity* of our thinking, speaking, and acting contains a *promise*. No more and no less. It becomes evident within our particular relations, within the awareness of our bondage. [57] It is not ours to remain onlookers *outside* the course of earthly events, but to exist in and among them. What compels us to take this position is our awareness of the joint responsibility that has been laid upon our souls regarding the depraved world.

More specifically, it is the thought of the Creator — who remains Creator even in this fallen world — that drives us to this position. Even if all that we do within the prevailing social orders is only *child's play*, it is a *meaningful* game when played correctly in relation to that which actually should be done. No good worker is going to be made out of a bad player. Loiterers, journalists, and gawkers on the battlefield of the mundane will not be turned into the storm troopers of heaven [cf. Mt. 11.22]. The problem we encounter in purely objective thought and deed breeds an amazement that must turn into a readiness to show the deepest respect for every honest achievement. Such honest achievements could be the purity of the Original that approaches us — that is, if we have eyes to see this approaching. Our profound insecurity about the worth of our own work ought to generate the strongest of wills to go about our work in a lawful and healthy way; indeed it could be that when that ray from above glints upon our mortal activities, it is the eternal appearing in that which perishes. "Fill up the earth and make it subordinate to you!" [Gen. 1.28]. "Whoever does not work should not eat!" [1 Thess. 3.10]. "The one who created humans in the beginning created them as man and woman!" [cf. Mt. 19.4]. "Honor your father and mother so that it may be well with you!" [Exod. 20.12; Deut. 5.16]. All these divine commands are fully legitimate. We will not let the consummate voice of the divine *wisdom*, the common sense of the Proverbs or Ecclesiastes so urged by Oetinger ring out in the streets for nothing, regardless of "late-Judaic" character of these texts.[53] Nor ought we to be too high-minded to receive the divine *blessing* that Isaac and Job received while still on this earth, after they had gone through the narrow gate.

This humble but clear-eyed and joyful freedom, this freedom to move even over the ground of this present age will never be fully prohibited or impossible for us: It is a freedom that allows us to live among the Philistines. It allows us to carry ourselves in a quiet superiority when we enter and leave the houses of tax collectors and sinners, [58] when we enter and leave the houses of unclean money, and the houses of the State, which — call them what you will — are the beast of the bottomless pit [Rev. 13]. In the same way, we will take on but then depart from an atheistic social democracy. We will keep company in the houses of the falsely famous sciences and liberal arts, and finally even in the house of the Church. After all, why should we not live in such freedom? This is *the* question. Why not! As it is said, "Come in, because the gods are here too!" [*Introite nam et hich dii sunt!*].[54] Our coming and going is accompanied by our fear of God. We therefore do not become the servants of such idols. We come and go as if we were not doing it [cf. 1 Cor. 7.29-31].

The fear of God is our freedom in freedom. "There is nothing better for mortals than to eat and drink, to find enjoyment in their toil. This also, I saw, is from the hand of God; for apart from him, who can eat or who can enjoy himself?" (Eccl. 2.24-25). We agree with the Romantics that the kingdom of God does not first begin today. We affirm the

---

53   See Friedrich Christoph Oetinger, *Inquisitio in sensum communem et rationem* (Tübingen: Fues, 1753); and *Die Wahrheit des Sensus communis, in den nach dem Grund-Text erklärten Sprüchen und Prediger Salomo* (Stuttgart: Steinkopf, 1754). Cf. Oetinger's lecture in *Friedrich Christoph Oetingers Leben und Briefe, als urkundlicher Commentar zu dessen Schriften*, Karl Christian Eberhard Ehmann, ed. (Stuttgart: Steinkopf, 1859), 198–211.

54   For more on this citation, originally found in Heraclitus but handed down by Aristotle in his *De partibus animalium*, I, 5, 645a 17, see also Georg Büchmann, *Geflügelte Worte: der klassische Zitatenschatz*, 42nd ed., re-edited by Winfried Hofmann (Munich: Ullstein, 2001), 499f.

Humanists' view that even the fallen human is the carrier of the spark of the divine light. We affirm life! Even the kingdom of nature [*regnum naturae*], that great stage of all temporal thinking, speaking, and acting, can at any moment become the kingdom of God [*regnum Dei*], if *we* are in the kingdom of God and the kingdom of God is in us [cf. Lk. 17.21]. This is not the wisdom of the world, it is the truth of Christ [cf. Rom. 9.1; 1 Tim. 2.7]. It is the fundamental, and thoroughly biblical, knowledge of life.

From our viewpoint on life, however, it would be wiser to speak quietly with the Bible than to speak loudly or even to shout about classical antiquity and German Idealism. This will save us from allowing a form of the *denial of life*, a form common in Russian and Eastern literature, from becoming a theme in its own right. Let us not watch the destruction of Sodom and Gomorrah, or the one who becomes a pillar of salt [Gen. 19.24-26]. On the other hand, the *affirmation of life* should not be turned into a theme in its own right either. We do not want to return to the Greeks or to a Goethe that lies behind the fundamental brokenness of Dostoyevsky. However, we are also not seeking a harmonious balance between the two moments. The question of how to relate the ancient Greek sense of tragedy to the brilliance of the humanity [59] with which the Greeks surrounded themselves is a fine and serious question. It is surely not something that can be solved through abstraction or reasoning, but can only be approached in connection to the history of God. Even so, these moments of affirmation and denial are not equal and symmetrical moments of the truth. Goethe on his throne of Jupiter in Weimar and the Dionysian Nietzsche may have thought that they were equals, and even Hermann Kutter may inform us that the divine humor likes to reveal itself by smiling through the tears shed at the conundrums of this world.[55] Nonetheless, we cannot afford to balance out the motion of these moments or smooth out the tension between them and bring them to rest — not even for the sake of achieving a complete philosophical concept of the human.

　　Formal reasons will not let us overlook the fact that the antithesis is more than a mere reaction to the thesis. It springs forth from the synthesis by means of its own original power. Then it encompasses the thesis in itself and thereby overcomes it, surpassing the thesis in worth and meaning every moment along the way. There is no rest here. Rest comes in God alone. Even if we try to understand our situation from the viewpoint of God, we must admit that we are more aware of our own tragedy than

---

55　Cf. Hermann Kutter, *Reden an die deutschen Nation* (Jena, 1916), 98, 113, 225.

of the sovereignty of God that helps us deal with it. The *tears* are closer to us than a smile. *We* stand more deeply in the "No" than in the "Yes," deeper in criticism and protest than in naïvety, deeper in our yearning for the future than in our participation in the present. *Our* reverence of the *Creator* of the original world is the same as our cry for the *Redeemer* of the present world. Our "Yes" to life has carried the divine "No" in itself from the start. It is this "No" which now breaks through in the antithesis. The antithesis points away from the temporary thesis toward the synthesis that is both original and final. To be sure, the "No" itself is not the final and most supreme thing, but is rather a cry to us from our homeland. It is the answer that comes to us when we seek God in the world. Surely, when we once again take up our old song about work and industriousness in the heavenly choir, about culture and our evangelical freedom in it, it will be in significantly muted tones. The unrest that we experience through God, through his grace and judgment, has been placed upon our paths in life as it unfolds. It is a promise and a warning such that we can no longer *not* think about this present moment.

With this fact pressing so strongly down upon us, [60] it is impossible for us not to see that our actions in this age stand as an analogy to the divine actions — but not in continuity. The presupposition to our affirmation of life, which consists of the fact that everything is vain, utterly vain, is *too* effective. Our present age is *overly* burdened by our knowledge that what we will become has not yet appeared to us [1 Jn 3.2]. Thus, this eon leaves no room for an Olympian mood. The power of Socrates admired by Alcibiades in the *Symposium*[56] emanates precisely from the knowledge of brokenness that comes with a Socratic view of life. It is a critical view that accompanies the Idea, and it is obvious in Michelangelo, Bach, and Schiller as well. This is what those blue-blooded Athenians did not recognize. We, on the other hand, want to see it, and we want to see it without confusing the parable with the thing itself. A genuine understanding of life is the bane of every abstraction. It says "Yes" to life in the first moment but only in order to say "No" even more loudly and clearly on the basis of it. For genuine knowledge of life does not pursue a kind of systematic completion but, rather, its own history, its place in the command of the hour. It has its own process, dynamism, and multidimensionality.

In this way, our uninhibited view onto the orders of creation leads us straight to the place where light and darkness are locked in a grueling but victorious *struggle*. It leads us beyond the kingdom of nature [*regnum naturae*] into the kingdom of grace [*regnum gratiae*], into Christ, where

---

56   See Plato, *Symposium*, R.E. Allen, trans. (New Haven: Yale University Press, 1991), 220 d 3–221 d 6.

life in its entirety becomes complicated and gets called into question but is, nonetheless, filled with promise. The same God who "looked upon everything that he had made, and behold, it was very good" (Gen. 1.31) is the one who "has rescued us from the power of darkness and transferred us into the kingdom of his beloved Son" (Col. 1.13). The very same force that gives us a trust in life takes that trust away again. When the answer is properly understood, it becomes a new question: The "Yes" becomes a "No." The same urgency with which we recognize the eternal beginning and eternal end in God must accompany us as we find our way within the fleeting nature of this present age, this "in between." At the moment when society becomes a mirror of the original thoughts of God, it will also then reflect our need and our hope.

What I have just been describing is the way the kingdom of God approaches in its *attack* upon society. But why is God so hidden from us? Why does it become almost impossible for us to recognize the original meaning of what we do every day and what we see others doing? Socrates and the authors of the Synoptic parables recognized it. [61] Is there something wrong with our eyes, or does the problem lay in the things themselves? Why is it that some are given to see but others not! And more often than not, those that do see, see so seldom, so poorly. The tremendous pressure that confounds us and inhibits us from doing the will of God here and now is merely a simple command when seen on its own terms. Who can explain this? Even the behavior of the most distinguished Christians in society leaves us in doubt as to whether their actions follow the will of God, taken so seriously in the Bible.

Why? When we contemplate this simple command, why do we turn our gaze, almost out of necessity, to the future? *Quod vixi tege, quod vivam rege!* "Guard what I have lived, guide what I shall live!"[57] Is tomorrow actually supposed to be better? Why are we always making preparations for a life which never actually begins? Why can we never land triumphantly with two feet in the kingdom of God, basking in the sun of Humanism, hands ready and eyes wide open? Instead, even in the best case, we limp into it, one-eyed, lame, and crippled, as ones who are demeaned, humiliated, and contrite [cf. Mt. 5.29f.; 18.8f.; Mk 9.43]. Why is it that only the Philistines can actually be satisfied with life and themselves? Why is it that *fundamentally*, despite our many *pen*ultimate objections, we cannot resist giving in to the protest raised by *Kierkegaard* against marriage and family, the protest raised by *Tolstoy* against the State, education, and art, and which *Ibsen* raised against the accepted middle-class morals, which *Kutter* raised against the Church, and which *Nietzsche* raised against

---

57   Often falsely attributed to Augustine, the origin of this prayer is unknown.

the entirety of Christianity, just as *Socialism* has raised it with particular vehemence against the intellectual and material structure of society as a whole? Why is it that we do not muster up the passion to fend off *Dostoyevsky's* shocking image of Christ passing in society as an idiot, or the actual understanding of Christ with its beginnings in the experiences of murders and prostitutes?[58] What is it in us that affirms the radical protest of the medieval *Mystics* and the original *Reformation* and *Anabaptism* against *the* only religion that is possible and conceivable in society? Why, with a *sacrificium* of our intellect and so much more than that, do we bow to the message of the *Sermon on the Mount*, which blesses individuals who do not even exist; which counters that which was said to our forefathers, [62] which we continually say to one another with the words, "Truly *I* tell you!" [Mt. 5.27f., 33f., 38f., 43f.] which we do not apply in today's society or in any conceivable one; which proclaims a morality that presupposes there is no more morality? Why are we so embarrassed and speechless at the accusation of the *social philosopher of the Old Testament*, who raises his voice not only against this or that present situation, but against life itself? "Again I saw all the oppressions practiced under the sun. Look, the tears of the oppressed — with no one to comfort them! On the side of their oppressors there was power — with no one to comfort them. And I considered the dead, those who have already died, to be more fortunate than the living, those who are still alive. But better than both of these is the one who has not yet been born, and who has not yet seen the evil deeds that are done under the sun" (Eccl. 4.1-3). How is it that we understand all of this without understanding it at all, and affirm it without affirming it at all? We participate — unwillingly — in the most profound of attacks directed at the very foundations of society. Why?

It is quite clear that facing this attacker puts us into the same dilemma as facing the defender, and that the attacker and the defender must be one and the same, with the attack acting as the advance of the defense. And it is also quite clear that this dilemma does not have its source outside of us but happens within our very own freedom. For the God, the Creator, whom we have been contemplating, is also God the Redeemer, whose footsteps we, in our freedom, must follow. For we have now entered into the history of God, and as part of this course, we must freely take steps from defense to attack, from "Yes" to "No," from naïvety to criticism of the social orders. We can deny this universal "No" as little as we can refuse that original "Yes." *Rebus sic stantibus*, we can deny the "No" even less! For the two are one, each following from the other.

58   This is an allusion to Fyodor Dostoyevsky's *Crime and Punishment*, Jessie Coulson, trans. (New York: Oxford University Press, 1980), and *The Idiot*, Anna Brailovsky, trans. (New York: The Modern Library, 2003).

The truth of Christ both warns us of a simplistic objectivity and at the same time propels us and our lives forward into an entirely different objectivity. We simply *cannot* rest content with seeing this transitory world *only* as a parable to something else. [63] Something in the concept of analogy wants to forge ahead to continuity, as with the example of the captain of Capernaum. The parable brings a promise, but promises demand fulfillment. After the child is conceived, it wants to be born. All that is creaturely anticipates the revelation of the Son of God. Its labor pains [ὠδίνειν] and sighs [στενάζειν] are no different from our own (Rom. 8.19-23). Mere images and parables are not sufficient: The *meaning* of what we think, say, and do presses forth into expression. There is a reason why transitory things offer up a likeness to eternal things; with them, we no longer forget the eternal. There is no other rest apart from the kingdom of God. We can no longer bring about rest through vague references to the realm beyond, for that "other side" now unsettles us with its absence, with its knocking on the closed doors of this present realm.

But pessimistic discrediting of the realm in which we exist does not help against our unrest. For it is on "this side" that we become aware of our fall away from the eternal, and likewise, of the promise given to us in parables. "*These* perishable things — τὸ φθαρτὸν τοῦτο — must take on imperishability, and *these* mortal things — τὸ θνητὸν τοῦτο — must take on immortality" (1 Cor. 15.33). If we do not want to be left behind and outside of the truth of Christ and the power of his resurrection, we will have no choice but to enter *fully into* the shock and the contradiction. We will fully enter into the judgment and grace that the presence of God entails here and now — and in every world imaginable [cf. 2 Cor. 11.10]. This shock and contradiction is not something we can simply *observe* from the outside as pious or jocular onlookers, nor can we *circumvent* it by strolling along the wide, sunny, bustling streets of the Romantics and Humanists.[59] Taking these side routes would mean consciously taking the position of those who are said to not know God [ἀγνωσίαν θεοῦ τινες ἔχουσιν (1 Cor. 15.34)]. In the face of God, we have no choice but to disrupt the safe equilibrium of our creatureliness. We *are* no longer free to simply call upon "reality" in the face of the *Reality* that wants to break out of "reality." We simply *must* take seriously the vehemence of the attack that is at one and the same time directed against us, as well as led by us.

How terrible it would be if among all the institutions, it is the *Church* which does not see this, but rather puts all of its effort into [64] *maintaining* the secure equilibrium of existence that humans are supposed to *lose*!

---

59   The second verse of the song, "Wenn ich ihn nur habe" by Fr. von Hardenberg (Novalis) concludes with similar imagery. See *GERS* (1891), 250.

But why even be concerned about the Church? The urgent question looming ever before us is whether we ourselves can see our situation, and it demands that we keep our eyes steadily straight ahead. Have we actually *heard* the call that has come to us? Have we *comprehended* that which we have understood — that the challenge of our day is not to stand in opposition to life or its details but to orient nothing less than our *entire lives* toward God? Have we comprehended that this orientation must be guarded and proved in its entirety by our frank criticism of the particulars, by making courageous resolutions and taking steps, by taking on ruthless challengers, by patiently doing the work of reform, which in our day in particular requires that we take an open-hearted, broad-minded and honest attitude toward *social democracy*, precisely not as disengaged onlookers or critics *of* it but as hope-sharing and guilt-bearing players and comrades *within* it? *Our* particular age is faced with the problem of the opposition to the old order, our age is given the parable of the kingdom of God. It is where it must be proven whether we have comprehended the problem in both its absolute and relative meaning. Who among us can boast of standing deep enough in the brokenness of life to really perceive the contradiction? *Domine ad te nos creasti*, "Lord, we are created for you" — this is the "Yes" to our perception of life. *Et cor nostrum inquietum est donec requiescat in te*, "But our heart is restless until it rests in you" — this is its paramount, urgent "No," which brings us back to the beginning.

Having said all this, we now say that a *new* day has surely begun. Jesus Christ *today* — Jesus Christ is *the same* today! [Heb. 13.8]. "Today, today as you hear his voice, do not thus hide your heart from it!" [Ps. 95.7f]. "...from the days of John the Baptist until now, the kingdom of heaven has been violently breaking in [βιάζεται] and the violent ones [βιασταὶ] take it by force" (Mt. 11.12). Further, I quote, "I came to bring fire to the earth, and how I wish it were already kindled!" (Lk. 12.49). This is the kingdom of grace [*regnum gratiae*]. "The kingdom of God has come near" [Mt. 4.17; Mk 1.14].

But now let us pause for one last time in order to come to terms with everything that we have just been considering. Our purely objective work within the bounds of the present social order is now accompanied by a radical [65] opposition to its very foundations. But with such a practicality and objectivity, we have had to guard ourselves from thinking that we could restore our toppled idols. By the same token now in regards to our opposition, we have to protect ourselves from expecting that our criticizing, protesting, reforming, organizing, democratizing, socializing, and revolutionizing can achieve a standard sufficient for the kingdom of God, *however fundamental and comprehensive they may be*. We simply cannot think that way. There can be neither casual naïvety about the present order nor unrestricted criticism. The problem into which God has cast us cannot be turned into an abstraction any more than can the orders of creation, into which God has placed us to live. The one must be understood through the other, and both must be understood as coming from God. Understanding them any other way, moves us from one kind of worldly wisdom to another. Our "Yes," like our "No," carries its limitations in itself. In so far as it is God who gives us our rest — and a greater unrest — neither rest nor unrest can be our final viewpoint of the world, no matter how necessary each one is.

One more thing is meant in the parables, in which we think, speak, and act. When we tire of them, we yearn for *another thing*, not just *any* other thing but the *wholly other* thing of the kingdom, the kingdom of *God*. The original, eternally productive power of the synthesis is the root of the power of thesis and antithesis alike. That which perishes is not somehow the penultimate stage to that which does not perish [1 Cor. 15.53]. Rather, when we hear that perishable things will put on the imperishable, we must keep in mind, in our desire for it, that the imperishable is "a house not made with hands, eternal in the heavens" (2 Cor. 5.1). It is fairly obvious what German theologians wanted to say during the War when they realized that it would be better to say the "side *within*" instead of the "*other* side."[60] But we still hold out the strong hope that this play on words — more serpent-wise than dove-innocent [Mt. 10.16] — does not find a following. "No, no," we say, "take your 'side *within*' away from us! *Apage Satanas!*" [Mt. 4.10, 16.23; Mk 8.33]. The "other side," *trans*, "beyond," *that* is the heart of the matter; that is what we live from. We live from that which comes from the *other* side of the realm of analogy, from that which even our own little *within* belongs to. There is [66] no continuity that leads from the realm of analogies into the divine reality. There is no objective relation between that which is *meant* in parable and that which *is*. We cannot even imagine some kind of objective, organic transition from here to there. The heavenly kingdom, like its promise, its revelation and the fullness of its presence, is a matter unto itself, but it does not and cannot remain so.

This is why when Paul talks about the goal of history, its *telos* (1 Cor. 15.23-28), he is not talking about some historical event among others but the summation of the history of *God* in our history, the glory of which is hidden from us, but not from him or from those whose eyes are opened. *Telos* does not mean "end" but "goal," and it is well known that the kingdom of goals[61] is a higher order not to be comprehended

60   P. Jaeger, *Innseits. Zur Verständigung über die Jenseitsfrage* (Tübingen: Mohr, 1917). Cf. Karl Barth,
     Antwort an Paul Jaeger (1924), reprinted in *V.u.kl.A. 1922–1925*, 381–390.
61   See Kant, *Grundlegung zur Metaphysik der Sitten* [BA 80, see astrisk]; ET *Groundwork of the Metaphysic*

within the system of time, space, and contingency. The synthesis lies in *God* alone, and in God alone can we find it. If we do not find it in God, then we will not find it at all. "If for this life only we have hoped in Christ, we are of all people most to be pitied" (1 Cor. 15.19). For the truth of creation and redemption lies in the fact that God is *God*, that *God's* immanence means his *transcendence*. "Flesh and blood cannot inherit the kingdom of God" (1 Cor. 15.50). Creatureliness and the revelation of the Son of God exclude one another [Rom. 8.19]. I say again: The synthesis is to be found in *God* alone, and it *will* be found in God. We are speaking here of the synthesis that is *meant* by the thesis and which is *sought* by the antithesis. Ernst Troeltsch put it most appropriately in his *Social Teachings*: "The power of the 'other side' is the power of 'this side.'"[62] We add: This power is the energy of affirmation, and the even greater energy of denial. The naïve and critical attitude that we take toward the order of lesser things when we are in Christ radiates the higher order of things, which is united with the lesser in God and God alone. Our naïve acceptance and criticism find their possibility, justification, and necessity in the power of the resurrection.

Therefore we say that the *resurrection* of Jesus Christ from the dead is the power that moves both the world and us. The most we can say is that it is the appearance of a corporality that is *totaliter aliter*, a corporality that is ordered in a completely different manner[63] than our corporality. Recall the Isenheim Altar and think about the way art historians would linger around this depiction and shake their heads in disapproval. [67] This is precisely the point! The *Holy Spirit* of Pentecost was *holy* precisely because it was not a human spirit, not even in the best, purest sense of humanity. It came in a *horribile dictum*, with a roar from heaven, shaking the house where the apostles and others were gathered [Acts 2.2f.; 4.31]. It came to them in tongues of fire, "perpendicular from heaven," just as Zündel pointedly noted.[64]

Because of this, we believe that there is a meaning that inheres our

---

of Morals, H.J. Paton, trans. (New York: Routledge, [1948] 1989) [BA 80 n. ★], 98: "Teleology considers nature as a kingdom of goals, and morality a possible kingdom of goals as a kingdom of nature. There the kingdom of goals is a theoretical idea, as an explanation for that which is there. Here, it is a practical idea about that which is not there, but which can become real through our deeds and being, and precisely which, measured by this idea, can even be achieved."

62   See Ernst Troeltsch, *Die Soziallehren der christlichen Kirchen und Gruppen*, in *Gesammelte Schriften*, Vol. 1 (Tübingen: Mohr, 1912), 979; ET *Social Teaching of the Christian Churches*, Vol. 2, Olive Wyon, trans. (Louisville, KY: Westminster/John Knox Press, 1992), 1006: "The other side is the power of this side."

63   According to legend, a dead monk appears to his fellow monk. The living monk asks about the "quality" of eternal life: "*Taliter? Aliter?*" The dead monk answers: "*totaliter aliter.*"

64   See Note 37, p. 42.

existing relations, but we also believe that there is evolution, revolution. We believe in the reform and the renewal of these relationships, in the possibility of friendship and fellowship on earth and under heaven. We believe in this because we are waiting for something completely different from these things: We are waiting for a new heaven and a new earth [2 Pet. 3.13]. We put our energy toward both daily and banal business and tasks, but also toward a new Switzerland and new Germany *precisely because* we are waiting for the new Jerusalem to come down from God out of the heavens [Rev. 21.2]. We have the courage to endure the limitations, bondage, and imperfections of this age *precisely because* we anticipate a time when the final enemy — death, that limitation of all limitations — will be destroyed, regardless of whether we have suffered or not [1 Cor. 15.26]. *Precisely because* we have been offered a view onto the day of Jesus Christ [1 Cor. 1.8; 5.5; 2 Cor. 1.14; Phil. 1.6, 10; 2.16; 2 Thess. 2.2], when God will be all in all [1 Cor. 15.28], we have the freedom of living either naïvely with God or critically with God. If we want to understand ourselves properly, we must follow from above to below, and never the other way around. For the final thing, the eschaton, the synthesis, is *never* the continuation, the outcome, the consequence or the next stage of the penultimate. It is exactly the *opposite*. It is the radical interruption of every penultimate thing, including its very own original meaning and moving power.

So we need not be anxious about pessimistically discrediting "this side" and the work we do in it if we place the Christian in society under the viewpoint of the *spes futurae vitae*, the hope of the future life.[65] The power of the consciousness of predestination comes from this place! The power to live in honor of God comes from this place! This viewpoint even binds us to our naïvety and our criticism of the present social orders. Being bound does not always have to mean a *loss* of energy but can mean a *gathering* of it, a salutary pooling of rushing waters to [68] prevent foolish squandering and dangerous flooding. At this very point it becomes entirely clear why we are bound. When we look out from creation and redemption toward perfection, when we look out toward the "wholly other" of the *regnum gloriae*, it means that our naïve as well as our critical attitude toward society — our "Yes" like our "No" — *is placed into a right relationship with God*. The one, like the other, will be liberated from the dangers of abstraction, where death lurks. It means that the one is related to the other, not in a systematic way but, rather, in an historical way, a God-in-history way, a way that is indispensable for life.

---

65   See Karl Barth, *Die Theologie Calvins*, H. Scholl, ed., *GA* (Zürich: TVZ, 1993), 204–207, 300, 331; ET *The Theology of Calvin* (1922) (Grand Rapids, MI: William B. Eerdmans Publishing Company, 1995), 154–156; 221–222; 244.

Clearly, this is what we need and what we have been seeking out in our theme of today. The more we are moved in God and God alone, the less we will get stuck in movements, either on the right or the left. We will no longer make the mistake of banging and drilling into the "Yes" with Naumann until it becomes nonsense. Nor will we follow Tolstoy into the "No" until it too is reduced ad absurdum. We will listen to the preacher, Solomon: "Do not be too righteous and do not act too wise; why should you destroy yourself? Do not be too wicked, and do not be a fool; why should you die before your time? It is good that you should take hold of the one without letting go of the other; for the one who fears God shall succeed with both" (Eccl. 7.16-19). Our decisions will be made at the *greatest* distance from things, and therefore with the *greatest* insight into them — they will be made with a view toward the *regnum gloriae* — and thereby, our short circuits to the right and to the left will gradually decrease. Then we will have the freedom to say "Yes" in this moment or "No" in that moment, without the hindrance of evil appearances. Neither will come out of some outward coincidence or some inner caprice, but, rather, they will grow out of the well-tested will of God — out of "what is good and acceptable and perfect" (Rom. 12.2). This is so because "For everything there is a season, and a time for every matter under heaven: a time to be born and a time to die; a time to plant and a time to pluck up what is planted; a time to kill and a time to heal; a time to break down and a time to build up; . . . a time to throw away stones and a time to gather stones together; . . . a time to tear and a time to sew; a time to keep silence and a time to speak; a time to love and a time to hate; a time for war and a time for peace." [Eccl. 3.1-8]. And the passage that was *Oetinger's*[66] favorite continues — if the Septuagint correctly translates the original: God "has made everything suitable for its time. Moreover he has put a sense of *eternity* [69] into their minds, without which they cannot find that which God does from the beginning until the end" (Eccl. 3.1-11). This then is our synthesis: God is the One who *can* be found by the eternity in our hearts. Jesus Christ is the same yesterday, today, and in eternity [Heb. 13.8]. This is the synthesis.

Implicit in our theme of today is one question that our lips are surely now secretly forming: "What should we do?" It is certainly true that this question, and all the great and small questions that burn within it and that urgently need answers, are not part of the fundamental answer of the Bible. That is, they *seem* not to be answered. After all, why should we not know what to do, *sub specie aeternitatis*? We are grounded in God, so why should eternity not be given into our hearts? We have been moved

66   See Ehmann, *Friedrich Christoph Oetingers Leben und Briefe*, 201 (see Note 53, p. 58).

by Christ, so why would we not be grounded in God? [cf. 2 Cor. 11.10] We cannot do much, but we can do one thing. It is a thing not done by *us*. For, what can the Christian in society do except follow closely that which is done by *God*?

CHAPTER 4

BIBLICAL QUESTIONS, INSIGHTS, AND VISTAS, 1920

The conference of Christian students in Aarau, where Barth delivered his lecture "Biblical Questions, Insights, and Vistas" on April 17, 1920, grew out of the activities of the international Student Missions Movement, in particular the first student conference of French-speaking Switzerland in Sainte-Croix in 1895 and the conference that followed by the International Student Missions Conference in Liverpool in 1896. In a circular letter to all students in German-speaking Swiss universities, an organization committee invited all to come to an inaugural conference in Aarau on March 23 and 24. The conference was intended to be "an opportunity where students who are concerned about the kingdom of God can get to know one another and make contact with teachers who are of the same mind." The circular letter continued: "We want to treat questions that employ the heads and the hearts of the students in a serious, sober way." At the inaugural conference, Barth's father, Professor Fritz Barth delivered a lecture on the topic "Obstacles of Faith." Fritz Barth remained in contact with the Aarau conference as a member of the governing committee and through lectures he gave during 1898, 1900, 1902, and 1910.[1] Karl Barth participated frequently in these conferences first as a student and then as a vicar in Geneva and later as a pastor in Safenwil. In 1910, he wrote reports about the tenth Aarau conference for the *Berner Tagblatt*, which make up his first written texts.[2] Later, Barth himself contributed to the conference on several occasions: in 1916 with a sermon on Gen. 15.6 ("The One Necessary Thing");[3] then at the 1920 conference with the lecture translated here, "Biblical Questions, Insights and Vistas; and again in 1927 with a significant presentation on "The Keeping of the Commandments."[4]

After Barth declined invitations to present at the conferences of 1917[5]

---

1   See P. Gruner, *Menschenwege und Gotteswege im Studentenleben. Persönlichen Erinnerungen aus der christlichen Studentenbewegung* (Bern: Stählin, 1942), esp. 154–193, 431f., and 453–456.

2   Karl Barth, *Vorträge und kleinere Arbeiten 1905–1909*, H.-A. Drewes and H. Stoevesandt, eds., *GA III* (Zürich: TVZ, 1992), 120–125.

3   Karl Barth, *Predigten 1916*, H. Schmidt, ed., *GA I* (Zürich: TVZ, 1998), 109–124.

4   Karl Barth, *Vorträge und kleinere Arbeiten 1925–1930*, H. Schmidt, ed., *GA III* (Zürich: TVZ, 1994), 99–139.

5   Letter from Karl Barth to Eduard Thurneysen, July 19, 1916 (*Bw. Th.* I, 46).

and 1918,[6] and after his brother, Heinrich Barth, held one of the keynote addresses at the conference of 1919,[7] he was once again issued an invitation on September 15, 1919. The president of the conference for 1919/20, medical student Mattheus Vischer, gave Barth the questions that would be discussed at the meeting in the spring of 1920: "What does natural science contribute to reliable knowledge in the interpretation of world events? What does history offer? What does the Bible offer?" He requested that Barth "take on the third of the morning lectures."[8] Barth accepted "without enthusiasm and without any illusion."[9] On January 30, Vischer communicated the names of both of the other morning readers of the conference: "1. Professor Baltzer from Freiburg im Breisgau (a Swiss), 2. Harnack from Berlin."[10] Barth commented about the "bombshell news" of Adolf von Harnack as the second presenter: "*Eheu me miserum*! And I'm the third! The days between the fifteenth and the twentieth of April will become days of great combat, only how shall I arm myself accordingly?"[11] On February 1, 1920, law student Ruth Speiser, in the name of the steering committee, requested from Barth the final formulation of his topic.[12] Upon this request, Barth noted several possibilities: "The message of the Bible in the present? The question of the Bible to the modern individual? *Biblical insights and outlooks*?" He ended up choosing "Biblical Questions, Insights, and Vistas." He kept the title even though the students found it "too weak" and asked for "a more concise, more positive sounding wording of the topic" (like "the Bible and contemporary times").[13]

Upon Barth's asking of the other two speakers about the direction of their remarks, Harnack answered on February 8, 1920 in a postcard that he would only be able to describe his treatment of the topic "two to three weeks before the lecture." But we "won't get in each other's way since I will adhere strictly to the topic."[14] Fritz Baltzer answered on February 20, 1920[15] with an overview of the material that he wanted to offer and his interest in a "sketch" of Barth's lecture, which Barth couldn't begin work on until mid-March.[16] Nevertheless, he was able to tell Eduard Thurneysen on March 17, 1920 that "the drill for the lecture is enormously active, and a continuous column of smoke rises from the whistle to

6   Letter from Karl Barth to Eduard Thurneysen, December 17, 1917, (*Bw. Th.* I, 252f.)
7   Heinrich Barth, "Gotteserkenntnis" (1919), reprinted in *Anfänge* I, 221–255.
8   KBA 9319.171.
9   Letter from Karl Barth to Eduard Thurneysen, September 18, 1919 (*Bw. Th.* I, 347). For Barth's changing and often skeptical opinion of the possibilities for the Aarauer student conference during this time, see also *Bw. Th.* I, 268, 284–286, 323, 325, 376.
10   KBA 9320.30.
11   Letter from Karl Barth to Eduard Thurneysen, January 31, 1920 (*Bw. Th.* I, 366.)
12   KBA 9320.32.
13   Letter from Mattheus Vischer to Karl Barth, February 9, 1920 (KBA 9320.45).
14   KBA 9320.43.
15   KBA 9320.51.
16   Letter from Karl Barth to Eduard Thurneysen, March 15, 1920 (*Bw. Th.* I, 373).

the roof as in the best times of my life."[17] The train of thought that was already taking shape — predestination, the language of the Bible, Christ, creation, redemption — apparently received a clear direction and its content acuteness[18] through Barth's work in particular on a sermon for Easter Sunday, which Barth delivered on April 4 in his congregation on 1 Cor. 15.50-58.[19] Barth's work on the sermon in particular seemed to answer his concerns about the perspective and the target audience, to whom he should "speak."[20] The rhythm of Barth's thought in the lecture was also significantly influenced by the Isenheim Altar of Matthias Grünewald, a print of whose crucifixion triptych had hung in Barth's study since 1919. The threefold reference to this unique piece of art gives order and shape to Barth's entire lecture.

Thurneysen's letter to Barth of April 20, 1920 gives an impression[21] of the truly unclear reception of the lecture by the "approximately 140 students and numerous guests who attended the twenty-fourth Aarau student conference (*Christliche Studentenkonferenz der deutschen Schweiz*)."[22] Barth himself remembered quite vividly "the horror" with which Harnack "in the discussion after my lecture expressed that since Kierkegaard (I still hear the Baltic sound of that name in his mouth) has the matter not been *so* bad as now! — but also the noblesse with which he responded to the many young people and random country pastors."[23]

Barth's lecture was published in July 1920 by Chr. Kaiser Verlag in Munich, who had previous agreed to publish *The Epistle to the Romans* and the pamphlet *On the Internal Situation of Christianity* by Barth and Thurneysen. The idea to print the Isenheim Altar triptych on the cover had to be dropped. Walther Köhler wanted the fact that Barth's lecture did not appear with the other papers in the conference publication[24] to be a sign of the conference's break with the one-sided

---

17   *Bw. Th.* I, 374.
18   See the letter from Eduard Thurneysen to Karl Barth, April 20, 1920 (*Bw. Th.* I, 382).
19   Karl Barth, *Predigten 1920*, H. Schmidt, ed., *GA* I (Zürich: TVZ, 2005), 126–134.
20   Letter from Karl Barth to Eduard Thurneysen, March 22, 1920 (*Bw. Th.* I, 376).
21   *Bw. Th.* I, 381–383.
22   This is part of the description in the preface to the publication of the lectures given at the conference (Barth's not included): *Aarauer Studentenkonferenz 1920. Referate von Prof. Baltzer, Freiburg, Prof. Ad. Von Harnack, Berlin, Prof. G. Hotz, Basel, XXIV. Christl. Studentenkonferenz in Aarau, 15–17. April, 1920.* (Basel, 1920), 3. The afternoon lecture from April 16, "A medical view of the personality" by G. Hotz, was not so tightly bound to the overall theme of the conference, which came to the fore in the morning sessions. On April 15, Baltzer dealt with the question: "What do the biological sciences have to offer as definite knowledge for the construction of a worldview?" On April 16, von Harnack dealt with the question: "What does history have to offer as definite knowledge for the interpretation of world history?" Barth spoke on April 17.
23   Letter from Karl Barth to A. von Zahn-Harnack, October 23, 1935 (KBA 9235.392). Barth's report about a second encounter with Harnack on April 18, 1920 in a letter to Eduard Thurneysen from April 20, 1920 depicts the distancing he experienced from von Harnack. See *Bw. Th.* I, 378–380.
24   See Note 21 above.

orientation of the "religious-social direction," with Barth speaking as its representat-ive.[25] In his review of "Biblical Questions, Insights, and Vistas," Köhler criticizes an "absentmindedness" characterized by the "imprecise title." Nevertheless, it was "too bad" "that some fine remarks contained in this lecture lose their value in the wasteland of paradoxes."[26]Among the relatively numerous discussions dedicated to the Aarauer lecture in 1920, there were some which interpreted its basic meaning as a manifesto[27] of a new biblical hermeneutic.[28] As such, "Biblical Questions, Insights, and Vistas" represents one of the milestones in the trajectory of radical change in hermeneutics and theology during the twentieth century.

[70] The question we are now considering is: What does the Bible offer us regarding the meaning of world events?[29] But the question turns right around and directs itself toward us, asking whether and in how far we are capable of making the knowledge that is offered in the Bible our own.

The immediate, spontaneous answer to our question is that the Bible certainly offers us knowledge of God and therefore it offers no particular knowledge of this or that. Rather, it offers us knowledge of the beginning and the end, the origin and the limit, the creative unity and the final problem of all knowledge. Why do we bother to ask?

"In the beginning God created the heavens and the earth" [Gen. 1.1] and "Amen, come, Lord Jesus!" [Rev. 22.20]. Such is the meaning of the world according to the Bible. It is our task to confirm this meaning by relating ourselves, our daily work, and our present moment in history to God the Creator and Redeemer. It has no place apart from other interpretations, and other interpretations have no place apart from it, for *all* other things — the natural sciences, history, aesthetics, and religion — have their meaning in *it*. They are conceived and preserved in it. In the final analysis, this meaning is also identical to that of philosophy — in

---

25   W. Köhler, *Von der Aarauer Konferenz 1920*, in the *Basler Nachrichten*,Vol. 76 (1920), afternoon edition, Nr. 429 (October 7, 1920).

26   *Basler Nachrichten*,Vol. 76 (1920), afternoon edition, Nr. 555 (December 28, 1920).

27   The term "manifesto" is actually more accurately applied to the form of Barth's "Biblical Questions . . ." than to the *Romans* [1919] commentary, which Hans-Georg Gadamer called "a kind of her-meneutical manifesto." See his *Wahrheit und Methode. Grundzüge einer philosophischen Hermeneutik*, 2nd ed. (Tübingen: Mohr Siebeck, 1965), 481.

28   This expression was used by O. Herpel in the *Darmstädter Zeitung*, Special Section to Nr. 288 (December 8, 1920); "the view of Paul" that Barth takes is now applied to "the entire Bible."

29   The twenty-fourth Aarau student conference from April 15–17, 1920, dealt with the questions "What do the biological sciences have to offer as definite knowledge for the construction of a worldview?" (given by Prof. F. Baltzer from Freiburg im Breisgau), and "What does history have to offer as definite knowledge for the interpretation of world events?" (Prof. A. von Harnack from Berlin). Barth related the formulation of his theme to these two issues, which was suggested by the steering committee of the conference.

so far as philosophy understands itself. This is the unrivaled, undisputed meaning, the viewpoint of eternity [*sub specie aeterni*]. What more do we want?

This is easily said, but how capable are we to truly hear it, to "do something with it," so to speak? Can we handle this answer? Its simplicity and universality is exactly what perplexes us. If it already comfortably dwelled within us, we would never even have come to the question, "What does the Bible offer us?" In fact, this question cannot actually be asked. It already has [71] offered something. Our entire knowledge *lives* from the knowledge of God. We are not outside but inside. The knowledge of God is not a possibility that we use in our search — or at worst in our *non*-search — for a meaning of our world. It is, rather, the presupposition that we always *start with* in our searching, however consciously, half-consciously, or unconsciously. As a matter of fact, instead of being a charter document of the self-evident, the Bible tends to become a historical document containing new, objective information. We approach it in our inquiry as if it could say something to us that we don't already know in a most profound way. Instead of being the presupposition that starts us on the road, the knowledge of God comes to be a philosophical or mythological tidbit which we must try to get somewhere with. When this is the case we demonstrate that we do *not* fully possess the simplicity and universality that make us capable of understanding the Bible in the way it understands itself, and in the way it alone can be understood. We demonstrate that we are not wholly qualified for or equal to the knowledge of God.

Our questions demonstrate that the answer the Bible gives — which we know even before we ask — perplexes us. I say 'perplex' — not more or less. Our question to it becomes its question to us. It strangely pushes us into the middle of the "Yes" and the "No," the "No" and the "Yes." This is something we have to admit from the outset.

We said that we are inside and not outside. That is, we are on the inside of the knowledge of God, on the inside of the knowledge of the final things about which the Bible speaks. The simplicity and universality offered to us by the Bible happily corresponds to the simplicity and universality in us. "The Spirit witnesses that it is the truth" [1 Jn 5.6]. But a puzzling, inexplicable, looming sense of "being outside" apparently contradicts this. The final things draw near: aloof, strange, problematic, immense. Our own complicated existence bristles against the simpleness of the knowledge of God. Our this-and-that culture and our individualism bristles against its universality. Splintered off from the Creator spirit, the unredeemed human spirit becomes a denier of its origin; it becomes a denier of itself. While this is all true, why does it only come to this and nothing more? Why is there no resolving of this contradiction, why does the "No" not fully consume the "Yes" once and for all, even though from the [72] oldest of days the "No" has had so much more power to convince than the "Yes"?

Moreover, why is there no breakthrough to the clear and final realization that our sense of being "inside" amounts to nothing? Doesn't the sheer fact of our continual quest for God indicate that we come from the "Yes" and not the "No"? This fact cannot be due to the influence of *theology* and the *Church* because ever since the beginning of the world, theology and the Church have done more to narcotize than stimulate on this particular question. The existence of *simple-mindedness* (in the crass sense of the word) also does not explain this fact, for it really needs more intelligence to "simply" believe in God in the face of the whole suffocating power of the "No" in us all rather than just declare the question of God settled. Were it in fact the faith of simplicity, finally, which has kept the question of God open then much could be said for the intelligence of this faith. But it still would not alleviate the pressure and actual dead weight of the question itself. The natural strength of the so-called *religious feeling* also does not explain the fact that God is continually sought. For, the religious feeling can just as well distract people from the question of God as it can lead them to it. Religion and a sense for God have never meant the same thing. It is apparent that the question of God is a *final inevitability*. It contains its own answer. We have been caught and taken captive by an original, presupposed "Yes," which we would not deny if it did not cause us such unrest. We cannot entirely forget the original unity and provenance of the soul in God. We cannot construct and preserve the boundaries of humanity[30] without keeping in mind what has been limited. We would not search if we had not already found.[31] Why then, is there no space within us for the knowledge of God?

In all of the above, we have merely expressed our perplexity. Isn't there indeed room in us for something next to the knowledge of God? By holding on to our partial "inside" position, are we not simultaneously declaring our position "outside"! Aren't we the ones setting up the dualism? Can't the knowledge of God dwell in us as more than just an antithesis to all other knowledge? Knowledge [73] of God contrary to other knowledge! How can it be that we honestly do not seem to get any further than this absurd self-contradiction? How is it that even our "Yes" is not capable of bringing us to rest, to fullness, to confirmation? Why

---

30   According to Paul Natorp, it is the task of philosophy to liberate religion from its guise of transcendence by guarding the boundaries of humanity, and thus to lead religion into the work of inner-worldly ethical human community. See his *Religion innerhalb der Grenzen der Humanität. Ein Kapitel zur Grundlegung der Sozialpädogogik* (Tübingen: Mohr, 1908).

31   See Chapter 3, Note 25 in this volume.

can't we even at this point break through to the clear realization that our being "outside," our naturalism, historicism, and atheism, amounts to nothing? Where does the opposing fact come from that we always manage to partly *not* ask about God? It is not due to the *triumph over dogmatic thinking* by philosophical enlightenment, ancient and modern. For when the human soul actually becomes aware of its autonomy and its freedom, the weight of the question about unity, about God, does not decrease but only increases. Our lackluster protest is also not due to *the progress of the theoretical and practical dominance of nature,* for it is five or even ten millennia older than the modern sciences and technology. The unreserved materialism of modern science is an affirmation, not a negation, of the truth that our existence hangs on the hinges of the beginning and the end. It is also not due to the natural *weakness of the religious feeling* in the majority of humans. For if the strength of this feeling cannot establish the sense for God, then its weakness cannot make this sense impossible.

There have often been expressly irreligious humans who have experienced the entire seriousness and weight of the question of God more keenly, and have expressed it more poignantly, than the most inward and fervent pietists. I think of the remarkably unsentimental mind of Immanuel Kant, or the frank and apparently unavoidable religious Philistinism of almost all the founders and leaders of socialism. I think of the reluctant theologian, the skeptic Franz Overbeck. Each one of these figures has, with or without emotion, truly lived the question of God. How does it happen then that we, with or without emotion, actually can live partly *outside* the question of God? Obviously, even our half-hearted protest is not an accident, historically and psychologically explained, but is *something final and unavoidable.* Our questions of God can also express the fact that we do not take our questions seriously [74] because we cannot or do not want to hear (can and want being the same thing) the answer that we know all too well. Instead, we use them to avoid it. We manage to ignore precisely what we know, namely, the original unity of the soul. We are capable of being satisfied to a high degree with a knowledge split in a thousand parts, directions, puzzles, each person clinging to their part with a jealous excitement; every man for himself, throwing the spiritual bond to the wind.[32] Biology for you! History for you! Religion for you![33] You in your corner and I in mine.[34] It is a fact as

---

32   J.W. Goethe, *Faust I,*V, 1938f. (scene in the study); ET, *Selected Works: Including the Sorrows of Young Werther, Elective Affinities, Italian Journey and Faust* (New York: A.A. Knopf, 2000), 792ff.

33   See Note 29, p. 74.

34   See the beginning of the song by G. Frei: "In der Welt ists dunkel;/leuchten müssen wir,/Du in deiner Ecke,/Ich in meiner hier [. . .]" in *Deutsches Kindergesangbuch,* 26th ed., J. Zauleck, ed. (Gütersloh: Bertlesmann), Nr. 227.

inexplicable as it is undeniable that there is also a presupposed original "No" which holds us captive. In the alleged interest of threatened religion or sometimes in the alleged interest of threatened culture, we resort to metaphysics and place as opposite a particular truth about the world to a particular truth about God. But this does nothing other than establish a system of double-entry bookkeeping that just converts the knowledge of God offered in the Bible into its opposite. The fear of the Lord that is offered in the Bible is not only knowledge next to other things. It is the beginning of wisdom [Ps. 111.10; Prov. 1.7; 9.10; Sir. 1.16].

As we find ourselves in the "Yes" and "No," "No" and "Yes," we become perplexed and are thrown into the crisis of the Word: "Whoever has *ears* to hear, let *him* hear!" [Mt. 11.15]. Every *penultimate* foundation and explanation of this perplexity has failed. When we question what the Bible has to offer, it answers with the question of *election*. What we call religion and culture belongs to everybody. But that simple and universal thing offered in the Bible — namely, faith — is not available to just anybody [2 Thess. 3.2]. At no time and in no way can just anyone reach out and take it. Simplicity is likewise not so simple. Universality, "the all," is not generality. The first thing given is never a "givenness." The ultimate presupposition is never a supposed truth among other truths. The self-evident is never obvious. The knowledge offered to us and demanded of us by the Bible pushes us out onto a narrow rock-ridge between the "Yes" and "No," between life and death, between heaven and earth. "Do it so that you will be blessed, with fear and trembling. For it is God who works in you the desire and completion, according to his [75] good will" [Phil. 2.12f.].

Our response to the fact of election is the vital core and the secret to both history and our existence. Augustine and the Reformers have related this in a drastic, over-hasty manner to the *psychological* unity of the individual.[35] In so doing they have indelibly stamped each individual's salvation or damnation with the rigid laws of nature. But as a matter of fact, our responses to election are related precisely to our individual *freedom*, and as such they are not made once and for all, but ever anew. Indeed, opposite responses can reside simultaneously *alongside each other* in the individual. There is never such a decisive "Yes" that it does not harbor the possibility of the "No." Likewise there is never such a decisive "No" without the possibility of toppling over into the "Yes." Being elected does not merely result from not being condemned. And being condemned does not merely result from not being elected. God's election alone is eternal: All the psychic and historical conditions that result from it are

---

35   See Barth's criticism of this issue in *Unterricht*, 183–186; ET 453–456.

temporal. Above all, what the Bible has to offer us is the insight that knowledge of God is the eternal problem of our most personal existence. It is the origin from which we live and yet not live, from which we are separated and yet are not separated. We learn from the Bible to tone down our affirmations of belief or unbelief, or better yet, to keep silent until we realize what it is actually about:

> Him, who dare name?
> And who proclaim,
> Him I believe?
> Who that can feel,
> His heart can steel,
> To say: I believe him not?[36]

We are dust and ashes with our "Yes" and "No" [Gen. 18.27; Job 30.19; 42.6; Apoc. fragments to Est. 3.2]. *This* is true. Who commands us to engage the Bible instead of quietly following our so-called religious or so-called cultural needs? Once we *have* engaged, however, there is nothing left to do but be perplexed. In fear and trembling we must come to respect the ultimate necessities under which we are living as a *previous* act before raising our questions or hearing the answer. We have undertaken the task of Christian theology today by asking what the Bible has to offer. We must be fully aware that no other endeavor is quite as dangerous and ambiguous [76] or brings judgment down upon a person quite the way this one does. Not a single word is spoken or heard from the Bible about the glory of God in the face of Jesus Christ [2 Cor. 4.6] outside of the distressing terms of election.

The Bible contains the literary monuments of an Ancient Near Eastern religion and of a religious cult of the Hellenistic epoch. As a human document like any other, it can lay no *a priori* dogmatic claim for special attention or consideration. Yet this very view is being proclaimed upon every tongue and believed in every place today [cf. 1 Tim. 3.16]. We don't have to continue trying to break down an open door. Now, when we turn our earnest, if somewhat dispassionate, attention to the objective content of the Bible we shall not do so in a way that riles up religious enthusiasm or scientific indignation into another battle against "rigid orthodoxy" and "dead faith in letters." It is all too clear that a rational and fruitful discussion about the Bible begins when we've admitted to and *gotten beyond* its human, historical-psychological character. If only the faculties in our grade and high schools and with them the progressive group among the

---

36   See J.W. Goethe, *Faust I,*V, 3432–3437 (scene in Martha's garden); *Selected Works*, 836.

clergy of our national church would from here on out resolve to quit the battle, which once had its time but now really *has had* it! The special *content* of this human document, its remarkable *object* which these stories are about, with their authors and the figures who stand behind them — the biblical *object* — is the question that engages and engrosses us today.

But we too, with the historians and psychologists, first hit up against the fact that at one time there were apparently individuals who lived with a quite extraordinary spiritual attitude and perspective. Without a doubt, the Bible is full of this kind of peculiarity. Upon and over the margins that are present in the Bible, the distinctive characteristics of its figures flow into the attitude of other humans. But one ought not to overlook an obvious and surprising uniformity of orientation among *these* particular figures. [77] Indeed, such instances of it are not confined to the biblical world. But along this single historical line — which disappears backwards into the darkness of the ancient East and forwards into the twilight of the modern West, its enigmatic middle point marking the turning point in our calendar time — this particular spiritual orientation shows up with a frequency, intensity, a unified diversity. Likewise, it is a diverse unity that is no less remarkable given that traces of it could be found in Greece, the wonderland of India, or the German Middle Ages.

Let me take a few random examples here. What kind of spiritual understanding could have produced such a book of "subdued enthusiasm"[37] like that of the preacher Solomon? What kind of human individual was it — even if it was only one of the infamous copyists! — that could commit such a blunder of such brilliance as is seen in the joining of the two parts of the book of Isaiah into *one* biblical writing? How could anyone be capable of coming up with something like 1 Cor. 15, and writing it down? What kind of public was it at one time who expected to read inspirational writings of such caliber as the letter to the Romans or the letter to the Hebrews? What kind of conception of God and the world made it possible for humans not only to tolerate the Old and the New Testaments next to one another but to understand the one in the light of the other? We all know the uneasiness that comes over us when we look out our window and see the people on the street suddenly stop, turn their heads, shade their eyes with their hands and look straight into the sky at something that is hidden from us by the roof. The unease is not necessary; it is probably an airplane. But in the face of the sudden stopping, focused gazing, and tense listening that is characteristic of individuals in the Bible, we are not so quickly put at ease.

---

37   This expression comes from Paul Wernle, *Einführung in das theologische Studium*, 2nd ed. (Tübingen: Mohr, 1911), 225, shaped with a view toward Calvin.

I personally have seen this first with Paul. This man apparently sees and hears something incomparable, which at first completely confounds my abilities to observe or rationalize. Try as I may to prepare myself as it advances, no, as it becomes present, no, indeed as it first comes, which Paul claims in cryptic words to see and hear, I still do not get past the fact [78] that he or anyone else for that matter — such as the author of Ephesians — was eyes and ears to an event which our expressions of excitement, horror, suspense, or astonishment simply do not sufficiently describe. Behind the screen in documents such as Paul's letters, there seems to be a personality who, by seeing and hearing that which I for my part do not see and hear, is thrown off of his — and every ordinary — course in order to be schlepped as a prisoner from land to land for strange, hasty, unpredictable yet mysteriously well-planned deeds. And were I to harbor any doubt about all this and think that I am delusional, I need only to look at the parallel course of secular history, with the widening circle of ripples in its pool. It tells me that in fact a stone of unusual weight must have been thrown into its depths somewhere. It tells me that among the hordes of Near Eastern itinerant preachers and miracle workers, who back then wanted to be pulled along the same Appian Way into the Rome of the Caesars, it was precisely this man, Paul, with his seeing and hearing, who was the cause of the most important developments — if not all — in that city's life.

This man, who goes by the name "Paul," is only one among many in the Bible. Next to him is a veritable vortex of entirely unique characters who in similar fashion saw and heard. One who goes by the name of "John." Next to him stands one with an eye original enough to combine the old and new, the author of the First Gospel. Then, next to the friends and followers of Paul is the one who is *more* than a "social-religious" doctor, Luke. Next among those who see and hear stands a more disturbing individual in his moral sobriety, James. Behind all of these individuals there are more figures in Jerusalem. And farther back on the shores of the Galilean Sea are those who stand nameless, their stories untold. But it is always the same seeing of the unseen, the same hearing of the inaudible, the same incomprehensible but undeniable mass standing still, looking up. "Jesus sent the twelve out" [Mt. 10.5p]. Or were there seventy, or five hundred? [Lk. 10.1,17; cf. 1 Cor. 15.6]. Who belonged? Who didn't? Enough said. If they can speak for us in strange tongues, we cannot *avoid* seeing that their eyes are strangely opened, their ears remarkably sensitive. Brushing aside every historical causality, these same eyes and ears existed before our time, in the time *before* time [79] — in the people of Israel. The people of Israel and Judea are certainly a people like any other. But they are a people who know well of such seeing and hearing. They are a people in whom full attention to a wholly Other was never completely erased. Or are we succumbing to another historical delusion when we say this? One look at those mysteriously moved and mobile people, the Jews and the Jewish Christians as they still live among us today, and we can see that at one time surely there must have been new, strange things at work. Whether they are prophets in the fruitful middle of the biblical line, or priests closer to the margins where the Bible stops being "Bible"; whether they say it in the Psalms or the Proverbs or in the comfortable stream of historical story-telling, the theme is amazingly similar throughout all its variations. What does it matter if figures like Abraham and Moses are models of later mythical epics — believe what you'd like! But once upon a time, a few centuries earlier or later, there were humans who had faith like Abraham, who were strangers in promised lands like Isaac and Jacob, and they made it clear that they were searching for their fatherland. Like Moses, they oriented themselves upon the one whom they did not see — behaving as if they had seen him. Once upon a time there were people who dared to do this. We may believe what we can and what we will about that "something" which moved these individuals who saw and hears, which moved them to dare. But the movement itself into which they all were drawn, the named, the unnamed, and the pseudonymous, cannot be denied any more than the rotation of the night sky around a central, unknown sun. The reality of this movement meets us in the Bible in an inescapable way. Think about John the Baptist in the crucifixion scene by Grünewald[38] and the way his pointing hand is twisted in an almost impossible manner. It is this hand that is documented in the Bible.

Yet this phenomenon needs to be interpreted. Simply drawing and describing the pointing fingers as religion, piety, experience, and the like does not help us interpret it, even if it is done with full expertise and love. Any attempt at an interpretation must presuppose that the phenomenon we are speaking of is never truly described or exhausted by religious categories, which are of little use for understanding the matter in the first place. The biblical experiences harbor a decisive element which is hidden and is not made visible through any psychological or emotional construct. [80] Biblical piety is not actually pious. It must be described more as a superior, qualified worldliness. At its deepest core, biblical religious history has the special characteristic of wanting to be neither religion nor history. Perhaps we should say reality instead of religion; truth instead of history. But I'm getting ahead of myself.

We are standing here before the decisive characteristic of the biblical line toward all that we call the history of religion. Everything we call

---

38   Barth is referring to Grünewald's Isenheimer Altar (Musée d'unterlinden, Colmar, France). See Odo Marquard, *Karl Barth und der Isenheimer Altar* (in *Arbeiten zur Theologie* 80) (Stuttgart: Calwer Verlag, 1995).

"religion" tends to have a deep current of "the other side," of worldly objectivity, of non-historicity. In every time and place religion has meant and means content and not only form. It has meant movement and not only the usefulness of the moved. It has meant the divine life, not only human life, not even a consecrated part of it. But always and everywhere, along with this inner tendency, there is an unmistakable trace of untruth. Religion forgets that its existence is only justified when it continually overcomes itself. Instead, it takes pleasure in its position within existence, holding itself for indispensable. It deceives itself and the world about its true character — and it is *able to do this* by virtue of the wealth of its sentimental and symbolic content, by the fascinating states of the soul, through dogma and cult, through morals and ecclesiastical authority. It refuses to tolerate its own relativity. It cannot bear the waiting, the wandering, the spirit of the stranger, which are the only things that justify its appearance in the world. It is not satisfied with references to the "x" that stands above the world *and* religion itself. It acts as if it were the owner of an other-worldly and super-ecclesiastical gold bar. And it actually begins to hand out jingling coins with its so-called "religious values." It appears as a power able to compete *next to* the other powers of life, as an alleged super-world *next to* the world. It drives missions as if it had a calling.

The extraordinary views of the Bible become recognizable, practical, possible and thus commonly seen attitudes *next to* other views. For the wondering world, trust in God becomes an attainable and entirely useful tool for life, and is utilized thoughtlessly as a great excuse. The pointing finger of John the Baptist becomes a common sight [81] in the pulpit. The experience of Paul is *also* had by earnest young people here and there. Prayer, the final possibility grasped at by those spirits imprisoned by God in their highest need and joy, is more or less a respected element of bourgeois households and church life. Without even a blush, one speaks of "Christian" ethics, "Christian" families, clubs, and institutions. "God in us"[39] — why not also I in you, you in me too?[40] Such religious mischief simply permits itself everything. Physics aligns itself with metaphysics as if it were necessary. Form dares to stand in for content. Experience becomes the enjoyment of itself, satisfaction in itself, and its own goal. The thing being moved wants to be the movement itself. The human has taken the divine into its possession. He has put it under his management.

No one notices, or wants to notice, that everything rests upon a

---

39   P. Ovidius Naso, *Fasti* VI, 5: "Est Deus in nobis . . ."

40   This comes from the fifth verse of the song, "Gott ist gegenwärtig" ("God Himself is Present") by G. Tersteegen (*GERS* 174; *RG* v. 4; *EG* 165; *LBW* 249), however this particular verse has not been included in the English version.

supposition, upon an enormous "as if"[41] and *quid pro quo*. How did it come to this? Who is responsible? Is it the people who broke out into a call to the gods, because they felt themselves utterly abandoned in the desert? Was it Moses' unavoidable brother, the priestly Aaron, who knew only too well how to show the people how to get such gods? Suffice it to say that the history-of-religions school starts here. It is the history of the unfaithfulness of religion against what it actually means. For, *the moment religion becomes conscious of itself as religion, when it becomes a psychologically, historically graspable matter in the world, it falls from its most profound tendency, from its truth, into idols. Its truth is its other-worldliness, its worldly objectivity, its non-historicity.* The decisive characteristic of the Bible as opposed to the history of religions — to which Christian history and the Church belong — is the visibility of a completely conspicuous line of faithfulness, perseverance, patience, waiting, and objective attention toward the incredible, non-psychological, non-historical truth of God. The mystery in the Bible, to which every religious perspective is oriented, achieved a fully successful resistance against the human attempt to betray and compromise it.

Biblical *piety* has its own limits and is aware of its relativity. Its substance is humility, fear of the Lord. By referring to something beyond the world, it points at the same [82] time and above all beyond itself. It lives entirely from and for its object. In the biblical *experience* there is nothing less important than experience as such. It is office and mandate, not goal and fulfillment. Therefore it is an elementary event, barely conscious of itself, which only ever makes a minimum of reflection and confession necessary. The prophets and the apostles do not *want* to be what they are called, they *must* be it. Precisely because of this they *are* prophets and apostles. Precisely on the typically central point of religion — the expression of a *personal relationship with God* — the Bible is remarkably reserved, sober, and colorless compared with the suppressed sexuality and shimmering wealth of rainbow colors that saturate the object of myths and mysticism. It is apparent that *the* relation to God, which biblical expressions aim at, does not take place in the crimson depths of the subconsciousness. Nor does it want to be somehow identical with that which depth-psychology today speaks of broadly or narrowly as the fulfillment of libido.

In this context the *concept of sacrifice* comes to mind, which is so important to the supremely vigilant and cautious handling of the entire history of religions. Already in the Old Testament, there is a standing reference beyond the sacrifice to some final fact. It is not settled with even the greatest and purest sacrifice, and it finally makes all sacrifice superfluous.

---

41   See Chapter 1, Note 21 in this volume.

God does not want a sacrifice but rather — rather what then? This is exactly what religious people back then were asking! [1 Sam. 15.22; Ps. 51.17,19; 40.6; 50.8; Prov. 21.3; Hos. 6.6]. Obedience, justice, love, open ears, gratitude, a reverent spirit, a broken heart are the puzzling, negative answers that precede the dawn of New Testament truth where all sacrifice is abolished through *one* sacrifice. "Where forgiveness is, there is no longer sacrifice for sin" [Heb. 10.18]. In remarkable isolation, the story of Stephen stands opposed to the entire flood of Christian stories of martyrdom [Acts 7]. Redemption through a sacrifice that *we* have to bring does not occur in the Bible from that point on. Thus, unlike religions up until this very day, the *polemic* of the Bible does not direct itself against the godless world, but precisely against the *religious* world, whether it now stands under the sign of Baal or under the sign of Yahweh. It directs its polemic against the heathens only in so far as their idols present those relativities, powers, and acts of violence that get raised into a metaphysical state, and as such are abominations to the Lord [cf. Deut. 7.25; 12.31; 17.1, etc.], abolished in Christ.

Furthermore, in the Old and the New Testaments, an [83] entire series of *heathens* must manifest a faith not found in Israel, and thus visibly demonstrate [Mt. 8.10; Lk. 7.9] how plainly the biblical person stands there fatherless, motherless [Heb. 7.13], without a race, as a newcomer, a rookie, and in contrast to all history, dependent only upon himself and God. Melchizedek, the king of Salem, is the classical prototype of this [Gen. 14.18-20]. Along the same lines lays the conspicuously low regard that the Bible shows for the *biographical* development of its heroes. There is no touching story of the childhood or conversion of Jeremiah, no report of an amazing death of Paul. To the disappointment of our theological contemporaries, there was in particular *no* "life of Jesus." What we hear about these people is never told by themselves, never as their "life and letters."[42] The biblical person stands and falls with his task, his work. Therefore even the biblical *conception of creation* is not developed into a cosmology anywhere. It zeros in on the ceremonious generation of the distance between the cosmos and the Creator, and precisely not on a metaphysical explanation of the world. God spoke: "Let there be!" [Gen 1.3, 6]. That's it. All being has the Word of God as its presupposition, everything perishable has the imperishable, and all temporality presupposes infinity.

"Where does one want to find wisdom and where is the place of understanding? No one knows where it lies, and it is not to be found

---

42   This formulation can be encountered for example in the work of Martin Rade, *Doktor Martin Luthers Leben, Thaten und Meinungen, auf Grund reichlicher Mitteilungen aus seinen Briefen und Schriften dem Volke erzählt*, Vols. 1–3 (Neusalza i.S.: Hermann Deser, 1890–1891; Tübingen and Leipzig, 1901).

in the land of the living. The depths say, 'it is not in me!' and the oceans say, 'it is not in me!'" [Job 28.12-14] The boundaries, the origin and the problem of the world — "the King of Kings and Lord of Lords, who alone has immortality who dwells in an inaccessible light" [1 Tim. 6.15f.] — this is "God" in the Bible. Precisely because of this, everything that has breath, praise the Lord! [Ps. 150.6]. And therefore the biblical *history* in the Old and the New Testament is actually *not* history but is, rather, seen from above as a series of free, divine actions. Seen from below, it is a series of unfulfilled attempts at an undertaking that is impossible in itself. From the viewpoint of development and pragmatism in its details and in its entirety, the Bible is absolutely incomprehensible, a fact which every honest teacher of religion knows only too well.

Thus, the biblical *Church*, namely the tabernacle, the wandering tent, exists only as an object to be attacked the moment it becomes a temple. One can glean that for the apostles, the whole of the Old Testament is summarized in [84] Stephen's speech in the Acts of the Apostles [Acts 7.44-50]. The central, undeniable concern in both the Old and New Testaments is not the construction of the Church but with its necessary and looming deconstruction. In the Book of Revelation, the characteristic of the heavenly Jerusalem is finally nothing more than its utter lack of a Church: "And I saw no temple in it" [Rev. 21.22].

Thus, biblical *thinking* and *speaking* is characterized by its flowing from a source that lies above every pair of religious conceptual opposites — from creation and redemption, grace and judgment, nature and spirit, earth and heaven, promise and fulfillment. Indeed, it initiates the contradictions, first on this side then on that side. Yet it does not lead them pedantically to their end. It never insists on the consequences, and it hardens itself neither in the thesis nor in the antithesis; it never stiffens into positive or negative finalities. It has no understanding for what our clumsy age calls "an honest either-or." It is equally concerned with the "Yes" as it is with the "No," for the truth does not lie in the "Yes" or in the "No." It lies in the knowledge of the beginning, out of which the "Yes" and the "No" come. It is an original thinking and speaking issuing out from the whole and pointing toward the whole. It is capable of agreeing with those philosophies that are worthy of their name, but it will never be marked by general psychologisms, however rough or fine they are. For it always wants to be completely serious but never taken at its word. It does not want to be merely accepted but understood; spirit through spirit! [1 Cor. 2.13]. It is through and through dialectical. "Be aware of the professors!" [*Caveant professores!*]. The biblical dogmatic is the fundamental overcoming of every dogmatic. The Bible has exactly *one* theological interest, and this interest is purely objective: the interest in God himself.

It is this that I would like to call the other-worldliness, the non-historicity, the worldly objectivity of the biblical lines. It is a new, incomparable, unachievable, not only heavenly but also supra-heavenly line: God has caught the attention of these humans for himself. God demands their *full* attention, their *complete* obedience. For God wants to remain faithful to himself. God is holy and remains so. God does not want to be seized, put into operation, and utilized. He does not want to serve, but he wants to rule. He himself wants to seize, confiscate, operate, and use. God does not want to satisfy any other need except his own. He does not want [85] other-worldliness next to this-worldliness, he wants every form of this-worldliness to be consumed by other-worldliness. God does not want to be *something* next to other things but wants to be *completely* other.[43] He is the infinite epitome of every mere relative difference. God does not want to establish a history of religions. He wants to be the Lord of our lives, the eternal Lord of the world. *This* is what the Bible is about. Is this true in other places too? Certainly. The only difference is that in other places it is a final, exalted background, an esoteric mystery and therefore only a possibility. In the Bible all this is the first thing, the foreground, the revelation, the one all-governing theme.

Indeed, for every named characteristic of the biblical line, there is also an opposing example that is also biblical. The biblical line is thus not identical with the book of the Bible. It is contained in the Bible itself, unprotected from the general history of religion seen there. There is hardly a point where it will not be penetrated by another, foreign line. The margins in the Bible where the biblical person looks very similar to not only *other* people but especially to *religious* people are often confusing and scattered about, especially in the Old Testament, though they certainly are not lacking in the New Testament. The myriad of variations lets the theme be almost forgotten along some stretches. The opinion that the Bible is only a part of the general religious chaos is therefore understandable but avoidable! It is avoidable at a time when the relative nature of Christendom that relies upon experience, metaphysic, and history has been so tangibly and unmistakably established; at a time when the question about God, about a *new* and *completely* different thing, about the reality of *God*, lays on our tongues like it does these days. We *can* avoid misunderstanding the character and the direction of the biblical line, avoid reading our own unfulfilled wishes into them.

A thoroughly enlightening confession of the Church from the time of the Reformation, the Synod of Bern from 1532, carries the motto

---

43   See Rudolf Otto, *The Idea of the Holy: An Inquiry into the Non-rational Factor in the Idea of the Divine and its Relation to the Rational*, 2nd ed., John W. Harvey, trans. (Oxford: Oxford University Press, 1950).

of a very non-churchly word of Paul: "Whether we have also known Christ according to the flesh, however, we no longer know him in this way" [2 Cor. 5.16].[44] Thus, despite its blurring throughout the history of the Christian Church, biblical insight has never been inaccessible, even in later centuries.

Let's let Grünewald speak again. Next to the haunting, pointing figure of its John the Baptist, stand the words: "He must increase, but I must decrease" [Jn 3.30: *Illum oportet crescere, me autem minui*]. This is the attitude of the prophets, the men of God, the seers and the hearers toward the One [86] to which this powerful pointing refers. This One, the object, the matter, the divine self as such is on the increase while the function, the piety, the Church as such is decreasing in meaning! We can call this the biblical line, the biblical insight.

He must increase! Yet who can fail to feel a profound fear in speaking and listening to this One who must increase? The One who was there, seen by the people in the Bible, and perhaps also seen — from a great distance — by us? Once we have turned our backs on the colorful carnival of the history of religions, we are surrounded by oppressive, sheer awe, stillness and solitude. We find ourselves in the loneliness of the desert, which is a significant location in the Bible for a good reason. In fact, it must be a *mysterium tremendum*[45] that drives the people of the Bible farther and farther out onto the margins of experience, thought, and deed, onto the margins of time and history. It drives them to step out into the air where obviously no one can stand. Wouldn't it be better for our peace of mind if we turned back at this point? Dare we let our eyes follow the pointing finger of the Grünewaldian Baptist? We know where it points. It points to Christ — but to Christ the Crucified we must immediately add. "Here it is!" declares the pointing finger. "He shall grow up before us as a tender plant, and as a root out of a dry ground: he has no form or comeliness; and when we shall see him there is no beauty that we should desire him. He is despised and rejected of men; a man of sorrows, and acquainted with grief: and we hid as it were our faces from him; he was despised, and we esteemed him not" [Isa. 53.2f.]. The one single source of unmediated, real revelation is in *death*. *Christ* has conquered it. He has brought *life* to light out of *death*.

Out of *death*! We cannot say this strongly and insistently enough. The

---

44 *Berner Synodus. Ordnung, wie sich die Pfarrer und Prediger zu Stadt und Land Bern in Lehre und Leben halten sollen, mit weiterem Bericht von Christo und den Sakramenten, beschlossen auf dem Synodus daselbst am 9. Jänner 1532. Cf. Der Berner Synodus von 1532. Edition und Abhandlungen zum Jubiläumsjahr 1982*, Vol. 1, G. W. Locher, ed. (Neukirchen-Vluyn: Neukirchner Verlag, 1984).

45 The *mysterium tremendum* is a moment of the Numinous in Otto's *The Idea of the Holy*, 12ff. See also Note 43, p. 87.

power and meaning of God is comprehended by the people of the Bible on the boundaries of humanity "where sensing and thinking dim in me like a light that flickers back and forth as its flame slowly dies."[46] The human correlate to the divine liveliness is not called virtue, enthusiasm, or love, but, rather, *the fear* of the Lord — namely, [87] the fear of death as the final, absolute fear. I am speaking of the particular fear that is expressed in Michelangelo's figures of the prophets.[47] "Our God is a consuming fire" [Heb. 12.29; Deut. 5.23 (cf. 26)]. "What is all flesh that it may hear the voice of the living God and remain living?" Humans can kill the body, but God can destroy body and soul in hell [Mt. 10.28; Lk. 12.5]. God befalls Jacob [Gen. 32.25] like an armed enemy [cf. Prov. 6.11; 24.34]. One hides his face from him but the brilliance of his light upon the face of Moses is overpowering [Exod. 34.33, 35; 2 Cor. 3.13]. Moses, Isaiah, Jeremiah, and Jonah all avoided serving him [Exod. 2.11ff.; Isa. 6.5; Jer. 1.6; Jon. 1.3], certainly not out of some moralistic, psychological inferiority complex but out of an ultimate inhibition toward the one into whose hands the falling is *terrible* [Heb. 10.31]. "The lion roars, who should not be afraid of him? The Lord Yahweh speaks; who should not prophesy?" [Amos 3.8]. "O Lord, you have enticed me, and I was enticed; you have overpowered me and you have prevailed . . . If I say, 'I will not mention him, or speak any more in his name,' then within me there something like a burning fire shut up in my bones; I am weary with holding it in, and I cannot" [Jer. 20.7, 9].

This is how it happens between God and those who belong to him! This is why they are all such broken, human, dissatisfying figures. Each one is an anti-hero. Their life histories are inconclusive. Their life's work is incomplete. The condition of their souls and their success are more than problematic, never mind the construction of or even the intention to construct *institutions* or an *historical* evaluation of the matter![48] Whether we think of Jacob, David, or Jeremiah, or of Peter and Paul, not one of them is in any way beautiful [Isa. 53.2]. Theirs is the liveliest

---

46   This comes from the fifth verse of the hymn "Christus, der ist mein Leben" (*GERS* 320, slightly altered from the original which was published in Jena, 1609, and was possibly written by Melchior Vulpius); *RG* 774; *EG* 516; *LBW* 263 (as "Abide with Us, Our Savior"; however, verse five has not been included in the English version).

47   Barth is referring to the ceiling frescos in the triangular spaces of the arches of the Sistine Chapel.

48   This is an allusion to the lecture by Harnack at the Aarau Student Conference, "What does history have to offer as definite knowledge for the interpretation of world events?" The emphases are Barth's. See Harnack's *Erforschtes und Erlebtes, Reden und Aufsätze*, new ed., 4 Vols. (Gießen: Töpelmann, 1923), 171–195. Harnack saw in institutions "the actual fruits of history's development, *which there-fore, the study of history must be in the first instance, and almost exclusively oriented toward*" (175). See page 186 where he says that "all history" is a "history of institutions"; "everything which is not merely ideology and which has not yet been brought into the form of an institution" is "not yet history."

witness — not from humanity but from the *limits* of humanity. Quite
honestly, with more than one of these men of God, it seems that that he
personally must have been a completely unbearable fogey.

For this reason even the epochs of the history of Israel are themselves as
unclassical as the others, with their various stages of human insufficiency,
or of Israel being sick for Yahweh, like Hosea has called it [cf. Hos. 5.12-
14].[49] Between the promise: "I want to be your God, and you shall be my
people!" [Lev. 26.12] and its fulfillment, the tangible reality of the decline
of this people pushes in. In a threatening manner over the entrance gate
to Solomon's wisdom of life, the tablet hangs, "Vanity of vanities . . . vanity
of vanities! All is vanity!" [Eccl. 1.2 etc.] The unmistakable [88] under-
tone of the Psalms, which so many people admire and claim they find
inspiring, reads "Lord, let me know my end and what is the measure of my
days; let me know how fleeting my life is. You have made my days a few
handbreadths, and my lifetime is as nothing in your sight. Surely, everyone
stands as a mere breath" [cf. Ps. 39.4-5]. The divine answer — "out of
the whirlwind" — to Job's theodicy question about the righteousness of
God in the world and in response to the apologetics and pastoral care
of his friends — thankfully making them fall silent [Job 42.6] — brings
Job to knowledge and confession in the dust and the ashes [Job 38.1].
For it refers to the final, absolute mysteriousness, incomprehensibility, and
darkness of all natural existence. And as the crown witnesses to this, as
compelling as they are ugly, the hippopotamus, crocodile, behemoth, and
mighty leviathan all march up [Job 40.15-24; 25-32]. "I have heard of
you, by the hearing of the ear," Job confesses, "but now my eyes see you"
[Job 42.5]. Certainly now he *knows* the righteousness of God!

After all this, the Prince of Peace of the final days [Isa. 9.5], the Servant
of God among the peoples [Isa. 53.11], the Son of Man who comes from
heaven in the Old Testament [Daniel 7], who stands at the center of the
New Testament, can be nothing other than precisely the *Crucified*. If this
particular correlation is taken into account, the New Testament proves
itself as the quintessence of the Old. "The axe is laid under the trees on
the roots" [Mt. 3.10; Lk. 3.9], the completion of the world [*consummatio
mundi*],[50] the overcoming of everything that is given, the breaking up
of every becoming, the decay of this world and time — all this is the
meaning of the "kingdom of God," as it has not only been proclaimed

49 See the title of the column that interprets Hos. 5.12–14: "Yahweh is the illness of Israel," in B. Duhm,
    Israels Propheten (Tübingen: Mohr, 1916), 124. Barth cited this in *Romans* 1919 as well. See *GA* II,
    366, 427. See also *Romans* 1922, 339 (1999 ed., 371); ET 354: "the sickness which men suffer at
    God's hands."
50 In the older Protestant Orthodoxy, this is the fourth of the five signs of the coming of the end of
    the world [*novissima*]. See SchmP 407. See also Mt. 13.39f., 49; 24.3; 28.20; 1 Pet. 3.12.

by the Baptist and by "Jesus of Nazareth," but also by Paul as well as by the author of the book of Revelation.

The work of Christ is, according to the corresponding Synoptic, Pauline, and Johannine witnesses, obedience to the will of the Father who leads him on a straight line to death. After briefly eyeballing the target and giving a great shove, the kingdom of God storms in [cf. Mt. 11.12], pushing through to the final questions, to the last doubt, to the ultimate insecurity. It pushes beyond the final boundaries to where all things cease, where only one thing remains to be said of the future of the Son of Man, namely, heaven and earth will die away! [Mt. 24.35]. It pushes to where even the question, "My God, my God why have you forsaken me?" [Mt. 27.46] will be possible and necessary, to where there is nothing more to know, nothing more to believe, nothing more to do, where the sin of the world will still only be *carried* [89], where only *one* possibility remains. But this possibility lies on the *other side* of all thinking and all things: *"See I make all things new!"* [Rev. 21.5]. *Everything that the New Testament affirms about God, humans and the world is related to this possibility without exception, which in the strictest sense is beyond all consideration. For this reason, it is always at the same time related to the greatest critical negation that the possibility of a new order unrelentingly presupposes.*

Whoever understands the New Testament "Yes" as anything but the "Yes" contained in the "No" does not understand it at all. Out of death comes life! *From here* comes knowledge of God as the Father, as the origin, as the one who created heaven and earth [Gen. 1.1]. *From here* comes its grace, as the first and the final, the radical, the decisive, and the inexpressible Word for the conquering, kingly relation of God to alienated humanity. *From here* comes the judicious but ground-breaking attack upon the law and upon the religious-ethical human righteousness of Judaism — an attack which secures the universality of grace. *From here* comes a clarity that is more than intuition, "I saw Satan fall from heaven like a rod of lightning" [Lk. 10.18]. *From here* comes the unheard-of prolepsis, "you *were* dead through trespasses and sins; in which you formerly had wandered according to the course of this world" [Eph. 2.1f.]. *From here*, comes the decision and the undertaking not to break into death's stranglehold on reality by miracle but by overcoming death and the world as a whole and by publically exposing its limitations, "to bring good news to the poor" [Col. 2.15]. "He has sent me to proclaim the release to the captives and recovery of sight to the blind, to let the oppressed go free, to proclaim the year of the Lord's favor" [Lk. 4.18,19. cf. Isa. 61.1f.].

From here comes the new and impossible perspective and standard for the distinguishing of good and evil, happy and unhappy, beautiful and ugly. What is highly regarded in the eyes of humans is an abomination in the eyes of God [Lk. 16.15]. But the poor, the abandoned, and the sorrowful, those who hunger and thirst for justice, are blessed! [Mt. 5.3-6]. *From here* comes the true warning against mammon, against having a god next to God, who in a materiality deceptively similar to death, hides the reality of life from us. [90] "In this night, you fool, your soul will be demanded; to whom do those things which you have prepared for belong then?" [Lk. 12.20]. *From there* comes the Savior's call to the weary and heavy-burdened to exchange their small yoke with the great yoke [Mt. 11.28-30]; to exchange the lowliness of the heart for peace, and to find the refreshment and quiet that is hidden from the wise and the clever but that is revealed to the lowly [Mt. 11.25]. *From there* comes the call to a *particular* penance that has little to do with the contrite, the ascetic, and the art of sacrifice, but consists of a radically new way of thinking, a new way of valuing all practical work, of becoming like children [Mt. 18.3], of beginning at the beginning with the insight that there is no good which we could do, that a camel cannot go through the eye of a needle [Mt.19.24], that God alone is the good. *From there* comes the subdued call of the Master to his disciples [Mt. 19.17] — a call laden with insistent warnings against hasty applause: "Follow me! [Mt. 4.19, etc.] you, to whom the mystery of the kingdom of God is given to be known [Mt. 13.11], to leave everything [Mt. 19.27], to deny yourselves, to lose your soul for my sake [Mt. 16.24, 25; 10.39, etc.] Everything comes *from this!* From the final thing! Or rather from the overcoming of the final things!

Therefore the Messiahship of Jesus must be a secret.[51] It would be better if his mission were not known rather than being understood as a possibility of the *old* order, as a *religious* possibility, *apart* from the great, critical, "from there." Jesus will be wholly understood or not at all. He first confesses this only at the moment when the danger of becoming a religious establishment is finally past, when the confession of his Messiahship is at the same time his condemnation to death, at the interrogation before Caiaphas. Only then does the Word first have its content: Jesus wants to be the Messiah only as the One given unto death. "*From now on* it will happen that you will see the Son of Man sitting at the right hand of the power and coming in the clouds of heaven" [Mt. 26.64]. Flesh and blood cannot — and ought not — inherit the kingdom of God [1 Cor. 15.50]. Through parables it meets those who are on the outside [Mic. 4.11; Lk. 8.10; cf. Mt. 13.13-16]. Flesh and blood did not reveal even to Simon Peter that Jesus was the Messiah, the living Son of

---

51   See William Wrede, *Das Messiasgeheimnis in den Evangelien. Zugleich ein Beitrag zum Verständnis des Markusevangeliums* (Göttingen: Vandenhoeck & Ruprecht, 1904).

God [Mt. 16.16-18] but rather Jesus' Father in heaven. The Christian community has been built upon the knowledge of the cliffs and the free air *"from there."* Even the gates of hell shall not overpower it. But when this same Peter calls into question Jesus' going to his death, he no longer speaks of divine things,[52] *"from there,"* [91] but rather of human things, in the role of Satan.

A thorough awakening to every penultimate thought and thing; a readiness for *final* questions and answers; a hastening that waits for *final* decisions [2 Pet. 3.12]; a listening for the tone of the *final* trumpet [1 Cor. 15.52] that announces *the* truth from the other side of the grave — this is the knowledge of God that comes to light as the conclusion and the epitome of the Old and the New Testaments. Franz Overbeck called it the "wisdom of death."[53] Indeed it is. The wisdom of death is the knowledge that the sacrifice demanded of us has been taken care of once and for all in the sacrifice of Christ. It is the knowledge that we ourselves *have been* sacrificed with Christ and that there is therefore no longer any sacrifice to be *brought* [Cf. Phil. 2.17; 2 Tim. 4.6]. Precisely because it is the wisdom of death, it is also an incomprehensible wisdom of life. I cite Kierkegaard: "The bird on the branch, the lily in the field, the deer in the forest, the fish in the sea, countless happy humans rejoice: God is love! But at the same time, *carrying*, like the bass part sounds under all of the sopranos, the 'out of the depths' [*de profundis*] out of the one sacrificed: God is love!"[54]

Really *love*? Can the ones who have been sacrificed really carry us? Is there anything else to be expected from the boundaries of humanity than only doubt and dissolution? Can absolute fear be fruitful? Can it conceive, or be creative? Is it *knowledge*, knowledge of God which is hidden in the great negation that approaches us, and which victoriously emerges from it? Is it true that out of death comes *life*? We think about the fact that on this point we stand with Buddhism, where so much profound reflection, so much supreme striving finds its last word in conscious resignation and skepticism.

The *Mater dolorosa*, Mary of Magdalene, and the disciple John, who make up the companion figures on Grünewald's altar panel next to the

---

52   In the original printing, the German *"was"* is present, whereas in the publication of *Das Wort Gottes und die Theologie*, *"als"* is mistakenly printed.

53   Franz Overbeck, *Christentum und Kultur. Gedanken und Anmerkungen zur modernen Theologie*. Carl Albrecht Bernoulli, ed. (Basel: Schwabe, 1919), 279, 318. See Overbeck's *Werke und Nachlaß*, Vol. 6/1. Barbara von Reibnitz, ed. (Stuttgart: J.B. Metzler, 1996), 66, 99. See also Barth's *Unerledigte Anfragen an die heutigen Theologie*, in *Th.u.K.*, 1-25, esp.15; ET 55–73, esp. 71.

54   Søren Kierkegaard, *Buch des Richters. Seine Tagebücher 1833–1855*, Hermann Gottsched, trans. and ed. (Jena/Leipzig: Diederichs, 1905), 100. Cf. Martin Luther, "Aus tiefer Not schrei ich zu dir" (*EG* 299).

pointing Baptist, all appear to suggest that it is possible to remain standing before the mystery of the cross in helplessness, horror, and despair. Where does the artist get the authority to show us this possibility in a depiction and at the same time to overcome it? Where does he get the authority to insert the Lamb of God who poured out his blood for many between the knowing and the unknowing? He literally opens his image of the cruci-fixion like a door and displays on the back the graceful annunciation to Mary on the one side and the resurrection of Christ on the third day on the other. But in the center, as a glimpse of the new thing that is waiting behind the gruesome door of death, the adoration of [92] the newborn child by people on earth and by angels singing hosanna — with a vista onto the infinite height of the throne of the glory of the Father. The unique rhythm of progress — out of life into death, then out of death into life — approaches us in the middle point of the Bible, there, where the New Testament in fulfillment of the Old speaks of the suffering and the glory of the Messiah. Is it believable? Is it rational? Is it real?

Let us not be too hasty in answering this question positively. Our positivity could otherwise lack its necessary gravity! Let us not contrast ourselves too rashly with those who consider the cross an irritation and foolishness [1 Cor. 1.23], for as a matter of fact, we belong to them. Let us not fool ourselves about the fact that all of our contemporaries stand in fear and need *before* the closed door of death, hardly aware of the new thing that may be waiting behind it. In any case, it does not do us well to rush past these people with speculative constructions, in evangelical or social activities, or in a supposed immediacy of our religious experience. For the sake of the suffering of millions, for the sake of much blood which has been spilled which cries out against us all, for the sake of the fear of the Lord, let us not rush. If there is any word that is in need of substantiation, of attestation and demonstration in corresponding ethical, social, and political action, it is the biblical word of death, that is swal-lowed up by victory [1 Cor. 15.55]. If we were aware of how difficult it is to substantiate, attest to, and demonstrate this word through *our* deeds, we must be clear about the fact that *we* can speak this word only in the deepest of shame, confusion, and reservation. In this case, what counts is only that which is done out of the possibility that lies beyond all con-sideration: "See, I make everything new!" [Rev. 21.5].

To really *name* the object of the Bible — the Easter message — would mean to give it, have it, show it. The Easter message becomes movement and truth as it is expressed — or else it is something *other* than the Easter message which is expressed. Therefore let us be satisfied that every bib-lical question, insight, and vista, in every direction is aimed at precisely this object. But let us not hide from ourselves, even for a moment, that obedience to this vision, that is, our acceptance of the Bible's proposal, is a leap into an abyss, a wager of unheard of consequences, an eternal undertaking. [93] Better to first stop and count the costs rather than not jump far enough [Lk. 14.28]. It is better to hear the "No" from all of this than to only hear an unreal, unconfirmed merely religious "Yes." It is better that we go away sadly but promptly because we have too many possessions [Mk. 10.22p.] than joining the innumerable greats of religion and the church — even the greatest in history — which turns out not to be joining them at all. Religion's blind and bad habit of eternally asserting that it possesses something, its feasting upon it and sharing it must eventually stop. It must give way to an honest, fierce seeking, asking, and knocking at the door.

With this reservation in mind, let us now turn the page and take up the Bible's final suggestion (as a suggestion!), and talk about something which we do not know, which *is* only true by *becoming* true. Indeed the God of Moses and Job, the awesome God of Gethsemane and Golgotha, is love [1 Jn 4. 8, 16]. Wind, earthquake, and fire come from the Lord, but the Lord is not in the wind, not in the earthquake, not in the fire. "After the fire came a quiet, soft sigh" [1 Kgs 19.12]. "After the fire?" Yes. That which is at the beginning for God comes into the consciousness of Elijah the human only at the *end. Behind the final things of humans stands the first thing of God.* Just as the tare coils up out of the earth from the dying seeds of wheat [Jn 12.24; cf. 16.21], just as the child comes out of the suffering body of the mother, just as thinking and law spring from the chaos of experience, resulting in something wholly new that alone makes experience possible, so the divine "first" lies beyond the final things of humanity. It is its fulfillment, its affirmation, its subversion, its overcoming.

The fear of the Lord is the beginning of wisdom [Ps. 111.10; Prov. 1.7; Sir 1.16]. The one who makes the patriarchs into pilgrims and foreigners, allowing them no rest, is also their shield and their exceedingly great reward [Gen. 15.1]. Those who gave themselves to be the prophets of judgment and evil will be legitimized and equipped as messengers of grace and salvation [cf. Isa. 52.7 and Rom. 10.5]. The one who calls to the Lord out of the deep finds courage in: "however, I will abide with you always!" [Pss. 130.1; 73.23]. Because Job looked the behemoth and the leviathan in the eye his imprisonment was reversed [Job 42.10]. In a final, intense unrest lies the first actual peace. The final, most radical question calls up the first real answer. Out of the final deadly terror, one can say for the first time: "Peace be with you!" The final day of humans [94] becomes the first day of God [Lk. 24.36; Jn 20.19, 21, 26]. *By the sound of the final trumpet,* says Paul, it will happen, that the dead will be resurrected incorruptibly, and be transformed [1 Cor. 15.52].

Resurrection is the *sovereignty of God.* Resurrection, God's sovereignty, is the meaning of the life of Jesus from the first day of his appearance on.

The older Blumhardt used to sing out: "Jesus is the victorious hero!"[55]
Indeed he is. He is the herald of the divine will, the fighter for the divine
honor, the authorized carrier of divine might. Jesus simply has nothing to
do with religion. The meaning of his life is the actuality of that which is
not in any actual religion. It is the actuality of the inapproachable, inconceivable, incomprehensible, the realization of *the* possibility that is beyond
all consideration: "See, *I* make all things new!" [Rev. 21.5]. There is barely
a word of Jesus that does not witness to the forcefulness of this claim. The
death of Jesus reveals its fundamental radicalism. "He must govern until
he brings every enemy under his feet. The final enemy which will be
conquered is death" [1 Cor. 15.25f.]. The boundary of our existence is
reached. Our existence is bound up in God. He holds it, determines it,
and rules over it. Reality is not ignored or laid aside, not extinguished
or disqualified, but is, rather, qualified. Its meaning is known, its determination is restored by being grasped and rolled out by the truth. The
truth gives up its distant, reserved, transcendent attitude toward reality. It
"rejoices" again in the inhabited world, as we read in Proverbs 8 [v. 8.31].
It rejoices as the living dialectic of every reality of the world by calling its
alleged answers into question and by answering its actual questions. The
spirit in every spirit, the humane in humanity, the creation in the cosmos,
the superiority of God — all of this as critical potential, as redemption
in action, as an increasing clarity of interpretation, as a pressing onward,
as knowledge that gains meaning — all this is Easter.

Resurrection means *eternity*. If the reign of God is the meaning of
time, then for this reason it is not in time. It is not a temporal thing
like other things. What is in time has not yet reached the boundary of
death. It is not yet taken up by God and ruled. It must still die in order
to enter into life. The moment in which the last trumpet blasts [1 Cor.
15.52] is the moment in which the dead will rise up and the living will
be transformed. This moment is not a moment[56] of time, it is not even
its final moment, but its *telos*, its [95] atemporal goal and end. It comes
ἐνἀτόμῳ, says Paul, in an indivisible, atemporal, eternal, and present
twinkling of an eye.[57] Is it yesterday, tomorrow, today? Is it always? Is it
never? We can answer all of this with a "Yes" and a "No." Our time is in

---

55   *RG* 856; *EKG* (Württemberg), 429.
56   In *W.G.u.Th.*, "is not a moment" does not appear.
57   This is an expression of Meister Eckhardt for the eternity of God (in the context of the "abiding
     instant" [*nunc stans*] of scholastic theology). Cf., for example, Thomas Aquinas, *Summa theologiae*
     I, q. 10 a. 2, 1, in *Existence and Nature of God (Ia. 2–11)*, Vol. 2, The Blackfriars, eds. (New York:
     McGraw-Hill Book Company, 1963), 139; Cf. also *Predigt 2* in *Meister Eckhardt, Werke I, Texte und
     Übersetzungen*, J. Quint trans., N. Largier, ed., in *Bibliothek des Mittelalters*, Vol. 20 (Frankfurt am Main:
     Suhrkamp, 1993), 24–37, esp. 30, lines 13–17.

God's hands, but God's time is not in our hands. Everything has its time,[58] but everything also has its eternity. The day of all days, the day of Jesus Christ [Phil. 2.16; 2 Thess. 2.2; cf. Mt. 16.16; Jn 8.58] was already seen by Abraham. However it may be with the historical Jesus, it is certain that Jesus the Christ, the Son of the living God, belongs neither to history nor to psychology, for what is historical and psychological is as such perishable. The resurrection of Christ or his *parousia*, which is the same thing, is not an historical event. The historians may rest assured as long as they do not prefer to be fully disturbed by this fact, that *here* we are dealing with *the* event which alone can allow us to speak of a real *happening* in history. The misunderstood Logos can bear to stand among those in the shameful corner of myth. Better this than to be shorn of its eternal character through a historicized explanation. The advent of a new world, the reign of him who was and is and is to come [Rev. 1.8] — this is Easter.

Resurrection is *the new world*, the newly conditioned and natural world. The uncovering of the meaning of the world, its life which comes out of death, the knowledge of *its* origin in God by the power of our *own* — this is fundamentally a revolutionary process. It is not a continuation of a given either in the spiritual or natural realm that is or becomes a new creation [cf. 2 Cor. 5.17]. Reality as we know it, even the optimistic, joyfully reforming reality will be neither confirmed nor explained through the truth, but it will be an entirely new reality in light of the truth. How? Completely different! [*Qualitater? totaliter aliter!*].[59] "What has been born of the flesh is flesh. What has been born of the spirit is spirit" [Jn 3.6]. There is no mixing, no bridge or stages in between. There is purely changing, deciding, new insight. There may be no keeping silent about the fact that what the Bible shows us from the other side of the grave is actually the absolute, pure miracle. The many *miracles* of the Bible are only illustrations of *the* miracle. The more they speak about the possibility of a new world order, the more we become aware of its consequences. They show in part what the resurrection shows entirely: [96] that it makes no sense to speak about its historicity and possibility. They lay no claim of being either. They signal the ahistorical, the impossible, the new time that is coming. Least of all are they relative, magical miracles, exceptions or rare special cases of the laws we know. Without the *absolute* miracle however, the Bible is *not* the Bible. Someday people will chuckle at the acceptable image of Jesus which we have presented to the cultured class by purging him of the miracles, the way miracle stories were chuckled at in the eighteenth and nineteenth centuries.

---

58   This is the refrain for verses 1–10 of the song "Sollt ich meinem Gott nicht singen?" by Paul Gerhardt (*GERS* 3; *RG* 724; *EG* 325 [vv. 1–9]).

59   See Chapter 3, Note 63 in this volume.

The highest expression of the totally other that comes in the form of words in the Bible is the sermon on the forgiveness of sins. Incidentally, let me say that forgiveness of sins is more astonishing than the resurrection of Lazarus [Jn 11.1-45]. The word of forgiveness is an unprecedented factor in the practical reckoning with life. Through the word of forgiveness, the moral subject is constituted anew by his being bound up into the order of the heavenly kingdom, by his becoming reckoned to God. The beginning of good is perceived in the midst of evil, the foundation of a royal freedom of humanity is established through the royal freedom of God. It becomes possible to understand all things in the light of God, to do the greatest and smallest thing to the glory of God, to temper our praise of the good person and our condemnation of the evil person, seeing both as brothers united in the reconciling light of God, seeing the human in our entire bondage, limitedness, and temporality. At the same time, however, we see the "all-exclusive way"[60] in which the human is oriented toward God, disquieted by God, and carried by God. We see the simplicity and the universality of grace. Who can possibly go along *with all this*? Is *this* — the forgiveness of sins — to be then diverted, demonstrated, proven by psychology? Doesn't this also stand outside of all history, as an absolute *novum* and original piece of data, where its traces are always recognized? It is precisely *this*, a *novum* that is unable to be established or achieved, that is understood as the entrance, προσαγογή, promise [Rom. 5.2; Eph. 2.18; 3.12]. It is a movement of our existence directed at the completely other. All this is Easter.

Resurrection is a *new embodiment*. We must at least indicate this rarely mentioned but indispensable implication. There is *one* Creator of all things, the visible and invisible.[61] Therefore there is one *redemption*: the redemption of our bodies [Rom. 8.22]. The [97] sighing of the creature cannot remain hidden from him. Just as it participates in the incomprehensibility, the absurdity, the darkness of our existence, so also it participates in the new possibility on the other side of the boundaries of our existence. The unity of the Creator and of the Redeemer is the Spirit [Eph. 4.3]. In the power of the Spirit, Christ is resurrected from the dead [cf. Rom. 8.11; 1.4]. For the sake of the Spirit, for the sake of the unity of God, the Bible emphasizes the physicality of the resurrection, the new world [1 Cor. 15.42]. An exchanging of the predicates is completed between being satisfied in perishability, and resurrection in imperishability (in other words, in the knowledge of God). The subject

---

60   The source of this expression could not be traced. Perhaps it was taken up by Barth from a critical comment by an audience member during the discussion session after the lecture.

61   See the beginning of the Nicene Creed in *The Creeds of Christendom: With a History and Critical Notes*, Philip Schaff, ed. (Grand Rapids, MI: Baker Book House, 1985), 58.

persists. If, however, it is the subject of the new world that is born "from above," ἄνωθεν [Jn 3.3, 7], if it recognizes itself in God, then there can *finally* remain nothing "from below" left over in him.

Every living being waits for his eternity [Jn 8.23]. Perishability cannot inherit imperishability [cf. 1 Cor. 15.50]. All perishability, however, is in a stream against the imperishable. There is not one tiny hair upon our heads [cf. Mt. 10.30p.] that does not want imperishability. *This* perishability *must* take on imperishability, as surely as it is perishable, as surely as it *must* die [1 Cor. 15.53]. The relationship of our *entire* existence to God, our conceiving of the length and the width, the depths and the heights [Eph. 3.18], the meaning of every appearance, thus not *merely* as appearance but rather as appearances of the idea, as works of the Creator who will preserve what he has made[62] — all of these things taken in turn as a reasonable act, as an acting consciousness, as faith and deed — all this is Easter.

There is one last thing to say: Resurrection is *the unique experience of humanity*. I trust I will not be misunderstood. The real experience begins when our alleged experiences cease. It begins in the crisis of our experiences, in our fear of God. But in God, the individual discovers not only his duty but his right. "Whoever loses his soul for my sake will gain it" [Mt. 10.39; 16.25; Mk 8.35; Lk. 9.24; cf. 17.33 and Jn 12.25]. The biblical history is the history of nature, spirit, and the world in so far as it first and foremost is the history of *humans*. God is the subject of this history, God alone, but as the God who is behind and above the *human* as the element in which the *human* originally lives, moves, and has one's being [Acts 17.28]. God is the One who should be sought and found by *humans*, who wants to bestow upon the *human* the spirit of the first-born. All things are in Christ [98] as the Son of *Man* [Rom. 8.23], the heavenly and the earthly together [Eph. 1.10]. The eternity of the heart is given to the *human*.[63] The new *human* should be put on [Eph. 4.24; Col. 3.10], who is created after the likeness of God. It is not the cosmos, not history in general, not even so-called humanity as a pile or a construct, as a stream or a movement.

It is not the organized or unorganized masses of the peoples, classes, and political parties, but is absolutely *the individual human* who knows himself in nature and history as a suffering, acting, and thinking subject of society, who carries his need and rejoices in his hope to be known

---

62   This is an allusion to the third verse of the song "Sei Lob und Her' dem höchsten Gut" by J.J. Schütz (*GERS* 9; *RG* 240; *EG* 326).

63   See Eccl. 3.11 (cf. Septuagint). For Friedrich Christoph Oetinger's interpretation of this verse, see *Friedrich Christoph Oetingers Leben und Briefe, als urkundlicher Commentar zu dessen Schriften*, Karl Christian Eberhard Ehmann, ed. (Stuttgart: Steinkopf, 1859), 201.

in God. *The God-fearing individual* is the first one to be moved [2 Sam. 12.7].[64] You are the man. *You* are the one meant; it is about *you*. It is promised to *you*, and in *you* it is to be fulfilled. *You* must believe, *you* must wager [cf. 1 Tim. 6.11; Heb. 10.36; 12.1], and from *you*, ὑπομονή, persever-ance, is demanded. *You* are the stage where it is decided, where the talk is of resurrection, of God. There are no onlookers to God, just as surely as there are no intrusive coworkers with God. There could, however, be the children of God [1 Cor. 15.10], who are what they are out of God's grace. This is our God-given existence, which has *not yet* appeared [1 Jn 3.2]. This is our experience — mine and yours — which may always *become* an experience of *God*. This is Easter.

Have we said too much? We know that every word that we say on this theme may already be saying too much. But even the most radical, comprehensive word on this theme could be saying too little. The Bible tells us more or less depending on how much or little we are capable of hearing and translating into deed and truth. We began with the question of election. It appears that we must also conclude with it. The *penultimate* biblical outlook necessarily becomes a renewed insight into the problem-atic of our own existence. Yet even the roots of this unrest are in God. Our seeking as well as our erring, our standing as well as our falling, our remembering as well as our forgetting, our "Yes" as well as our "No" are surrounded and upheld by God. He knows what kind of creatures we are, he is aware that we are dust [Ps. 103.4; cf. 1 Cor. 8.6; 13.21; Gal. 4.9]. We *are* known before we *know*. This is saying neither too much nor too little. This is the *ultimate* biblical vista.

64   This is an allusion to the concept of the "first mover/cause" [*primum motum*] in Thomas Aquinas's proofs of God. He introduces the proofs based on a discussion of "change." The "first cause" is the first of the five proofs. See Thomas Aquinas, *Summa theologiae* I, q. 2, a. 3, c, The Blackfriars, eds., Vol. 2, 14, 15 (see Note 28, p. 74).

CHAPTER 5

THE NEED AND PROMISE OF CHRISTIAN PROCLAMATION, 1922

[65] On June 19, 1922, D. Julius Jacobi,[1] the general superintendent of the southwest parish [*Suedwestsprengel*] of the province of Saxony, sent Barth a letter, in which he wrote the following:

> I am considering holding a Pastors' conference for my parish from the 24th to the 26th of July in the *Schulpforta*[2] by Koesen, which has been kindly rented out to us from the Rector until the beginning of the school vacation. The deep, recent interest which your theology has awakened, even in our province, especially among the younger pastors, as well as the important discussion about the relation between God and the world that your book[3] offers, and which is appropriate for the deepening and clarifying of faith in God, occasions me to request you to introduce your theology to a large group of my spiritual charges . . . Which core topics you choose and how you formulate them, we leave by all means up to you, dear Professor.[4]

Barth accepted the invitation a few days after receiving it and committed himself to July 25, and gave as his theme, "The Need and Promise of Christian

---

1   A critical edition of this essay in German can be found in *Vu.kl.A. 1922–1925*, 65–97. Page numbers in brackets in this essay run according to the *GA*. August Julius Justus Jacobi (1850–1937): In 1877 he became pastor of the German-Reformed congregation in Magdeburg; 1884 chaplain to the court and garrison in Weimar; 1889 pastor at St. Stephani church in Bremen; 1893 pastor at the Zion's Church in Berlin; 1901 superintendent of the diocese of Berlin III; 1902 pastor in Schoeneberg and superintendent of the diocese of Friedrichwerder II; 1907–1924 general superintendent of the southwest parish of the church province of Saxony (the federal state of Saxony-Anhalt in today's Federal Republic of Germany).

2   Schulpforta lies between Bad Kösen and Naumburg in the Saal Valley (in the former German Democratic Republic). The facilities of the former Cistercian cloister reception room served as a nationwide educational facility with a boarding school. It was founded in 1543 as a school for the ruling class by Moritz of Saxony.

3   Jacobi is referring to the second edition of Barth's Romans commentary, published in 1922.

4   Letter from D.J. Jacobi to Barth, June 19, 1922 (KBA 9322.203). Barth included this correspondence in his own letter to friends in Switzerland on June 28, 1922. See *Bw. Th.* II, 87.

Proclamation."[5] Under the pressure of his various lecturing obligations, he later complained: "how am I supposed to get anything sensible onto paper now, for Schulpforta, for example? I brooded over the Tambach lecture[6] for three weeks; this time I will have to be glad if I can spare three days."[7]

The lecture was scheduled to take place [66] at nine in the morning on the agreed-upon day after morning devotions. Afterward, a question-and-answer session took place.[8] In a thank-you letter from August 3, 1922,[9] Jacobi wrote to Barth:

> It was the fruit of knowledge and experience [γνῶσις καὶ αἰσθήσεις]. And when I asked with curiosity about the difficulties of your theology in order to open the discussion, you had the right to reject this curiosity of mine because you wanted to offer a seamless cloak. The echo from the world of pastors is already there. It's been reported that some gray practitioners moved through the cloister deeply moved and were of the opinion that it is time they hang up the their official hats, whereupon their "better half" appeased them, like Bartholome's wife on the *père lachaise*, patting him on the shoulder saying, "It was probably not so badly meant!"

The trip to Schulpforta began Barth's extended lecturing activities which accompanied his obligations at the university from then on. The first publication of this particular lecture was also the prelude to the journal, *Zwischen den Zeiten*, at the beginning of 1923.[10]

The friendly invitation extended to me by the general superintendent, Mr. D. Jacobi, contained the request to give you an "introduction to the understanding of my theology." It always embarrasses me to hear such serious talk about "my theology." This is not because I think that what I do is something different or better than just rough-and-ready theology. I think I have already overcome to some degree the teething troubles of being ashamed of theology. A few of you may have had this too, and perhaps have also overcome it. The embarrassment comes, rather, because I am taken aback, and wonder what my theology should actually consist of; where the cathedral or fortress could be that has earned this name, and

---

5   See *Bw.Th.* II, 87.
6   He is referring here to "The Christian in Society" (Chapter 3 in the this volume). Also published in *W.G.Th.*, 33–69; *Anfänge* I, 3–37.
7   See *Bw.Th.* II, 92 (July 7, 1922).
8   See the complete program in the brochure of the pastors' conference in *Amtliche Mitteilungen des Evangelischen Konsistoriums der Provinz Sachsen*, 1922, Nr. 9, p. 77f.
9   KBA 9322.203.
10   *Zwischen den Zeiten*, 1 (1923): 3–25. Cf. *Bw.Th.* II, 115 (October 26, 1922).

how I could — by means of an outline, for example — "introduce" it [67] to you. This already gives me enough to sigh about; but I must frankly confess to you, that when I look at it closely, what I might conceivably call "my theology" consists of a single point, and not even a *standpoint*,[11] which would be the minimum demanded of a proper theology, but rather only a *mathematical* point that one cannot stand upon. It is a mere *view* point. I have barely made a start with proper theology, and I don't know if I will ever get beyond it, indeed, if I even desire to get beyond it.

I really do not presume to set something equal or commensurable next to the venerable thinkers who have created and still create great theological programs and systems. Do not mistake my contribution to the theological discussion, including what I would like to say today, as an endeavor to compete with positive, liberal, Ritschlian or history-of-religion types of theology. I want you to understand my contribution as some *notes in the margin* and a gloss, which in its own way both agrees and disagrees with all these other types of theology — and which, I am convinced, loses its meaning the moment it becomes something more than just a gloss, the moment it wants to fill the room as a new theology and make an appearance next to the others. Should Thurneysen,[12] Gogarten,[13] and I[14] ever really make up a "school" in the ordinary sense

11   For a critique of a Christian, or theological, "standpoint" [*Standpunkt*], see *Romans* 1919, 703 (index). The concept of *Standpunkt* was not carried into the index of the English edition. Cf. also *Romans* 1922, 35, 116 (1999 ed., 38–39, 126–127); ET 60, 139, for example. See also the preface from the third edition of *Romans*, which was also written, like "Need and Promise," in July 1922: "The '*pneuma Christou*' is not a standpoint which one can stand on in order to correct Paul or anyone else, like a teacher" (XXII [1999 ed., XXX]; ET 19).

12   Eduard Thurneysen (1888–1974): In 1911–1913 he was assistant secretary of the Christliche Verein Junger Menschen [hereafter CVJM] in Zurich; 1913–1920 pastor in Leutwil-Dürrenäsch (Kanton Aargau); 1920–1927 pastor in St. Gallen-Bruggen; 1927–1959 pastor at the Münster in Basel (from 1941 on he was simultaneously Professor for Practical Theology in Basel). Barth and Thurneysen, whose parents were already friends (cf. Busch, 14, 17; ET 3, 5), became acquainted with one another during their studies as members of the "Zofingia" fraternity (Busch, 48, 62; ET 37, 50).

13   Friedrich Gogarten (1887–1967): In 1917 he was pastor in Stelzendorf (Thüringen); 1925 pastor in Dorndorf an der Saale and Privatdozent for Systematic Theology in Jena; 1931 professor in Breslau; 1935 professor in Göttingen. Barth met Gogarten for the first time in September 1919 at the Tambach conference. Cf. Busch, 124; ET 112.

14   Gogarten, Thurneysen, and Barth had not published anything together until July 1922. In August of that year, at "Bergli," the summer retreat house by Oberrieden (on Lake Zurich), the journal *Zwischen den Zeiten* ("Between the times") was founded. It was a quarterly journal from 1923 until 1926, when it became a bi-monthly journal until 1933. The name of the journal came from Gogarten's essay "Zwischen den Zeiten," published in another journal, *Die Christliche Welt* (*CW*), 34 (1920): 374–378; reprinted in *Anfänge* II, 95–101; *BDT* 277–282. This particular reference however is not part of the English translation. Georg Merz headed up the publication operations for *Zwischen den Zeiten*. Georg Merz (1892–1959): In 1918 he was pastor in Munich as student chaplain; 1930 Assistant lecturer in Bethel; 1939 provost in Schweinfurt; 1947 rector of the Augustana-Hochschule in Neuendettelsau; 1923–1933 head of *Zwischen den Zeiten*, edited by Barth,

of this word, [68] then we are finished. I think that everyone should *stay* in their schools and by their masters. They need only perhaps to put up with my theology as a *corrective*, as "a pinch of spice" to the main meal, as Kierkegaard says;[15] as something significant that is contained in every note in the margin. "My theology" is related to the other mainstream theologies something like the way the Bohemian Brethren are related to other mainstream confessions and church congregations;[16] it does not constitute a new type of its own.

And now I must make a second request: That it not be construed as pride and conceit on my part that I refuse to be placed in the series of other theologies. Naturally, I realize that one cannot just stand in the air; one stands somewhere on earth whether one wants to or not, even if it is only with one foot. I know that I am not the first and only one who imagines a "theology of wanderers" [*theologia* [69] *viatorum*][17] cutting straight through the existing theological possibilities to the left to the right and in the middle, understanding all, encompassing all, and overcoming all as the goal of a desire. Who doesn't want to find a way to stand "over the trends" of today? I also know that not one of these real or supposed *theologi viatores* — if the gods did not love it enough to let

---

Thurneysen, and Gogarten. Barth became acquainted with Merz in Munich in February 1920. See *Bw.Th.* I, 367 (February 2, 1920). See also Georg Merz, *Wege und Wandlungen. Erinnerungen aus der Zeit von 1892–1922*, J. Merz, ed. (Munich: Kaiser, 1961), esp. 238ff. See also *V.u.kl.A. 1905–1909*, 39, n. 3. For the circumstances under which *Zwischen den Zeiten* was founded, cf. Barth's letter to Georg Merz in *Bw.Th.* II, 97f. (September 14, 1922), and Barth's retrospective look at it in his "Abschied," *ZZ*, 11 (1933): 536–544; reprinted in *Anfänge* II, 313–321; *BDT*, 277–282.

15   Søren Kierkegaard, *Buch des Richters. Seine Tagebücher 1833–1855 im Auszug*. Hermann Gottsched, trans. and ed. (Jena/Leipzig: Diederichs, 1905), 99f.:

> Oh, the world leadership is one enormous household, a grandiose painting. Indeed the master, God in heaven, works just like the chef and the artist; he says, "There I still need to add a little spice, add a little bit of red!" We do not understand, we barely see it, in degrees, the little bit of spice disappears into the whole. But God knows why [. . .] They are the correctives. It is a disastrous error when only the one who added the corrective becomes impatient and wants to turn the corrective into the norm; this is an attempt to confuse everything.

16   The members of what was once the Zinzendorf Brethren normally belonged to the respective State churches as well [*Landeskirchen*]. On June 17, 1922 the Brethren celebrated its two-hundredth anniversary, which was recognized in several different journals and newspapers. See for example, Th. Steinmann, "In necessariis unitas, in dubiis libertas, in omnibus caritas. Gedanken zur Zweijahrhundertfeier der Brüdergemeine (1722–17. Juni-1922)," in *Theologische Blätter* 1 (1922): 121–124. The entire issue of *CW*, 36 (1922) was dedicated to Zinzendorf and the Herrnhutern.

17   With "*theologia* ἔκτυπος" ("the theology of creatures' knowledge of God") the dogmaticians of Orthodoxy distinguish between the still-to-come "*theologia beatorum*" ("the theology of the saints"), i.e. "*comprehensorum*" (a theology of those who have arrived conceptually) and that which is already possible in this life, the *theologia viatorum*. See HpB, 6; ET 4; and SchmP, 28. Barth is using the phrase here with a different meaning.

it die early[18] — has yet been successful in completing its course without constructing a cathedral or a fortress or even a gypsy tent somewhere, and which then, whether it liked it or not, came to be understood as the text itself, as a *new* theology, instead of remaining a gloss. Even the most bold of knights on the chessboard, Kierkegaard himself, did not fare any differently.

So "we" too must deal with the fact that in the eyes of many, nothing new will appear on the program; just another instance of a somewhat quaint theology filling out the spiritual room, appealing to the breadth of history and being questionable enough next to its many old and new stately neighbors. It will probably be seen as something like a mystical or even biblicistic neo-supernaturalism,[19] not to mention neo-Marcionism.[20] We cannot help it that it looks this way. [70] If the issue is about wanting to understand what one sees in my theology, we can only ensure that we are not coming from the construction of a school or system but precisely from the "*need and promise of Christian proclamation*," about which I would like to speak to you today.

May I briefly explain something about that to you? It is relevant to the topic. I was a pastor for twelve years,[21] just like you all, and *had* my theology; not my own of course, but that of my unforgettable teacher, Wilhelm Hermann.[22] I was engrafted into the theology of my land. I subscribed — more unconsciously than consciously — to the direction

18   Ὃν οἱ θεοὶ φιλοῦσιν, ἀποθνῄσκει νέος: this goes back to Menander, from Plutarch. See Plutarch, *Consolatio ad Apollonium*, chapter 34 (on handed-down verse).

19   See Reinhard Liebe, "Der Gott des heutigen Geschlechts und wir. Vortrag gehalten im Bund für Gegenwartchristentum zu Eisenach am 5. Oktober 1921," in *CW*, 35 (1921): 850–853, 866–868, 883–889. Liebe called Barth's theology a "biblicistic neo-supernaturalism" and categorized it along with Gogarten's expression of a "*mystical* neo-supernaturalism" (867).

20   Barth was accused of Marcionism until 1922 by Adolf Jülicher, "Ein moderner Paulus-Ausleger," in *CW*, 34 (1920): 467 (cf. *Anfänge* I, 95f.; *BDT*, 78f.); Erich Foerster, "Marcionitisches Christentum. Der Glaube an den Schöpfergott und der Glaube an den Erlösergott. Vortrag auf der Eisenacher Tagung des Bundes für Gegenwartchristentum am 3. Oktober 1921," in *CW*, 35 (1921): 813f.; K.L. Schmidt, "Marcion und wir. Die Gegenwartsbedeutung von Harnacks Marcion," in *Kartell-Zeitung. Organ des Eisenacher Kartells Akademisch-Theologischer Vereine*, 31 (1920/21): 83–85; A. Hein, "Moderner Marcionitismus und praktische Theologie," in *Theologische Blätter* 1 (1922): 124–130, 145–152. From 1921 the accusation was made with reference to Adolf von Harnack's *Marcion: Das Evangelium vom fremden Gott* (Leipzig: Hinrichs, 1921). See also Barth's remarks to this in *Romans* 1922, XVIf. (1999 ed., XXIV); ET 13.

21   Barth was a vicar [*pasteur suffragant*] in Geneva from 1909–1911, and from 1911–1921 pastor in Safenwil (Kanton Aargau). During his time in Safenwil he was also a member of the religious movement of Hermann Kutter and Leonhard Ragaz.

22   Johann Wilhelm Hermann (1846–1922) was Professor for Systematic Theology in Marburg from 1879 on. Barth studied in Marburg for three semesters (summer 1908–summer 1909). His intention to do a doctorate in philosophy under Hermann after his vicarage in Geneva never came to fruition. See Busch, 69; ET 58.

of Reformed theology, which I indeed still represent, gladly, due to
my official standing. *Independent* of my habitual way of thinking about
theology, I have been pushed by various and sundry circumstances more
and more strongly toward the specific *pastoral* problem of the *sermon*,
and have tried to properly find my way, as you yourselves most certainly
have as well, between the problematic of human living on the one side
and the content of the Bible on the other. As a pastor, I am supposed to
speak to *individuals*, I am to speak into the egregious contradiction of
their lives. But I must speak from the message of the *Bible*, which is no
less outrageous, which stands over this contradiction of life like a new
riddle. Often enough these two greats, life and the Bible, have appeared
to me (and still appear!) like Scylla and Charybdis: If *that* is the "Where
from?" and "Where to?" of Christian proclamation, who should be a
pastor? Who could preach? I am convinced that you are all familiar with
this situation and this plague. Many of you *silently* know this much more
profoundly, intensely, and more vividly than I do.

   To those of you who already know this, I actually will have nothing
substantial to say. You have already been introduced to my theology. While
you have remained silent, I have been speaking. Remaining silent has its
time, and speaking has its time [Eccl. 3.7]. I do not overestimate the value
that lies in the freedom to choose to speak; I have indeed sometimes
wished to remain silent.[23] But that is just how it is. The well-known
situation of the pastor [71] on Saturday at his desk and on Sunday in the
pulpit was fully consolidated for me into the form of marginal notes to all
theology in the voluminous form of a commentary on Paul's letter to the
Romans. My friends fared in similar fashion. It is not as if I found a *way
out* of that critical situation. I *precisely* did not. Rather, this critical situation
of the pastor became an illustration of the substance of all theology to me.

   What can theology be except the expression of this desperate situation
and the question of the pastor when he dares to take on this task? What
can it be but a description as true as possible to the pressure under which
the human sinks; a cry therefore, a great need and hope for rescue? What
can theology do differently for the fulfillment of its *cultural* function —
a function which it indeed has — as well as its *pedagogical* function for
those eager youth who have decided to "study 'pastor,'" as it is said around
here? What can theology do except to remain constantly aware of this

23   See similar declarations by Barth, which were not recorded until later: for example *Bw.Th.* II, 99
     (September 29, 1922): "Oh how I sometimes silently curse being a professor, academic caps and
     fame (especially the latter!) and covet, with Richard Rothe, not peace but silence, being allowed
     to keep silent"; *Bw.Th.* II, 222 (February 5, 1924): "If only we had kept silent back then . . . but we
     never kept *silent* and that was the calamity, and now we have a nice mess [. . .]". See also *Bw.Th.* II,
     391, 393, 650.

pressure as its most essential and authentic being as it works though its traditional, historical, systematic, and practical substance? What situation is more characteristic than *this* for the vocation for which it wants to prepare people? But how come the theological enterprise communicates so little about the preparation for *this* vocation, which leads to *this* situation? I had to wonder back then, how did it simply come about that all the question marks and exclamation points already set in theology, of which I was aware and which are part of the existence of the pastor, played absolutely no role, so to speak, so that, when I became a pastor, I had to be assailed by the truth itself as if by an armed warrior [cf. Prov. 6.11]? Was my question really *my* question²⁴ and [72] did others *know* the way out that I myself could not find? I saw other theologians taking a way out, but they were ways I could not affirm. Then why did the theologies familiar to me seek to represent the conundrum of the pastor's situation, if they even addressed the situation at all, as bearable and able to be overcome instead of first just trying *to comprehend* it; to look it in the face? Had they looked exactly there, they would have discovered theology's very own object in its entire, unbearable and insurmountable nature. I asked myself further, is it not worth being satisfied with the light shed on theology from *this* particular viewpoint? Wouldn't it be better for the sake of theology's own salvation to be nothing more than the knowledge of the quest and questioning of the Christian preacher, full of need and promise? Shouldn't everything else be the result of this knowledge?

Being besieged by this question — and I ask yet again: Is it merely *my* random question? — I worked at that time on Paul's letter to the Romans,²⁵ which at first was only supposed to be my own attempt to understand myself. Of course many other, apparently very different, things stand in that book, like New Testament theology, dogmatics, ethics, and philosophy. But you will understand it best when through it all you

---

24   This is an allusion to an accusation against Barth's *Romans* 1919 made by A. Jülicher, in a review of it in his "Ein moderner Paulus-Ausleger" (468f). It can be found in *BDT*, 81:

> He who in holy egoism thinks only of his own problems and chides the dead, who can no longer answer him, can surely not demand that a product of the past — as the Letter to the Romans most surely still is — should become alive for him. I hear — from the past — besides my own questions, the questions which the men of the past ask of me, and because I do not limit the duty to love my neighbor as myself to my neighbors living and future, my conscience compels me to answer their questions, or at least to attempt to do so. My own questions I answer as well as I can in the privacy of my own room.

See *Anfänge* I, 98.

25   See the preface to *Romans* 1922, XIIf. (1999 ed., XIX); ET 9: "I know what it means to have to undertake the way of the pulpit year in and year out, having and wanting to understand and explain, but not being able to . . . Indeed, out of the need of my task as a pastor, I have come to understand and explain the Bible more keenly."

consistently hear the pastor with his question: What does preaching mean? Not: How does one *do* it? But rather how *can* one do it? The other things which stand in the book are already reflexes and not the light itself to which I saw myself pointing, and to which I would like to point. So it comes down to something that wants to broaden out as "my theology," or let us say, a "corrective theology."

I am not telling you all this in order to enlighten you about my biography but rather to show you how far my intention, at least primarily, is not a new theology. It is, rather, [73] an *illumination* so to speak, throwing light upon theology from the outside, an illumination from the very spot where you already stand — perhaps not as theologians but certainly as pastors. I believe that we here *cannot* do otherwise than agree, if you have the humor to kindly *overlook* some random details and grant me this one thing, that I *fundamentally* do not come armed with a new, amazing theology but rather with that which may also be *your* theology. I simply step up *next to* you with understanding and empathy for your situation as pastors. Understand clearly that I speak to you today more as a pastor to colleagues than as a professor. According to the facts of the case, *this* is without a doubt the most sensible way to carry out my task today. If I not only have a *view*point but somehow also a *stand*point, then it is simply the well-known one of the man in the pulpit, before whom stands the mysterious Bible and the mysterious minds of his more or less numerous listeners. Indeed, which one is more mysterious? In any case, the question is: "*What now?*" If I succeed in making you acutely aware of the whole content of this "What now?" then I have won you over not for my *stand*point — because it is yours already — but to my *view*point, no matter what you might think of my theology.

On Sunday morning as the bells start to ring, calling the community and the pastor to church, the moment heaves with *anticipation* of a great, meaningful, even decisive *event*. The anticipation has nothing to do with how strongly the people feel it, or indeed with whether there are even people present at all who consciously foster this anticipation. The anticipation is real; it permeates the entire scene. Here is an ancient, venerable *institution*, frequently and severely attacked from the outside and still more frequently and more severely compromised from the inside, but which has an indestructible power of life — we should say power of existence. It is able to transform and persevere at the same time. It is ancient and modern as well (whatever "modern" currently means) even though it does not like either word.

Up until now, it has victoriously withstood the most difficult intellectual, political, social, and even religious shocks — and why shouldn't it continue to do so in the future? Its existence is grounded on a claim that appears to stand in grotesque contradiction [74] to the actual facts. But only very few — and little recognized — people loudly and unequivocally dare to wholly reject its right and potential to make such a claim. Here is a *building* whose very design, whether in old or new language, already reveals architecture that is meant to be an arena for extraordinary things, regardless of the symbols, pictures, and furniture with which it is decorated. Here are *people*, perhaps only two or three as is the case in this country, but perhaps a few hundred, who stream into this building driven by an odd instinct or will — where they seek *what*? The satisfaction of an old habit? Perhaps, but from where does this habit come? Do they seek entertainment and instruction! A very strange entertainment and instruction indeed! Edification? Yes, it is claimed, but what does edification mean? Do they know somehow? Or do they have other reasons for being here? In any case, they are here — even if it is only a little old lady — and their presence already points to an event which they anticipate or appear to anticipate, which at least at one point in time had been anticipated here, even if now the whole place is dead and deserted.

Above all, here is a *man* upon whom the anticipation of that apparently imminent event rests in a very special way. He appears to be burdened by it, not only because he has studied the technique of this event and is supposed to have mastered it, not only because he is salaried and employed by the community, or tolerated with hardly any opposition in his office — an office that finds its meaning in connection with this event. In play here is not only mechanics but freedom: This man chose to take up this vocation, God knows out of what understanding and misunderstanding, but he did so, and has now completely and wholly bound his short life, his only life, to the expectation of this event. In front of the congregation and for the congregation this man will *pray*, you heard it right, pray — to God! He will open the *Bible* and bring words of infinite significance to his reading of it, words that refer to God, each and every one of them. Then he will climb into the pulpit and — what a risk! — *preach*, that is, he will add something out of his head and heart to that which was read out of the Bible.

One time there will be "biblical" thoughts according to his knowledge and conscience, and at another time there will be thoughts that boldly or feebly flutter by the Bible. One will have prepared a "positivistic" sermon just yesterday and another will have prepared a "liberal" sermon. But does it really matter when [75] one considers the object? In either case, the talk here perhaps *nolens volens* must be about God. After that, the pastor will let the congregation *sing* ancient songs full of difficult, weird conceptual cargo, peculiar, ghostly witnesses of the suffering, struggle, and triumph of fathers long passed on, all at the edge of an unfathomable initiating event, all full of memories of God — whether pastor and congregation understand what they sing or not — again and again of God. "God is present!"[26] Yes, God *is* present. The entire situation bears witness, calls, indeed clearly shouts this out, even if it still appears questionable, beggarly, and bleak from the pastor's or congregation's point of view — perhaps more so in such moments than in moments when abundance and human success partially or fully obscure the problem of the situation.

But what is the meaning of this situation? To what kind of event does this anticipation point? What does "God is present!" mean here? Obviously it does not quite mean the same thing here as it does when we take the liberty to use it in speaking of a blossoming cherry tree, Beethoven's Ninth Symphony, the State, or the honest, daily work of ourselves and others. What else are the superfluous accessories for? Why the special particulars in *this* particular situation if it were not aimed at a special, specific, bold "God is present!"? Isn't it the case that when people come together in *this* situation — church — they have, whether they know it or not, left cherry trees, the symphony, the State, daily work, and many other things *behind* as possibilities somehow exhausted? The answer, "God is present!" undoubtedly is somehow given in all these possibilities — their truth-content, their witness to meaning in life. But it has once again become the question, the great riddle of existence. The inscrutable muteness of the so-called nature that surrounds us, the accidental and shadowy nature of all everything that exists in time; the suffering and fate of peoples and individuals; radical evil;[27] death — they are all there again, and this time they speak louder than anything that [76] might assure us that God is present.

No, we cannot supress it any longer: The question burns, *is it true?* Is it true, the vision of unity for those who are scattered; the anticipation of a steadfast pole amid the flight of phenomena [*Erscheinungen Flucht*];[28] a righteousness that does not lie somewhere behind the stars but within the events that make up our present life; a *heaven* above the earth — *above* the earth, indeed above the *earth*? Is it true, the speaking of the love and goodness of God who is more than some friendly deity of transparent origin and short-lived dominion? *Is it true?* This is what people want to

---

26   See Gerhard Tersteegen's song "Gott ist gegenwärtig" ("God is present") (1729) (*EKG*, 128; *GERS* 201; *LBW* 249).

27   See Immanuel Kant, *Die Religion innerhalb der Grenzen der blossen Vernunft*, in *Werke. Schriften zur Ethik und Religionsphilosophie*, Vol. 4, Wilhelm Weischedel, ed., (Wiesbaden: Insel-Verlag, 1956), 645–879; ET *Religion within the Boundaries of Mere Reason*, Allen Wood, trans. (New York: Cambridge University Press, 1998), 31–191.

28   See Friedrich von Schiller's poem, "Der Spaziergang" (1795): "Aber im stillen Gemach entwirft bedeutende Zirkel/Sinnend der Weise, . . . /Sucht den ruhenden Pol in der Erscheinungen Flucht." For English versions see Marianna Wertz's translation entitled "The Walk" in *Fidelio*, VI, No. 3 (Fall 1997) and http://www.schillerinstitute.org.

hear, to know, to understand. *Therefore* they grasp, not knowing what they do, at the unheard of possibility to pray, to open the Bible, to speak of God, to listen, and to sing. *Therefore* they come to us, placing themselves into the highly grotesque situation of Sunday morning, which is indeed only the expression raised up toward this possibility.

Indeed, they want to hear, know, understand. They do not want to simply receive mere assertions and advice, no matter how heartfelt and sincere they may be. In this hearing, knowing, and understanding, they want to know *if it's true,* and not something else that beats around the bush. But let's not get distracted by the fact that this desire seldom, if ever, openly meets us with such urgency. *This* is not something that people simply cry out, least of all into the ears of us pastors. But let us not be deceived by their silence — blood and tears, the deepest despair and highest hope, their passionate desire to grab hold of *that* which, no, rather *him*, the one who has overcome the world [cf. Jn 16.33] because he is its Creator and its Redeemer, the Beginning and the End [cf. Rev. 1.8, etc.], the Lord of the world. They passionately desire to have *the* Word be spoken to them, *the* Word, which promises grace in *judgment*, life in *death*, the beyond in the *here and now.* This is what stands behind our churchgoers, no matter how spiritless, bourgeois, or commonplace their desire seems to be in so-called reality. There is no wisdom in stopping at the next-to-last and next-to-next-to-last desires of the people, and they will [77] not thank us for doing so. They expect us to understand them better than they understand themselves.[29]

We are lacking in love not when we reach deep down into the wounds with which they come to us but rather when we brush them aside as if we did not know why they are coming to us. We are deluded, not when we embrace the fact that they come to us with ultimate and profound

---

29   This hermeneutical expression has precedents in history. Cf. Immanuel Kant, *Kritik der reinen Vernunft*, in *Werke*, Vol. 2, Wilhelm Weischedel, ed. (Wiesbaden: Insel, 1956), 322; *The Critique of Pure Reason*, Paul Guyer and Allen W. Wood, trans. and eds. (New York: Cambridge University Press, 1998) [A 314], 396:

> I only make a note of the fact that it is not at all unusual to understand an author better than he understands himself through common conversations as well as in writings, through the comparison of the thoughts that the author expresses about his object, after having not determined his own concept sufficiently enough, and therefore, he has spoken or even has thought contrary to his own intentions.

Other precedents can be found in Frederich Schleiermacher and Johann Gottfried von Herder, and these are laid out by Barth in *Das Christliche Leben, Die Kirchliche Dogmatik IV/4, Fragmente aus dem Nachlaß. Vorlesungen 1959–1961*, Hans-Anton Drewes and Eberhard Jüngel, eds. (Zurich; TVZ, 1979), 440, n. 109; ET *The Christian Life: Church Dogmatics IV/3: Lecture fragments*, Geoffery W. Bromiley, trans. and ed. (Grand Rapids, MI: William B. Eerdmans Publishing Company, 1981), 254, n. 4.

questions, but when we think that they will be put off with temporary, easy answers. Oh yes, these methods work for the time being: The people are moved, pleased, satisfied, even if they do not find what they are actually looking for but rather that which they could basically get in a better way elsewhere (in religious, Christian, or Christian-fundamentalist forms perhaps). Catholicism is a powerful example of how the church, if need be, can succeed in putting people off, lulling them into choosing to forget their actual desire by presenting them with something pleasant — and for the time being — ultimate. But do not be fooled: *We* are not Catholic nor are our congregations.

Despite any appearance of backsliding we are in an advanced stage of the situation, in which the administration of even the highest-quality narcotic only partly and temporarily still has an effect on us. Do *not* believe the good-natured individuals who assure us that we have done our work well even when all of our skills have been directed at avoiding the true meaning of the situation! Do *not* listen to the anxious ones who complainingly warn us of letting the situation become somehow too serious who, indeed, warn us not to abandon our usual blind shooting for sharp shooting! It is *not* the voice of God's church that [78] speaks through them! The most serious meaning of the situation for *us* is this: The people desire to hear the *Word*, that is, they want the answer to the question which moves them whether they know it or not: *Is it true?*

The situation on Sunday morning is, in the most literal sense of the word, "the end of history." It is eschatological, even from the point of view of humans, quite apart from the Bible for now. When this situation occurs, history — the remnant of history — comes to an end. An *ultimate* desire of the people for an *ultimate* event now becomes the standard. If we do not understand this ultimate desire, if we do not take people seriously in the pressure of their existence that has driven them to us (and I say it again, more seriously than they take themselves!), then we ought not wonder that a majority of them, without becoming enemies of the church, basically learn to give it the cold shoulder and leave us behind with the well-wishers and hand-wringers. Is it a psychological condition that even the sons of enlightened pastors and theologians continually join this army of silent deserters? Or does it come from the fact that they know first-hand that people will seldom find among us what they are actually looking for! Am I not at least partly correct when I say that people, both the educated and the uneducated, are *disappointed* in us — deeply disappointed! All too often, perhaps for centuries now, they have been *appeased*. All too often our words have been spoken right past them, precisely in the well-meant intention of getting closer to them. And instead of concentrating on new appeasements for the disappointed out of an alleged love for humanity, wouldn't it be better for once if we considered the fact that they might be waiting to be taken more *seriously* by the church, to be better *understood* by the church in their great unquenchable restlessness of life than they are in their normal lives (contrary somehow to methodistic, communistic, or anthroposophistic gatherings)?

It is amazing enough that in letting us at least baptize, confirm, marry, and bury them they demonstrate that their expectations of us have not been completely extinguished. It is amazing enough that there still are so-called church congregations and parishes. Maybe it would be better if they no longer existed so that we would finally realize that the bell has tolled. But we should not let the patience of God, which meets us pastors many times over in the patience of our congregations, perhaps even in [79] the drowsiness of our listeners, keep us away from penance. This, certainly, is the first order of business for people today.

Yet this is only one side of the situation on Sunday mornings. The other side is even more significant. It consists outwardly of the fact that on Sunday mornings the *Bible* is opened, at least in our Protestant churches. It is worth pausing for a moment to make it clear what an immensely dangerous event it was when the Reformers risked proclaiming the Word of God expressed in the Holy Scriptures as the ground and goal of the church. Whoever has not *gasped* at this move does not have the right to *celebrate* it with the happiness of the Reformation. With this move, the Reformers pushed the latch of the door into its socket, and us with it, so that we in good conscience can no longer be satisfied with temporary performances, just as our congregations also cannot be satisfied with them.

How incomparably more securely, smoothly, and confidently the other church goes its way, having wisely left this dangerous principle of the Word undiscovered! And we have absolutely no reason to wrinkle our noses without further ado at this well-known Catholic certainty. What comes to mind is a story which was told to me by a Benedictine from Alsace about the time during the War. As the lead cantor of his cloister, he sang the Magnificat in harmony one evening with his fellow monks, and suddenly a French grenade crashed through the roof and exploded in the middle of the nave of the church. But the smoke dissipated and the Magnificat was continued. One may certainly ask, would the Protestant sermon have also been continued? [79]

When our task as *verbi divini ministri*, as we Reformed say,[30] once again

---

30   "Verbi Divini Minister" (VDM) is the statutory title for a pastor in Switzerland up until this very day. For more historical background of this characterization, see Barth's *Christliche Dogmatik*, 38.

begins to hassle and depress us, hasn't each one of us experienced a silent
homesickness for the "beautiful worship" [Ps. 27.4] of Catholicism?[31]
Haven't we all longed for the enviable [80] role of the priest at the altar,
who becomes a "creator of the creature" [*creator creatoris*][32] when he
elevates the holiest of hosts [*Sanctissimum*] before all the people with the
entire weight of meaning and power always possessed more strongly by
the objective symbol than the symbol of the human word as such! And
not only does he proclaim in words the double grace of the sacrificial
death and the incarnation of the Son of God but consummates it as well.
I heard it literally proclaimed one time at an installation of a priest: "The
priest is another Jesus Christ!" [*Le prêtre un autre Jésus Christ*]. If only we
could do that as well! Yes, there too, the Bible is being interpreted on
the side. But how insignificant, how indifferent is the task of the sermon,
how meager is the homily, covered and rescued from the start through
the reflection of the Eucharistic miracle in which it occurs. For the sake
of this miracle alone, the people actually come to church. How visible,
brightly lit, how orderly and possible is the way of God to humans and
from humans to God!

The Catholic priest goes daily upon this way, out from this center, and
points it out to others. How brilliantly the problem is solved there! It is
solved using the most profound understanding of what people are looking for in the church. It keeps them there — for the time being — with
an enormously ultimate act. It radically shakes the equilibrium of souls
and the world by not actually shaking it, and thus inspires the appearance
that now the ultimate, redeeming word has been spoken.

Which one of us would have the nerve to call into question the
kerygmatic content and success of the Catholic Sacrament of the Altar
with the suggestion that *we* might actually have something better? But
let us be clear about this: The better thing, which the Reformers wanted
to have securely in place in the exact position where the abolished Mass
used to be, is the proclamation of the word. For, "the visible word"
[*verbum visibile*],[33] [81] objectively clear verbal proclamation, is also that

31 This might be an allusion to the publications of the Marburg historian of religion Friedrich Heiler
    and his position on Catholicism. Cf. for example, idem, *Katholischer und evangelischer Gottesdienst*, in
    The World of Christian Piety, Vol. 1 (Munich: Kaiser, 1921), 16. There he states that in the Catholic
    Mass, the "fine arts" are united "with the mystical piety of the heart to form a fruitful bond." He
    adds: "The one who stands outside of this, the one who visits a Catholic worship for the first time,
    has the impression of a peculiar, staged drama. Each form of art works together to incorporate the
    mysteries of viewing God and being united to God into a world of beauty."
32 This is an allusion to Paschasius Radbertus (b. 790–856/59) and his concept of the Lord's Supper
    (he accused it of being "absurd"). See Friedrich Loofs, *Leitfaden zum Studium der Dogmengeschichte*,
    2nd ed., (Halle: Niemeyer, 1906), 473.
33 The characterization of the sacraments as "*verbum visibile*" goes back to Augustine. See for example,

which continues to be a sacrament in our church. The Reformers took everything away from us and somewhat cruelly left us nothing but the Bible. Do we not want to turn back the wheel of history, even if only a quarter or eighth? Is it only a growing sensitivity and tolerance, or even a waning sense of mission [*Exusia*] that we refrain from labeling the papal Mass, in the bold words of Question Eighty in the Heidelberg Catechism, with a "complete denial of the once for all sacrifice and passion of Jesus Christ (and as such an idolatry to be condemned)?"[34] In an understandable faintness of heart, our well-known endeavors to broaden the narrow — terribly narrow — basis of the Protestant, Christian preaching betray all too clearly the homesickness to which many of us have succumbed. For instance, could anything else more clearly prove the direction in which we are traveling than the absolutely facetious suggestion to fill the painful hole in the church of the *Word* with the so-called "sacrament of — *silence*?"[35] Isn't [82] the deep impression left upon us by Heiler's

---

Augustine, *C. Faustum Man*, 19:16: "For what are the sacramental things except some visible words?" (*CSEL* 25, 513).

34 *BRSK* 704, 30–32; *BRC* 41: "Therefore the Mass is fundamentally a complete denial of the once for all sacrifice and passion of Jesus Christ (and as such an idolatry to be condemned)."

35 Experiments with such a "sacrament" were occurring in circles of the Freunde der Christlichen Welt, among others; for example, at their yearly convention from September 29 through October 1, 1920 in Eisenach. See the convention's minutes recorded by G. Rade in "Eisenach," *CW*, 34 (1920): 670:

> The third day began with a devotional of friends in the Kreuzkirche. Fine music, selected poetry and an address by Fuchs led the way to the 'sacrament of silence.' Through a general joining of hands, the inner community became visible. But the community was not all that inner and the atmosphere not all that unified. Such highlights of common worship cannot be forced; the fruit must first ripen before one is allowed to pick it.

With reference to the "silent worship" of the Quakers, Rudolf Otto promoted a "spiritual form of worship, which has never yet been exercised. It has a moment in it that ought not be absent from any cultus, and which is profoundly neglected in the Protestant cultus." See his "Schweigender Dienst," *CW*, 34 (1920): cols. 561–565. On the occasion of the Lord's Supper, Otto suggested,

> The congregation kneels down and a complete silence follows until the prayer bell has rung three sets of three. For those who are inexperienced, such silence consists of the ceasing of all external words and every external distraction, but still with an inner speaking, as a prayer of self-surrender to the Present One. Then an inner silence meets up with the outer silence, along with the entire keeping of the Sabbath and silence of the soul and all of its powers, and the quiet immersion into the eternal foundation, the high miracle of the union itself.

He added:

> The cultic silence can be of a three-fold type: the numinous-sacramental silence, waiting silence, and the unifying silence. The *numinous-sacramental* silence has its meaning in the words of the Psalms, "The Lord is in his holy temple; let all earth keep silence before him!" [Hab. 2:20] Such great acts of silence . . . are the sacramental highlight of the cultic action. It characterizes the moment where the presence of the Numinose is experienced [. . .] Everything that precedes this in the cultic act is only a preparation . . . for the moment about

sultry book on prayer[36] more noteworthy than the book itself? What is one supposed to think when one hears serious men seriously considering the introduction of liturgical dance, regressing even further back in history than Catholicism?[37]

It is all too easy to imagine the confusion out of which this all grows! It is tough to bear the fact that the Reformation shut and bolted a door which will not be easily unlocked, that our situation cannot fundamentally change even though it still tends to move in the direction of Catholicism despite its four-hundred-year history. And indeed, the Reformation continues to be obscured through the various aromas of holy incense which some people today would like to see rise up again.[38]

which it can be said, "that which is impossible becomes an event here" [. . .] Such an "event" of the impossible is the sacrament. And what it brings either accompanying or preparing, is sacramental. Therefore such a silence is a sacramental silence (col. 562).

See also Rudolf Otto, "Schweigender Dienst in der Christvesper," *CW*, 35 (1921): col. 61f.; U. Altmann, "Schweigender Dienst," *CW*, 35 (1921): 242f.; see also Otto's follower, Friedrich Heiler, *Der Katholizismus. Seine Idee und seine Erscheinung* (Munich: Reinhardt, 1923), 411.

36   Friedrich Heiler, *Das Gebet. Eine religionsgeschichtliche und religionspsychologische Untersuchung.* (Munich: Reinhardt, 1919). On Barth's reading of this book in May/June 1920, see *Bw.Th.* I., 368, 386f., 395.

37   Dance was of great significance in the "Freistätte des persönlichen Lebens" community founded by Johannes Müller (1864–1949), first at Mainberg Castle, and then from 1916 at Castle Elmau, which he built. Müller regularly held lectures about the "being of the dance" for his guests, and offered weekly, specially arranged and performed evenings of dance. Müller characterized this "being of the dance" as "the shutting off of the ego with the saving, redeeming results of the return to the origin of one's being and to the immediacy of personal life, from where a receptivity of the past is born for the creative ideas and impressions; here the in-born geniality of life is awakened again" (idem, *Vom Geheimnis des Lebens. Erinnerungen II: Schicksal und Werk* [Stuttgart/Berlin: Verlag der Grünen Blätter, 1938], 76). On the dancing at Mainberg and Elmau, cf. ibid., 73–83, 89f. Müller does not give an "introduction of the dance," but he does explain a theology behind it. According to Müller, "there, if somewhere, the *Creator Spiritus* binds us in his kingdom and work and without our being aware of it, influences, heals, and redeems, and turns us back to the originality of our created existence" (77). About the dance evenings, he says,

It is no wonder that sometimes a roar, a chiming, a singing goes through one's heart. No one thinks in that moment of the "Holy Spirit." It was for everyone a festive occasion out of the worship services in dark rooms, where one seeks forgiveness of sins and protection from the demons in one's own heart. [. . .] They [the dance evenings] became almost like events of Pentecost, not only for the dancers but also for the onlookers, who experienced it as well (73).

See also J. Müller, *Die Erlösung des Leibes*, Flugschriften Heft 9 (Elmau), 31–36; B. Müller-Elmau, *Das Wesen der Elmau* (Elmau), 61–64. Barth perhaps found out about the dance evenings at Elmau from Georg Merz who occasionally attended. (See also G. Merz, *Wege und Wandlungen. Erinnerungen aus der Zeit 1892–1922*, J. Merz, ed., (Munich: Kaiser, 1961), 166–171.

38   In the framework of the contemporary liturgical movement, which Barth is generally alluding to, the reintroduction of holy incense into Protestant worship was occasionally demanded. See for example, O. Mehl, "Weihrauch," *Die Hochkirche. Monatsschrift der Hochkirchlichen Vereinigung*, 3 (1921): col. 308f.; and R. Otto, "Schweigender Dienst in der Christvesper," *CW*, 35 (1921): col. 62. Cf. also Note 35, p. 115.

NEED AND PROMISE OF CHRISTIAN PROCLAMATION 117

[83] It is tough to bear the fact that the boundaries which cross over from the land of Yahweh into the land of Baal, even if not hermetically sealed, as we clearly see, are still effectively closed up. The proclamation of the biblical Word of God is laid upon us in the entire dead weight of its historical reality, no longer to be shaken off. It is tough to have to stand in the dusky shadows of the Reformation — even if it were only as epigones — instead of in the bright light of the Middle Ages, the way it shines at the end of Goethe's *Faust, Part Two*. Indeed, as tough as the other matters mentioned here is the fact that our present and former audiences expect to hear the Word from us and our church, and wait for an answer to the question, "*Is it true?*" Scylla and Charybdis! They behold one another from opposite sides, and we have to find our way through them.

Yet we must look more closely at the side of the situation that is shown through the book of the Bible as it lies there, opened upon pulpit and altar. What makes it so difficult for us to remain true to the Reformation principle of Scripture alone? Please, spare us any platitudes in your answers! It is not the age, distance, or alien nature of the Bible that makes it so difficult for us (for example the strangeness of its "worldview"). Nor is it the enticing competition facing the Bible by Goethe and Schiller, Buddha, and Nietzsche. Nor is it typically the overly abundant flow of our own inspiration that may perhaps feel a little cramped within the biblical line of thought.

No, the Bible is strange to us because it carries in from the *other* side a new, great (*greater!*), exciting *expectation* to the church situation. While the congregation primarily *brings* to the church the great *question* of life and *seeks* an *answer* for it, on the contrary, the Bible primarily *brings* an *answer*, and it *seeks* the *question* to this answer. [84] It seeks questioning *people* who want to seek and find this answer; who in so doing understand that its seeking of them is the very answer to their question. The thought-world of the Bible moves along a line that also seems to run through an entire series of great and valuable possibilities which are called into question by the preponderance of negative factors in life's reckoning. Thus it runs precisely along the side of humanity where the question arises, "Is it really true?" With an uncanny one-sidedness, the Bible skips over all the stages of human life in which this crisis is not quite acute, in which the human can still comfort himself with unbroken naïvety in the presence of God with cherry trees, symphonies, the State, or daily work. With an uncanny urgency, the Bible is primarily interested in *the* stage — the highest or the lowest? — where doubt has washed over the human.

Indeed, praise and gratitude, jubilation and certainty are present in the Bible, but not on this side of the line, rather on the other, where the human has become a seeker, an inquirer, a knocker at the door [cf. Mt. 7.7], where he is overcome by precisely the difficulty that drives him toward help, which, let us say, drives him to church. Just to name one prominent example, notice where the line of the Bible intersects the human lifeline in the Psalms: There we have the unambiguous answer. It intersects in the consciousness of sin and sickness, in hardship brought on by personal circumstances and enemies of the nation, in the distance of God and divine things, in doubt and despair, in transitoriness and dying. In this way, the Bible first and foremost simply sets itself down next to the individual who has just become aware of his condition, for whom certainty has everywhere begun to waver. It asks with him (think of Psalm 42, think of Job), *is it true*? True that there is a meaning, a goal, and a God in all this?

Now the Bible *differentiates* itself from the consciousness of the individual awakening to his condition in two respects. First, it differentiates itself in that it gives this human question its primary clarity and meaning. It does it in such a way that it leads the most shocked, humiliated, despondent person once again to the edge of an abyss which he cannot even imagine. It does it in such a way that every contradiction we see in our existence, the joy and suffering, good and evil, light and darkness, yes and no, all at once shuffle in close together. Even our most burning question, which eventually makes us throw up an entreating hand to God [85] must turn cold and fall silent in a way that we cannot ignore. All our questioning was preparation and practice. Only now we can see whether we are asking *seriously*, whether we want to ask about *God*. When Job, the patient sufferer, laments in his suffering, he clearly means a suffering that, humanly speaking, has no end. When Paul speaks of sin, he does not mean some straw-man sin,[39] with which we plague ourselves, but with the sin of Adam from which we originate and in which we are born, the sin which we will not get rid of as long as time lasts. If the writings of John know enough to speak of the darkness of this world,[40] they are not speaking of just any darkness in which and next to which there are all kinds of friendly little lights for everyone who does not want to act like a completely rabid pessimist. Rather, the talk in these writings is about *the* darkness in the face of which the question of more optimism or more pessimism becomes entirely meaningless. And when Jesus Christ

---

39   See Martin Luther, WA.TR 6: 106, 33–107, 3 (Nr. 6669):

> Since I was a monk, I wrote often to Doctor Staupitz. One time I wrote to him: "Oh my sins, sins, sins!" To this, he replied, "You want to be without sin, but you have no real sins; Christ is the forgiveness of genuine sin, like the murder of parents or their public burdening, or the despising of God, breaking up a marriage, etc. These are true sins. You must keep a list where genuine sins stand, then Christ shall help you; but you must not go about so slovenly [*mit solchem Humpelwerk*], and your doll's sins [*Püppensünde*], and make every fart [*Bombart*] a sin!"

40   See Jn 1.5; 3.19; 8.12, etc.; and 1 Jn 1.5; 2.8f.

dies on the cross, he does not merely ask whether it is also true, but he cries out "My God, my God, why have you forsaken me?" [Mt. 27.46]. It has been believed that Jesus must be excused for this outcry that has obscure roots, that it is not yet the expression of a real desperation.[41] In fact, it has been completely overlooked that this outcry is not less but even *more* than doubt and desperation. It is dereliction [*derelictio*]. It is doom and abandonment, as the old dogmaticians still knew.[42]

In the Bible, suffering means to suffer under *God*. [86] To sin means to sin against *God*. To doubt means to doubt *God*. Offense means offense against *God*. The painful insight into the boundaries of humanity[43] that people can more or less gain with the rising and falling of life's experiences becomes the message of the *cross* as the order of the holy God in the Bible. Humanity is placed under this, here and now, once and for all. The cross is God's demand on us to ask about it, to ask about God. Throughout our entire lives, even if every other question may be able to be answered, we shall not unwind and tear ourselves away from *this* question. In the Old and New Testaments, this message struggles ever more clearly into the light, becoming unambiguous and unmistakable in Jesus Christ. It searches for the persons who can and want to seek God, who are in the position to let their *minor* questions — and which ones *are not* minor? — merge into the *major* questions; persons who surrender themselves at the foot of the cross, and that means before God. "Come to me, all you that are weary and are carrying heavy burdens!" Why? "Take *my* yoke upon you!" [Mt. 11.28f.]. It is not obvious, not even to the most mature, most earnestly seeking individuals, that they are *the* weary and heavy-laden ones, that they take upon themselves *his* yoke, the yoke of *Christ*. We will never comprehend this, even if we have already comprehended it a thousand times.

The second decisive point is that even in their highest form, the profound questions of human life are only questions, against which the sought-after answers stand as second, as different, as those things which must be arrived at. Contrary to this, the *Bible* understands the questions of human life by translating them into the question of *God* and then

41 See for example, Augustine, *Enarratio in psalmum XXI, MPL* 36, 172. For an interpretative-historical overview, cf. Erich Vogelsang, *Der angefochtene Christus bei Luther* (Berlin: de Gruyter, 1932), 23; Günther Bornkamm [Meditation upon] *Mark 15: 20–39* in *Göttinger Predigtmeditationen. Die altkirchlichen Evangelien*, 4 (1949/50) (Göttingen, 1966), 121f.

42 For example, compare the documents in K.A. von Hase, *Hutterus redivivus, oder Dogmatik der evangelisch-lutherischen Kirche. Ein dogmatisches Repertorium fuer Studierende*, 10th ed. (Leipzig: 1862), 273; and Christoph E. Luthardt, *Kompendium der Dogmatik* 8th ed. (Leipzig: Dörffling & Franke 1889), 207.

43 See J.W. Goethe's poem "Grenzen der Menschheit," in *Selected Poems*, Christopher Middleton, ed. (Boston: Suhrkamp/Insel Publishers, 1983), 83–85.

subjecting them to it. The Bible does not allow us to speak or hear a "question" at all without already hearing an *answer*. Whoever can say that the Bible only leads us to hear a big "No," to see a big hole, proves only that he himself has not yet been led there. *This* "No" is precisely "Yes." *This* judgment is grace. *This* condemnation is forgiveness. *This* death is life. *This* hell is heaven. *This* fearsome God is the loving father, who takes the lost son into his arms [87] [cf. Lk. 15.20]. The crucified one is the resurrected one, and the word of the cross [1 Cor. 1.18] as such is the word of eternal life. No additional thing needs to appear. The question is the answer. The truth and reality, the establishment of this reversal — is this the sense of the entire Bible? I do not know any other reality but the reality of the living God, the One who *is* who he is [Exod. 3.14], the One who constitutes himself. The Bible renounces any and every foundation for God. It witnesses to revelation. We have seen his glory [Jn 1.14], and *therefore* we saw it as the answer in the *question*. How can one hear, recognize, or know it any differently than this? But the *answer* is the *primary* thing. It would not be a question if it were not the answer.

Only by encountering the human as a question, can it really *be an answer* for the human. God is the fullness of the "Yes." Only by going through his "No" do we *understand* him as God. The narrow way [cf. Mt. 7.14; Lk. 13.24] does lead to life. Only because it is *this gate*, it must be so narrow. "I will give you rest!" [Mt. 11.28] and "My yoke is tender and my burden is light" [Mt. 11.30]. Only by taking this yoke and burden upon ourselves will it become true for us. "'In that you *seek* me with all your heart, do I want to *let* myself to be *found* by you!' says the Lord" [Jer. 29.13f.]. Only the *Lord* can speak in such a way. Only he can put seeking and finding, questioning and answering all into one. The Bible, however, witnesses *that* he speaks in such a way.

This is what makes up the *other* side of the situation of the church. Have I given an accurate portrayal? It is the still *greater* expectation that is carried into this situation through the *Bible*. It asks this: Where are the people who recognize their own questions in the questions of the Bible, and then in turn recognize God's answer *in* this question; an answer that is final, redemptive, creative, enlivening, blessed, shining the light of eternity upon time and everything in time, generating hope and obedience? Where are the individuals who have eyes to see what no eye has seen, ears to hear what no ear has heard, hearts to understand what has not yet occurred in the human heart [cf. 1 Cor. 2.9]? Who are the people who want and are able to receive the Holy Spirit as the pledge of that which still has *not yet* appeared even to the children of God, which has *not yet* appeared *precisely* to the children of God [cf. 1 Jn. 3.2]? Who are the people who *in the midst* of their need want and are able to believe in the *promise*? *God* expects, *God* seeks out such individuals. The Bible is not asking about *our* life, *our* [88] opportunities, needs, and wishes, but about the *Lord* who seeks workers for *his* vineyard [Mt. 20.1].

The expectation that the congregation carries into the situation of the church is minor. Despite any profound understanding we might have of it, it is actually meaningless in light of *the* expectation that comes from the side of the open Bible. Although it is just as mute as every other, this expectation is very different and more real. In other words, if the awakening of the human characterized by this situation is great and meaningful, then it is so only in the light of what *God* expects. Therefore, the expectation of humans is to be taken seriously and cannot be taken seriously enough. For it is a shadow of the great expectation with which God comes upon the scene. This is an uncanny situation, who dares misjudge it? It is understandable that we would like to avoid it, but we cannot kick against the goads [cf. Acts 26.14]. *We* are the ones held fast by the very side from which the uncanny element in this situation originally comes, exactly from the side of the Bible. I say it again, *we* are held fast by that which came over Christianity four hundred years ago.

The event toward which this expectation is directed from both sides is Christian proclamation. And the man who is not the middle point in this event but who nevertheless stands exposed at the front line is the Christian preacher, the pastor. From a human perspective, he is certainly the first one who gives an *answer* to those who come to church — or not — on Sundays. Seen from the perspective of the Bible, he is the first one who must be prepared to place himself under the *question* posed by God, to place himself into a line of those seeking God. Without this, God's answer cannot become true for us. Were the pastor to answer what *humans ask* as one who himself is *questioned by God*, then may it be said that he speaks God's Word; a Word which people seek in a pastor and which God commissions him to speak. For as a human truly questioned by God, and as a human who seeks God, the pastor would indeed know God's answer. By virtue of this, he would be able to give an answer to other people who await *God's* answer with *their* questions, even when they do not realize it. Indeed, if *that* were the case, would there then be a more meaningful, more decisive event than Christian [89] preaching! All at once the entire situation of the church would become understandable if it were seen in the context of *this* event. The existence of the pastor would be justified if he were the servant of *this* event and if he sensibly carried out the deed that should build the center of the pastoral office in Protestantism, that is, if he preaches a sermon as the interpretation of the Bible. It must happen in this way if the sermon is going to be proclamation of the Word of God.

It is almost a banality when I now say that, from the perspective of heaven as well as earth, there is nothing more important, urgent, necessary, helpful, redeeming, sanctifying, or appropriate to the situation than that of speaking and listening to the Word of God in the power of its truth that tears down and builds up, in the way it uproots and reconciles all things, in the power it has to shine a light upon *time* and time's troubles, but beyond that to shine in the clarity of *eternity*, and always both *at the same time,* with the one *through* the other and *in* the other — the Word, the Logos of the living God. Let us ask ourselves, with Jesus Christ in mind at this point, isn't the will of God pushing forth, and isn't the plight of humanity, that of modern people here in Germany in 1922, crying out for this event?

What a proclamation it would be if our Christian preaching *were* this event! And it is indeed this event, for this is the promise it holds: If we take our situation as pastors seriously, then we *could* do no other than *affirm* this promise. It is *given* to us in our taking seriously our situation between the congregation and Bible. "Taking seriously" here can mean nothing else than to seize upon and believe God's promise that stands behind this remarkable situation, to trust in it and to be obedient to it.

But here we must pause. The *promise* of Christian proclamation is this: That we *speak God's Word.* Promise is not fulfillment. Promise means that fulfillment is promised to us. Promise does not do away with the necessity of believing but establishes it. Promise is the *human* part; fulfillment is *God's* part. It can only be believed that what belongs to God also belongs to humans. "*We* have such a treasure in *earthly* vessels" [2 Cor. 4.7]. Do not get confused between God's part and humanity's part, between the treasure and the earthly vessels! Why does this confusion occur most readily in those of us who are theologians and careless philosophers, in those of us who are supposed to know better? It is certainly [90] clear: We can only believe that we can speak of God. God's Word on the lips of a human? This is not possible. This does not occur. This is not something one can fix one's eyes on or set into motion. The event is *God's* act toward which the expectation of heaven and the earth are directed. Nothing else will suffice for the waiting crowd, and God wills nothing else than that he himself produces this event. God's Word is, will, must be, and remain *God's* Word. When it seems to be something else, no matter how brilliant, Christian, or biblical, it turns the situation into something opposite. A premature fulfillment robs us even of the promise.

Now we must address the terrible *danger* of the situation of the church. Isn't the church completely taken with inspiring that appearance? Humans intend and — who knows? — may have already achieved taking God's Word upon their lips as their own. Indeed, the more success, achievement, and fulfillment that get bound up with the appearance of this event, the more dubious it becomes, and the more threatening the situation becomes. It becomes even more perilous when our churches are fuller, when our work is more blessed and satisfying. What does blessing mean? What does satisfaction in the pastoral office mean? Do the prophets and the apostles, not to mention Jesus Christ himself, give us the impression that they are people who were successful, who could look back on their lives as blessed and satisfied? How curious it is that we are so much better at it than they! What can this mean?

It means that in any case, we at first should be shocked. What are you doing, you human, with *God's* Word upon *your* lips? How do you come to play the role of the mediator between heaven and earth? Who has authorized you to place yourself in that position and generate a religious mood! And to do so with success and achievement? What can this mean other than the greatest presumption, the highest Titanism, and — less classically but more clearly stated — the highest kitsch! One does not cross over the bounds of humanity[44] and tread on the rights of God without being punished! Don't they both unavoidably belong to the call of the pastor? [91] *Is* not the situation of the church an illustration of the chronic presumption by humanity, worse here than in any other field? I would answer: With God it is possible that this is not the case, that we *as* pastors *in* the situation of the church have been plucked like a brand from the fire [cf. Zech. 3.2]. But it is impossible to be saved in such a way by humans [cf. Mt. 19.26].

From what *we* know, we can now ask: Who deserves the wrath of God more than us pastors? Or should we ignore just how directly *we* stand under the judgment of God, not in any spiritual, religious, or otherwise harmless sense, but in the most real sense? Moses [cf. Exod. 4.10, 13] and Isaiah [cf. Isa. 6.5], Jeremiah [cf. Jer. 1.6], and Jonah [cf. Jon. 1.3] truly knew why they did *not* want to find themselves in the situation of the pastor. In fact, church is actually an impossibility. There can be no such thing as a pastor. As for preaching, who dares, who can do this knowing what preaching is? The critical situation of the church has still somehow not yet been sufficiently impressed upon us. Will we ever recognize it?

Which one of the many objections raised against Christianity and the church today by their cultured and uncultured despisers[45] contains the objection which we must finally raise against ourselves if we were more

---

44   See the writings of Paul Natorp and Emil Brunner for Barth's allusion here. Paul Natorp, *Religion innerhalb der Grenzen der Humanität. Ein Kapital zur Grundlegung der Sozialpädagogik* (Freiburg, i. Br., 1894); Emil Brunner, *Die Grenzen der Humanität. Habilitationsvorlesung an der Universität Zürich* (*SgV* 102) (Tübingen: Mohr, 1922); reprinted in *Anfänge* I, 259–279. See also Barth's own words in his 1922 lecture, "Über Kirche," in *V.u.kl.A 1922–1925*, 10.

45   An allusion to Friedrich Schleiermacher's 1799 *Über die Religion. Reden an die Gebildeten unter ihren Verächtern*, in *PhB*, Vol. 255 (Hamburg: Meiner, 1958).

conscious of the risk we take as pastors? Wouldn't it be better for once to accept the objection, however just or unjust, clever or dumb it is, with an acknowledgment that there is something to it, as David did with the stone-throwing of Shimei the son of Gera [2 Sam. 16.5-14], instead of immediately getting defensive with the weapons of our equally subtle but questionable apologetic? Wouldn't it be more advisable to quietly let certain threatening storms overcome us with their purifying power and have an effect on us for once, instead of immediately fending them off with an ecclesiastical counter-storm? Wouldn't it be better for us, instead of reading the likes of pastoral and theological journals, to pick up Feuerbach,[46] for example, and read him without [92] immediately trying to pull our heads out of his snare?

If God has elected us and wants to justify us — and yes, the miracle is *possible* for *him* to elect and justify us *as* pastors and *in* the situation of the church — then it must happen only in *judgment* upon ourselves, in *judgment* about the state of the pastor. For only *then* can we grasp the promise, only *then* can we believe. Only by taking upon ourselves the great, humiliating, indeed deadly question that God poses to everything, not as humanity in general — that would be all too convenient because no one is a "human" in general — but exactly as spiritual beings, exactly in our position as mediators, do we first become capable of being true priests [*Geistliche*]. This means understanding God's *answer* and then also giving an answer to the human with his question. Only if proclamation comes as a real need does our office become a *mission*, and only mission can legitimize our proclamation.

It makes sense that on the Day of Atonement, according to Leviticus 16, the high priest must first present a bull, slaughter it, and sacrifice it as a sin-offering so "that he purifies *himself* and *his* house" [Lev. 16.11]. Only *after that* does the priest present the ram as a sin-offering for the people [16.15]. Wouldn't it be advisable to first present this bull and in the meantime let the ram live! Are we somehow denying that the judgment of God must begin in the House of God [1 Pet. 4.17]! Are we refusing to place ourselves and our office and our church in the position where all flesh must stand? Should that *not* be the first thing that we constantly *begin* with, about which we constantly think about *first*, which must come

---

46   The "Stange-Kränzchen," a discussion group organized by Professor Carl Stange to which Barth belonged in Göttingen, dealt with Feuerbach on February 5, 1922. See Barth's comments in his 1922 essay, "Feuerbach," in *V.u.kl.A. 1922–1925*, 6ff. On Barth's later contention with Feuerbach, see his "Ludwig Feuerbach," *ZZ* 3 (1927): 11–33. Reprinted in Karl Barth, *Th.u.K*, 212–239; and his *Die protestantische Theologie im 19. Jahrhundert. Ihre Vorgeschichte und ihre Geschichte* (Zurich: Zollikon, 1947), 484–489; ET *Protestant Theology in the Nineteenth Century: Its Background and History* (Grand Rapids, MI: William B. Eerdmans Publishing Company, 2002), 484–489.

before our work at the study desk and in the pulpit? Wouldn't we secretly or openly like to avoid, with a worldly or Christian reason, the fundamental disillusionment that this entails? Should we fling an accusation against the world, against an unchristian worldview, the unreligious masses and all that goes with it; an accusation which has not yet hit us with all its vehemence, which will knock out of us the breath we need for condemning others? Should we speak of sin, the sin of "being like God" [*Eritis sicut Dei*, Gen. 3.5, Vulgate] without [93] first having said to ourselves: "*You* are the man [2 Sam. 12.7], you *more* than all the others!" And once we've started out in this way, how then do we stop *staying* under the judgment out of which and from which the Word of God wants to rip us and rescue us, together *with* all other flesh?

Refusing to examine ourselves first can only mean that we do *not* want to let ourselves be satisfied with the promise; that we do *not* want to believe. How then can we hear and speak the Word of God and our congregations recognize and understand it? How can anyone believe us? How can we be able to really proclaim — and not just in words — the forgiveness of sins, the resurrection of the body, and the everlasting life?[47] We become *worthy* of being believed only by acknowledging our own unworthiness. *Compelling* talk of God only occurs when Christian proclamation itself stands in the middle of *need*, under the *cross*, in the *question* that God himself first poses so that God could answer it. We dare not wish to get *out* of this need.

This is precisely the accusation of the young Martin Luther against the Catholic Middle Ages. They wanted *out* of this need. Almost every page in his interpretation of the Psalms and Romans[48] speaks from the appall that seized him when he made the discovery that what the Scholastics and the Mystics did was indeed a "theology of glory" [*theologia gloriae*],[49] as he called it in the *Heidelberg Disputation* of 1518. They sought to produce a naïve religious mood, a *flight* from the questions which God poses in order for God to be able to give his answer. *Here* is where he dug in the spade and defined his theology as a "theology of the cross" [*theologia crucis*], the Reformation theology upon whose ground we allegedly stand. It is drafted from the place where the human gives up precisely the highest and the best things and places them under judgment. By

---

47   See the Apostles' Creed, *BSLK*, 21: 21–23; *BC* 21–22.

48   In 1922 Barth possessed a copy of *Luthers Vorlesung über den Römerbrief 1515/16*, Johannes Ficker, ed. in *Anfänge reformatorischer Schriftauslegung*, Vol. 1 (Leipzig: Dieterich, 1908), and *Dr. Martin Luthers erste und älteste Vorlesung über die Psalmen aus den Jahren 1513–1516*, 2nd ed., 2 Vols., Johann Karl von Seidemann, ed. (Dresden, 1880); see also *Bw. Th.* II, 90 (June 30, 1922) and 94 (July 7, 1922).

49   Martin Luther, *Heidelberg Disputation* (1518), Thesis 21: "A theologian of glory calls evil good and good evil. A theologian of the cross calls the thing what it actually is." WA 1: 354, 21f.; *LW* 31: 40.

doing this, humans grasp the promise in faith *alone*, because the human is grasped by the groundless [94] mercy of God[50] that is only grounded in itself.

We are grasped because *Christ* the *Crucified*, in his dereliction, is the bearer of the promise. "It is he that has made us and we are his; we are his people and the sheep of his pasture" [Ps. 100.3]. How are the people supposed to hear this from Christian proclamation in the church when the church itself has perhaps not yet heard it at all?

Do we stand on the ground of the *theologia crucis*? This appears to me to be the question of destiny that is posed to our Protestant church today, where we have the real opportunity to see what the cross is. We need *serious* pastors today. However, this seriousness must be a *matter* of the church and it can in no way mean that it is about the church itself. Applied to the church, the very human seriousness of the pastor is no longer a match for the almost terrible seriousness of today's situation. We need hard-working pastors. But not with *business*-smarts. The administration of the Word is not a business, even if it worked brilliantly. The hard work will have to prove itself in situations in which businesses tend to come off as not hard-working, in failure and ineffectiveness, in the deepest of isolation and negative results, perhaps until the end of one's life. Indeed, if devotion means obedience to the call, "Follow *me*!" [John 21. 22], which can lead us out from everything that conservatives and liberals call devotion, then we need pastors who are *devout*.

Consider for yourself, however, what seriousness, hard work, and devotion might mean on the basis of the *theologia crucis*. If we want to stand there, then we must in any case make a departure from all that lies along the lines of the Catholic Sacrament of the Altar, this most genial of symbols of the glory of the church. This sacrament believes it can *withdraw* itself from the judgment of God and therefore withdraw itself precisely [95] from *grace*. It is a symbol that is not satisfied with the promise but wants to have, enjoy, experience — yes even live in — the fulfillment, as if the way to dwelling in the fulfillment did not go through the dying of all human glory, and first and foremost the glory of the church! We

50   See Barth's *Romans* 1922, 70 (1999 ed., 68, 74); ET 93: "The righteousness of God is the *nevertheless!*, with which God declares himself to be our God and with which he turns us to himself; and inconceivably, unprovoked, only in himself, only grounded in God, especially 'therefore' purely in this 'nevertheless!'" The expression, "groundless mercy" may be traced back to the general formula of confession found in the Nürnberger Messe by Andreas Döber (1525), included in some liturgies; Barth could have heard the expression in Göttingen in a general confession, which at that time came before the Lord's Supper (according to the celebration of the Lutheran liturgy of high worship). This information came to the editor of the *GA*, Holger Finze, from Pastor Dr. Joachim Stalmann, Hannover, Germany.

are not supposed to want to be *creatores creatoris* in any way or under any circumstance. We are not to *create* God, but to *witness to* God. In these two words lies all the difference.

What lies along the lines of the Catholic Sacrament of the Altar is a *flight* from the need of Christian proclamation and therefore a flight also from the *promise* of Christian proclamation. Do not let yourselves be fooled: Many things lie along this line, things that do not look Catholic at all, but rather very evangelical and especially very modern. I will leave it up to you to decide whether this line has been drawn deep into the features of our most customary homiletics and pastoral care, into our *traditional* forms of the church, and still much more into the *new* and *newest* endeavors in exactly that area of church formation, as well as deep, very deep into the systematic and historical presentation of our theology. It runs through all those places where "having" appears that is not at the same time "not-having"; hurrying without waiting [cf. 2 Pet. 3.12]; giving without taking; possessing without lacking; knowing without not-knowing; having a right without a wrong; sitting without getting up; a presence of the kingdom of heaven where there are not any "poor in spirit" [Mt. 5.3]. No security, no victory can come along this line. For the God who brings security and victory lives in a light which no one can approach [1 Tim. 6.16], and as such God wants himself to be recognized and worshipped. This is the crisis of Christian proclamation.

Of course, I would not like to level any direct accusations at any side when I speak of this fatal line. The subject matter does not commend itself to making accusations. I do not mistake that much can be said and made out of the need and therefore the promise of Christian proclamation, which at the first glance appears to lie uncannily close to that fatal line. May everything then, which is said and done today about the matter of Christian proclamation, on the right and on the left, in the community churches and in the high-church community,[51] from the old [96] and from the young, take its course. *Fiat! Fiat!* "One is not appropriate for all. Each one must see to it where he stays, each one must see to it that he does his thing, and each one must stand so that he does not fall."[52]

The situation cannot be about setting up a new position or even

---

51   In October 1918, the "Hochkirchliche Vereinigung e.V." [High-Church Union] was established with its publication "Die Hochkirche." It advocated an ecclesiastical constitution for bishops, the reintroduction of the Deutsche Messe [German High Mass], hourly prayer, and a renewal of private confession, among other things. Cf. W. Drobnitzky's article, "Hochkirchliche Bewegung. II. In Deutschland und anderen Kirchen der Ökumene," in *RGG*, 3rd ed., Vol. II, cols. 379–382.

52   From J.W. Goethe's poem "Beherzigung," in *Lyrics and Epigrams: After Goethe and Other German Authors*, M. Gray, ed., (Edinburgh: n/a, 1890). The German citation runs, "[. . .] Sehe jeder, wie er's treibe/ Sehe jeder, wo er bleibe [. . .]."

putting forth a polemic negation. It is, however, about *reflection*, about that which is spoken of and done there, reflection about the One, necessary, inescapable thing [cf. Lk. 10.42], that which our church, that which our pastors and theologians, especially today more than ever, actually face. Reflection means *remembering* the *sense* of our speaking and doing.[53] Perhaps with such reflection, things that have been said can no longer be said and done, or must be said differently. Perhaps the same things that have already been said and done will be done from a new perspective. Reflection means fundamentally neither position nor negation, but precisely a mere note in the margin, "a little spice."

In any case reflection need not separate us from one another, even if differs in its theoretical and practical results among us. I believe that it must be fundamentally possible to come to an understanding with a Catholic theologian, even about the Sacrament of the Altar finally, and without wanting to take the Sacrament away from him. In the end, the need and promise of Christian preaching, divine judgment, and divine justification will stand behind the Church of Trent too. There is enough "Catholic" within us Protestants for us to have to accept that Reformation concerns cannot be simply dead, even in the Church of Trent. What justifies us in this supposition? Supposing so only makes a rapprochement even more difficult. But such a rapprochement is made no less difficult if we suppose that the concerns of the Reformation were somehow obvious to us. They are *not* obvious to us. We can [97] *not* take it for granted that we know them and that they are alive in us. They must awaken in us again and again, today, tomorrow. Reformation is truly no less possible and necessary today than four hundred years ago.

Reformation occurs where reflection occurs. If the longing for reformation approaches you today, perhaps as no more than a bitter care, do not think that it is supposed to be something different. Utter the words, "*Veni creator spiritus!*" [Come Creator, Holy Spirit!],[54] which is for now, according to Romans 8 [v. 26], more hopeful than triumphant, as if one already had it.

Once you have heard this sigh, you have been introduced to "my theology." If you have heard it and understood it, perhaps better than you care to, then you will also understand it when I close with a confession of *hope*. There are a few sentences from *Calvin's* exegesis of Mic. 4.6 ("In

---

53   "Reflection" [*Besinnung*] would become a controlling concept in Barth's first dogmatic lecture cycle a few years later, in the 1924 prolegomena of the *Unterricht in der christlichen Religion* (see the index, 388, and esp. 30); ET 24. The concept *Besinnung* was carried over as "reflection" into the English edition, but was not included as an entry in the index.

54   This citation comes from the beginning of a Pentecost hymn, "Veni creator spiritus," by Hrabanus Maurus (c. 776–856). Cf. *EKG* 97.

that day, says the Lord, I will assemble the lame and gather those who have been driven away, and those whom I have afflicted"). "Although the church," says Calvin, "up to this day is hardly to be distinguished from a dead or invalid man, one must not give up hope; for all at one time the Lord will arrange those who exist, like the way he wakes the dead from the grave. This is, however, to be paid attention to, for, when the church does not shine, we quickly hold it for extinguished and finished. But in this way the church is maintained in the world, that, *it all at one time*, will be raised up from death. Indeed, at the end, its being sustained will happen every day, among many other such miracles. Let us remember that the life of the church is not without resurrection. Even further, it is not without many resurrections. *Tenendum est, ecclesiae vitam non esse absque resurrectione, imo absque multis resurrectionibus.*"[55]

---

55 CR 71 (= *Calvini Opera* 43), col. 353:

This is the highest thing: However much the church under these conditions is almost indifferent to the mortal human, or at least to the mutilated human, there is no reason for desperation. Just how the Lord lifts up his own again and again, he also summons the dead out of the tomb. And this is closely to be noted, even though the church of God does not shine, we nonetheless cleanse it, the one which is utterly destroyed and abolished. Nevertheless, the church presents itself in the world in such a manner so that it be resurrected again and again from the dead. Finally, the conservation of the church through almost every single day is the consequence of many miracles. But this is to be held without many resurrections, one should say.

CHAPTER 6

THE PROBLEM OF ETHICS TODAY, 1922

[98] For the lectures in the German cities of Wiesbaden, Lüneburg, Emden, Nordhorn, and Bochum, to which he was invited in September and October of 1922, Barth had originally envisioned handling different themes.[1] Due to a lack of time, however, he finally restricted himself to repeating the Wiesbaden lecture of September 26, 1922 on "The Problem of Ethics Today" four times. The writing of it "cost" Barth "*bad, bad* weeks"[2] because it was being written very nearly at the same time as the preparations for "The Word of God as the Task of Theology" given on October 3.[3]

I. Wiesbaden, September 26, 1922

The first group to whom Barth gave this lecture — the working group of pastors, "Theologische Arbeitsgemeinschaft zu Wiesbaden" (also known as the "Arbeitsgemeinschaft nassauischer Pfarrer") — [99] goes back to a private

---

1   A critical edition of this essay in German can be found in *V.u.kl.A. 1922–1925*, 98–143. Page numbers in brackets in this essay run according to the *GA*. The theme for Wiesbaden was apparently stated from the beginning; cf. *Bw.Th.* II, 87 (June 28, 1922). It can no longer be verified whether it was formulated by Barth himself. For Emden and Nordhorn, he had in mind "something Calvinistic." The people at Bochum assigned Barth the topic "revelation and faith" (cf. the introduction to the *GA*). For Lüneburg, he had planned on repeating a lecture from the start. As late as September 12, Barth implied as such when he wrote to his mother, "I've arranged it so that I hold the one lecture three times, so I only have to write three lectures for five occasions. But even that is enough for me" (KBA 9222.63). Within two days, however, Barth decided to change his plan. On September 14, he mentioned in a letter to Georg Merz his intention to give a lecture about "'revelation and faith' in Emden and Bentheim [i.e. Nordhorn], and on October 22 in Bochum" (*Bw.Th.* II, 97). So, after having given up planning a lecture about "something Calvinistic" — Barth had given a lecture course on the theology of Calvin in 1922 — he also dropped the theme of "revelation and faith" at a later, unknown date.

2   Barth's letter to his mother, October 5, 1922 (KBA 9222.67). See also his complaint in a letter to Thurneysen from just a week before the Wiesbaden date (*Bw.Th.* II, 99 [September 20, 1922]): "I'm doing *badly*. There has thus far been *nothing* on paper and not even in my head on the lectures (it all starts next Tuesday)! Only a formless waving and driving, which has almost made me physically ill . . . I'm afraid I stand on the eve of a battle of Sedan of the worst degree." See *Bw.Th.* II, 97 (September 14, 1922).

3   See Chapter 7 in this volume.

initiative of Julius Rumpf,[4] pastor of Langenschwalbach, when he invited Barth to a "pastor's retreat" in 1921. After his call to the Wiesbaden Marktkirche in the spring of 1921, he and other pastors then organized annual conferences open to all theologians in the region, which took place in Wiesbaden for the first time from September 25–28, 1922.[5] Supposedly, the invitation to Barth for a lecture on the 26th came from Rumpf personally.[6]

2. Lüneberg, September 28, 1922

In the last week of September, 1922, "several members of the theological faculty of Göttingen"[7] were invited to Lüneberg for a "continuing education seminar for those holding the office of pastor." "The evening lectures are directed toward a larger public audience, whereas the afternoon lectures are mainly for theologians. However, both are open to anyone to whom these important questions are of interest."[8] In the morning of September 28, Barth repeated his lecture from Wiesbaden. Among the audience was "an entire table filled with candidates for the office of teacher, who found themselves in the dark urge of this [100] festival of intelligence."[9] Barth later said to Thurneysen about the concluding discussion round, "Until then, everything was going well, I did not have any trouble handling the speakers in the discussion here like in Wiesbaden (who, by the way, were all very respectable!)."[10]

4   Julius Rumpf (1874–1948): In 1903–1921 he was pastor in Langenschwalbach (what is today Bad Schwalbach); 1921–1939 (with an interruption in 1934 and 1938/39 due to a suspension of the staff) pastor of the Marktkirche in Wiesbaden; 1934 chairperson of the Pastors' Emergency League of Nassau; 1936–1940 chairperson of the Regional Fraternal Council in Nassau-Hessen.

5   According to the wording of the invitation, Barth's lecture took place on the 26th at 8:30 in the morning (found in the central archive of the Evangelical Church in Hessen and Nassau 1/72). On the following Wednesday, assistant lecturer Dr. Heinrich Frick (Gießen) lectured about "Catholic and Protestant worship"; on Thursday, pastor licentiate, Herrmann Schafft (Wilhelmshöhe) on "the meaning and the inner development of the Youth Movement." See the report on the conference in the *Wiesbadner Zeitung* 75, Nr. 271 (October 3, 1922), 2f. The conference was held in the congregational hall of the Bergkirche, Steingasse 9.

6   In any case, Rumpf was the one whom Barth thanked for coming to the lecture in a letter on October 6, 1922 (KBA 9322.231). See *Bw. Th.* II, 100, 102 for Barth's remarks on his stay in Wiesbaden.

7   *Lüneburgische Anzeigen*, Nr. 224 (September 25, 1922), 3: "On Tuesday and Thursday evenings in the fellowship hall at 8:30, lectures open to the public will take place. On the 26th, Professor for Old Testament, Professor Bertholet will speak on Israel and its environment, and on the 28th, Licentiate Piper will speak on the evangelical faith."

8   *Lüneburgische Anzeigen*, Nr. 223 (September 23, 1922), 2.

9   *Bw. Th.* II, 103 (October 7, 1922).

10   *Bw. Th.* I I, 100 (September 28, 1922).

3. Emden, October 11, 1922

In a letter from May 11, 1922, the pastors Garrelt Leemhuis[11] and Diedrich Siebo Rödenbeek[12] informed Barth in the name of the moderators of the "Coetus Reformed preachers in Ostfriesland"[13] that

> from several sides the wish has been expressed to come into personal contact with you as the representative of Reformed theology at the university of our home province.[14] We imagine that it is a wish of yours as well to have the occasion to get together with this, the oldest cooperation of the Reformed pastors of Ostfriesland. Therefore we would like to kindly request that you hold for us a lecture in Emden on a topic chosen by you.[15]

Upon receiving this invitation, Barth repeated [101] his lecture on ethics in the orderly session of the Coetus on October 11, 1922. It was held in the *Konsistorienstube* of the great church.[16] After the lunch break, he repeated his "The Word of God as the Task of Theology."[17] "Fifty one members and a few candidates" were present.[18] "The 'elders' claimed that the 'Coetus' had never seen such a large assembly . . ."[19]

---

11 Garrelt Leemhuis (1871–1954): 1899–1902, pastor in Veenhusen; 1902–1947 pastor in Oldersum; 1919–1938 president of the Coetus.

12 Diedrich Siebo Rödenbeek (1873–1958): 1902–1945 pastor in Westerhusen; 1919–1934 secretary of the Coetus.

13 This group had existed since 1544, and was founded by Johannes a Lasco (1499–1561). For a history of him, see M. Schmid, *Ostfriesische Kirchengeschichte*, in *Ostfriesland im Schutze des Deiches. Beiträge zur Kultur- und Wirtschaftsgeschichte des ostfriesischen Küstenlandes*, Vol. IV, J. Ohling, ed. (Pewsum, 1974), 157ff.

14 The Reformed part of Ostfriesland belonged at that time to the Evangelical-Reformed church of the province of Hannover (today it is the Evangelical-Reformed church in Northwest Germany). The seat of the church government was Aurich. It was responsible for the administration of the honorary chair in Göttingen, which was financed by American Presbyterians and was Barth's first professorship (Busch, 135ff.; ET 123). Barth used the occasion of this stay in Ostfriesland to speak with the president of the Konsistorial, Dr. Lümko Iderhoff, and the general superintendent, Gerhard Cöper, on October 12 in Aurich regarding concerns he had about the Göttingen chair. See *Bw. Th* .II, 112 (October 16, 1922).

15 KBA 9322.132. The invitation was preceded by a lecture by Gerd Hesse Goemann (pastor in Oldenrop/Nenndorp) on April 24, 1922, for the theological "conference for Emden and the surrounding area" about the "presuppositions and foundations of Karl Barth (Göttingen)," which mainly thematized Barth's *Romans* 1922 commentary. See G.H. Goemann, "Die Anfänge Karl Barths in Ostfriesland," in *Sonntagsblatt für die evangelisch-reformierten Gemeinden*, Emden, Vol. 60 (1956), Nr. 19 (May 6, 1956), 2ff. (The entire Nr. 19 was dedicated to Barth by the Coetus for his seventieth birthday.) Thus Barth's remark to Thurneysen, "The Romans commentary is read very industriously there . . ." (*Bw. Th*. II, 111 [October 16, 1922]).

16 This church was destroyed by the Allied air raids in 1943. On its ruins, the present Schweizer Kirche was built.

17 See Chapter 7 in this volume.

18 Minutes from the protocol book of the Coetus (handwritten and unpaginated), from October 11, 1922 by Pastor Alfred Rauhaus (Weener), to the editor.

19 *Bw. Th.* II, 111 has further remarks by Barth about his stay in Emden. See ibid., 110 and *Bw. R.*, 179

4. Nordhorn, October 13, 1922

On October 13, 1922, Barth repeated this lecture in Nordhorn, "where the *Bentheimische Geistlichkeit* had gathered," among them "my *special* friends, the 'Kohlbrüggianer,' storm troopers of about four to six pastors who are saying the same thing as us, in a very *astonishing* way."[20]

5. Bochum, October 24, 1922

Johannes Müller,[21] in an auxiliary office of provincial pastor for apologetics, wrote to Barth in a letter from July 6, 1922[22] that

> The popular first Westphalian Week of Worldviews, your visit to which you unfortunately had to cancel before the end of the year, is supposed to have a follow-up in this year. May we request of you this time that you not turn us down, and speak for about two hours [102] on "revelation and faith"? The general topic should be: "revelation and the modern person" . . . You have some friends in Westphalia who would be happy to sit at your feet on this occasion. The week will be introduced on October 22nd with an opening worship, for which the general superintendent, Mr. D. Zöllner,[23] will hold the sermon. Your lecture is planned for October 24th, at half past three in the afternoon.

Barth at first agreed to the suggested topic, but then decided to repeat his Wiesbaden lecture one more time.[24] In Bochum, "a hall completely pressed full"[25] awaited him.

(October 16, 1922).

20   *Bw. Th.* II, 112 (October 16, 1922). Further details about the occasion of this lecture in Nordhorn are not known.

21   Johannes Müller (from 1924 Johannes Müller-Schwefe) (1874–1955): In 1905 he was pastor in Punschrau (Sachsen); 1911 pastor in Werne (Westfalen); 1918 pastor in Bochum, where from 1920 he was responsible for theological apologetics on the local committee for inner-provincial missions; 1921 pastor in Schwefe by Soest and at the same time auxiliary provincial pastor for apologetics; from 1927 in the provincial office of pastor for apologetics in Münster; from 1934, pastor in Klein-Quenstedt (Sachsen).

22   KBA 9322.174.

23   Wilhelm Zöllner (1860–1937): In 1886 he was pastor in Friedrichsdorf by Bielefeld; 1889 pastor in Barmen–Wupperfeld; 1897 leader of the Diaconate institution in Kaiserswerth; 1905–1931 general superintendent of Westphalia.

24   See the Introduction to this essay, p. 131.

25   See Barth's report about his stay in Bochum in *Bw. Th.* II, 116–118 (October 26, 1922). On p. 116, Barth wrote that he attended the lectures of his colleagues from Göttingen: Carl Stange's "Christianity as an Absolute Religion," and the assistant professor, Johann Wilhelm Schmidt-Japing's "Revelation and Theosophy," in the context of the "Second Westphalia Worldview Week." See also the reports in the newspapers, *Bochumer Anzeiger* and *Märkischer Sprecher*, both from October 25, 1922.

The problem of ethics is a critical question under which is placed all human action, that is, one's entire temporal existence. This question asks about the meaning and law of individual actions as well as the extent of the truth in one's existence. It makes the individual responsible for the presence of the truth in his existence. If the truth of human life comes to expression, even under the conditions placed on it by nature, it would still become problematic in light of the ethical question. The apparent "given" gets transformed into a task. That which is conceived as "being," with its demand of highest worthiness and prestige, steps[26] into the shadow of another, superior, non-being. The True, even if it were [103] the truest, must subject itself to the critical question of whether it is then also *good*.[27] The legitimacy of this question is based on the very fact that it is posed. Even the logical question, the question of the truth of things as they are, is not accidental and arbitrary, but necessary, not the object but rather the presupposition of sense experience, which is grounded in itself and nothing else. But this is the case only insofar as this question refers back to the truth of the True and so includes the ethical question, in which the thought of what-is-not-yet but should-be lays a claim on the human's life in terms of the human's act.

When the logical question, namely the question of that-which-is, is grounded as a critical one within the question of that-which-might-be, namely the question of the Good and the ethical problem, it is then no longer something that can be called into question. Therefore it makes no sense, no sense whatsoever, to logically subordinate the question of the Good to the question of the True right from the start, as if it were not the question of truth already in itself, as if it did not ground the first question (of the Good) in itself first. No sense in turning the question of obligation and rights, the question of the moral subject and object, into the question of the reality and the possibilities *of* the human as the object of our sensory experience, as if none other than this individual as such were not called into question by *the* question that is the ultimate presupposition of all sensory experiences. There is no sense at all for us to position ourselves as mere onlookers who are somehow considering the ethical question as if this very ethical question did not already have its basis in the fact that we *cannot* stop at merely considering our lives, at merely being onlookers to our actions, but rather have already been compelled to understand ourselves as the ones living our lives, as the actors of our deeds.

Not even for a moment can we lose sight of the seamless nexus of

---

26   In the earlier manuscript, this reads, "prestige, it steps." Barth corrected his copy.
27   In the earlier manuscript, this reads, "the truest were, it must." Barth corrected his copy.

being [*Seinszusammenhang*] in which we intertwine our existence and do no more than make it comprehensible, and within which the Good about which the ethical question asks is *not* given; what is given here and what is able to be given can indeed *not* as such be the Good. But this does not change the fact that our comprehensible existence within the nexus of being is precisely that which is measured on a standard that is not given at all, either with our existence itself or with anything that is given as existing concepts. [104] Nothing changes with the fact that the human as human is placed into the situation in an irredeemable way, where his "being" is understood as those activities he is responsible for; where his desires are questionable; where that-which-does-not-yet-exist wants to engross that which should be, namely, as the *truth* of the trueness of his actions.

The problem of ethics itself does not stand[28] or fall with its genesis within the context of this existence, and especially not with the attempts at a solution set up yesterday, today, or tomorrow, even if the historical-psychological processes by which the human becomes aware of the ethical question, and even if the goals, goods, and ideals of yesterday, today, or tomorrow, i.e. the answer to the ethical question that the human thinks he knows, are derivable from existing concepts or things able to be conceived, or out of contingent, secondary, non-original sources, out of fate or nature or randomness or accident, out of hunger or love. The problem of ethics fundamentally reaches out beyond its temporal emergence as well as beyond any real and possible, temporal answers. In its origin as well as its goal, it has its own right, its own dignity. It resists skepticism, which every ethical ideology is prone to, because long before the skeptics awaken, it is already the merciless crisis of all ethical ideologies. Indeed all real and possible *content* of human action, every occurrence in the fulfillment of time in the history of the individual and in society is called into question with the question of the Good.

"*What* are we supposed to do?" is the question that is asked here. This "what" directs itself aggressively and corrosively; it hollows out the entire portfolio of that which we did yesterday and what we will do tomorrow; it lays everything on the scale. The moment it stumbles across given or real action, it splits the good from the evil right then and there in order to immediately place exactly that which is recognized as the good as well as the evil under the same critical question, like it has never happened before, now or in eternity. We start noticing absolute life when the ethical problem poses itself; but can it mean anything else for us except

---

28   In the earlier manuscript, this reads, "the problem of ethics itself, it stands . . ." Barth corrected his copy.

that we must die! Absolute edification rises up; but how can it complete itself in any way except through [105] a gradual degradation! Absolute infinity opens itself up; an infinity which would be better called the end of all things.

By posing this risky question, "What are we supposed to do?" the human has made himself available to and has placed himself into the service of this absolute. He has entered into a relation with it, a step next to which the entire range of every sort of interaction with the invisible powers of the heavenly or demonic becomes child's play. Indeed this question has as its object human action, existence, and interaction in the world and in every possible underworld. But if the human makes this question his own, he has not only admitted that he has noticed the eye that is watching him from beyond all worlds, but that he *also* sees all that this eternal eye sees, the weight of the contents of our entire lives, the crisis in which we find ourselves in every deed in every moment. The human is not only completely called into question, but he *himself* must pose the question that, if he properly understands it, actually cancels him out. By asking himself this simple question the human sets in motion his association with the *eternal* observer of his life in a specific way. Precisely because of this, the question inevitably becomes the end of all his *own* contemplation, even the end of contemplation itself. With this question, the human sets in motion his relationship to *God* and takes the necessary, uncanny, radical consequences upon himself. If we could conceive of an individual who in all seriousness gives himself to this question in real correspondence to the question's absolute content, we would say he were bound to God, lost in God. But if he does this, how could we think of him in any other way than as knowingly and willingly *dying?* On the other hand, how should the knowing and willing death of a human (as we know the human) be that which somehow could seriously correspond to the absolute content of this question? What awaits us in the problem of ethics is the mystery of the impossibility of humans as we know them, of the living and the perishing; the mystery that *this* human can only perish before God.

Now one thing must be cleared up. We do not have the choice to pose or not pose to ourselves the problem of ethics. Therefore we do not have the choice to accept or shake off the crisis of our lives' content that comes with this problem. Nor do we have the choice to take or leave the unavoidable relationship to God that lies within this problem. The problem of ethics [106] does not wait for our ethical reflections. The crisis in which our deeds find themselves does not somehow become critical only once we are ready. Our relationship to God does not somehow wait for our so-called religious experiences. All this comes *first* in our most fundamental considerations; they are *a priori* part of the plan. We *have* already posed the problem of ethics to ourselves. We already *stand* in that crisis and relationship. Our reflections and critique, our so-called experiences, can only consist in the fact that we bow down once again before the truth that exists without our contribution; that we look the facts in the face; that we *are* asked and *have* asked. There is not one moment in which we are released from the burden of this question. We *live*, indeed, from moment to moment.

And life means *doing*, even if it is by chance a not-doing. A life which was not identical to our actions would be absolutely incomprehensible to us; it would not be *our* life. All action, however, stands unavoidably under the question of meaning, order, and truth. It is a question that is inherent in the goal of every act. This question is *not* exhausted by the knowledge of the meaning and order of our action by virtue of its orientation towards this goal, the next goal, or the final goal. For in the final goal itself lies the question about its own goal, and beyond that, the question about the epitome of all goals, which indeed, is the question of the Good that reaches out beyond all being. This larger question slumbers in every temporal phenomenon and question of "What are we supposed to do? No arbitrary or temporal "that!" can give a satisfactory answer to *this particular* "What?" because it is the necessary and eternal "What?" And with the question comes the crisis of the content of our existence, and with this crisis, our relationship to God. We *stand* in this relationship. Let us now see how we can find our way through this.

What kind of sense can it make to speak of the problem of ethics *today*! Apparently, at its most basic, the only sense it makes is in its emphatic reminder to us that this problem cannot simply deal with a perspective on life and the world or other harmless things. Rather, it deals with our very existence, our most personal and most real situation in this moment; it deals with our plight, the actuality of which we cannot even for a moment abstract from if we really want to speak of *it* and not of an entirely different problem. It does not deal with *a* problem but *the* problem. When we say "the problem of ethics *today*," we want to override, if at all possible, every temporal distance, every distance from the onlooker [107] which could save us from our plight. But obviously we do this with the reminder [*Gegenerinnerung*] that we can only be partly successful. For we do not know of a present time that does not immediately split into past and future; a present time which it not itself a time, even if it is *our* present time.

We must also keep in mind that it is dangerous to put the perennial problem of all temporality into the perspective of a particular time, even if it is our time. The problem of ethics today can, in fact must, not be anything different than the problem which it has been and which it will be throughout all time. Through its being posed to us, we enter into *the* history and community where there is no becoming and no transforming. We cannot do anything different today than what Jacob did by wrestling with the Lord: "I will not leave you until you bless me!" [Gen. 32.26]. We cannot occupy ourselves with this problem in a way that is any more historically appropriate than by fixing our eyes with all earnestness on its timelessness, or rather on its address to every era. The temptation from which we must protect ourselves today is a philosophy of revolution[29] or even a philosophy of reaction.

But none of this can release us from the task of facing the ethical question only as humans of *our* time and none other, bearing in mind that by this we mean not our *time*, but the *present*, the eternal "between the times."[30] Why can't we allow ourselves to be [108] exempt from gazing upon *our* time? Because we are not to be separated from the ethical question; we are the ones being asked and the ones doing the asking; we are the very definite human individuals to whom the ethical question is posed, the ones who are disquieted and pressured by this very question. We are these very definite human individuals as people of *our* time. As surely as the problem of ethics is posed to humans as a question of existence, it is posed to them in the light of a definite time, *their* time; they deal with it in a way that is corresponding to a *particular time, to this* time. That being said, however, we add that this particularity can be nothing other than a particular emphasis and underscoring within the problematic that remains the same throughout all time.

---

29   On October 7, 1922 (shortly after the writing of the lecture), Barth wrote in a newsletter to his friends: "Hirsch attempted a controversy with us, mentioning our names ... in his epilogue to the second edition of *Deutschlands Schicksal* with the title 'philosophy of revolution.' Not very instructive ..." (*Bw. Th.* II, 106). See Emanuel Hirsch, *Deutschlands Schicksal. Staat, Volk und Menschheit im Lichte einer ethischen Geschichtsansicht*, Göttingen 1922, 2nd ed. (Göttingen: Vandenhoeck & Rupprecht, 1922), 159, 161.

30   This is an allusion to Friedrich Gogarten's "Zwischen den Zeiten," *CW*, 34 (1920): cols. 374–378 (reprinted in *Anfänge II*, 95–101; *BDT* 277–282). In August of that year, Gogarten, Thurneysen, and Barth founded a journal with the same name, which was published from 1923 until 1933 under the editorial leadership of Georg Merz. At the time of this lecture, the title had, however, become controversial again, because Gogarten wanted to change it to "The Word." See *Bw. Th.* II, 111 (October 16, 1922). See also *Romans* 1922, 485 (1999 ed., 483; 526; ET 499):

This tension between the "back then" of our peaceful being and the "now" of the disturbing memory of our non-being is *always* there; the tension is *always* there between the times of the "already" occurred revelation, the "already" done deeds, of the "already" known God on the one side and on the other side the times of the thoughts, expectation, and looking forward to the existential becoming of the only supposedly "already" existing, namely, of the eternal moment of the appearance, the parousia, and the presence of Jesus Christ (483 [1999 ed., 481]).

Here Barth speaks of the "'*moment*' between the times," and from the "*present* 'between' the times."

The particularity of our time lays in the fact that the problem of ethics is a concern of much greater measure than it seems to have been in earlier times. Simply said, it is a real *problem*. There are no longer many humble hours left for us to *imagine* that we are able to escape the question, "What are we supposed to do?"; and not many more hours where we become aware of this question as easy and solvable, where it is anything other than a burden and need. I would like to spare myself and you from "reporting in the newspaper what we ourselves have experienced with a shudder."[31] With the Negro standing on the Rhine,[32] and Lenin [109] where the czar once stood,[33] and the dollar topping out over 2,000,[34] there is no need to comment on the fact that the question as to our next move has already been posed with quite a bit more gravity than it was at the pinnacle of the turn of the century, in the glitter and security of the Wilhelminian era. Even the deeper problematic that stands behind those very moves cannot remain untouched by all this. It has become deeply problematic for us; difficult, bitter, and painful. By saying this, I do not want to suggest that this question was not difficult, bitter, and painful for those who have gone before us. But one cannot get past the general conclusion that we are more perplexed, more out of sorts, and more insecure compared to the generation that was over by the time 1914 came around. We are troubled by the ethical question today. We sense more clearly the unavoidable final sense of being at a loss, out of sorts, and insecure. And without wanting to deny that the former generation also sensed these things, we are amazed that they, in

31   Friedrich von Schiller, *Wallenstein. Die Piccolomini*, V, 1059 (Act 2, scene 7): "Spare us from reporting in the newspaper what we ourselves have experienced with a shudder."

32   The First Moroccan Division was stationed on the Rhine as a French occupation power according to the Versailles Peace Treaty (1919). Several angry protests were made against their presence. See B.E.D. Morel, *Der Schrecken am Rhein,* 3rd ed., (Berlin 1922); A. Ritter von Eberlin, *Ein Welt-Problem: Schwarze am Rhein* (Heidelberg 1921); the "Deutsche Notbund gegen die schwarze Schmach" (Barth himself was encouraged to join this group). See *Bw. Th.* II, 75 (May 9, 1922): a monthly journal was published in Munich from 1921–1926 under the title "Die Schmach am Rhein." On the occasion of his stay in Wiesbaden for the giving of this lecture, Barth saw "Moroccans and Annamites" (= Vietnamese), members of the occupation troops. See *Bw. Th.* II, 102 (October 7, 1922).

33   The 1917 "October Revolution" in Russia sealed the fate of czarism. Under Vladimir Ilyich Lenin as the chairperson of the Council of the People's Commissars, and the leader of the Bolshevik party, the Russian Soviet Socialist Federal Republic, was founded in July 1918. In December 1922, the Union of the Soviet Socialist Republics (U.S.S.R) was founded, with Lenin as its leader until his death in 1924.

34   "20,000" was mistakenly printed in *ZZ*. When Barth gave this lecture for the first time on September 26, 1922, the U.S. dollar was valued at 1,460 German Reichsmarks. With a reference to the repeat of this lecture on October 24 in Bochum, Barth reported, "The new increase of the dollar in these last days gave the entire lecture a strange feeling of the end of the world" (*Bw. Th.* II, 116). Inflation was advancing so quickly that on the day Barth gave this lecture in Bochum, the U.S. dollar had already reached a value of 4,600 Reichsmarks.

their behavior and speaking, let on so remarkably little of such things.

Allow me to characterize our present era with a few points. There was a time when the problem of ethics was something that used to be called an academic problem, at least by the theologians and philosophers. Whatever pessimists, grumblers, literary types, and other agitators, inspired by Nietzsche, Ibsen, or Tolstoy, liked to argue, there was at least an entity of human culture in that era which was arranging and building itself up into a State, an economy, technology, and science. It did not swerve from the general line of progress. It was romanticized and lionized through art, and apparently it projected above and beyond itself through morals and religion into yet higher regions, the existence [110] of which, however, was substantially simplified by the question of the Good, and the sharpness of which, in any case, was dulled. Ethics were done well against this background.

At its most basic, however, it was not really about asking *what* was to be done, as if one did not know what to do. Rather, it was a matter of asking about whether the more philosophical or theological way, the Kantian or Schleiermacherian way, would provide the enlightening formula for doing that Good which was to be done, that which was quite evidently to be done in the certain, infinite need for improvement in culture as a whole. This was a culture which was quite evidently infinitely capable of improvement, whereby the avoidance or abolishing of the great New Testament obstacles to such a perspective on the state of affairs only made the matter more interesting, particularly for the theologians. Could one imagine, even for a moment — to name only two examples — the ethics of the *Ritschlian* school[35] without the solid background of the merrily ascending German middle class at the time of the country's consolidation under Bismarck's rule? Or the ethic of *Troeltsch*, with its great "as well as!" without the background of the Christian faith, and in particular the impact of Christian Socialism, which did not entirely renounce the culture of capitalist economics, and which found its prophet in the likes of Friedrich Naumann?[36] [111] To put it another way, in which of the

---

35   See for example, Theodor Haering, *Das christliche Leben. Ethik.* (Calw: Vereinsbuch, 1902); Wilhelm Herrmann, *Ethik* (Tübingen: 1901); Otto Kirn, *Grundriß der Theologischen Ethik* (Leipzig: Deichert, 1906); Hans Hinrich Wendt, *System der Christlichen Lehre* (Göttingen: Vandenhoeck und Ruprecht, 1906), 408ff. Cf. *KD* III/4, 347; *CD* III/4, 307, where Barth comments on "the authoritative German theologians at the turn of our century from the school of A. Ritschl ... W. Herrmann, Th. Haering, Otto Kirn, H.H. Wendt," who "were all true German nationalists in the sense of the post-Bismarckian era."

36   On the political proximity of Ernst Troeltsch (1865–1923) to Friedrich Naumann (1860–1919), see the numerous documents by Hartmut Ruddies, "Karl Barth und Ernst Troeltsch. Aspkete eines unterbliebenen Dialogs," in *Troeltsch-Studien*, Vol. 4, *Umstrittene Moderne. Die Zukunft der Neuzeit im Urteil der Epoche Ernst Troeltschs*, Horst Renz and Friedrich Wilhelm Graf, eds., (Gütersloh:

well-known ethics of that time do we find the question, "What are we supposed to do?" posed in any other way than that which fits almost exactly the answer to all the preceding questions about the State, society, and Church, namely, "*That* is what we want to do!"? With all the faltering, wobbling, and fading that has appeared in the meantime, any such background that would give us nerve to answer the ethical question with a similar "*That!*" is gone. We believe we have seen fewer occurrences of the Good, which would seem to make the question easier. Our "What?" has become more hollow and emptier. We sense more clearly that we are not spared from *asking*, with bitter seriousness, as ones who do not know, "What are we supposed to do?"

Further, there was a time which essentially thought out the ethical problem with Kant and still more with the cheerful Fichte as an expression and witness to the special worthiness and majesty of the human being. They felt happy and uplifted, not insecure and pressured, when they spoke about what we should do out of who we are, and when they spoke about norms based on things 'given,' when they spoke about history out of nature. Back then, they saw themselves on the safe ground of the distinction between humans and animals, or even on the safe ground of the cultured individual compared to the wild. They even believed they had found the Archimedean point with which a material world- and life-view in its desolation and godlessness could be lifted from the hinges. Today, we wonder whether such a patent of nobility, which was thought to be able to certify humans on the basis of their proper knowledge of the transcendental origins of the ethical problem, might just have been obtained by fraud. It makes us think that this problem is nothing more than the *problem* of humanity.

Then when and where does the question of the Good begin to mean something other than the *judgment* upon humanity as we know it, even upon *moral* humanity as we know it? *We* apparently have gotten to know the savage and immoral human. More specifically, we have *not* gotten to know the moral human in a way that would make us proud of his achievements. We remember from Genesis chapter three that the possibility of being able to distinguish between good and evil [cf. Gen. 2.17], that the majesty and dignity of the human being based on such distinguishing, while establishing his superiority over nature, could just

Gütersloher Verlagshaus Mohn, 1987), 230ff., esp. 241–245. On 242, Ruddies writes, "Troeltsch worked together with Naumann in the evangelical-socialist Congress, he held war lectures next to Naumann, belonged to Naumann's party as a member of Parliament and after Naumann's death, temporarily cooperated in the editing of the journal, 'Hilfe'." Here, Barth makes a further play on Naumann's *Neudeutsche Wirtschaftspolitik* (Berlin-Schöneberg: 1902), and the fully and newly worked-over, substantially thicker work of 1906 which carries the same title.

as well mean the human's fall from God.

Moreover, there was a time which regarded dogmatics as difficult compared to the easier knowledge of ethics. [112] Paul's letter to the Romans was considered to be dark and burdened by the issues contemporary to it, but the Sermon on the Mount was seen as enlightened, preaching very much to the present time. It was considered an apparent benefit to reduce the Gospel to a few religious-ethical categories like trust in God and love for one's neighbor [37] from its discountenances of the superfluous metaphysical efforts of the Church Fathers and the Scholastics. They believed they had figured out Christianity by basically presenting it as a religious ethic and could warmly recommend it to our race of humanity as especially worthy of praise.

To us, however, the proven impossibility of Christianity precisely as *ethics*, or rather, the proven impossibility of the deeds of our European race, precisely in the face of the *ethic* of Christianity, has been placed in an awkward situation and called into question. This has suggested that maybe the impossibilities of the old-style Christian dogmatics still correspond more closely to our real situation than the comfortable assertions of the possibility of so-called "following Jesus." Shall I continue? The view beyond all that is human, which the ethical problem opened up for those who felt the need for an apologetic for God, spirit, and the Beyond, was at one time a comfort and a foothold. But now it is merely human and it frightens and shakes us to the core. We fear that the problem of ethics truly and inexorably points to a realm beyond all that is human, including our most beloved religious ideologies. We fear that it is not so easy to utilize apologetics in order to come to the help of *humans* who are deeply threatened by this very ethical problem.

Further, at one time there was a Schleiermacher, [38] a Rothe, [39] a Troeltsch [40] who could [113] not help but be fair at any cost to the mani-

---

37   The conceptual pair, "trust in God and love for the neighbor" came up in the young Barth again and again, but was seen for the first time in 1915/16 in his confirmation curriculum, *Konfirmandenunterricht 1909–1921*, J. Fangmeier, ed. (Zürich: TVZ, 1987), 69; and in a polemical sense again in *Romans* 1919, 209, 396; *Romans* 1922, 356 (1999 ed., 388); ET 372. See Paul Wernle, *Einführung in das theologische Studium*, 2nd ed. (Tübingen: Mohr, 1911), 175, "One must hear the same joyfulness in God in the Pauline apologetic and the same love of the neighbor in the Pauline work in the church which Jesus blessed and incited." Wernle also spoke of the "spiritual kingly reign in which the faith in God and the love of neighbor that Jesus had, is supposed to take over every heart" (493).

38   See Friedrich Schleiermacher, *Die christliche Sitte nach den Grundsätzen der evangelischen Kirche im Zusammenhange dargestellt* (from Schleiermacher's hand-written legacy and students' notes of his lectures), Ludwig Jonas, ed., in Schleiermacher's *Sämtliche Werke*, I, Vol. 12 (Berlin: G. Reimer, 1884).

39   See Richard Rothe, *Theologische Ethik*, 3 Vols. (Wittenberg: Zimmermann, 1845–1848) and the 2nd ed., 5 Vols. (1867–1871).

40   On Ernst Troeltsch, who did not write a systematic ethics, but dealt again and again with

fold riches of life's content and to the entire fullness of creation and the creature. They were so fair to all this, in fact, that Christianity, with its somewhat different intentions, fell into a most difficult housing shortage, so that we can no longer see the rich man in the modern European; we only see the poor Lazarus [cf. Lk. 16.19-31]. What has now become urgent is our concern about how ethics are to be fair to the truth of the *Creator*. For now, the field of ethics has taken on for us the image of a modern battlefield. The entire foreground in the face of the actual fronts has become frighteningly empty. Whereas at one time Ritschl and his followers saw a pure clarity in dealing with humans who trust in God for their calling, for their participation in the kingdom of God,[41] we see the deepest darkness. We often want to say with the letter to the Hebrews [10.31] that it is terrible to fall into the hands of the living God, instead of the much-recommended "Commend your ways . . ."[42]

I will stop here. It is not about the individual points I just named, but about the *line* drawn by them, from which it becomes clear that the problem of ethics today is a lack of peace, a pressure, an attack. It is the uncanny, disturbing appearance of a *strange*, uncomplimentary guest[43] in the sensitive circle of our lives.

Whoever seriously poses the question today, "What are we supposed to do?" and wants to answer it must have *noticed* something of this change in the situation, whether one now still reads too much of Dostoyevsky and Kierkegaard or not. [114] It is not appropriate to continue speaking in a secure and casual manner as if nothing has happened. The time of *these* ethics is once and for all *over*. Whoever wants to be secure now must have become especially *insecure* at one time. And whoever wants to speak now must have at one time *been silent*. For, in the meantime, something *has* happened. It is not the end of the world and not the death of the old human, as some have thought under the first impression of so many rapidly changing events. In the face of the confidence with which the human individual believes in himself, there is now the writing, large and clear, on the wall [cf. Dan. 5.25].

Of course, it is not about skepticism in the face of the authority and urgency of the ethical problem, for we think we see better than ever how

---

fundamental ethical questions, see the presentation of Walther Köhler, *Ernst Troeltsch* (Tübingen: Mohr, 1941), esp. 192–219.

41 See Albrecht Ritschl, *Unterricht in der christlichen Religion* (Bonn: Marcus, 1875), 53f., (new edition edited by Gerhard Ruhbach [Gütersloh, 1966, 30f.]). Among the followers of Ritschl (see above Note 25, p. 141), cf. Theodore Haering, *Das christliche Leben. Ethik*, 2nd ed. (Calw: Vereinsbuch, 1907), 214–222; Wilhelm Herrmann *Ethik*, 118–122; Otto Kirn, *Grundriß der Theologischen Ethik* (1906), 48f; Hans Hinrich Wendt, *System der Christlichen Lehre*, 565–570.

42 See the beginning of the song by Paul Gerhardt, "Befiehl du deine Wege" (*EKG* 294; *KGB* 275).

43 See L. da Ponte and W.A. Mozart, *Don Giovanni*, Act 2, Finale 1.

irrefutable it is. Truly, it is also not about skepticism toward the fact that the ethical problem involves our relationship to God. On the contrary: It is the very fact of this relationship which *frightens* us today, which fills us with skepticism toward *ourselves*, toward *humans*, and toward our human relationship to the idea of an ethical personality, an ethical goal. This is now *our* situation, and we dare not abstract from it. For, how could we solve the ethical problem of *our* situation if we have comprehended that the *ethical* problem is only a problem posed to *us*? It is not about absolutizing the impressions and voices of this time. They are relative, like everything else in history. Perhaps our children and children's children will be lucky enough to again view life in a more harmonious and naïve fashion than we do, as long as they do not totally neglect to see more clearly than those who went before us that which is almost impossible to overlook today, namely, that the problem of ethics is the sickness of humanity: the sickness unto *death*.[44] For we do not regard this as a mere temporary effect of the post-War period, but rather as a temporally conditioned and limited form of a captivating insight into a part of the truth which has been won — an insight that by all means would rather be forgotten. As we have seen, it is based within the context of the matter at hand and it will now be developed in connection to the matter at hand. [115] As humans of *our* time, however, we are not only permitted but required to use *this* insight. The one thing valid for *all* time cannot be accessible to us in any other way than in the form of the particular, in which it speaks to *us*.

One more observation: When I interpret the problem of ethics as the crisis of humanity, as humanity's sickness unto death, and when in so doing I describe what is particular about our present time, namely that it turns us away *from* every other easygoing interpretation to *this*, I ask that we do not neutralize this particularity by means of a *theological-philosophical* process. Indeed, one such operation is "crisis," a term with which I am familiar and which is possible and appropriate for any time. I have heard that "crisis" is a dialectical concept which not only allows an inversion but demands an inversion, which *takes* away every false dignity from the human deed and thus *gives* the human deed a new — no — its original dignity, which not only means "question" but also could mean "*answer*," not only abolishing but *establishing*. We will need to speak of this process as well, but I want to warn you at the outset about hastily invoking the concept of dialectic for the sake of logical symmetry and perfection, as if this inversion corresponded to the all-too-real *reality* for us humans today, as if we were in the position to accept without hesitation

---

44   See Jn 11.4 and the title of the work by Søren Kirekegaard, *The Sickness Unto Death* (1849).

the "No" of the ethical problem as a "Yes," or as if we were in the even bolder position to tackle this problem from a height which lay on the other side of "Yes" and "No."

Holding out the possibility of the reality of an ultimate inversion (but not by *us*!) among other possibilities, we are assigned a *definite* position, and namely one that is "deeper in the 'No' than in the 'Yes.'"[45] Through the problem of ethics, *we* know *more* about the negation, more about the judgment over everything human, than about any paradoxical justification or new possibility that it might bring, for surely we do not want to be blind to all that to which it witnesses today. [116] It seems that words of *comfort* are not permitted to me — even if I based it on something thoughtful! — because the need and confusion of millions of people and our own dilemma is *so great*. Therefore, let us take the truth from the side where it shows itself, in the ways that it presents itself to us who are looking to the streets, fully aware that even *then*, *precisely* then, we are dealing with the *entire* truth.

But now let us return to the basic consideration that may be a sole deciding factor. The problem of ethics is the dangerous, deadly *attack* on humans. It is the question posed to humanity, the answers to which are questions themselves. It only gives an answer that the human himself cannot even ask. The human cannot live where only questions and more questions are asked. But he also cannot build his existence upon *the* answer, which is so final in its nature that it cannot be an answer for him at all.

We can gain clarity about the actuality and consequences of this attack from the perspective of the questioning *subject*, and best orient ourselves to it based on the ethic of *Kant*,[46] in which this side of the matter appears in a uniquely sharp light. What I am referring to here is Kant's basing of the concept of the moral personality on the idea of the autonomous will. He taught that the only will which can be called good is one that defines itself based on a law that is *pure form*, without any content. For, only a law that displaces all arbitrariness, which is universally valid,

---

45   See Chapter 3, p. 88 in this volume. See also *W.G.Th.* 59; *Anfänge* I, 28: "We put up with the awareness of this tragedy in our situation. The tears are closer to *us* than the smile. *We* stand more deeply in the 'No' than in the 'Yes.'" See also *Romans* 1919, 216.

46   Barth summarizes the basic lines of the ethical teaching of Kant in the following remarks, especially as they are drawn out in Kant's *Kritik der praktischen Vernunft* (1788), and *Grundlegung zur Metaphysik der Sitten* (1785), in Kant's *Werke in sechs Bänden*, Vol. 4, W. Weischedel, ed. (Darmstadt, 1970); ET *Critique of Practical Reason*, T.K. Abbott, trans. (New York: Prometheus Books, 1996), *Fundamental Principles of the Metaphysic of Ethics*, Otto Manthey-Zorn, trans. (New York: Appleton-Century, 1938).

which is conceivable as a law of humanity, can be "good." To displace all arbitrariness leaves only the pure form of the obligatory moral law as such. By contrast, a *material* will, determined by the demand of this or that *object*, characterizes itself as being individually arbitrary, as self-love, as heteronomous. The good will directs itself away from every finite purpose and therefore away from every desire for such purposes, out of a pure, immediate esteem for the *ultimate purpose*, which is *identical* with the categorical *imperative* of duty. [117]

Kant sees the human, whose will is determined in this way, as being grounded in the intelligible world of freedom, with its own causality that is superior to that of nature. The human[47] is the moral personality, the subject of the deed to which the ethical question refers, and therefore the human is the subject which the ethical problem brings up in the first place. The seriousness with which this question is shot through is seldom spoken of more clearly. But if it is the human who is grounded in the world of freedom, who raises this ethical question, and who places himself as the subject of the deeds of which the ethical problem speaks, what then shall become of all the real and possible *ways to answer* this question, out of all the real and possible *actions* of humans?

To state it clearly, does this subject then somehow bring the causality of the world of freedom with him into the world of nature where the actions of humanity as we know it play out! And can *this* subject be conceived as being identical in a comprehensible way, in a way that can be experienced, with the human as we know him? Does it, therefore, come to a will and activity of the human as we know him, which is directed purely to the observance of the law and not defined at all through a demand of this or that object? In other words, does it come to a will and an activity *of the* human whom we dare name "*I*" or "*we*" which is directed immediately to the ultimate purpose — a purpose which in itself is not a purpose at all but the epitome of everything for which we aim? Kant strictly held back from making any positive assertions in this direction, and this is what makes his ethics so credible. A personality whose will is governed by the idea of humanity, and who therefore has a *pure, autonomous, good* will, and *moral* personality, who has stepped over the threshold of the world of freedom into our world, has never existed anywhere, and will never exist anywhere. It is certainly impossible to imagine or conceive of a human without interests, or of a human with an interest in the moral law as such. And thus it is impossible to track down a human will and deed that sometime, somewhere has been determined purely by practical reason.

47   In an earlier manuscript this reads "It." Barth corrected his copy.

According to Kant, freedom is a *presupposition* which is completed
when the human becomes conscious of a duty that is actually different
from what can only ever be imagined as his desiring will. But what
does [118] completion of this presupposition mean? Kant protected
himself from the kind of Titanism we later see in Fichte, who claims,
"One decision — and I am superior to nature!"[48] As if acquiring this
superiority only needed a tug at some depth of the soul or conscience!
No, if we dare to set freedom as the causality of *our* will and deeds here,
then it is about a presupposition, an *a priori* in the strictest sense. Even if
we have with good reason an *idea* about this freedom, we nevertheless
do not have the slightest *knowledge* of it. We do not know any main-
spring of our will or some other imaginable one that could be suitable
as freedom and freedom-producing. Obviously, we are only *cognizant*
of the stimulation of our appetites, which do not come from freedom
and do not lead into freedom. The only human we can *know* is the
one who proves with all of his desires and possessions that he wants
and has that he is not the personality grounded in the world of freedom. We can *comprehend* only the incomprehensibility of the categorical
imperative.

This is where the ethics of Kant reaches its peak: in the doctrine of
the *postulates*.[49] It peaks in the postulate of *God*, that is, in a final unity of
the kingdom of freedom and the kingdom of nature, and therefore also
in the unity of morality and blessedness. It also peaks in the postulate
of *freedom*, that is, the true determination of ourselves as physical beings
through ourselves as rational beings. It peaks in the [119] postulate of
immortality, that is, in the harmonizing of our real aptitude for the moral
law with an infinitely unending process of sanctification.

What exactly do these postulates — which indeed all say the same

48   It appears that Barth summarized a central thought of Fichte here. See Johann Gottlieb Fichte, *Die
      Bestimmung des Menschen*, revised by Erich Fuchs on the basis of the edition by Fritz Medicus, 5th
      ed., in *PhB*, Vol. 226 (Hamburg: Meiner, 1979), 31, where there is a reflection upon the conflicting
      systems of freedom and determinism:

      . . . according to this, the capacity and effectiveness of my senses are subject to the dominion
      of nature; they are continuously set in motion by the same powers which brought them forth,
      a motion which my thoughts can only ever watch. According to the present state of things,
      this ability, once it has been available, falls under the dominion of a liberating power which is
      superior to nature and all its laws, namely the power of the concept of goals, and of the will.

      Fichte adds:

      I *am* immortal, everlasting, infinite, as long as I take hold of the decision to obey the laws of
      reason; I shall not first *become* it [. . .] I reach eternity through that decision, and peel away the
      life in dust and all other life which still could be ahead of me, and set myself high above it (125).
49   For more on these "postulates" or "regulative ideas of reason," which Kant mentioned again and
      again, see especially his *Kritik der praktischen Vernunft*, 107–302; ET 147–160.

thing — actually mean, other than that Kant sees the human being called upon in the most unheard-of manner through a challenge directed at the human's natural will? But at the same time the human cannot tackle this challenge in any other way than with the aid of a still much more unheard-of act of faith. In this act of faith, he must think, *first*, of a God as a warrantor of this challenge that mocks the reality of humans. *Secondly*, he must think of himself as capable of adopting this challenge as his own. *Third* and finally, he must think of his actual will and action as at least approaching the content of this challenge (under the presupposition of an infinite series of moments in time). For now, let us put aside the difficulty of the fact that the challenge of such an act of faith levied in this theory of postulates is truly more impossible, more superhuman than the moral challenge which it is supposed to reinforce. I do not clearly see the extent to which Kant gave an account of this difficulty. In any case, once again: If this act of faith, which points on all sides into infinity, establishes and makes up the moral personality, then what will become of that which we have characterized as "I" or "we" in some moment of time? What will become of the real human as we know him if we can only *believe* in a human who alone is good? Is not this singularly good person the overcoming of all the predicates of the human as we know him? Is the action of *this human* the negation of all *real* acting in history? Is the norm of *his* action the disintegration of all *possible* norms? Which *answer* to the ethical question, which human act, could, from this perspective — and it *must* be seen from this perspective — evade the fate of transforming itself into a new set of *questions*?

How could such an idealistic ethic unfold other than as a *critique* of all other ethics? What is its deepest presupposition other than the knowledge of the *bondage* of the human will in regard to the Good, the *bondage* of the will [*servum arbitrium*]?[50] And when questions, ever new questions, are the final thing that the human can find as the answer to the [120] ethical question, then how can he *live*? Can the human only live from questions? Can he somehow do it? Somehow with stoic resignation under whatever circumstances he finds herself? Somehow falling into God's left hand saying, "The truth is for You alone!"?[51] Or is there another way?

---

50   See Martin Luther, *De servo arbitrio* (1525), WA 18: 600–787; *LW* 33: 15–297.

51   This is an allusion to Gotthold Ephraim Lessing, *Eine Duplik* (1778), in his *Gesammelte Werke*, Vol. 8, Paul Rilla, ed. (Berlin: 1956), 27:

> If God held the entire truth in his closed right hand, and in his closed left hand the individual drive which always stirs for the truth — although with the addition that I will always and forever will go the wrong way — and said to me, "Choose!" I would fall into his left hand and say, "Father, give it to me! The pure truth is indeed only for you alone!"

One can approach the situation from the perspective of the ethical *object*. With this, I would like to touch upon the apparently — but only apparently — obscure idea of the *thousand-year reign*. This has become relevant for many of our contemporaries — including me — in the form of a socialist hope for the future. It played a role in Kant,[52] and is by no means something that can be circumvented by those who consider the ethical problem with any seriousness (despite Article 17 of *The Augsburg Confession* with its "condemnation"[53]). It is about the thought of a *goal of earthly history* which has no prejudice toward hope of an eternal life in a new world. Just as the ethical question as an individual question is by no means a question about the individual (which we have just seen), but about that which is generally valid and generally human, so it includes, more or less determined by itself, the question of an historical *ideal*. It is a question about a *final condition* that does not lay outside of time but inside it, and which is to be actualized inside of time. It is a question about an interpretation of human *society* based on our usual stammering about [121] truth and justice, spirit and love, peace and freedom. It is already contained in the "we" that stands in the question: "What are we supposed to do?"

In that the individual tries to set himself as the subject of the ethical question, he connects himself to his *fellow* humans, and he places himself as the *subject* of the *community*. But that means he more or less knowingly sets what he does as the ethical *object*, as a goal of *history*. Ethics cannot exist without millennialism — even if only a tiny bit of it — just as it can exist even less without the idea of a moral personality. Whoever claims with a cheerful heart to be completely free from this "Jewish opinion" can be said to not yet truly see, or no longer see, the ethical problem. When the question of "What are we supposed to do?" is taken seriously, then the event in time, both the outer as well as the inner event, ceases to be in the "givenness." It will itself become a question, and remain a question all along the line. This question may not be killed off from the start by

---

52   See for example, Kant, *Die Religion innerhalb der Grenzen der bloßen Vernunft*, Bd. IV, 802; ET *Religion Within the Boundaries of Mere Reason*, Allen Wood, trans. (Cambridge/New York: Cambridge University Press, 1998), 139:

> The appearance of the Antichrist, the millennium, the announcement of the proximity of the coming of the end of the world could, before reason, adopt its appropriate symbolic meaning, and the latter as an ... event not to be seen before this; it expresses very well the necessity for every time to stand ready, but in fact ... to see us every time really as citizens called to a divine (ethical) state.

53   *The Augsburg Confession* (1530), Article 17, "Concerning the Return of Christ for Judgment": "They also condemn others who are now spreading Jewish opinions, that before the resurrection of the dead the godly will take possession of the kingdom of the world, while the ungodly are suppressed everywhere" (*BC*, 51: 5–8; *BSLK* 72: 5–9).

someone saying that its responsibility lies on the other side of all temporality, as if that were obvious. No. By all means, the ethical question must be valid for an event in *time* if it is meant seriously. Let one beware, lest one limit this occurrence in time to a matter of the right inner disposition or to the personal morality of the individual. However closely or distantly it stands in relation to the possibility for an *answer* is its own concern. We have no authority or basis to draw boundaries around the *question* that is directed at us. It inexorably directs us as much to the idea of a pure will as to the idea of a totality of good action. And this totality is obviously what is meant by the idea of the millennium and all of its derivatives. It is therefore not to be snuffed out.

It is necessary in this context for me to add here a word concerning the understanding of my countryman, *Leonhard Ragaz*,[54] from whom I am separated by not a few things aside from this. Should being an unabashed non-Enthusiast,[55] and *not* believing in the Social State and world peace in the depths of one's heart, already be [122] a sign of ethical maturity?[56] In any case, skepticism does not allow itself to be ethically based upon the "what should be." And again, I see many people whose future ideal is different from that of Ragaz only by way of a certain narrowing of the field of vision and therefore only by way of having somewhat different shades than his. If they want to content themselves with a future of Germany or the Church or faith-generating missionary activities, for example, don't they have to ask themselves whether it could be permitted, perhaps even necessary, to make the radius somewhat bigger, or to set the circle of hope on a different point, and to consider the People's Alliance[57]

54 After a short period as a pastor in the Bündner congregation in Flerden-Urmein-Tschappina and Chur, and then as religion instructor at the Canton school in Chur, Leonhard Ragaz (1868–1945) was called in 1902 to a position of associate pastor at the Basel Munster, which was under the direction of the Free Reformed church. In 1921 he gave up his position as professor for theology in Zurich, which he took up in 1908, in order to dedicate himself to the education of society and the public. On Barth's relationship to Ragaz, see *Bw. Th.* I, 538 and II, 733 (the index). On Ragaz's representation of the Social State, see in particular his book, *Die neue Schweiz. Ein Programm für Schweizer und solche, die es werden wollen* (Trösch: Olten, 1917). For "world peace," see the summary by Markus Mattmüller, *Leonhard Ragaz und der religiöse Sozialismus II: Die Zeit des Ersten Weltkriegs und der Revolutionen* (Basel/Stutgart: 1968).

55 Emanuel Hirsch occasionally called Barth (along with other religious socialists) an "Enthusiast." So, for example, he makes an allusion to the concept of "disturbance" which he encountered in *Romans* 1922 in the heading of chapters 12–15, 412ff. (1999 ed., 447ff.); ET 424ff. In his *Deutschlands Schicksal*, Hirsch wrote, "whoever encounters the relation to the earthly things only under the perspective of 'interruption' instead of as a making alive of the community of God, must finally lose oneself in an Enthusiastic spiritualism, which can contain love, spirit and eternity only as empty words" (158).

56 See Hirsch on the "Social State" in *Deutschlands Schicksaal*, 2nd ed., (Göttingen: Vandenhoeck and Ruprecht, 1922), 109–125. On "world peace" cf. 84–109.

57 The grounding of a People's Alliance goes back to the encouragement for it shown by the American

or something similar, as a hopeful pre-stage of the millennium? Why not! *All* ideas from a target state of history [123] are "chimerical."[58] So are all ideas today of the pre-stages that can lead there. And the *content* of the ideas can eventually *not* be that different on either side, as long as they have ethical intentions. The question is — and Ragaz can say this as well — whether one can really see the ethical problem without taking such ideas very seriously. It is not as easy to deal with the religious socialists, as Althaus[59] would like to make it, for example, or the unfortunate attempt by Schlatter to make it even easier in his article in the *Furche*. However, this is just a side issue.

It is necessary now to consider the following. The inspiring sense of the millenarian expectation is not a eudemonistic dream of a throwback to a golden age of universal happiness. It is rather the conscious perspective on the reality of the epitome of all goals, whose possibility is indeed the question that slumbers in a hidden manner in every daily, banal action based on the goal. Already according to Revelation 20 [vv. 2-4], the thousand-year reign is in no way an island of the blessed, but rather the kingdom of saints and martyrs, built on the abyss in which the old dragon is chained. According to Kant, this is the kingdom of practical reason. The enthusiastic, idealistic, communistic, anarchistic, and, to be noted again and again, *Christian* hope (despite all true Lutheran teaching) is meant as a reality which stands here on earth before our eyes, in the sense of a task, not as an object wished for, but as a goal, and not as the end of the ethical struggle. It means freedom in love and love in freedom as a pure, *direct* theme of social interaction. It means a community built upon justice as its *direct* object. It means the overcoming of paternalism, or

president, Woodrow Wilson, in the year 1916. The articles of the People's Alliance from April 28, 1919 make up the first part of the Treaty of Versailles. The People's Alliance, which took on its responsibilities on January 16, 1920, belonged in the beginning to the Allied and associated powers of the First World War (with the exception of the U.S.A.). Germany was a member from 1926 until 1933. For more on the repeated appearances of Ragaz in the People's Alliance, which was decisive for the entrance of Switzerland into the alliance in 1919/20, see his work, "Sollen wir in den Volkerbund?" *Neue Wege. Blätter für religiöse Arbeit*, 13 (1919): 569–600; as well as other articles in *Neue Wege* such as "Zur Diskussion über den Völkerbund," 14 (1920): 26–33; "Die Schweiz vor der Lebensfrage," 14 (1920): 182–188; and his *Sozialismus und Völkerbund* (Zurich, 1920).

58   See the essay by Adolf Schlatter which Barth expressly alludes to here in his remarks, "Die religiös-soziale Bewegung in der Schweiz," *Die Furche. Monatsschrift zur Vertiefung des christlichen Lebens und Anregung christlichen Werkes*, 12 (1922): 173–177. Schlatter accuses the religious socialists of having a goal that is a "misty chimera," with which they replace "the need that bedevils us with a wobbly picture of the future" (175).

59   Paul Althaus, *Religiöser Sozialismus. Grundfragen der christlichen Sozialethik*, Studien des apologetischen Seminars in Wernigrode, Monograph 5 (Gütersloh: Bertelsmann, 1921). See Barth's response to it in *Grundfragen der christliche Sozialethik. Auseinandersetzung mit Paul Althaus*, in *V.u.kl.A. 1922–1925*, 39ff.

rather the exploitation and oppression of the one through the other; the overcoming of the differences in class and the borders of countries, of war, bondage, and violence altogether. It means a culture of the spirit instead of a culture of things; humanity in the place of objectivity, brotherhood in the place of the oppression of one person by another! The colors of this target state in which one paints oneself may be vivid or pastel. Whether one thinks of the way there [124] as being long and another thinks of it as short; whether one may spend more time thinking about the end goal itself and another about the way there, for instance, thinking about the indispensable nation state fulfilling the soul, one thing is certain: The question of the Good cannot be seriously posed without some primitive or refined, fantastical, or sober idea of a good that is becoming real within history. There is no Plato without the platonic state![60] There is no Calvin without the City of God on Lake Geneva.[61] There is no Kant without the idea of perpetual peace![62]

It was an unfortunate hour when *Schiller* wrote his "Words of Delusion,"[63] abstractly overemphasizing the *one* side of idealistic knowledge, while denying what moral reflection is not permitted to deny. As certainly as the question "what should we do?" calls into question our action on *this side* of eternity, in *time*, so too we *cannot* allow the thought on what is to do on *this side*, in *time* — a moral object in *history*, in which the two lines *intersect* — to be put off by the promise of heaven. Nor can we let it be taken away through a reference to so-called inwardness. This kind of thinking has always had the notorious effect of letting the question as *question* doze off and finally fall asleep.

But now it becomes necessary to evaluate what *this* very ethical thought wants to say. What does freedom mean? What do love, spirit, peace, brotherhood . . . mean! All these words which give off a meaning, but which do not yet stand with final clarity behind the different images of the future, words in which the human, in the discord of his being called into question and his questioning, stammers what by all means needs to

60   Barth gained important knowledge of the philosophy of Plato from his brother, Heinrich (see the preface to *Romans* 1922, VII; ET 4). On the central meaning of the state in the thought of Plato, see Heinrich Barth, *Die Seele in der Philosophie Platons* (Tübingen: Mohr, 1921), where the paragraph, "Die Seele und der Staat" stands emphasized at the beginning (4–49).

61   This is an allusion to the theocratic program of Calvin for the city of Geneva. Calvin himself did not characterize his ideas for that city as "the city of God."

62   See Immanuel Kant, *Zum ewigen Frieden. Ein philosophischer Entwurf* (1795), in *Werke in sechs Banden* Vol. VI, 191–251; "Toward perpetual peace (1795)," in *The Cambridge Edition of the Works of Immanuel Kant: Practical Philosophy*, Mary J. Gregor, trans. and ed. (New York: Cambridge University Press, 1996), 311–352.

63   See Friedrich Schiller's poem, "Die Worte des Wahns." (1799). See *Vu.kl.A. 1922–1925*, 124–125, n. 63 for the entire poem.

be done if the seriousness of the question is to correspond to the seriousness of the answer? Even if we imagine the human building up a Social
State, bringing in world peace, perhaps even with one of those groups
that belong to the religious league of humanity,[64] how should [126] we
imagine him as doing *that* which all those words say! And what would
the whole vision of the future be, if now somehow the very meaning
of these words is *not* supposed to be acted upon? Is it not the closely
guarded, bitter secret of every goal-oriented, human moral will that the
more intently and genuinely humanity sets its sights upon the future and
the words that stand behind this future vision that give it meaning, be
it a realistic or far-fetched vision, the more it feels rebuffed by this very
vision? Is this not painfully obvious with the growth of every enthusiastic
and revolutionary movement? Further, the more clearly he becomes
conscious of the fact that what we are supposed to do is to be free and
act in freedom, to love ourselves, to be people of the spirit and of peace
(that, *that* was it!), the more he feels thrown back into an ever growing
distance from his vision. Indeed, this vision can really only rebuff us. The
more removed the human feels from this vision, the more clearly the
work appears to him in its impossibility — not these words, but the *work*
which these words demand of him, and he himself as the *doer* of this work.

When he gets at least a certain and genuine glance of the reality of the
thousand-year reign; when it has become clear to him that those words
alone can give meaning to these visions of the future, then it must be
said, "Good for him!" Good for him when he at least does not abandon
himself at that point to any illusions about *his* ability, when he recognizes
what he sees, when he has not underestimated the distance and has not

---

64   The alleged plan of a "religious alliance of humanity" which Rudolf Otto pushed for was often
     discussed in 1922. For more on the setting of his goals, see R. Otto, "Ein Bund der guten Willen in
     der Welt," in *Die Hilfe. Zeitschrift für Politik, Literatur und Kunst*, Vol. 27, (1921): 205–208. On p. 206
     he writes,

     The goal and the sense of the matter are, very briefly put, to produce a human-*conscience*, to
     produce the validity of this conscience and to unify the strongholds of conscience throughout
     the world, in order to impose the law of justice and the feeling of reciprocal responsibility
     upon the relationships of the peoples, social layers and classes to one another, and to solve
     the great new collective ethical task of cultured humanity through binding effects [...] We
     welcome any "good will", wherever it comes from. But we believe that the strong roots of
     the correct will lay in the religious will, and we therefore are searching primarily for people
     with religious enthusiasm and an inner-burning, as they are only generated (consciously or
     unconsciously) in religion.

     For further discussion on this topic, see also W. Schücking, "Der religiöse Menschheitsbung," *Die
     Hilfe* 27 (1921): 198–200; W. Gundert, "Mission und religiöser Menschheitsbund," *CW*, 36 (1922):
     cols. 61–63. On August 1, 1922, a variety of local groups and individual members of the "Religious
     Human Alliance" [*Religiösen Menschheitsbundes*] gathered in Wilhelmshagen by Berlin. Cf. P. Gastrow,
     "Tagung des Religiösen Menschheitsbundes," *CW*, 36 (1922): cols. 743f.

falsified the lofty words, and when he has not somehow cut down and minimized the ideal in the name of his limited possibilities, when he has not somehow gambled away and squandered the ethical impulse for a bowl of lentils! [cf. Gen. 25.34]. Good for him if he recognizes that *he* the *human*, is the incapable and impossible one, when he does not somehow reject and blaspheme hope by blurting out words of delusion as if *it* were the deceiver and impossible thing! In a word, good for him if he at least perishes waving a flag, and, without compromise and capitulation, deceives himself and that which he is supposed to want! Much that is low-minded lurks near the human in the moment that he begins to realize what [127] the ethical object means for him. But whether honorably or with low-mindedness (in reality it is always both!), the human perishes on these shoals, from which he cannot and may not steer himself away. For one only needs to conceive of the very idea of "purposes" as the object of human willing to make crystal clear the utter contradiction between every penultimate purpose, which alone the human can will, and that ultimate purpose. This can happen earlier or later, but it does finally happen when the individual takes the first step in this direction, even if it is only in thought.

But let us ask ourselves: What *could* we then want and do? In particular, we want to eat, drink, sleep, beget and bear children, and everything which belongs to these things. This is the broad foundation which is generally gently ignored or rapidly glorified by ethics with the help of a few truisms, as if it were child's play to "glorify" this very sphere of goals that occupies at least ninety percent of all humans almost entirely, and surely the rest of us too; as if it were child's play to bring them into relationship to things like spirit and justice! Above this foundation is a significantly thinner layer of science, technology, politics, and art. It is said that these goals could serve the ultimate goal, namely, the Good. In theological ethics they are even happily placed in the "service of the kingdom of God,"[65] which is supposed to be even more than the thousand-year reign![66] Indeed, what if these goals were to be separated from us *humans*; what if they were not always and everywhere goals which were willed by *us*! But as such, they are certainly nothing else than wonderful bubbles of *our* genius, which in itself can also mean the greatest senselessness —

---

65   On the use of the phrase "placed in the service of God," see for example, Wilhelm Herrmann, *Ethik*, 2nd ed. (Tübingen: Mohr, 1901). His particular ethics is divided up between chapter 1, "The Service of God within the Natural Human Communities," including "The Service of God in Marriage and Family" (152–163), and "The Service of God in the State" (163–182), and chapter 2, "The Transformation of the Christian in the Service of God" (191–203).

66   The *GA's* phrasing of this sentence is taken from the published version of Barth's lecture in *W.G.Th.*, not from an earlier manuscript.

I recall here the use of technology in the War. And regardless of such abuse, doesn't this senselessness open up in broad daylight everywhere where a human desolves entirely into a scientist only, artist only, politician only [128] in these goals! An even *thinner* layer of *moral* goals lays over this one. Even these are *our* goals. And therefore there are such things as bourgeois morals, as Bolshevistic morals, as Negro morals.

Accepting for now that our morals have nothing at all to do with certain more deeply-seated ends, which of course is always questionable, our moral certainly is primarily an aspiring of the *human* to our own heights. Thus, our morals are not exactly friendly, not exactly enjoyable for our fellow humans to look at, not exactly peace-making and light-spreading the more we become conscious of them and the more we want them. Is there a more powerful negation of the kingdom of freedom and love than a human in whom the will is somehow supposed to be completely moral? Perhaps yes, because over the moral layer there is as the outermost and thinnest layer the *religious* goal. The human can also search for God, become pious, and pray in every key of every religion and confession. Even *this*! We hear religion commended as the indispensable ferment of culture. We are exceedingly happy when occasionally even a scientist or politician offers religion this compliment.[67] This may very well be, but then in any case, the concept of "culture" must be expressly understood as being one of the *sub*-spheres. It can*not* then be the kingdom of love, and *not* be the ultimate purpose.[68] Or does the religious human as such understand himself as a station on the way to the kingdom of love — call him Luther or Ignatius of Loyola, or Kierkegaard — *he* with his quirkiness, his fanaticism, his imagination, his almost unavoidable tendency toward the finest Pharisaism, the highest, most arrogant Titanism because *this* is religion when considered as human will and deed? Is it not perhaps so, tragically, that he is the greatest obstacle to the coming of the kingdom of love because the religious goal is the most contradictory of all in relation to the ultimate purpose?

What the *human* can want are things, not the spirit. What the *human* can do is the highest unfolding of himself, but this is not love. What the *human* can achieve occurs in history, which is the colorful image of a community with its manifold variations, [129] including the cry of injustice that is unavoidably bound to it, or, it could be the constraint of the tedium and boredom of the barracks, where more than ever the highest

---

67   The statements by Bismarck about questions on religion were watched with great interest. See for example, *Bismarck's Religion* by Otto Baumgarten, in the series, *Die Klassiker der Religion* (Göttingen: Vandenhoeck and Ruprecht, 1922).

68   See for example, Wilhelm Herrmann, *Ethik*, 168: "If the work of building up culture stands in the service of the ethical ultimate purpose of personal communion, then it is a form of worship for us."

right becomes the highest wrong.[69] But all this is in no way freedom in love and love in freedom. The only possible love of *humans* is Eros. The only possible justice of the *human* is civil justice. The only possible prayer of the *human* is the ardor of a feeling (see Heiler!),[70] which is like any other feeling and is not even a very sympathetic feeling. The inventory of human possibilities — from our everyday act of going to sleep to immersion in a mystical experience — is simply not appropriate for the realization of the ethical object, of the goal of history.

This inventory is certainly in itself very capable of developing and improving, but in relation to the ultimate purpose, it stands like the number one stands in relation to infinity. The human wants to do nothing other than to *live*; that is what it is. This will to live lets itself be neither spiritualized nor glorified, nor, as it is said, "be placed into the service of God." It is only and exactly what it is. It seals the human as *creature*. The image of this seal is the fact that every person must *die*, one after the other, without having seen the purpose of history. The human cannot begin to deal with anything like a real answer to the ethical question. He can only comprehend over and over that he is in absolutely no position whatsoever to ask about this answer. What can be gained from the concept of the ethical object is the knowledge of the *fall into sin*, as the Bible puts it, which precedes all of history and which determines all of history [cf. Gen. 3.1-7]. The human cannot even live knowing the answer for which he is no match. Or can he? Maybe he can by choosing crudeness, compromise, and capitulation in order to avoid knowledge of the fall, by learning to turn a blind eye to it. How else can he live with it? [130]

We have now come to the moment when we should recall our train of thought, which we have already covered briefly in light of the situation just described. It arises from the *dialectic of the thought of God*. It is the way of *Paul, Luther*, and *Calvin*, roughly parallel to which I also see the way of *Plato* running. As far as I can in my own words, I would like to describe this to you in the following way. This way begins with the unconditional affirmation of the insight which we have now gained in a double way: Through the question of the Good, the human condemns himself to

---

69   See Marcus Tullius Cicero, *De officiis*, I, 10, 33: "Summum ius summa iniuria."
70   See Friedrich Heiler, *Das Gebet. Eine religionsgeschichtliche und religionspsychologische Untersuchung* (Munich: Reinhardt, 1919), 41; ET *Prayer: A Study in the History and Psychology of Religion*, Samuel McComb, trans. (New York, Oxford University Press, [1932] 1958), 2:

> A *concrete moment of need* always creates the original occasion to pray, in which the fundamental life interests of an individual or a group are severely threatened . . . The spiritual results which are conditioned by such situations, which motivate prayer, are characterized as momentary *affects* (sometimes even are habitual or ongoing affects) of high intensity: fear, terror, horror, anxiety, annoyance, rage, hate, worry, grief, sorrow (my translation).

death, because the only secure answer which exists is that he, the human, is *not* good, and is impossible. But this very insight, this comprehensive critical negation under which we place ourselves and the entire world, this fear of death that the entirely sincere conscience produced within us by means of this insight, is said to be that very small way and narrow gate to the truth [cf. Mt. 7.14], to the real and redeeming answer.

The primary, and essential, challenge is to bear up under this insight, to look it in the face, to not dodge it, *neither* by weakening the seriousness and radicalness of the question posed to us, *nor* by ceding something to the pure and lofty presupposition of the object of a real, ethical action, *nor*, in that we find ourselves between Scylla and Charybdis, by making illusions about our own real capability. It is necessary to understand the complete intolerableness of the human situation, to confess it, to accept it. It is necessary to immediately *bow* under the judgment that arises in the problem of ethics. Precisely in the inescapable sharpness of this judgment, we hit upon the reality of *God*. This reality is confirmation that the problem of ethics posed to us is about our relationship to God. Remember that we must die: in this way we become wise [Ps. 90.12]. Precisely in this way we break through to that which is not only gradually but principally superior to us and the entire world.

What is it then, this relentless border, this unbridgeable abyss at the edge of which we are demanded to "stop!"? What else is it except a different boundary from the ones which divide and must divide God and the world, Creator and creation, the holy ones and the sinners, the idea of the Good[71] that exists beyond the heavens and all of its [131] necessarily broken and infinitely incomplete phenomena? Would God still be God if he encountered us differently? Would God not still be the origin of all that exists? Would God not still be the Creator of all things[72] if, compared to him, all being had to disqualify itself as non-being, if all things had to disqualify themselves as alienated and fallen away from the life of God, which alone is good and perfect! And would there be any relationship of the human to God other than the one which goes through the gates of the death and hell of the individual's knowledge of his own elimination, damnation, and impossibility?

If, however, this judgment is the rock of the eternal *truth*, and if our doom at hitting this rock is our *rescue* from the sea of illusion and betrayal, then the negation under which we are placed, which is enough to make one tremble, must also have its positive, reverse side. That God does not

71   See the description of Plato by Heinrich Barth, *Die Seele in der Philosophie Platons*, especially the paragraph, "Der Erkenntnisweg der Seele und die Idee des Guten" (70–104).
72   See the third verse of the song by N. Herman, "Lobt Gott, ihr Christen alle Gleich": "Und nimmt an sich eins Knechts Gestalt/ Der Schöpfer aller Ding" (*EKG* 21; *KGB* 113).

abandon us, and that we cannot let go of God:[73] *This* is the meaning of our situation. Because *God himself, God alone*[74] is the possibility of our lives, our remaining alive has been made impossible. Because *God* has said "Yes" to us, we must radically, inescapably stand in the "No." Because *God* is the answer, and *God* works upon us, we can only give answers to our deeds that immediately turn themselves back into questions, or for which we are no match. Because the immortal life of *God* is the true part of us, the fact that we must die reminds us so implacably of the sinful limits of our [132] will to live. In this way, that which is above judgment appears *in* judgment, namely, God's love. Forgiveness appears *in* the knowledge of sin; the beginning of the new and original life appears *in* death and the end of all things. In this way, God's mercy finds the human precisely in his distance from God.

God has been only waiting for the humility which can restore his honor, an honor he cannot allow any other to have [cf. Isa. 48.11]. God has been only waiting for the penance in which the human waits on grace or disgrace and allows God to take him captive. God has only been waiting for the "despair in trust" [*desperatio fiducialis*],[75] that comforted desperation to which the human gladly gives himself over — gladly because he has finally comprehended what this state of being lost means. God has been waiting for all these things, if one can even speak at all of a "waiting" by God, in order to make the positive relationship to him *all the more real in grace*, that is, in none other than in its love, forgiveness, life, and mercy. If this is the state of things then a new light shines forth from the ethical question, precisely from that point at which it is *entirely* destructive. This new light falls on everything that we actually do within its dark shadows. If the human's original, positive relationship to God becomes visible precisely in that final crisis, with its entire negative vehemence, then apparently the entire action of the human participates in the promise, in the justification *within* the brokenness brought forth through that crisis. The entire action participates in the saving meaningfulness

---

73   See the beginning of the hymn by L. Helmbold, "Von Gott will ich nicht lassen, denn er läßt nicht von mir" (*EKG* 283; *KGB* 227).

74   "God self, God alone" is the formula in *Romans* 1922, which is "repeated *ad nauseum*" (413; 1999 ed., 448; ET 424). Cf. also 16, 36, 39, 50, 56, 65, 70, etc. (1999 ed. 16, 37, 40, 53, 60, 68, 75); ET 39, 59, 62, 73–74, 80, 88, 94. This "formula" comes up again in a wider context in the paragraph headings of the trinity and revelation in Barth's first two dogmatic cycles. See Barth's *Unterricht I*, 105; ET 85: "The content of revelation is God alone, wholly God, God himself. But as God solely and wholly reveals himself, he makes himself known in the three persons of his one essence . . ." This is similar in Barth's *Die christliche Dogmatik im Entwurf*, 165: "God's Word is God himself in his revelation. God reveals himself as the Lord. He alone is the revealer. He is entirely revelation. He himself is the revealed one."

75   See Martin Luther, WA.B 1: 35, 33ff.; *LW* 48: 13; WA 39/I: 430, 7ff.

gained by the existence of the human in this valley of death.[76]

Understand that here it is about a *participation*, in which the infinite distance between the righteousness of God and the righteousness of humanity is *not* overcome, but rather is recognized ever more deeply in its infinity. Here it is about promise, not fulfillment, about meaningfulness, not about the "given"; about explaining the right and not about making things right. The positive relationship of God to the deeds of the human is just like the new creation of humanity itself seen in "forensic justification" [*justificatio forensis*],[77] imputed justification [*justificatio impii*] [cf. Rom. 4.5], as the height of the paradox of the human's "becoming other" while not becoming other. [133] The human will is and remains in bondage.[78] He stands and will remain standing until the end of his days under the annihilating effect of the fall into sin. His goals will remain contradictory from the least of them to the greatest; his deeds, not only incomplete but evil, will pervert his perfection. In turn, however, the law is and will remain directed in inseparable unity with the Gospel.

In other words, the ethical question with its gravity, obligation, and demand, will remain *posed* as strong as ever. There is no escape from the problematic of life, no pillow to slumber on for the comforted conscience, no security, not even religious security. The doctrine of the old and new Lutheranism which says that now there are so-called "offices," a hierarchy of holy functions, beginning with the "office" of father and mother to the office of the pastor, up until the divinely graced office of the king, which is supposedly read off of an alleged "order of creation,"[79] and within which human deeds would then be justified in

76   For the use of the phrase "valley of death," see Ps 23.4 (in older translations it is the "valley of the shadow of death"). See also the ode by Fr.G. Klopstock, "Frühlingsfeier" in his *Oden und Epigramme*, R. Boxberger, ed. (Berlin, 1879), 168: "Du wirst die Zweifel alle mir enthüllen,/O Du, der mich durch das dunkle Thal/Des Todes führen wird!"

77   See the support of this concept by Friedrich Loofs, *Leitfaden zum Studium der Dogmengeschichte*, 4th ed. (Halle: Niemeyer, 1906), 835f., 847f., 884.

78   See Note 50, p. 153.

79   Cf. in Luther's works the interpretation of the Fourth Commandment (according to the Lutheran ordering of the Commandments). For example, in the *Large Catechism* (1529), we read: "So we have introduced three kinds of fathers in this commandment: fathers by blood, fathers of a household, and fathers of the nation. In addition, there are also spiritual fathers . . ." *BC* 408: 158–161; *BSLK*, 601: 24–27. On the doctrine of the "*ordo triplex hierarchicus*" in Lutheran Orthodoxy with the differentiation between "*status ecclesiasticus*," "*status politicus*," and "*status oeconomicus*", see the evidence in SchmP, 381–393. On the "orders of creation," see Paul Althaus, *Grundriß der Ethik* (Erlangen, 1931), which is a new edition of his earlier *Leitsätze zur Ethik* (Erlangen, 1929), and *Die Krisis der Ethik und das Evangelium* (Berlin, 1926). For the Lutheranism of that time, see also Friedrich Brunstäd, *Die Idee der Religion,* (Halle: Niemeyer, 1922), esp. 203f., 248; Emanuel Hirsch, *Deutschlands Schicksal*, 2nd ed. (Göttingen: Vandenhoeck and Ruprecht, 1922), 76. Cf. Friedrich Gogarten, *Politische Ethik. Versuch einer Grundlegung* (Jena: Diederichs, 1932), esp. 108–132. On September 28, 1922, Barth wrote to Thurneysen about this lecture:

some particular way, is alarming. What is all this [134] but an avoidance of
the question, "What are we supposed to do?", which one may *not* avoid
because the justification of the sinner is inseparably bound to it. Only in
the knowledge of the grace of God is this question taken seriously. Only
once we know how merciful God is, do we know how holy he is, and
how awesome he is in his holiness. How should the *religious* individual in
particular, with his more than questionable "certainty"[80] be justified in a
particular way before God, as if it is not him or anyone else who is in the
greatest need of imputed righteousness! And how should any relation in

You will find all kinds of strange things in it: an illumination of Kant's ethic, a defense of the
thousand-year reign, in which even Ragaz is expressly praised and defended; a "however!"
which is directed at the Platonic-Pauline-Lutheran dialectic; an urgent warning about
[Gogarten's] teaching on the orders of creation; and finally a "punctuated line" that announces
the Christological problem" (*Bw. Th.* II, 100).

Gogarten did not express his views on the "orders of creation" in writing until 1922. However,
cf. Barth's report about a visit from Gogarten in Göttingen in a letter to friends on February 11,
1922. There he wrote:

Gogarten told of his correspondence with Grisebach, who twice worked through the Romans
commentary. He highly praised him, but somehow finds him too Kantian. Both of his claims
(*claims* for now!) are to be seen as further places to build upon, on the other side of the "great
disturbance," where a type of natural law of the family, calling, and state as orders of sin, and
therefore of God (!) are supposed to experience their establishment and justification (*Bw.
Th.* II, 38).

See Gogarten's later works, *Die Schuld der Kirche gegen die Welt* (Jena, 1928; 2nd ed. 1930), 18; *Wider
die Ächtung der Autorität. Eine politische Kampfschrift* (Jena, 1930), and the programmatic expression
of the "orders of creation" in his *Politische Ethik. Versuch einer Grundlegung*, 108–132.

80   For more on the "certainty" of the "religious human" (and the "so-called 'religious certainty'"), see,
      for example, Paul Althaus, *Die Prinzipien der deutschen reformierten Dogmatik im Zeitalter der aristotelis-
      chen Scholastik. Eine Untersuchung zur altprotestantischen Theologie* (Leipzig: Scholl, 1914). The third
      part of this work (pp. 179–273) is titled, "Die Lehre von der religiösen Gewißheit"; cf. also Fr. H.R.
      von Frank *System der christlichen Gewißheit*, 2nd ed., 2 Vols. (Erlangen, 1881–1884); Karl Heim, *Das
      Gewißheitsproblem in der systematischen Theologie bis zu Schleiermacher* (Leipzig: Hinrichs, 1911); and his
      Glaubensgewißheit. Eine Untersuchung über die Lebensfrage der Religion (Leipzig: Hinrichs, 1916); Ludwig
      Ihmels, *Die christliche Wahrheitsgewißheit, ihr letzter Grund und ihre Entstehung* (Leipzig: Deichert,
      1901). "Certainty" is also a typical concept of Barth's theological teacher, Wilhelm Herrmann.
      See the following works by him: *Die Gewißheit des Glaubens und die Freiheit der Theologie* (Freiburg
      i. Br., 1887), 18–52; *Religion im Verhältnis zum Welterkennen und zur Sittlichkeit. Eine Grundlegung der
      systematischen Theologie* (Halle, 1879), 39–67; *Der Verkehr des Christen mit Gott. Im Anschluß an Luther
      dargestellt* (Stuttgart: Cotta 1886), 51, 53, 66, 91, 93, 101, 146, etc.; ET *The Communion of the Christian
      with God*, Robert T. Voelkel, ed. (Philadelphia: Fortress Press, 1971), 58, 61, 101, 103, etc. See also
      authors such as B.J. Gottschick, "Die Heilsgewißheit des evangelischen Christen, im Anschluß
      an Luther dargestellt," in *ZThK*, 13 (1903): 349–435; Karl Holl, *Die Rechtfertigungslehre in Luthers
      Vorlesung über den Römerbrief mit besonderer Rücksicht auf die Frage der Heilsgewißheit* (1910), in his
      Gesammelte Aufsätze zur Kirchengeschichte, I: Luther (Tübingen: Mohr 1916), 111–154; the description
      of "certainty" as "certainty of God and certainty of salvation" by K. Leese, *Die Prinzipienlehre der
      neueren systematischen Theologie im Lichte der Kritik Feuerbachs* (Leipzig: Hinrichs, 1912). For Barth's
      critique of the "certainty of salvation," see *Romans* 1922, 398 (1999 ed., 432); ET 411.

life that is based on irrationality as such have any advantage before God
over those that are based on rationality? The dignity of the individual
who finds no other basis than himself can only amount to *one*. The
answer is never and nowhere the creature but the Creator *alone*. No,
here there cannot and may not be any rescue or any security besides the
one, divine forgiveness with which the sin of the pious and the impious,
the sin of *all* life-relations, and the sin which is the presupposition of the
entire system of any humanly possible goal, are *covered*. Forgiveness is only
to be found by *God*. But God can only be found in *need* — a need into
which the human is thrust by the problem of ethics.

This saving need can only be found where one seriously struggles
with it. And this secures our struggle against being confused with a
cheap quietism. This makes any acceptance of particular "offices," which
come from above and sink into human existence, [135] fundamentally
superfluous. Now more than ever, this struggle secures the residual
relative dignity and validity of the thoroughly profane system of human
goals which are set squarely "from below" by the fallen human. *But* it
also secures the justification and the necessity of the fight for a relatively
higher goal, let us say for example, for political or social progress with or
without a revolution. In my opinion, the insecure[81] connection between
the light of forgiveness and the shadowy kingdom of ethics secures the
unbroken continuity of the ethical task,[82] which is broken only by that
to which it adheres.

Covered by the forgiveness (which is always forgiveness of *sin*!), there is
also a justified action of the human. There is a *sanctifying obedience*, which,
of course, is different than that which is meant by the moralists. This
sanctifying obedience begins our climb down from every height, and
namely from the highest one first, as the first ones to urge religious
and moral disarmament, and in no way its opposite. There is a *love of
one's fellow human* which is capable of works. Its "helping" will begin

---

81   In Barth's copy, this word is underlined and has a question mark next to it in the margin.

82   For more on the concept of "the ethical task," see Wilhelm Herrmann, *Ethik* 2nd ed. (Tübingen:
     Mohr, 1901), 10f.:

> Ethicality can, however, only be in a human individual who has the energy to want to assert
> himself. However, the most elementary ethical challenge is that the human is capable of this
> will at all. One becomes capable of this through work. Ethical humans are therefore, in any
> case, only humans who work. Already before we know what the ethical form of life is, we
> could say to ourselves that it is in any case, only possible through work.

Herrmann adds:

> The most important forms of the natural life of humans for Christian ethics are the family,
> the cultured society and the state. With them, we already have a match for the natural drives
> in the band of the community among humans, and therefore we already have set for us forms
> of our ethical task (152).

as the opposite end of the well-known Christian charity, namely, that we — with empty hands! — forgive those who sin against us, just like we ourselves are forgiven [cf. Mt. 6.12]. There are *worse* and *better* goals, a conscious choosing and a serious advocating of the better ones. There is a working together on the tasks of the technological, scientific, artistic, political, and even religious *culture.* Their own dignity is not manifested as "orders of creation" but is a *witness,* a *reflection* which lies entirely on *this* side. We see its reflection in the here and now of a lost and hidden "order of creation," [136] but we also see that it does not need to be and is not capable of being Christianized.

There is therefore the *possibility* and this possibility is the *necessity,* not only to ask the ethical question, but to look for ethical *answers,* despite, no, *because* of its questionability; despite, no, *because* we are no match for the decisive ethical questions. There is the possibility to say a "yes" to it uninfected by pessimism or skepticism, because the "no" under which everything stands for now does not grow out of pessimism or skepticism but is born out of knowledge.

I see, in this fundamentally Pauline-Reformation line of thinking, which perhaps can be better formulated with a richer dialectical unfolding of the details, the only possibility to do justice to the difficulty of the problem of ethics today, *precisely* today, in its urgency for us today. If I had a hope for the church and theology, it would be what I have just expressed: I would like my train of thought, which Christianity has more than once taken up, to become lively and effective once again. I do not believe I am mistaken when I say that innumerable people of our day, Christians and heathens, wait for this thought to be finally spoken to them again.

However! — indeed is there yet another "however"? Have not the *final* words been spoken with our unfolding of the Pauline-Reformation dialectic? I am also of the opinion that yes, the *final* words have been spoken. It is possible and necessary to reach down much more deeply and comprehensively into them than we first did, but it will still always be about this great reversal: from the end to the beginning, from sin to grace, from judgment to righteousness, from death to life, from humans to God, from time to eternity. However, shouldn't we be unsettled that the final things encountered in the problem of ethics today are *words,* and in the best case, *these* words?

Just in the past year, I have had to hear much opposition against the perspective represented here. Most of this opposition has not left an impression on me because it apparently rests upon the mishearing or misunderstanding of some point or other. Which points from today's lecture do not lend themselves to be misheard and misunderstood by many to whom this entire series of thoughts is fairy-tale new,[83] even though the New Testament and some edition of Luther [137] most certainly stand on their bookshelves? Other objections have occasioned me to take a step upon the well-worn way and then go another step further. *The* particular opposition, however, which gives me the most difficulty, and I mean an insurmountable difficulty, is that which is more obvious than them all. It is the most banal, not to mention the dumbest, namely, the contention that sees this endeavor as simply a grand intellectual game, which has been played much better long ago by Hegel and his peers, and which does not lead us any further in the real problematic of the situation.[84]

What stands behind this opposition? It is basically a laziness of thought, which lags behind, waiting to turn the next corner so that it can then speak down from above about anti-intellectualism: "Not teaching but life . . .?" One recognizes the entire melody in the first few notes![85] Or is bare [138] godlessness behind this opposition, the agnosticism towards God [ἀγνωςία θεοῦ] [cf. 1 Cor. 15.34] which calls for that which Kierkegaard condemned as "direct communication,"[86] and which calls for clearly arranged comforts and admonitions to be readily available without having to think about God and eternity?

But, if we don't want to be seen as students caught in the act, where

---

83   *Bw. Th.* I, 368 (February 19, 1920). The use of the expression, "fairy-tale new" [*fabelhaft neu*] goes
      back to Barth's first encounter with Georg Merz and Albert Lempp, the leader of the Christian
      Kaiser publications, in February 1920 in Munich. Back then, Barth gave one of the sermons he gave
      in Safenwil, "which made an impression on all of us, that we must agree upon with our enthusi-
      astic friend, Lempp, who suddenly laid his arm on the table, looked Barth straight in the eye and
      exclaimed, '*That* is fairy-tale new to me!'" See also *Bw. Th.* I, 431,488 and *Bw. Th.* II, 27, 60, 169.
      See also Georg Merz, *Wege und Wandlungen. Erinnerungen aus der Zeit von 1892–1922,* J. Merz, ed.,
      (Munich: Kaiser, 1961), 212.

84   See L. Heitmann, "Kulturkrisis und was dann? Eine Absage" *Blätter für religiösen Sozialismus*, 3
      (1922): 21–24. See also A.D. Müller, "Streitpflicht auf die religiös-soziale Bewegung Deutschlands.
      Selbstbesinnung und Ausblick," *Neue Wege. Blätter für religiöse Arbeit*, 15 (1921): 270–283. Müller
      spoke of a "very dangerous type of intellectualism" in Barth (277), adding:

      > Intellectualism is there everywhere where an available life impulse remains stuck in thought,
      > where the way into life is not channeled for it, where thinking presents itself practically as a
      > goal unto itself instead of as a medium which serves life, where the drive for living embodi-
      > ment of that which is thought is swallowed by the work of thinking which is exercised in
      > the highest satisfaction . . . This all appears to apply to Barth, despite all assurances to the
      > contrary (278).

85   See the poem by J.V. von Scheffel and set to music by K. Attenhofer, "Die Maulbronner Fuge,"
      in *Liederbuch für die schweizerische Studentenverbindung Zofingia (Deutsche Sectionen)*, 4th ed. (Zurich,
      1891), part 2, no. 144, p. 132f.). Cf. *Vu.kl.A. 1922–1925*, 137, n. 85 for the entire verse.

86   On the impossibility of "direct communication," see Kierkegaard, *Einübung im Christentum*,
      H. Gottsched, trans., in *Gesammelte Werke,* Vol. 9 (Jena, 1912), 119–131; ET *Practice in Christianity*,
      Howard V. Hong and Edna H. Hong, trans. and eds. (Princeton: Princeton University Press, 1991),
      133–144.

would we get the authority and the confidence to slap our fellow human with this second accusation, or, even the first, despite the fact that a "theology of the unregenerate" [*theologia irregenitorum*][87] stares out from the holes of our opponent's coat? In spite of it all, couldn't he somehow be right compared to *us*, compared to the Pauline-Reformation dialectic in *our* mouths? Couldn't it be that in *our* mouths there is at least as much a "theology of the unregenerate" as there is in his, another kind of poverty! And couldn't the annoying phenomenon of his laziness of thought actually call attention to the fact that our way has pushed us hard up against the boundaries of our thinking, and perhaps not only ours?

Against the accusation that all of this may just be "only words," we must not defend ourselves by resorting to talk of the divinity of the Logos because it could be that what *we* say, were it literally the words of Paul or Luther, is not the divine Logos. This results from the fact that what we say constantly breaks apart into a multiplicity of *logoi*, first into two, but then immediately into an unending system of paradoxes which we can only hold together through continual reversals and, to be honest, by the sweat of our brows [cf. Gen. 3.19], so that they may [139] at least point to the one single and complete thing. Even out of the most stalwart admirers of Paul, who could escape this accusation? What does Paul's letter to the Romans keep expecting from us? Or Luther's commentary on it for that matter, every page of his work in fact, and Calvin just the same (just read his chapter, "*De fide*, Institutes III, 2" which in and of itself is a true set of paradoxes)? I will not even mention the nineteenth-century master of this Pauline-Reformation dialectic, Kierkegaard! The Word of God is a two-edged sword [Heb. 4.12], but its very nature as two-edged means that it does not need to be turned around to cut along the other side as well, as is the case with our words — even the meaning of our final words, including "the Word of God," no matter how emphatically we might express it. The *appearance* that everything is "just words," as if this is all a game here (the matter has even been expressly compared to a soccer game[88]) must, in any case, be applied to us. For, it cannot be denied that these words are often played in clever and foolhardy, pious and impious ways.

---

87   In Lutheran Orthodoxy, the possibility of correct theological work, also that of the "*theologus irregentius*," was emphasized (in contrast to the "*theologia regenitorum*" demanded by Pietism). This possibility was expressly acknowledged and established first in J.A. Quenstedt, *Theologia didactico-polemica sive systema theologicum*, P.I,c.I,s.II,q.III, Ekth.V. (Wittenberg, 1691), 16.

88   See L. Heitmann "Kulturkrisis und was dann? Eine Absage," *Blätter für religiösen Sozialismus*, 3 (1922), 22: "This dialectical thinking is apparently the transitional sickness of the German youth, and plays its role as the corrosive ferment of the eons which have passed by . . . just like the soccer game of the West has roused the robust youth, likewise the dialectic of the West has aroused the spiritual."

But there is still more: We have to reckon with the very real[89] possibility that the appearance might be the *truth*. We do not have any protection against it, not even the slightest. This is the case because the *reality* that corresponds to what we say when we speak according to Pauline-Reformation paradoxes does not stand by us, but by *God*. And we do not have God at our disposal, even if we splendidly have the dialectic of our thoughts about God at our disposal. That the question is the *answer*, the "No" a "*Yes*," that judgment is *grace*, death is *life*, and all the rest, that there is a desperation born of faith and on its basis a justified life in sanctification and obedience amidst this valley of death which in turn is also the world of God, does not become true by our thinking and saying it.

All this stands logically — and do not be mislead here — as a *reality* on the same level as Kant's postulate about God, freedom, and immortality or the idea of an historical goal. If we establish it as real, then we appeal to an instance that we can *only* appeal to, without forcing a decision [140]. The temptation of Fichtian insolence once again threatens to seize something here which does not belong to us. Therefore, because we have come so close to the burning bush [cf. Exod. 3.2], it must once again be remembered with particular urgency that the human is not in a position to solve the ethical problem, not even through his thinking, and not even by his arrival at a correct solution. There is no way to God from our position, not even a negative way [*via negativa*].[90] There is no "*via dialectica*" or "*paradoxa*." If even a way were to be found, the god who stands at the end of the human way will have already ceased being God.

Seen from where we stand, the apparently correct solution *could* simply remain as the establishment of the intractability of the ethical problem. It *could* also be interpreted in a Feuerbachian manner. The promise which we grasp at in hope, in its culmination, *could* be a nice mirage from where we stand. Likewise, from where we stand, it is *possible* that at the very moment when we lose ourselves to our trust in God, we underwrite our own damnation to eternal death. The desperation that comes with this — not comforted desperation but simply desperation — is now not only our last word, but our final reality, our fate. It is indeed so, that without fail we hit up against the reality of God — namely up against God's *judgment* — when we face the problem of ethics. It is a dangerous nautical maneuver, like Goethe described in the two last verses of the

89   In *W.G. Th.* this is mistakenly written as "first." The *GA* has been corrected according to the version in *ZZ*.

90   This concept derives from the teaching of the divine characteristics, where "*tres viae*" is divided into "*causalitatis*," "*eminentiae*," and "*negationis*." For more on the history of this topos, cf. Chr. E. Luthardt, *Kompendium der Dogmatik*, 8th ed. (Leipzig: Dörffling & Franke, 1889), 97. See also Barth's later critique of it in *KD* II/1, 389–391; *CD* II/1, 346–348.

Tasso: "the captain still clings to the cliffs upon which he crashed."[91] We are anticipating God's *grace*. But does it lie in our power at all to anticipate God's grace? *Everything* hangs on this!

God's grace will certainly not let itself be produced through a simple dialectical reversal. He *is* and *remains free*, otherwise he would not be God. "So then he has mercy on whomever he *chooses*, and he *hardens the heart* of whomever he chooses" [cf. Rom. 9.18]. This is the concept of double *predestination*, which we can [141] also perceive from the peak of the Pauline dialectic. The knowledge that we are not damned but chosen; in other words, the knowledge of the *reality* to which our last words correspond; the knowledge that we may *risk* it to hold onto these last words, to *live*, is *not* to be gained in this way.

I would like very much to stop here, and as a conclusion read to you my interpretation of the story of the raising of Lazarus from John 11 [vv. 1-44]. With this I want to say to you what now still must be said. I do not want to leave you with a puzzle, but I do want to claim that I know what I have done by leading you to this point of no return. You cannot expect me to now offer you a so-called "positive supplement."[92] No, there is nothing here to supplement. The circle of our consideration of the question, "What are we supposed to do?" must remain open at this point. What must now be said is found in another book. I do not mean this as a way to flee. It simply is the way it is. I just want to intersect the curve of an entirely different circle which is crossed over at this point by our circle. Two central concepts of the Pauline-Reformation dialectic that I have intentionally not yet named because they refer to another center, although they themselves are also dialectical, make up the curve which belongs to that other circle: the words "faith" and "revelation." I take what *faith* is from that place in the Gospel [142] where it says, "I believe, Lord, help my unbelief!" [cf. Mk 9.24]. And I take what *revelation* is from a sentence of Luther's: "I do not know or understand it,

91   J.W. Goethe, *Torquato Tasso*, V, 3452f.
92   In July of 1922, Alfred Daniel raised up a similar challenge to Barth in a letter exchange with him. See "Ein Briefwechsel," in *Weltwende. Kampfschrift des Christ Revolutionärs*, Vol. 3, Nr. 7 (Balingen, 1922): found on the final 4th and 5th pages of this non-paginated printing. Daniel wrote to Barth, "You have adamantly raised up the *one* pole of the Christian faith: all the flies are buzzing. Now the other pole! Moved out just as far at the first. *You must know it.*" Barth answered him:

   Do you actually mean that I am some train station machine from which one could first pull out a cigar and then (with another ten pence) also the matches? Does it work with spiritual things at all to order like that, "I have heard A, so please, now I wish to hear B?" And now, think what it is about in my case! I can only say to you, you completely err when you think that I yet have some kind of B *in petto*, which I have, out of some kind of malice, kept from the public and which you could now draw out from me *per postcard*!

but I hear that it rings down from above, and echos in my ears, what no human has ever thought."[93] Faith and revelation are the clear rejection of a way from humans to God's grace, love, and life. Both words say that here we are only considering the *way of God to humans.* But between these two words, stand two other words — and this is the innermost core of Pauline-Reformation theology. They are *Jesus Christ.*

These two words themselves are dialectical. They were already for Paul. A flood of biblical proportions of discussion and counter-discussion has washed over them. How is it supposed to be easy for us, bolting from one problem to another? *We* in particular will not be driven with any other *words* onto the far bank, where there are no more problems, not even with these two words. We can only say what Paul meant with these two words. Luther and Calvin intended to clearly and decisively point over to the far bank, to that other circle which cuts across the circle of the ethical problem. They intended to point to the way of God to humans; to the circle where all reality is positive; to that which they thought they could say about the will and deed of humanity along *its* ways. If I may speak in foolishness here [2 Cor. 11.23], they meant Jesus Christ *himself,* when they proclaimed the turn from "No" to "Yes," from judgment to grace, from death to life and all this with a certainty that there is a solution to the problem of ethics, a certainty that has nothing to do *at all* with so-called "religious certainty," because this certainty is not ours but *God's* certainty.

It is a certainty about the solution because certainty is *salvation.* Certainty is the salvation of humans, flesh, the creature, the imprisoned, the lost creation of God. It is salvation because the presence of the new humanity from above, the new heaven and the new earth [cf. Isa. 65.17 etc.], the kingdom of God not yet broken in but infinitely close [cf. Mt. 4.17], is not to be glimpsed without [143] believing [cf. 2 Cor. 5.7]. It would otherwise need no more words, no more dialectic. Therefore, as a *human* word, its witness is as fragile as every other word. But as a witness to *God's* Word, it is the truth. Hence its proclamation of the forgiveness of sins, which is the cardinal answer to the ethical question. However, note: All this is about the *way of God to humans,* and in no sense does the way come from anywhere else. And indeed note further: There is no way to this way. Rather the way itself is the way to this way. *I* am the way! [cf. Jn 14.6]. All of *our* ways lead somewhere else.

---

93   Barth cites the Erlangen edition of Luther's works, 20, 133. Cf. WA 37: 39, 40–40:1 (Sermon from April 1533): "But in the matter which I cannot approach with my cleverness, I must leave it at home and say, 'I do not know it and do not understand it. But I hear it, that from above it makes a noise and rings in my ears, which no human has ever thought.'" Barth mentioned this citation of Luther also in a letter to Thurneysen from that time. See *Bw. Th.* II, 99 (September 20, 1922).

Jesus Christ is *not* the crowning capstone in the arch of *our* thinking. Jesus Christ is *not* a supernatural miracle which we can try to believe to be true. Jesus Christ is *not* the goal that we would come across at the end of the history of our hearts, consciences, and conversions. Jesus Christ is *not* a figure of our history with whom we can build a "relationship." Jesus Christ is *least of all* an object of religious and mystical experience. If he is somehow all this to us too, then he is not Jesus Christ. He is God who becomes human, the Creator of all things,[94] who lay in the manger as a child [cf. Lk. 2.12, 16]. But this word is interpreted through the others: He is the crucified, the one who died, the one who was buried, the one who went down to hell, the one who was resurrected from the dead.[95] Certainly *this,* and nothing else, is what Paul and the others meant when they said "Jesus Christ." *From there* they have the solution, because *from there* they have spoken of *salvation.* If we do not learn once again to mean *this* as well, then today's theology will not help us more than any other. But even if we do mean this, we are only helped by Jesus Christ being *it,* before we even begin to form our thoughts about him.

And now as I close, back to the story of Lazarus. If you can, do *not* interpret this conclusion as merely edifying: "And everyone who lives and believes in me will never die," which is followed by the question "Do you believe this?" [cf. Jn 11.26].

<hr />

94   See Note 72, p. 162.
95   See the Apostles' Creed, *BC* 22: 5; *BSLK* 21: 13–15.

CHAPTER 7

THE WORD OF GOD AS THE TASK OF THEOLOGY, 1922

I. Elgersburg, October 3, 1922[1]

[144] The weekly magazine *Die Christliche Welt* (*CW*) was founded in 1886. In the following years, under the editorial leadership of Martin Rade, it was widely circulated and became the main organ of liberal Protestantism in Germany. Rade remained the editor until 1931.[2] An auxiliary group, the "Association of Friends of the Christian World" (Vereinigung der Freunde der Christlichen Welt [FCW]),[3] was created in Eisenach over the two days of September 29 and 30, 1910, in order to promote theological discussion among the readers of "Die Christliche Welt"; a group to which Karl Barth belonged from 1910 until its dissolution in 1934.[4] Barth and Rade had had a close connection ever since Barth's days as Rade's editorial assistant in Marburg in 1908–1909.[5]

At Eisenach on October 1, 1920, the FCW general assembly decided to form an alliance with other liberal Protestant associations and groups in the region,[6] which then held annual conferences under the name "The Alliance for Christianity Today" (Bund für Gegenwartchristentum [BGC]).[7] The first general assembly of the BGC took place in Eisenach in the beginning of October, 1921, together with an assembly of the FCW. In the two keynote lectures by Erich Foerster[8] and [145]

---

1   A critical edition of this essay in German can be found in *V.u.kl.A. 1922–1925*, 144–175. Page numbers in brackets in this essay run according to the *GA*.

2   Martin Rade (1857–1940): In 1882 he was pastor in Schönbach; 1892–1899 pastor in Frankfurt am Main; 1900 assistant lecturer, and later professor for systematic theology, in Marburg.

3   See J. Rathje, *Die Welt des freien Protestantismus. Ein Beitrag zur deutsch-evangelischen Geistesgeschichte. Dargestellt an Leben und Werk Martin Rade.* (Stuttgart: 1952), 123–127.

4   See *Bw.R.*, 194, n. 1.

5   See Busch, 58, 61; ET 46, 49, and the correspondence between Barth and Rade in *Bw.R.*

6   Among these other groups were the "Friends of the People's Free Church" [*Freunde der Freien Volkskirche*] in Thüringen, and the "Friends of Evangelical Freedom" [*Freunde evangelischer Freiheit*] in Anhalt, as well as the "The People's Free Church League" [*Bund Freie Volkskirche*] in the church province of Saxony (Saxony-Anhalt). See Rathje, *Die Welt des freien Protestantismus*, 274. The BGC alliance existed until 1930.

7   Rathje, *Die Welt des freien Protestantismus*, 276.

8   See Erich Foerster's "Marcionitisches Christentum. Der Glaube an den Schöpfergott und der Glaube an den Erlösergott", a lecture from a conference of the BGC in Eisenach on October 3, 1921, printed in *CW*, 35 (1921): cols. 809–827. For references to Barth, see cols. 813–819. According to Foerster, Barth's *Romans* 1919 commentary displayed a "renewal of Marcionism" (col. 813).

Reinhard Liebe,[9] as well as in the discussion period that followed, the dispute with Barth (who was not present) came to play "a significant role."[10]

Soon after, on October 13, 1921, Rade wrote a letter to Barth: "I am already writing you to say that we will be asking you to hold a lecture for us sometime over the coming year."[11] Rade made his earlier invitation official on January 9, 1922:

> The theme remains up to you. You also have the choice as to whether you would rather speak in the special assembly of the FCW (presupposing that it is a more professional, theological audience), or in one of the two assemblies of the BGC . . . for a wider circle of lay members . . . I strongly advise you to accept this invitation. Reasons for not doing so can be easily found, but I think that it will not be received well among the broader circles if you do not respond at such a moment.[12]

Barth accepted the invitation, writing in a letter on January 10, "I see clearly that I cannot very well decline this, although many things do actually speak against accepting it . . ."[13] To Barth's question about the theme, Rade answered,

> In my opinion, it should be about an answer to Foerster. But even so, not an *answer*. Rather, it should deal with a continuation of the thoughts which occupied us back then, their pros and cons. So, a direct confrontation with Foerster must be put aside, and what must come victoriously to the fore is that which *moves you the most*, that which drives you to lift your voice up and write books, and where you see yourself united with others like Gogarten.[14]

[146] Barth waited until the end of June[15] to formulate a theme for the lecture, at

---

9   See Reinhard Liebe's "Der Gott des heutigen Geschlechts und wir," a lecture given to the BGC in Eisenach, October 5, 1921 and printed in *CW*, 35 (1921): cols. 850–853, 866–868, 883–889. For references to Barth, see cols. 867, 888 (where Liebe calls Barth a "biblicistic new supernaturalist").

10   See the letter from Rade on October 13, 1921 (*Bw.R.*, 161). A discussion of the lectures by Foerster and Liebe can also be found in *An die Freunde. Vertrauliche d.i. nicht für die Öffentlichkeit bestimmte Mitteilungen*, Nr. 71 (1921): cols. 777–779, 782–786.

11   *Bw.R.*, 161.

12   Ibid., 168.

13   Ibid., 169. Upon Barth's acceptance, Rade claimed in the "Miscellaneous" column of *CW* that Barth would be a speaker at the Elgersburg conference. Cf. *CW*, 36 (1922): col. 87.

14   *Bw.R.*, 171 (January 21, 1922).

15   See *Bw.R.*, 175 (April 3, 1922). "Can you have a bit more patience about Elgersburg? I am still rather at a loss about what should actually happen there, and would much rather crawl into my snail shell. As soon as an appropriate intuition comes into my head, I will contact you with it." Again, in a letter from June 3, 1922 to Nelly Barth, Rade asked, "Has your husband, Karl, considered a theme for Elgersburg in the meantime?" See also *Bw.R.*, 177.

which point he "finally settled on 'the Word of God as the task of theology.'"[16]

At the end of June, the BGC announced in *CW*[17] that it would host a conference in Elgersburg[18] from October 2 to 5, 1922. Barth's lecture was planned for the third at 6 o'clock in the evening. As late as September 28, Barth wrote to Eduard Thurneysen, that "the matter of Elgersburg" filled him "with great worry." "*Four* complete days lay ahead of me, in which the whole caboodle must be produced. *What* in the world am I supposed to say to them?"[19] With a manuscript which was not yet complete, Barth traveled from Göttingen: "The last third of the Elgersburg lecture I wrote on my lap with the courage bred from desperation in the train, only a few hours before I gave it!!"[20]

In attendance at the conference were "three to four hundred 'Friends of the Christian World.'"[21] The lectern from which Barth spoke had "plaster angels on the left and on the right, each carrying a sign that pointed at me, which read, 'Confess!'"[22] "Afterwards, there was a great festival of conversation in the ballroom of the castle,"[23] with numerous contributions from the audience.[24] In the crowd was Foerster himself, "who smoothly repeated his accusations from last year."[25] [147] Barth appeared to be dissatisfied with the discussion.[26] "My closing remarks were, accordingly, quite angry."[27]

Later on, Rade refused Barth's request that *CW* cede its implicit right to exclusive publication of his lecture to the journal *Zwischen den Zeiten*.[28]

16   *Bw. Th.*II, 87 (June 28, 1922).
17   See the program in *CW*, 36/30 (June 27, 1922): col. 567.
18   Elgersburg lay by Ilmenau in the area of the Forest of Thüringen, south of Erfurt (in the former East Germany). The event took place partly in the area near Elgersburg Castle, and partly in the Deutscher Kaiser locale.
19   *Bw. Th.* II, 100.
20   *Bw. Th.* II, 107 (October 9, 1922).
21   See Barth's letter to his mother, October 5, 1922 (KBA 9222.67).
22   *Bw. Th.* II, 102 (October 7, 1922).
23   See Barth's letter to his mother, October 5, 1922.
24   See Barth's report on the evening in *Bw. Th.* II, 103–106 (October 7, 1922); the exchange of impressions from Elgersburg between Barth and Rade in *Bw. R.*, 179–182 (October 16 and 18, 1922); and the summary report about the discussion in *An die Freunde*, Nr. 75 (1922): col. 818 (which only appeared later due to failures on the part of the one reporting).
25   *Bw. Th.* II, 104 (October 7, 1922).
26   See *Bw. Th.* II, 105 (October 7, 1922) and *Bw. R.*, 179f. (October 16, 1922).
27   See Barth's letter to his mother from October 5, 1922. This closing remark was printed in the *An die Freunde* in the following manner: "Barth was generally shaken by the discussion! How confidently the pastors spoke! Jesus Christ makes it possible for me to be stuck in such need but still not to despair."
28   On September 13, Rade asked Barth, "Regarding your Elgersburg lecture, it is set up so that right after the conference, I receive it very rapidly in order to print it in *CW*. Every Elgersburg lecture appears in *CW*. (Afterwards you can use the text further as you wish.)" (*Bw. R.*, 178). Thereupon, in a letter circulated to friends, Barth wrote:

I must hand the Elgersburg lecture as loot over to the "Christian World" as soon as I have

2. Emden, October 11, 1922

Barth gave this lecture again to the "Coetus of Reformed pastors in Ostfriesland" in one of their regular sessions on October 11, 1922, in Emden.²⁹

[148] We theologians endure hardship because of our vocation; a vocation in which we can perhaps soothe ourselves, but never really find comfort. Even as students we vaguely recognized that it would come to this, but as we have grown older, it has become more difficult than we thought. We are pastors or assistant lecturers, but it is always the same dilemma; the one group can sidestep it no more easily than the other. I am amazed that there still are theologians who go to the Catholic church and goodness knows where else to find the so-called Numinous,³⁰ as if it did not already completely surround us, quite inconspicuously, but nevertheless really there — when we are sitting at our desks, when we go to bed at night and wake up in the morning, before we resume work in our official capacities, and after our work is done. It is simply there, without any fuss, by virtue of the fact that we are theologians.

The dilemma of our situation is completely independent of the circumstances in which we may find ourselves. Surely psychology (to get this out of the way), is able to illustrate this dilemma, but it can *explain* it no better than it can explain the question of the certainty and immanence

held it again in Emden. This is certainly not right in the opinion of our editor in Munich [Georg Merz, editor-in-chief of the planned journal, *Zwischen den Zeiten*], and not right to me either, but barely able to be circumvented without trampling on the head of Rade (*Bw. Th.* II, 103 [October 7, 1922]).

Despite the implicit promise which Barth made to Rade ("But only if it can happen in *friendship* should it happen"), Barth requested of him:

With our soon-to-be-public journal, we are poor people, I mean poor in necessary manuscripts, and not really in the position to just give up such a superior manifesto like the Elgersburg lecture to a rich man like *The Christian World* . . . Thus I come to you with the request as to whether you would not be willing to set free what you have taken into custody (*Bw.R.*, 179 [October 16, 1922]).

Rade, however, still rejected this; cf. *Bw.R.* 181 (October 18, 1922). Barth saw his lecture "now getting moldy in *The Christian World*." See *Bw.Th.* II, 115 (October 26, 1922).

29 See the Introduction to Chapter 6 in this volume.
30 This is an allusion to Friederich Heiler, *Katholischer und evangelischer Gottesdienst*, in *Die Welt christlicher Frommigkeit*, Vol. I (Munich: Kaiser, 1921), 17f.: "Every aesthethic pleasure surrounds the mystical, primal feeling of the *numinous* and *fascinating* only in a holy awe that breaks through in its undifferentiation into Catholic worship, as it seldom does elsewhere." The concept of "the Numinous" was lastingly shaped by Rudolph Otto, in *Das Heilige. Über das Irrationale in der Idee des Göttlichen und sein Verhältnis zum Rationalen* (Breslau: Trewendt u. Granier, 1917); ET, *The Idea of the Holy: An Inquiry into the Non-rational Factor in the Idea of the Divine and its Relation to the Rational*, 2nd ed., John W. Harvey, trans. (Oxford: Oxford University Press, 1950).

of death that is written upon the soul of every human individual. The strange up-and-down in the life of the soul, to which we theologians are subject like everyone else, moves in its own way alongside this plight of ours and has essentially nothing to do with it.[31] Even issues in the technical aspects of our vocation sidestep this plight and do not cause it. Take the systematic side of theology, for instance. It has been improved and completely restructured often enough, just as theological praxis has as well. And every possible variation of our personal attitude toward our vocation has long since been tried out and tested. [149] Do these things really amount to anything more than just a turning of the sick man in his bed from one side to the other for a little diversion? Have we not yet noticed, in the church as well as in the university, that yesterday's peace will certainly be tomorrow's unrest! At any rate, we cannot hope that a change of method or orientation, unavoidable though such changes always are, will free us from our plight.

Our plight is not simply a dilemma unique to the present day. Throughout history, theologians have believed that their particular era made it especially difficult to fulfill this calling. In fact it might even be easier to be a theologian today than ten years ago, particularly here in Germany rather than in one of the neutral countries. The churning up of the ground beneath our feet due to the events from which we are still emerging has opened up incomparably more favorable opportunities for us. Our plight does not stem from our questionable position in society. It is not due to the fact that we theologians are not particularly loved and respected by the majority of people but are surrounded instead by a cloud of suspicion, about which Franz Overbeck has said so much.[32] Being good readers of the Gospel, we should not be surprised at this situation, even if we are secure about the rest of our affairs. As a matter of fact, the situation is not all that unfortunate. Even in the new Germany there was recent outrage at a so-called survey [Bedürfnisfrage] that questioned whether the likes of us were needed at all.[33] On the whole, [150] we certainly do not

---

31   In an earlier copy Barth had an incorrect gender for the German word "Bedrängnis," translated here as "hardship," "plight," or "dilemma."

32   See Franz Overbeck, Christentum und Kultur. Gedanken und Anmerkungen zur modernen Theologie, Carl Albrecht Bernoulli, ed. (Basel: Schwabe, 1919), p. 273:

> [The theologians] are the mediators of Christianity to the world in the best case, and exactly because of this no one properly trusts them along the way, even if the circumstances are such that there is a great trust in them in this regard, like it seems to be at the moment. But next to this there always remains the fact that they themselves are mediators — a kind of human which has a reasonable mistrust against them.

33   Perhaps this is an allusion to the movement to leave the church after the end of the First World War. See Hans Georg Haack, Die evangelische Kirche. Deutschland in der Gegenwart (Berlin: Mittler, 1929), esp. 107–114. "The full breadth of the exit from the church after the war is recognized by

have anything to seriously complain about regarding the treatment we receive by the educated and uneducated public.

The real and genuinely alarming question is posed to us from an entirely different side. The need that I have in mind here does not come from the church, from the antiquated spirit of its leadership, its bureaucracy, or from the limitations of our creed. I come from the land of paradise, where everyone, from theologians and university professors to village pastors, can essentially do what they want within their own sphere,[34] where there are no preambles,[35] and where even the mildest and most elastic middle-of-the-road theology leads the way among the ranks of clergy. And I warn you: it is an illusion to think that the burden of the theologian can be lifted, even slightly, by such friendly conditions. On the contrary, even if all the struggles against the old church in the name of the new finally lost their meaning outwardly, as they already have inwardly, and even if all the zeal directed at such fights gets directed [151] toward more serious matters, the essential need of theology will continue to eat away at us all the more fiercely. Our need comes from the content of our task. But in how far this or that individual *feels* the need is another question altogether. Regardless of whether we feel this way or that, it should

the frightening fact that from 1919–1922, 931,146 Protestants in Germany turned their backs on the church" (ibid., 110).

34   In the nineteenth century the obligation to pledge oneself to certain confessional writings was partly alleviated by officials and also increasingly neglected in the churches of the different Swiss Cantons. Confessional formulations have been found only in the introductions of the respective organizational documents of the church since then. See Barth's own interpretation in "Die kirchlichen Zustände in der Schweiz," *V.u.kl.A. 1922–1925*, esp. 21ff.

35   In the year 1922, the preamble of the constitutional committee of the "Evangelical Church of the Old Prussian Union" became the subject of great controversy between different ecclesiastical factions. See *CW*, 36 (1922): col. 228. See also in *CW* 36 the collection of various positions on the issue, in "Erklärungen zu dem Verfassungsentwurf der altpreußischen Landeskirche," cols. 307–309; "Wider die Präambel," cols. 479f., 659; H. Schuster, "Eine dringliche Warnung. Ein Wort der Religionslehrer zum Streit um die Präambel," cols. 451–453; "Kundgebung der Theologischen Fakultät Berlin zur Bekenntnisfrage," col. 454; and Otto Baumgarten, "Vom Präambelstreit," cols. 534–538. The formulation of the preamble of the "Constitution of the Evangelical Church of the Old-Prussian Union," which was accepted after three drafts on September 29, 1922, reads:

Being true to the inheritance of the church fathers, the Evangelical church of the district of the old-province of Prussia stands on the Gospel given in the Holy Scripture of Jesus Christ, Son of the living God, who was crucified and resurrected for us, who is the Lord of the Church. We recognize the continuing truth of its confessions: the Apostles' Creed and the other creeds of the ancient church. We further recognize the *Augsburg Confession*, its *Apology*, the *Smalcald Articles* and the *Small* and *Large Catechism* of Luther in the Lutheran churches; and the *Heidelberg Catechism* in the Reformed congregations, where these creeds stand in authority (cited according to Karl Kupisch, *Quellen zur Geschichte des deutschen Protestantismus 1871–1945*, in *Quellensammlungen zur Kulturgeschichte*, Vol. XI [Göttingen: Musterschmidt, 1960], 146f.).

be possible for me to talk with you about our *situation*, which I would like to characterize by the following three sentences: *As theologians, we ought to speak of God. But we are humans and as such cannot speak of God. We ought to do both, to know the "ought" and the "not able to," and precisely in this way give God the glory.* This is our plight. Every thing else is child's play in comparison. I will attempt to explain my statements in order.

We ought to speak of God. Our title claims this, but not just our title. We should all face the fair and simple question, "*What is our purpose?*" What kind of sense do the design and activity of our office make? What do the people who support us for what we are — or at least recognize us — really expect! And when they feel deceived, what do their scorn and despising tell us? Naturally, we may not ask about what they primarily want from us, as if they could tell us offhand. It is about the motive of their motives. It is about understanding the people around us and what they expect better than they understand themselves.[36] Isn't it true that our existence as theologians is to be understood only on the basis of the existential needs of other people? They do not need us to construct their lives and everything that belongs to life. They take care of that without our advice, better than we usually think. But they know that on the other side of their existence, on the other side of every question asked in their daily lives, the "What?" "Why?" "Where from?" "Where to?" stand like a minus sign before the entire equation.[37] It is a question that turns everything that stands inside the brackets into a new question, even those which may have already been answered. [152]

The people know that they have no answer to this question of all questions, and they are naïve enough to accept that others could give answers, so they thrust us into our peculiar, unique existence, and place us into their pulpits and lecterns where we are supposed to speak of God and give answers to the ultimate question. Why do they not try to come to terms with this ultimate question themselves, like they do with all other questions? We may well ask, why do they come to us, even though they must have recognized for some time now that they cannot use us as they would a lawyer or to a dentist, that when it comes to this question, we can answer it no better than they themselves can? We may well ask. Apparently, by coming to us they are somehow expressing their

---

36   On the history of this hermeneutical formulation, cf. Immanuel Kant, *Kritik der reinen Vernunft*, in his *Werke*, Vol. II, Wilhelm Weischedel, ed. (Frankfurt a. M.: Suhrkamp, 1956); ET *Critique of Pure Reason*, Paul Guyer and Allen W. Wood, trans. and eds. (New York: Cambridge University Press, 1998). See Chapter 5, Note 27 in this volume.

37   On the use of the expression, "a minus sign outside the parentheses" [*Minus vor der Klammer*], see, for example, *Romans* 1922, 468–471 (1999 ed., 508); ET 482–483.

realization that the human cannot answer this question alone. Coming to
another with this question is seeking something greater than an answer
that the other person might be able to give.

Whatever the case may be, we are being *asked*. Therefore it is essential
to consider *what* we are being asked. People clearly do not need us to
live. But it seems like they want to use us to *die*; their entire lives stand in
the shadow of death. History marches along at its pace without us, but
when the eschatological, the *final things*, appear on their horizons — and
which problems in history do not ride the wave of the final things? — we
apparently ought to be there and have open and decisive words to say.
They are for the most part well adjusted in themselves and their own
capacities and life possibilities. But amazingly, when it comes to the state
of the gossamer upon which the entire net of this life hangs, when it
comes to the razor-sharp ridge between *time* and *eternity* along which
they suddenly find themselves wandering, after having long forgotten it,
they want to hear from us. The theological problem comes into being[38]
on the *boundaries*[39] of humanity. The philosophers know this, but quite
often, it appears that we theologians do not.

Obviously the people have *no* real need for *our* observations on things
like ethics and the spiritual life, religion and piety, or even on the possible
knowledge [153] of higher worlds.[40] Even all these things belong to their

38   In the earlier manuscript, the word "raised" was mistakenly printed as "called." Barth corrected this
     in his copy.
39   On this wordplay see the publications of Paul Natorp, *Religion innerhalb der Grenzen der Humanität.
     Ein Kapitel zur Grundlegung der Sozialpädagogik* (Freiburg i. Br.: Mohr, 1894); and Emil Brunner, *Die
     Grenzen der Humanität. Habilitationsvorlesung an der Universität Zürich*, in *SgV* 102 (Tübingen: Mohr
     1922); reprinted in *Anfänge* I, 259–279.
40   See Rudolf Steiner, *Wie erlangt man Erkenntnisse der höheren Welten?* (1904/05) (Dornach/Schweiz:
     Rudolf-Steiner-Verlag, 1961). On this allusion to anthroposophy and Christian community, see
     also Friedrich Rittelmeyer, "Die religiöse Krisis und die Anthroposophie," *Die Drei. Monatsschrift
     für Anthroposophie, Dreigliederung und Goetheanismus*, 1 (1921/22): 889–904.

     One can certainly wish that religious proclamation would want to awaken and build this
     receptivity in humans through itself. The fact is, however, that religious proclamation in our
     present time is simply no longer capable of exercising this effect on most people. The reason
     for this can be that the strong materialism of the present makes certain inner powers of the
     soul weaker and weaker, and that the contemporary governing intellectualism which is its
     accompaniment makes this inner power uncertain again and again, whenever it wants to stir. Is
     there a knowledge in humans that teaches them to know and recognize the deeper powers of
     the soul, which religion also applies itself to with its clear, necessary connection to the entire
     spiritual organization of humans? If there were an upbringing of the human which brought
     these inner powers to a new development and unfolding, then without question, religion
     itself would benefit. Such knowledge and such an upbringing is what anthroposophy wants
     to be. This is its answer to the need described above. This is the powerlessness of religion in
     the face of modern life (ibid., 897–898).

     See also *V.u.kl.A. 1922–1925*, 314f., n. 31, and 315, n. 32, for further references to Rittelmeyer's work.

lives, and have been pulled into the one *need* of their existence, whether they know it or not. It may be that we bring help and happiness to this person or that person, or even to a hundred people when we attempt to give them more or less useful suggestions and reliable information to the questions which occupy them in this sphere. We are able to do this, so why shouldn't we? But we must do so without forgetting that the *one* question actually brought to us by people is *not* settled. It is *not* by virtue of our office as ministers that we practice the art of giving answers *here and now* or that we are able to minister to *these* needs (religious needs included!).

Let us not be too quick to cite love as our excuse. We must first ask, what *is* the love that *we* owe the people? It could be that *we* are being *unmerciful* when in the name of love we merely help people to exist, even if thousands were to thank us for our help. When they come to us, they are not asking about *their* existence but about the other side of their existence, *God's* existence. As village or city sages, we are unwanted, superfluous, and ridiculous. We have misunderstood our office if we fail to see it as an index and sign of the truth. We must see it as a distress signal of the dilemma that extends over the *entire* range of actual and possible human circumstances in which[41] the human finds himself as one among many: the moral *with* the immoral, the spiritual *with* the unspiritual, the pious *with* the impious, the human in his humanity, which means limitedness, temporality, creatureliness, and separation from God, whether he knows it or not. His situation only gets worse the less aware he is, the less he can tell us what he is missing. It then becomes easier for his fellow human, who is eager to help, to misunderstand him.

The human in his humanity cries out for God, not for *a* truth, [153] but for *the* Truth, not for *something* good, but for *the* Good, not for answers but for *the* Answer that is directly connected to his questions. For he himself, the *human*, is the question. Therefore the answer must be the *question*. It must be *himself*, but himself as answer, as answered question. The human does not cry for solutions, but for *salvation*; not for something human again, but for God as the Savior of his *humanity*. He may be told a thousand times that in order to step into infinity, he only has to give in to temporality in all directions.[42] He does this, oh yes, he goes forth along a way that is in fact only possible for him. All the splendor

For Barth's reading of this essay in February 1922, see *Bw. Th.*II, 52.

41   The first publication of this essay inadvertently had the phrase, "in which the moral, however . . ." Barth corrected the "however" with a "therefore" in his exemplar from *CW*, while in the reprinting of *W.G. Th.* it disappeared altogether.

42   This comes from J. W. Goethe's poem "Gott, Gemüt und Welt": "If you want to step into infinity/ Go into temporality in all directions."

and horror of his deeds and accomplishments are witness enough to the unearthly vehemence and driving force of this search for the impossible.

Yet over and over, in spite of all guidance and instruction, he is not satisfied with the path of finitude — why not? He continually runs into the unbearable fact that the thing sought relates to the seeker like the number one to infinity, and he cannot believe that one equals infinity. How could he believe that? How could he, how dare he, when over and over again, the entire ocean of answers to which he has access turns to a single drop in his hands, a drop which is still only a question? This question is himself, his existence. And beyond this, on the other side of every ocean lies the answer. It is the reality to which every one of his relationships in life points. It is the subject of every predicate, the meaning of the symbols of his life. It is the origin of all the false starts, all of which make up life as he knows it.

But this answer, this reality, this subject, this sense, this origin, is precisely *there* and not here. The answer is not the question. *The "there" is not the "here."* When the human asks about God, he is asking for the answer that would be the answer to his *question* about the infinite that would — as infinite — be finite. He is asking about the One there, who is the same One who would be *the One here.* When he asks about God, he is asking about God who as God would become *human.* If we meet him with an answer that commends or condemns the great things such as culture, the spiritual life, and piety, [155] no matter how well-intentioned our answers may be, aren't we simply sending him back again to where he came from? Do we want to play such a game with him endlessly, never understanding the reasons why he tolerates us or thinks he needs us? Why don't we tell him openly, since we secretly believe it, that we do not want to or cannot speak of God? If we have good reasons not to tell him, or not tell him openly, then why don't we at least make his *question* about God our own? Why not make it the central theme of our vocation?

Up to this point, I have had primarily the proclamation of the *church* in mind. Everything I have said, however, is also fundamentally true for *academic theology*, even if one wants to disregard its educational task for future pastors. Theology is a sign of need in the university, a sign that all is not well, even in the *universitas literarum.* In the final analysis, the academy stands in an existential need that is identical to the need of the rest of humanity. Genuine science is admittedly *not* certain of its own affairs, and not just of this or that point, but of its *fundamental*, ultimate *presuppositions.* Every field of science is keenly aware of the minus that stands before their entire parenthesis. It is spoken about in hushed tones that betray the fact that *it* is the nail upon which everything hangs; *it* is the inevitable question mark standing behind an otherwise logically structured whole. If one recognizes that this question mark is the ultimate fact of each of the sciences, it would become quite apparent that the so-called academic cosmos is really nothing but a whir of individual pages fluttering over an abyss! These question marks really *are* the ultimate fact of every science.

Therefore, to appease its bad conscience — or rather comfort its anxious one — the university tolerates theology within its walls. Although it is somewhat vexed at the way in which theologians unreservedly lay their finger upon the ultimate things, which are not spoken about,[43] it is nevertheless (or am I kidding myself?) [156] secretly happy about the fact that someone is willing to be unscientific enough to talk loudly and distinctly about this ultimate thing, this indemonstrable center to which everything refers. It is secretly happy that someone is a living reminder that the whole academic system may have a meaning. Even here — regardless of what the private opinion of this or that non-theological academic may be — theology is faced with the general expectation that it exercises its office (let's see how it will come to terms with this!) and gives an answer to that which remains a question in the minds of others who would like to keep it under wraps in the background, if they can. It is expected to represent as a *possibility* that which the others only know as an impossibility, as a limit concept. Theology is surrounded by the expectation that it not only whisper and rumor about God, but that it *speak* of him, that it not only refer to God but *witness* to God by being grounded in him, not leaving God somewhere in the background but disregarding methodological and scientific presuppositions and placing God in the *foreground*.

Obviously, the existence of theology in the academy is not to be justified and established *a priori* but is only an emergency measure, a permanent exception to the rule, because the need will never be remedied. As such, however, the existence of theology is justified and established, as is the existence of the Church in society, out of a notion that is not its own. It is paradoxically but inevitably true that theology has *no* right to exist in the academy the way other sciences do. It is a completely unnecessary duplication of a few disciplines that belong to other faculties. A *theological* faculty has a reason to be in the academy only when it is charged with the task of expressing that which the others dare not say under the circumstances, or say it in a way that is not heard, or when it at least signals that such things *must* be said. It cautions that chaos, though wonderful, is not a cosmos, and it stands as a question mark and exclamation point on the outer edge of that which philosophy does — no, in contrast to it, precisely beyond the bounds of scientific possibilities. A *religious studies*

---

43   An earlier manuscript mistakenly reads "lay their question" and not "finger." Barth corrected this in his copy.

faculty,[44] on the contrary, really makes *no* sense. Although it is true that knowledge [157] about the phenomenon of religion is indispensable to historians, psychologists, and philosophers, all these researchers are in the position to gain and cultivate this knowledge on their own, without the support of theology. Or, should so-called "religious" insight somehow be the rented property of the random, theologically oriented historian or psychologist, because the secular scientists are not capable of studying the original documents of religion with the same love and knowledge of the object?

If we believe that theology should merge with religious studies, then we forfeit the right of our existence in the academy. Religion is a phenomenon that is just as instructive, but also just as questionable, as any other. Indeed, it is necessary and possible to know about religion. But precisely by studying religion as something that *can be* known, I admit to the fact that I find myself in the existential need of every other science — like the study of beetles, for instance. New, special, and quite remarkable questions may then occupy me, but they are questions like any other; they are questions that refer back to my final, unsolved question. But they are not *the* question which is nothing else than the ultimate answer, and for the sake of which theology — once the mother of the entire university — still stands as first and unique among the faculties, even if its head hangs a little lower. Regardless of how theology places itself as a science in the academy, I have not yet lifted a finger toward the venture that the other faculties fundamentally expect of me, the theologian — think of me what they will.

I would like to conclude this discussion with a historical footnote. If my reflections here are decisive in any way, then the line of ancestors upon which we have to orient ourselves runs through *Kiekegaard* to *Luther* and *Calvin*, to *Paul* to *Jeremiah*. Many are used to calling upon these familiar names. I would like to add for clarification therefore that I do not trace this line back through Martensen[45] to Erasmus,[46] or to those who are

---

44   See Christoph Ernst Luthardt, *Kompendium der Dogmatik* (Leipzig: Dörffling und Franke, 1889), 4: "Since the eighteenth century, theology has been understood as the science of religion (Wegscheider)." Georg Wobbermin made this thought programmatic in his *Systematische Theologie nach religionspsychologischer Methode I: Die Religionspsychologische Methode in Religionswissenschaft und Theologie* (Leipzig: Hinrichs, 1913); the heading of chapter 6 of this book is "Theology as the science of religion" (99–117).

45   Hans Lassen Martensen (1808–1884) was the Lutheran bishop from Seeland (Denmark) from 1854. The sermon on the occasion of the burial of his predecessor, Jakob Peter Mynster, on February 5, 1854 led Søren Kierkegaard to make a sharp and final attack on the contemporary church, which is found in his 1855 *Øieblikket*; ET *The Moment and Late Writings*, Howard V. Hong and Edna H. Hong, trans. and eds. (Princeton: Princeton University Press, 1998).

46   Desiderius Erasmus of Rotterdam (1469–1536). Here Barth alludes to Erasmus' dispute with

disputed in First Corinthians 15 [vv. 12–34], [158] or to the Prophet Hananiah who took the yoke from the neck of the prophet Jeremiah and broke it [cf. Jer. 28.10]!

To make my point crystal clear, I would like to expressly refer to the fact that in the list of ancestors recommended here, the name of *Schleiermacher is missing*. With all due respect to the brilliance of his life's work, I hold Schleiermacher to *not* be a good theological teacher for now, because as far as I can see, his work leaves fatally unclear the fact that the human as human finds himself in *need*, that is, in inescapable need. His work also leaves unclear that the entire stock of so-called religion, including Christianity, *participates* in this need. Thus he is vague on the point that speaking of God means something *other than* speaking about the human in a somewhat higher pitch. Those of you who locate Schleiermacher's special accomplishment in the fact that he overcame the so-called dualism in which Luther is said to have remained stuck, and that his particular concept of religion allowed him to build the long-wished-for bridge between heaven and earth over which we may now reverently cross, will now certainly have to disavow what I am presenting here, if you have not already done so. I cannot stop you from doing this. I can only express my wish that you not call upon Schleiermacher *and* the Reformers, or on Schleiermacher *and* the New Testament, or on Schleiermacher *and* the Old Testament prophets, but rather that you seek out a new line of ancestors before Schleiermacher, whose previous representative may be *Melanchthon*.

What is illustrated with the names Kierkegaard, Luther, Calvin, Paul, and Jeremiah is unequivocal, and shows complete "un-Schleiermachian" clarity about the fact that the service of humans must be the service of *God*, that is, *worship*, and not vice versa. The negativity and loneliness with which Jeremiah confronted the kings of Judah, their princes, the people in the land, and especially the *priests* and *prophets*; the sharp turn against the world of *religion*[47] embodied in Judaism which characterized Paul's entire life; [159] Luther's break, not with impiety but with the *piety* of the Middle Ages; Kierkegaard's attack on *Christianity*[48] are all undertak-

---

Luther in 1524/25. See Erasmus of Rotterdam, *De libero arbitrioDIATPIBH sive collatio* (1524), in *Ausgewählte Schriften*. Vol. 4, Werner Welzig, ed. (Darmstadt: Wissenschaftliche Buchgesellschaft, 1969); and Martin Luther, *De servo arbitrio* (1525), WA 18: 600–787; *LW* 33: 3–297.

47 See. Barth's exegesis of Romans 7 in *Romans* 1922, 213–255 (1999 ed., 230–276); ET 229–270, for the sense of his reference here.

48 See the title of the edition of Kierkegaard's work begun by August Dorner and Christoph Schrempf, but not completed: *Sören Kierkegaards Angriff auf die Christenheit I: Die Akten*, (Stuttgart: Frommann, 1896). J. Herzog alludes to the title of this edition in his article, "Abwehr von Sören Kierkegaards 'Angriff auf die Christenheit.' Ein Beitrag zum Verständnis der Mission Kierkegaards an die evangelische Kiche," *ZThK* 8 (1898): 271–381.

ings which Schleiermacher would never have embarked upon. They are the characteristics of the way in which *God* is spoken of here. To these thinkers, the human is a riddle. His universe,[49] be it ever so vividly beheld and experienced, is nothing else but a question. God stands facing the human as the *impossible* to the possible, as the *death* of life, as the *eternity* of time. But the solution to the riddle, the answer to the question, the end of the existential need, is the absolutely new event: The impossible *itself* becomes possible, *death* becomes life, *eternity* becomes time, and *God* himself becomes human.

There is *no* way that leads to this *new* event; *no* human faculty that can apprehend it. For the way and the faculty are themselves the new thing. They are the revelation and the faith, the knowing and being known by the new human. I only want to point out the *seriousness* of these thinkers' attempt to speak of God, their impulse to do so. Success is another question. What was *understood* in each of their cases is the need that the human as human finds himself in. They *understand* the question that the human raises up in his need. They link their attempt to speak about God to this *need* and this *question,* and nowhere else, dispelling all illusions that could prevent them from being seen as the need and question that they really are. This is the seriousness I am talking about. This is why we are orienting ourselves upon this historical line, and why we heed this historical imperative: We ought to speak of God! This command is enough of a burden, even if we were in the position to obey it.

[160] Now I turn to the second claim which I would like to use to characterize our situation: *But we are humans and as such cannot speak of God.* Think of the words of the oldest one in our lineage: "Oh Lord, Lord, I am no good for preaching!" [Jer. 1.6]. Jeremiah kept up that kind of speaking even after twenty-three years of preaching [cf. Jer. 25.3]. "I cannot say it": This protest was certainly not meant to document how he had developed but to preface everything that came after it. And Jeremiah was someone called and consecrated by God himself! We do not want to get into the question here as to how easy it is to establish the ecclesiastical office on the basis of being called by God himself, or whether one can be identified with the other, even though Luther did so using quite illuminating arguments.[50] Let our understanding of our office assume the

---

49   See Friedrich Schleiermacher, *Über die Religion. Reden an die Gebildeten unter ihren Verächtern*, ed. Hans-Joachim Rothert, in *PhB*, Vol. 255 (Hamburg: Meiner, [1799]1958), 29 (original ed., 50); ET *On Religion: Speeches to Its Cultured Despisers*, Richard Crouter, trans. and ed. (Cambridge: Cambridge University Press, 1996), 22: "The being [of religion] is neither thinking nor acting but beholding and feeling. Beholding, religion wants the universe, it wants to reverently eavesdrop on the universe's action and presentation of itself . . ."

50   See for example, Luther, *Auslegung des dritten und vierten Kapitels Johannis in Predigten* (1538–1540),

knowledge that even in the precise moment of the divine calling and equipping, we still cannot speak of God.

It is indeed amazing that people, the community, believe they could push us into saying that which we know all too well must indeed be heard at any cost. It is amazing that they delegate us, just as the university does, to tell them *that* which no one else can or dare say. But we are also only human, and we theologians are no more capable than they of that which they want from us, and which we ought to want from ourselves. We cannot speak of God. To speak of God in all seriousness would mean to speak on the grounds of revelation and faith. To speak of God would mean to speak that Word which can only come from God himself: the Word, *God becomes man.* We can say these three words, but it does not mean we have spoken the Word of God that contains the *truth.* Our theological task is to say that *God* becomes *human* and to say it as the Word of *God*, as *God* would say it. [161] This would be the answer to the question put to us by terrified consciences. It would be the answer to the human's question about the redemption of his humanity. It is precisely this which must be sounded with trumpets in our churches and in our lecture halls — but differently than the way we scribes are used to — beyond the churches and lecture halls, out into the streets where people today are waiting for it. We stand in our pulpits and lecterns in order to say *this* to them. As long as we do not say *this* to them, we are speaking past them, and thus disappoint them.

This alone — note, God's Word alone — is the answer that possesses genuine transcendence and thus has the power to solve the riddle of immanence. This answer does not eliminate the question, nor merely underline and sharpen it, or even audaciously assert that the question itself is the answer. It is an assertion, which, although true, has a way of being too explicit or too ambiguous when it comes from our mouths. No, the question must *be* the answer. It must be the fulfillment of the promise, the satisfying of the hungry, the opening of the blind eyes and deaf ears [cf.

WA 47: 191, 27ff., 38ff.; and *Luther's Works, Vol. 22: Sermons on the Gospel of St. John: Chapters 1–4*, J. Pelikan, O. Hilton, and H. Lehmann, eds. (Saint Louis: Concordia Publishing House, 1957), 482:

> John is speaking here about calling or sending . . . There are two ways of sending. First, God sent His messengers, the prophets and apostles, like Moses and St. Paul, directly and without the help of an intermediary. . . . The other way of sending is indeed also one by God, but it is done through the instrumentality of man. It has been employed ever since God established the ministry with its preaching and its exercise of the Office of the Keys. This ministry will endure and is not to be replaced by any other. But the incumbents of this ministry do not remain; they die. This necessitates an ever-new supply of preachers, which calls for the employment of certain means.

See also Wilhelm Brunotte, *Das geistliche Amt bei Luther* (Göttingen University Dissertation, 1959), 118–126, for further evidence.

Isa. 35.5]. We must *give* this answer, but this very answer we cannot give.

I see three ways in which we can attempt to provide this answer. All three end up with the insight that we cannot give the answer. They are the ways of dogmatism, self-criticism, and dialectic. But note that this differentiation is only a conceptual one. No actual, respected theologian has taken only one of the three ways. We will encounter Luther, for example, in all three.

The first way is the way of *dogmatism*. This way seeks to properly understand the human in his need and questioning by leaning more or less explicitly upon the Bible and dogma, presenting the familiar Christological, soteriological, and eschatological perspectives that have been developed out of the claim that God became human. Being reminded of Luther's sermons, I consider it better to go down *this* way — if one does not know any better — than to revert back to cultivating the spiritual life and piety with the help of history — even biblical history. For when we revert back, we lose sight of the things that are necessary and *not necessary* for humanity, and thereby forget [162] what people are really asking of us: that we as theologians ought to speak of God. It is true that there are things to question in orthodoxy. However, orthodoxy contains a powerful, living memory of what is necessary and not neeceessary — more so than some of its theological opponents. It is this particular memory, and not merely custom or lazines that allows orthodoxy to be so effective time and again, religiously, ecclesiastically, and even politically. Orthodoxy simply digs deeper.

We cannot but notice here that even the most convicted anti-orthodox thinker will not be able to avoid using dogmatic expressions, especially when he wants to cross over from his customary psychologisms to decisive messages, when he speaks — even if against his will — of God instead of piety. When the theologian gains the decisive insight that theology is not about the divinization of the human but the incarnation of God, he acquires a taste for objective things, even if this insight only comes as an occasional twinkle. He ceases to view objectivity as a mere psychic instrument for use in analyzing the Bible and dogma. He begins gradually but almost effortlessly to understand and find meaning in the "supernatural" world in which he dwells; a world that was previously ominous and uncomfortable. He sees its ideas from the inside out, from behind, so to speak, and thus comprehends that it must stand as it is written and not otherwise. He begins to feel at home in the farthest corners of this world, in places he would never have allowed himself to dream of. And he moves through these strange places with a newly acquired freedom. Finally, perhaps he is able to find the Apostles' Creed in all its rigidity as simply truer, deeper, and spiritually richer than anything that modern huffing and puffing could put in its place.

But obviously, the human cannot speak of God, even with the most powerful and lively supernaturalism that could be imagined. We can only witness that we would like to do so. The weakness of orthodoxy is not the so-called supernaturalistic content of the Bible and dogma. That is actually its strength. Its weakness lies in the fact that we (in that we are all a bit dogmatic) cannot get past making this content into an object, a thing, even when it is the word "God." Then, in our pragmatic way, we approach it like we would a myth: Here it is! Now believe it! [163] For instance, we have all come across such places in Luther, in his teaching on the Trinitarian dogma for instance, where we have been left standing with the message that one must simply greet this particular topic with a lift of the hat, and say "Yes."[51] There, amidst our readiness to beat the whore of reason to death,[52] we sense that this is not how it works. And we think with consternation about how often we have done so, openly and in secret, even without being Luther.

Why is this not how it works? Because the human's question about God is abolished by this kind of answer. He no longer has a question, for an answer stands in its place. But he is a human and as such, he cannot let the question go. For he himself, the human, is the question. If there is an answer for him, then it must take on his nature: it must itself become a question. But this does not mean simply speaking of God, or placing something before the human, even if it is the word "God," and demanding that he believe it. This is precisely the point: The human can*not* believe what merely stands *before* him, even if what was *there* is also *here*. The human can*not* believe what is not *revealed* to him, what does not have the power and perfection to come *to him*. God alone is not God. He might be something else. The God who reveals himself — this is God. The God who becomes human is God. Dogmaticians do not speak of this God.

The second way is the way of *self-criticism*. This way does indeed pro-vide clear, terribly clear, statements about the incarnation of God. With this way, anyone who wants to participate in God is bid to die, to

---

51   See for example, Martin Luther, *Von Jesu Christo eine Predigt zu Hofe zu Torgau gepredigt* (1533), WA 37: 40, 17ff.:

> There you have the word and reason against one another, still they should be the ones to cause a fight, and not become the judge or doctor, but should lift the hat and say, 'two are one,' whether I see and understand it or not, I still believe it. Why? For the sake, which it above spoke about . . . Now, since it sounds from heaven, I want to believe what it says to me that two, yes all three persons are only rightly one God, and not two or three gods." Cf. WA 37: 44, 41–45, 2: "But it is not valid for one to want to pull it [understanding the Trinity] into this art which does not grow out of our heads, but rather God's word, revealed to us from heaven; rather it is simply lifting your hat and to say 'yes' to it, simply let it be true.

> See also WA 30/I, 118: 19; *LW* 51: 189 and 34/II: 102, 14, 24.

52   See WA 9: 559, 28f.; WA 18: 164, 25–27.

surrender[53] all individuality, every sense of self, all egoism; [164] he must fall silent, become simple and open in order to become as purely receptive as the Virgin Mary when the angel appeared to her: "I am the servant of the Lord; let it be according to your word" [Lk. 1.38]! God is not a This or a That, an object, a thing, an opposite, or a second thing. God is pure, all-filling Being. God is without physical qualities. Only the particular individuality of the human stands in God's way. Were this obstacle to finally and ultimately be eliminated, the birth of God would certainly occur in the soul. Even the way of mysticism is truly remarkable! Who has a right to berate it outright, when even the young Luther[54] enthusiastically played with the best of them in the Middle Ages for awhile?[55]

It is quite remarkable that even the mystical way possesses the insight that when it comes to speaking of God, it can in no way be about the building up of the human but must fundamentally be about helping in the deconstruction of his existence. It possesses the insight that when it comes to speaking of God, the human is asking for the one who is *not himself.*

That is why I call this way the way of mysticism, which can also be understood as a form of idealism. It is a self-critical way. For the human places himself under judgment, he negates himself, because it is seen so clearly here that what must be overcome is the human as human.[56] But each one of us has had encounters at various points along the way, and we will never be able to give it up altogether. Even Luther could not do so. To the one filled with pride in his culture or non-culture, to the one stretched out [165] like a Titan toward heaven in his morals and religiosity, it will have to be said over and over that he must learn to move from one negation to the next [*von Aufhebung zu Aufhebung*]. He must learn to wait, become small, become nothing — he must die. This idea of the catastrophe of the human contains a partial truth. Regardless of the

---

53   See the compendium by Friedrich Loofs for this and other allusions to the late medieval mysticism which Barth used here for advice, among other things: *Leitfaden zum Studium der Dogmengeschichte* (Halle: Niemeyer 1906), 628–633.

54   *CW* mistakenly reads "the entire Luther" here.

55   In 1516, Luther published — at first incompletely — the writings of an unknown priest of the Teutonic Knights in Sachsenhausen by Frankfurt, which were rooted in German mysticism from around 1400; see WA 1:153ff. Luther described its content as "according to the kind of the enlightened doctor Tauler." In the preface to the larger 1518 edition, which at first carried the title *Eyn deutsch Theologia* (WA 1: 378ff.; *LW* 31: 75–76), Luther explained that for him, "next to the Bible and St. Augustine there has never been a book from which I have learned more about, and have wanted to learn more about, what God, Christ, humanity, and all things are" (378: 21–23). See also a letter from Luther to G. Spalatin from December 14, 1516 (WA.B. 1: 79, 58–63; *LW* 48: 75–76).

56   "The human is something which ought to be overcome"; see Friedrich Nietzsche, *Also sprach Zarathustra*, IV, 10, in *Nietzsches Werke*, Vol. II, Karl Schlechta, ed., (Darmstadt: Wissenschaftliche Buchgesellschaft, 1963), 279; ET *Thus Spoke Zarathustra: A Book for All and None*, Walter Kaufmann, trans and ed. (New York: Viking Press, 1966), 12.

objections made against mysticism, the neglect of this aspect will bring consequences with it. The strength of mysticism lies where dogmatism is at its weakest. Something happens here, we are not left standing with the message that we must simply believe. The human is attacked in the most serious way here. God becomes human so energetically that nothing is left of the human at all, so to speak. Obviously, even this is infinitely better than the paganistic cult of the spiritual life and piety.

But the human cannot speak of God even in this way. The mystic wants to *claim* — and we are all a little bit mystic — that *God* is that which wants to fulfill the human who is himself annihilated, that *God* is the abyss into which the human has collapsed, the darkness into which he gives himself, the "No" under which he ought to stand. But we are in no position to *demonstrate* this. The only thing we are *certain* of, that which we can *demonstrate,* is always only the negation, the negativity of the human. When we consider that the human *emerges* precisely *from* this negativity of his existence, *from* this question mark on the other side of all that makes up his life, we are stunned to discover that we are doing nothing else by following the self-critical way but making the question mark even more gigantic. Of course it is good to continually remind the human that the question with which he approached us is still radically different from how he imagines it within the random confusion of life. It is good to continually push his culture and coarseness into the blinding light of the infinite distance between Creator and creature,[57] and [166] to make clear to him what it is that he actually wants when he cries out to God in his need. But let us not forget: No self-negation that we can

---

57   See Søren Kierkegaard, *Einübung im Christentum,* Hermann Gottsched, trans., in *Gesammelte Werke,* Bd. 9 (Jena, 1912), 114, 126; ET *Practice in Christianity,* Howard V. Hong and Edna H. Hong, trans. and eds.(Princeton: Princeton University Press, 1991). Kierkegaard states:

> But take away the possibility of offense, as has been done in Christendom, and all Christianity becomes direct communication, and then Christianity is abolished, has become something easy, a superficial something that neither wounds nor heals deeply enough; it has become the false invention of purely human compassion that forgets the infinite qualitative difference between God and man (ibid., 140).

And further:

> To be the individual human being or an individual human being (in a certain sense it is a matter of indifference whether he is a high-ranking or low-ranking person) is the greatest possible distance, the infinitely qualitative distance from being God, and therefore is the most profound incognito (ibid., 127–128).

See also Barth's explanation in the Preface to *Romans* 1922, "If I have a 'system,' it consists of the fact that I hold in view, as persistently as possible, that which Kierkegaard called the 'infinite qualitative difference' of time and eternity, in its negative and positive meaning" (XIII; 1999 ed., XX; ET 10). See also 16, 28, 75, 184, 271, 317, 343, 401 (1999 ed., 15, 27–28, 79–80, 198–199, 293–294, 344, 372–373, 435); ET 38, 49–50, 98, 203, 286, 330–331, 356.

recommend to him (even if we recommended suicide!) is as great, as fundamental as *the* one negation to which all negations can only point to, the one negation which is immediately fulfilled by the positivity of God. Even with the sharpest criticism of the human, we do not get beyond the violent sharpening of the question as question.

What this means, then, is that when the human is called into question, we must show — properly show — the place where the speaking of God can happen. But even this is not yet speaking of God. It is not yet it. Even Luther's and Kierkegaard's attacks upon Christendom were not it! The cross is erected, but the resurrection has not yet been proclaimed. And ultimately, it is not the cross of Christ that is being erected here, but some other kind of cross. The cross of Christ certainly does not need to be erected by *us* first! The question has not yet received an answer here. *God* has not yet become human. But now more than ever, the *human* has again become human. And that is not a salvific event. More than ever now, the human's subjectivity towers like a glorious, broken column toward heaven. There is speaking of God only where *God* becomes human (in that objectivity which orthodoxy knows so much about!); only where he enters into our emptiness with his *fullness*,[58] into our "No" with his "*Yes.*" The mystics, and we with them, do not speak about this God.

The third way is the way of *dialectic*. It is by far the best way, not only because it is the Pauline-Reformation way, [167] but also because the content is superior. This way presupposes the great truths of both dogmatism as well as self-criticism in their fragmentary nature and relative sufficiency. From the outset, this way takes seriously the positive unfolding of the thought of God on the one side and the critique of the human and all things human on the other. Neither one, however, happens on its own accord but with constant reference to their common presupposition, to the living truth itself, which itself is naturally not a reference. Rather, it stands in the center and gives each one its position and its negation, its sense and meaning. Here we consistently see the living truth, the decisive content of a genuine speaking of God — that God (really God!) becomes human (really human!).

But how should we establish the necessary relationship of each side to the center? The true dialectician knows that this center is incomprehensible and invisible. He will let himself get carried away into direct communication as seldom as possible,[59] for he knows that every dir-

---

58   See the expression in *Romans* 1922 which corresponds to this use regarding faith as the "crater": 11, 19, 27f., 39, 64, 88, 99, etc. (1999 ed., 10, 18, 27, 41, 68, 92, 105); ET "void": 33, 42, 50, 62, 88, 110, 121; "empty space": 102 (1999 ed. 109); ET 124; "empty channel," 42f., 64, (1999 ed., 44, 68); ET 65, 88; and "a vacuum," 127, 224 (1999 ed., 136, 242); ET 149, 240.

59   See Note 57, p. 189.

ect communication about *it*, whether it is positive or negative, is *not* communication *about it*. Instead, it will always be *either* dogmatism *or* self-critique. Only along this narrow cliff ridge can we walk — and keep walking, for if we stand still we will fall. It might be to the right or to the left, but it will definitely be down. Thus the only thing left is an appalling spectacle for all those overcome by dizziness, where we *keep looking* from one side to the other, from the position to its negation and the negation to its position. The only thing to do is to clarify the "Yes" in the "No" and the "No" in the "Yes," pausing no longer than a moment in the gaze of the "Yes" *or* the "No." The only thing to do is to speak of the glory of God in creation (recalling Romans 8 [vv. 19–22]) only to swiftly and strongly emphasize the complete hiddenness in which we perceive God in the natural world; to speak of death and transitoriness only to remember the majesty of an entirely different life that meets us in death. In the same way, the image of God in humans is by no means to be spoken of apart from the warning once and for all that the human as we know him [168] is a fallen creature, whose misery we know more about than his glory. That being said, however, sin should not be spoken of except to point out that we would not recognize it if it were not already forgiven us. According to Luther, that God has made the human righteous means nothing else than "imputed righteousness" [*justificatio impii*; Rom. 4.5 in the Vulgate]. Once the impious person realizes that he is impious and nothing more, he can then hear that he is righteous and nothing more. The only possible answer to the genuine insight into the imperfection of every human work is to eagerly get back to work. However, even after we have done everything we are required to do, we will still have to say that we are worthless slaves [Lk. 17.10]. The present is only worth living in view of the eternal future, the beloved Last Day.[60] But we are mere dreamers if we think that the future of the Lord is not standing right outside our door, today. "A Christian is a free lord over all things, subject to none. A Christian is a perfectly dutiful servant in all things, subject to all."[61]

I need not continue. Whoever has ears to hear will understand what I am getting at here. He understands that the question is the answer because the answer is the question. The moment the answer becomes audible to him, he becomes more eager than ever to ask new questions. Indeed, he would not have had the answer if he did not continue to have the question.

---

60   See Martin Luther's letter to his wife, July 16, 1540; WA.B. 9: 175, 17.
61   See M. Luther, "Freedom of a Christian" (1520), WA 7: 21,1–4; LW 31: 344: "A Christian is a perfectly free lord of all, subject to none. A Christian is a perfectly dutiful servant of all, subject to all."

Faced with all this, an onlooker — a "prairie dweller" probably[62] — will [169] stand there confused, not understanding a thing. Maybe he will whine about supernaturalism[63] or atheism. He will see old Marcion emerging from his grave, and after him, Sebastian Franck,[64] who are actually not the same. Perhaps he will even see it as Schelling's philosophy of identity.[65] He will be shocked about the negation of the world that is so terrible that he no longer knows what is happening to him, and then he will be annoyed about the fact that an affirmation of the world ought to be possible precisely by this means, in a way he never could have dreamed of. He will rise up against the positive, then against the negative, and then again against the "unforgivable contradiction" with which each confronts the other.[66]

---

62   For the following allusions that Barth makes, see Erich Foerster, "Marcionitisches Christentum. Der Glaube an den Schöpfergott und der Glaube an den Erlösergott," *CW* vol. 35 (1921): cols. 819:

> Barth compares the wandering upon the dividing boundary between position and negation of culture one time as a hike on a ridge. In fact, only with such a thing can one compare a life according to this rule, a wandering upon a razor-sharp ridge, where every step too far to the right or the left without fail falls into the abyss, where no standing still, no lying, no sitting is possible, but only an unceasing climbing further. The son of the Swiss mountains may not take this aspect to be as terrible as the millions who live in the flat land. But they will certainly say that the proving of Christendom in life has become an act of virtuosos and a refined technique through this. How ought they go about keeping the balance upon this narrow base?

63   This is an allusion to Reinhard Liebe, *Der Gott des heutigen Geschlechts und wir*. See Note 8, p. 171.

64   The suggestion here is that Barth's theological opponents saw him as having some theological affinities with the theology of Sebastian Franck (1499–1542), but there is no clear archival evidence to support such a suggestion. Perhaps Barth meant here Franck's Anabaptist contemporary Kaspar von Schwenckfeld (1489–1561), who was brought into connection with Barth's theology by W. Köhler (pseudonym Justinus). See Köhler's article, "Zur religiösen Lage der Gegenwart," *Neue Zürcher Zeitung* (October 21, 1920). There Köhler states, "With Barth, the pastor from Safenwil, every Zündel, Schwenckfeld and old Mystic has come alive again . . ."

65   This is perhaps an allusion to A. Albers, "Johannes Müller und Karl Barth, was sie uns heute sind," *CW*, 35 (1921): col. 498–501:

> Nietzsche's friend Franz Overbeck has a strong effect on Barth. Both stand on Lutheran ground and are no strangers to German Romanticism (Fichte, Schelling, and Kierkegaard). That said however, I will not have wanted to say that they are "dependent" upon these men. They belong, even if strongly modified, to the spiritual type of these men (col. 499).

See also Barth's comment on this in a letter to Thurneysen on January 22, 1922: "willingly one lets oneself be handled as a 'type' (by Hirsch, for example, as a religious agnostic . . . by Stange as a philosopher of identity, etc.)" (*Bw. Th* II, 29f.); and Barth's letter to Thurneysen from a few months later on June 21, 1923:

> I get a whiff, behind his [E. Grisebach's] claim that our teaching is a Schelling-like philosophy of identity (Heim also gave the same oracle), . . . of *his* complete incapability (for which our speaking is not entirely innocent), to really listen for what could be meant when God is the talk by us [. . .] It appears to have become fashionable to encumber us with the horror of the philosophy of identity (*Bw. Th* II, 178).

66   See Foerster, *Marcionitisches Christentum*, "What an unbearable contradiction — this theoretical

What should the dialectician — a "son of the mountains" probably — answer, except to say: "My [170] friend, you must understand that when you ask about *God*, when the talk is really from *God*, then you ought not to expect anything different from *me*. I have done all I could to alert you to the fact that my affirmation, like my negation, does not claim to be the truth of God. It only claims to be a *witness* to the truth of God who stands in the center, on the other side of every "Yes" and "No." For this very reason, I have never affirmed without negating, never negated without affirming, because the one, like the other, is not the ultimate thing. I apologize if my *witness* to the ultimate thing is not enough for you and the answer you seek. It could be that I have not yet given clear enough witness to prevent any misunderstanding; that I have not yet lifted up the "Yes" strongly enough through the "No" and the "No" strongly enough through the "Yes." It could be that you in fact could see nothing but that upon which the "Yes" and the "No" depend.

"It could be, however, that my failure lies in the fact that you have not yet properly *asked*, that is, that you have not yet properly asked about *God*. If you had, we would have understood each other." Such is the way the dialectician could answer the onlooker, and he would probably be right.

He would *probably* be right, but maybe he *wouldn't* be[67] — even in the face of the onlooker! For even dialectical speaking suffers from an inherent weakness. This becomes apparent when the dialectician wants to persuade, for then he is dependent upon having his conversation partner *first approach* him with the question of God. If he really speaks of God here, his answer will be the question at the same time. If he really speaks of God here, he will not be allowed to leave his conversation partner standing there shaking his head at the message that he does not yet have the right question. The dialectician would be better off shaking his own head about the fact that *he* apparently does not yet have the right *answer*, the answer which is the very question of his conversation partner. The dialectician's speaking [171] would rest precisely on a very significant presupposition, namely, on the living, original truth, there in the center. His speaking itself is not, could not be, and should not be the framework for this presupposition. Rather, it should be an affirmation and a negation that obviously refers to this presupposition, this origin. But it must come

negation of culture at the same time as a practical affirmation!" (col. 820).

67 Barth alludes here to an anecdote from his Safenwil days that he shared with Thurneysen in a letter from May 30, 1921:

You know, that among our friends . . . The anecdote is circulating that the two of us sat one time for an entire afternoon face to face just smoking. After an hour of this, *I* said, "Perhaps!" and after another hour of silence, *you* said, "But perhaps not!" and that is supposed to have been our conversation and the concentrated content of our system! (*Bw. Th.* II, 492).

primarily in the form of a *claim* that it is all this. The claim will sound *clear* to the right and to left, but a final claim showing that the right and the left are saying the same thing will sound *ambiguous*, very ambiguous.

How does human speaking become meaningful in a necessary and compelling way? How does it come to have power as a witness? This is the problem that arises with particular force out of the dialectical method, because everything that could be done to make human speaking carry meaning and bear witness is done. On those occasions when dialectical speaking *has* proven itself to be meaningful and bear witness — as in the case of several interlocutors of Plato, Paul, and of the Reformers — it did not do so on the basis of the abilities and activities of the dialectician or his claims, which are in fact questionable, more questionable than any indignant onlooker could imagine. When it happens, it is because the dialectician's unambiguous and ambiguous claims allow the living truth in the center, the reality of God, to assert *itself*. It creates the question that is raised about it, and *gives* the answer that the human is looking for, because it already *is* precisely both: the right question and the right answer.

But the possibility that God *himself* speaks when the human speaks of him is not contained in the dialectical way as such. It arises where even this way *comes to an end*. It is evident that one can also elude the claims of the dialectical theologian. In this respect, the dialectical theologian himself is no better than the dogmatic or self-critical theologian. The actual weakness of the dogmatic and self-critical theologian, his own inability to truly speak of *God*, and his compulsion to speak always about something else, appear in even more pronounced ways in the dialectical theologian. Precisely *because* he wants to say *it all*, and in view of the living truth itself no less, he becomes only more painfully aware of the unavoidable *absence* of this living truth in his saying it all. Even if [172] God were to suddenly speak his own Word and give a sense and meaning to everything, beyond anything his conversation partner could say about it all, even then, *precisely* then, the dialectical theologian as such is proven wrong, and can only confess: "We cannot speak of God." Even if God himself speaks, it can only happen beyond that which could be said by the dogmaticians and the self-critics, and perhaps even more primitive speakers.

There is no reason why dialectical theology should be the *preferred* leader, even if it simply leads *up to* the front of this door that can only be opened from the inside. If it somehow imagines itself to be of special importance, even if only as preparation for that which God does, let it be clear that with all its paradoxes it can do no more *to this end* than a simple, direct word of faith and a humility. In relation to the kingdom of God, any pedagogy can be good or bad — a stool may be high enough and the longest ladder may be too short to take the kingdom of heaven by force.

Now who — and this is more or less clearly every theologian — after seeing all this, after testing all the possibilities available in these three ways (and I have only given the viable possibilities) would not be distressed?

I now turn to the third claim which I would like to use to characterize our situation: *We ought to do both.* We ought to speak of God but cannot, and *precisely in this way, give God the glory.* There is not much to say about this statement. It can only stand there as a concluding stroke and confirm that everything is meant the way it all has been said.

The Word of God is the necessary but impossible task of theology. This is the conclusion to everything I have said up until this point. It is actually all I have to say on this topic. Now what? Does it mean a return to the low country where one appears to be a theologian but in reality is actually something completely different, something that others can be too, causing them to fundamentally *not* need us? I am afraid that even if we were capable of such a tour de force, the logic of the matter would soon lead us right back to where we stand now. Or should we move from a service of the *word* to a service of *silence*?[68] As if it were easier and more possible [173] to be still before God (really before *God*), than to speak of him! What kind of game is this supposed to be? Should theology just bid its farewell? Should we hang up our hats and become happy, like other people? But people are not happy. If they were, we would not be here. The pressure of our task is a sign of the plight of every other human task. If we were not here, other theologians would then be in the same situation. A mother cannot walk away from her children and the shoemaker cannot walk away from his block, and we cannot be convinced that the dialectic of the children's nursery is any less effective than the dialectic of our theological study halls. Giving up theology makes as little sense as taking of one's life — nothing will come of it, and nothing will change by doing so. So, persevere. That is all. We ought to *know* both the necessity and the impossibility of our task. What does this mean?

It means we hold our gazes steadfastly on that which is expected of us since we have been set in the place where we are now standing. The question is not what will come of it, and whether people will be satisfied with us. Our task only makes sense within the context as we know it of human life in its entirety, only in nature and culture, where questions arise about how this entirety as such makes sense within the world and God's creation. This question can only arise in the human. Therefore our task can be categorized only as that which cannot be categorized. Such logic, such a categorical imperative of objectivity,[69] is a part of our vocation just like any other vocation. But ours has *this* particular content. We must fix our eyes on this categorical imperative, like every railroad conductor does. More cannot be demanded from us; neither can any *less*.

As we consider our task, it must be equally remembered that only *God* can speak of God. The task of theology is the Word of God. This means the certain *defeat of all* theology and *of every* theologian. Even here we must not avoid the things that are meant to be seen, or divert our attention to one side or the other, toward the array of enlightening or unenlightening veiling [174] and disguising of the facts of the matter. We must be clear about the fact that no matter which way we pursue, even if our names were Calvin or Luther, we would no more reach the goal than Moses did the Promised Land [cf. Deut. 34.4]. Even though it is truly worthwhile to be careful about choosing the way we must go, not settling for the first thing we find, we must keep in mind that our goal is the speaking of *God himself*. So we ought not to wonder when at the end of our ways, even if we have performed our task well (especially if we have done it well) our mouths *close*.

Allow me to conclude with three observations.

1. I hardly dare to hope, and yet I still do, that no one will approach me after this and ask: "So, what should we do now? What do you think should happen in the Church and the academy if *this* is the situation?" I have no suggestions for you, neither about the reform of the office of the pastor nor about the reform of theological education. It is not *about this*. It appears to me that the question is not, "What do we do now *if* this is our situation?" but rather whether we want to recognize *that* this is our situation. Once we acknowledge this, perhaps there would be several things to change in the Church and in the academy from what they are; but maybe not. A conversation about these things would only be possible and useful on the basis of our acknowledgment of the situation, but again, it is not dependent upon *this*.

2. Our plight is also[70] our promise. When *I* say that, it is a dialectical statement just like any other — and we now know what dialectic is. You may say, "Thank you for the promise which I only experience as perplexity!" and I will not be able to answer you. Yet indeed, *I* may not be the only one saying that our plight is also our promise. It might be possible that it is the living truth which dwells beyond the "Yes" and "No." It might be the reality of God which I cannot enact, even

---

69   "Objectivity" [*Sachlichkeit*] would soon become a leading concept in Barth's first dogmatic cycle, given in Göttingen, 1924; see *Unterricht*, 398 (index), for example. The English translation of Barth's Göttingen dogmatic cycle did not carry this term over into the index.

70   *W.G. Th.* mistakenly reads "is our promise." This was corrected after the first printing.

through a dialectical reversal. [175] In this dialectical reversal, out of no power or love of ours, it might be possible that the promise enters into our perplexity. It might be possible that the Word — the Word of God that we will never speak — has taken on our weakness and perversion, so that *our* word becomes capable of the Word of God precisely *in* its weakness and perversion — or at least become the mantle and earthen vessel of it [cf. 2 Cor. 4.7]. I say it might be possible. If it were so, we would have every occasion to speak loudly and strongly from the hope, from the hidden glory of our vocation, instead of speaking from the need.

3. Although I have touched upon the *actual* theme of my presentation a few times, I have not expressly named it. All of my thoughts circle around the one point which is called "Jesus Christ" in the New Testament. Whoever says "Jesus Christ" may not say, "It might be possible," but, rather, must say, "It *is*." Yet which one of us is in the position to say "Jesus Christ?" *We* must satisfy ourselves with the fact that "Jesus Christ" *has been said* by his first witnesses. Our task is to believe in their witness, to believe in the promise, and to be witnesses of their witness — to be theologians of *Scripture*. My lecture today is given in the vein of the Old Testament and Reformed theology. As a Reformed theologian (and in my opinion, of course, not only as that), I must maintain a certain distance toward the Lutheran concept of real presence — the Lutheran "is"[71] — as well as toward the Lutheran *certainty of salvation* [*Heilsgewißheit*].[72] The question now, is whether

---

71   See the report on the Marburg Colloquy on religion from 1529, for example, by Osiander (WA 30/III: 147, 15–17; *LW* 38: 63–68): "Luther lifted the velvet cover and showed him the words, 'this is my body,' which he for himself had written in chalk, and said, here is our Scripture." For a further report on this, see WA 30/III, 147: 112; *LW* 38: 63; and WA 21: 137, 9–13.

72   See for example, B.J. Gottschick, "Die Heilsgewißheit des evangelischen Christen, im Anschluß an Luther dargestellt," *ZThK*, 13 (1903): 349–435; Karl Holl, *Die Rechtfertigungslehre in Luthers Vorlesung über den Römerbrief mit besonderer Rücksicht auf die Frage der Heilsgewißheit* (1910), in his *Gesammelte Aufsätze zur Kirchengeschichte I: Luther* (Tübingen: Mohr, 1916/1932), 111–154; and the presentation by Kurt Leese which emphasizes the "certainty of God as the certainty of salvation", *Die Prinzipienlehre der neueren systematischen Theologie im Lichte der Kritik Feuerbachs* (Leipzig: Hinrichs, 1912). For more evidence on the question of "certainty," see Paul Althaus, *Die Prinzipien der deutschen reformierten Dogmatik im Zeitalter der aristotelischen Scholastik. Eine Untersuchung zur altprotestantischen Theologie* (Leipzig: Wissenschaftliche Buchgesellschaft, 1914), 179–273, the third part of which carries the heading, "Die Lehre von der religiösen Gewißheit"; Franz Hermann Reinhold von Frank, *System der christlichen Gewißheit*, 2 Vols. (Erlangen: Deichert, 1881–1884); Karl Heim, *Das Gewißheitsproblem in der systematischen Theologie bis zu Schleiermacher* (Leipzig: Hinrichs, 1911); and idem, *Glaubensgewißheit. Eine Untersuchung über die Lebensfrage der Religion* (Leipzig; Hinrichs, 1916/1923); Ludwig Ihmels, *Die christliche Wahrheitsgewißheit, ihr letzer Grund und ihre Entstehung* (Leipzig: Deichert, 1901/1914). "Certainty" was also a typical concept of Barth's teachers. See Wilhelm Herrmann, *Die Gewißheit des Glaubens und die Freiheit der Theologie* (Freiburg i. Br.: Mohr, 1887), 18–52; *Die Religion im Verhältnis zum Welterkennen und zur Sittlichkeit. Eine Grundlegung der*

theology can and ought to get out beyond being a prolegomena to
Christology. It could also indeed be the case that with the prolegomena
everything is already said.

systematischen Theologie (Halle: Niemeyer,1879), 39–67; *Der Verkehr des Christen mit Gott. Im Anschluß
an Luther dargestellt* (Stuttgart: Cotta, 1886), 51, 53, 66, 91, 93, 101, 146, etc.; ET *The Communion of
the Christian with God*, 2nd ed., J. Sandys Stanyon trans., R.W. Stewart and Robert T. Voelkel, eds.
(Philadelphia: Fortress Press, 1971), 58, 61, 101, 103, etc. Barth had already given a critique of the
concept of "certainty of salvation" in *Romans* 1922, 398 (1999 ed., 432); ET 411.

CHAPTER 8

THE SUBSTANCE AND TASK OF REFORMED DOCTRINE, 1923

[202] In the year 1884, a "Reformed Alliance"[1] was founded in order to bring the Reformed churches, congregations and individuals that were scattered throughout Germany, more closely together. Its general assembly was held biennially at various locations.

Sometime around the beginning of summer, 1923, Barth was invited to give a lecture at the nineteenth general assembly of the Reformed Alliance, held on September 16–19 in Emden. He accepted the invitation and gave a description of the theme, which he personally chose.[2] The lecture was worked out during a visit Barth made to Switzerland, in St. Gallen-Bruggen at Eduard Thurneysen's home.[3] Barth finished it during a "prolonged work day"[4] in Göttingen.

Barth arrived in Emden on the afternoon of September 16 and participated

---

1   A critical edition of this essay in German can be found in *V.u.kl.A. 1922–1925*, 202–247. Page numbers in brackets in this essay run according to the *GA*. For the Reformed Alliance, see R. Steiner's article, "Reformierter Bund," in *RGG*, 3rd ed., Vol. V, cols. 894f.

2   Barth first mentioned his obligation to give a lecture in Emden to Thurneysen on June 18, 1923 (*Bw. Th*. II, 176). Professor Dr. August Lang, moderator of the Reformed Alliance since 1920, informed Barth in a letter from July 5, 1923 of the final dates of the general assembly and of Barth's lecture, which had already been basically agreed upon. In the letter it says, among other things, "You already know from Pastor Heilmann, that at this year's conference, we are especially looking to you, and that you have indeed already given your acceptance, along with a nice formulation of the theme of your lecture." The original is in the Karl Barth Archive, Basel. Johann Adam Heilmann (1860–1930): In 1884 he was pastor in what was formerly known as the Waldenserkolonie, Waldensberg; 1887–1891 pastor in Spanbeck; 1891–1920 pastor in Göttingen. In Göttingen he was effective in promoting the forming of the chair for Professor of Reformed Theology, and was involved in dealings with regard to the calling of Barth to that position. In the Karl Barth Archive, Basel, however, there is no letter about these dealings from Heilmann. Since Barth and Heilmann were both in Göttingen, and met up with one another occasionally, most likely the invitation to the Emden lecture was passed on to Barth from Heilmann directly in conversation. See *Bw. Th*. II, 5, 19, 28, 71f., 74, 138, 145, 361.

3   See a postcard from Barth to Lukas Christ from September 3, 1923, written in St. Gallen-Bruggen: "I have been sitting here by Thurneysen and will stay until around the tenth, working on my lecture for the Reformed Alliance, which shall go out from the batch on the seventeenth in Emden . . . Eduard and I are working here in two attic rooms next to each other, not without the exchange of information of the deepest kind" (KBA 9223.50).

4   *Bw. Th*. II, 183 (September 24, 1923).

in most of the events of the following days,[5] which [203] brought him into contact for the first time with a great number of leading representatives of Reformed
Protestantism in Germany. He gave his lecture on Monday September 17 at
nine o'clock in the morning in a small hall at the house of the Blue Cross (after
a morning devotion led by the general superintendent, Gerhard Coeper, from
Aurich). "Not until the third day was there any discussion of my lecture. The whole
affair was poorly organized, as there was never the proper amount of time to
have conversations."[6] Afterwards, Barth expressed the following to Thurneysen:

> my Emden lecture was the voice of the preacher in the wilderness [cf. Isa.
> 40.3]. The leading men of the Reformed Alliance are completely unbroken
> people who in no way allow themselves to be rattled. They would rather
> be satisfied with praising me to the skies, and then go about their ways
> as if nothing had happened.[7]

In the discussion, he was able to "hinder, at least formally and with effort, the construction of a rainbow of peace over the differences which have become visible."[8]

It was reported in the business meeting on September 18, among other things,
that a position of Honorary Professor of Reformed Theology at Göttingen had been
formed, and that Barth had been called to begin teaching in it.[9]

Barth sent over to Georg Merz a completed manuscript of the lecture to be
printed for the fifth issue of *Zwischen den Zeiten* on September 24.[10]

[204] Let me begin by reading a short snippet: "Any observer who has
been paying attention could not come away without seeing just how
tiny a role *unfruitful theological discussion* plays these days. The conference
was pervaded by a heavily spiritual streak, which seized and revived in
as *untheological a manner as possible* the old truths of the Reformation in
their religious meaning for today; with this turn back to the old and

---

5   See the conference schedule in *Reformierte Kirchenzeitung*, 73 (1923): 193f., and Barth's own report
     about his stay in Emden in a letter to friends from September 24, 1923 (*Bw. Th.* II, 182–187). About
     the course of the general assembly, see the report of H.A. Hesse, "Die Emdener Tagung," in
     Reformierte Kirchenzeitung, 73: 232–234, as well as the *Rhein-Ems-Zeitung*, Emden (September 18
     and 22, 1923).
6   *Bw. Th.* II, 186.
7   Ibid., 189f. (September 25, 1923).
8   Ibid., 187 (September 24, 1923).
9   See J.A. Heilmann, "Die Ausbildung der reform. Theologen. Vortrag auf der Tagung des
     Reformierten Bundes in Emden" in *Reformierte Kirchenzeitung*, 73 (1923): 262–264, esp. 264; and
     Bw. Th. II, 187.
10   The request from the *Reformierte Kirchenzeitung* for rights to the first printing was refused by Barth.
     See *Bw. Th.* II, 183. It appeared in the *Reformierte Kirchenzeitung*, 74 (1924): 2–5, 9–11, 13–17 as a
     reprint of its publication in *ZZ* Vol. 2, No. 5 (1924): 8–39.

sacred legacy, the conference allowed itself to be led by a spirit of resolute decisiveness that presses *on* and that wants to test out[11] in practice these old truths through new relations."

This statement stands in a report on the recent conference of the eastern section of the Reformed World Alliance in Zurich, and comes from the pen of one of the leading personalities of this event.[12] If the position expressed here is characteristic of the affinity and aversion of the widest and most authoritative circles among modern Reformed churches to date — and there is no doubt that this is the case — then the task given to me today is a thankless task. Indeed, I am to speak about Reformed doctrine, theology, preaching, and proclamation, and thus exactly about that which those in Zurich have been as silent "as possible." I am also to speak about that which they would much rather and with increasing measure keep silent about. Why do they prefer to keep silent?

I believe I see three reasons for this: *First*, they prefer to keep silent because in Protestantism, mainly among theologians remarkably, the flood of conviction is still on the rise [205] that "doctrine" is something different, something worse and less important than "*life.*" The concepts "theological" and "unfruitful" appear to many of us to be neighbors, at least. Along with it is the question of the proper *content* of preaching, which, if we are not fully indifferent to it, we are willing to defer while we discuss the good will and the best ways to understand all kinds of other church practices, the inner and outer union, the actions in our shared struggle against "Rome" and the modern lack of faith, the spiritual and material support of one another, the organization and development of our potential in "the conviction to move in the direction toward which the *spirit* of Jesus Christ directs us," as the report states in its conclusion.[13]

---

11   Barth's manuscript had "test in" not "test out." The *GA* took the corrected version from the *Neue Züricher Zeitung* Nr. 1055 (August 3, 1923).

12   See Adolf Keller, "Der Reformierte Weltbund in Zürich," *Neue Züricher Zeitung*, Nr. 1055 (August 3, 1923). The emphases are Barth's own. Adolf Keller (1872–1963): In 1896–1899 he was an assistant pastor in the German evangelical congregation in Cairo; 1899–1904 pastor at the castle in Stein am Rhein (Canton Schaffhausen); 1904–1909 pastor at the German-speaking congregation of the National Church [*église nationale*] in Geneva, where Barth was assigned to him as a vicar; 1909–1924 pastor at the Church of St. Peter in Zurich. In 1920 he became the first secretary of the newly founded "Swiss Evangelical Alliance of Churches" [*Schweizerischen Evangelischen Kirchenbundes*]. Keller dedicated himself from that time on to ecumenical concerns. Among other things, he was the first general secretary of the "European Center for Ecclesiastical Assistance Projects" [*Europäische Zentralstelle für kirchliche Hilfsaktionen*] in 1924. Because of the polemical use of this article by Barth in 1924, a partly public and partly private dispute was carried out in a letter exchange between Keller and Barth. See *Zur Kenntnisnahme*, in *V.u.kl.A. 1922–1925*, 395ff.

13   Keller wrote in "Der Reformierte Weltbund":

This alliance [of the European continental section of the Reformed World Alliance] strives without aggressive goals towards the Reformed family for now. But visible on the horizon

Secondly, they prefer to keep silent because based on past experience, the question of proper doctrine is primarily not conducive to the Christian *unity* so wished for today because any attempt at a serious understanding of *what* the members of the so-called "Reformed family" — those of the eastern section (not to speak of the western one!) — want to agree upon, of *what* they want to fight for together, of *what* they want to support in one another would probably arise much less harmoniously and impressively than the agreement on strategy and tactics, which no doubt was met quite happily in Zurich, and which even happens at festivities that take place in picturesque, historical places where the praises of Christian brotherhood are inevitably sung. Whoever adheres to the Reformed doctrine in its uniqueness[14] conjures the ghosts of [206] Marburg as well,[15] along with other unfriendly shadows. And who would not rather avoid these if he could?

Thirdly, and most importantly, the question about proper doctrine cannot be raised without uncovering and confessing a great — perhaps the greatest — *dilemma* of modern Protestantism. The contempt of "doctrine" uses the same reasoning as the judgment of the fox about the grapes.[16] If we *had* something more substantial and authoritative to say, if we *had* a compelling and recognizable theology beyond specific groups and circles, if we *had* a message that we *had to* proclaim, we would not think differently. On the whole, our churches *do not* have any of this. I think it is not a mistake to say that this is true even for those who are irreverent enough — or frank enough — to declare our inherited doctrines obsolete by doing away with them.[17] The question about proper

are indeed the further goals of a generally more intimate connection of the Protestant world, like they are already in motion in the larger movements towards unity, without the demand for power, without superstition and towards organizing without a suspicious overconfidence based on forms and formulas, but rather in the conviction to move oneself in the way which the spirit of Jesus Christ directs us.

14   Keller wrote in "Der Reformierte Weltbund":

The Reformed spirit is stirring again, and is becoming religiously as well as sociologically effective and fruitful today. After the Reformed uniqueness had to pay for the cost of the union, namely in Germany, it is now discovering obvious tasks that need to be solved, especially by the inherent principle of Reformed theology.

15   At the Marburg Colloquy in 1529, the union between Luther and Zwingli about the Sacrament of the Lord's Supper broke down. Luther explained in the end that "I am not your Lord, your judge, or even your teacher, thus our spirit and your spirit do not sing the same song, but it is apparent that we do not have a unified spirit . . ." (cited according to Walther Köhler, *The Marburg Religionsgespräch 1529. Versuch einer Rekonstruktion* in Schriften des Vereins für Reformationsgeschichte, Nr. 148 (Leipzig, 1929), 129.

16   See Aesop's Fables, Nr. 33, "The Fox and the Grapes"; ET *The Fables of Aesop* (London: Paddington Press, 1975), 167.

17   On the "doing away with" and the silent omission of the obligation of individuals and congregations

doctrine leads us directly to the vacuum at the *center* of our churches and of Christendom.

The shame and embarrassment at just the sight of this vacuum could lead to setting a *deeply* disturbing question mark after the spirited call to "the old and sacred legacy" and to "press on" with practical tests of our inheritance. Therefore, an "Oh touch, touch it not!"[18] calls from every side! And am I now to stick my finger exactly into this wound? Wouldn't it be better to follow the well-founded instincts of the majority of our Protestant contemporaries and hurry along like the priest and Levite past the one who fell among thieves [cf. Lk. 10.30-32]? Wouldn't it be better to bracket out the question of doctrine as "somehow" already solved [207] or able to be solved, and turn with "resolute decisiveness" to *the* question of Christendom and our Reformedness, which people can speak about in an interested, peaceful, and happy manner — especially in these times when life, even the life of the Church, is already complicated enough, and when simple watchwords and ways should enjoy a more excellent name?

But I think that no matter how the chips fall, we have occasion to be thankful to the moderators of the Reformed Alliance for their courage to place this wound onto the agenda of this conference. It is a question that at some point must be taken up again. Why shouldn't we start the conversation? Sooner or later even the Reformed International[19] group and Protestant Christendom in general will not be able to avoid facing this question more earnestly than they do now, cost what it will and come what may. The gloomy seriousness of the age into which we have entered will not allow the churches (those of Europe in any case!) to appease themselves with false solutions, even if they have the advantage of an enlightening simplicity. But the talk of pressing on to a practical testing of the old truths in new relations *is* only a *fake solution. What* is supposed to be tested here? In the long run, will it escape the sharp eyes of the children of the world, and our own, the children of the house, that we have here a predicate without a subject? Is it then so absolutely certain that even where the confessions still hold power or do so at least on paper, our Reformed churches still reverberate with the "old truths of the Reformation?"

"In their religious meaning for today," is stated further. What is this supposed to mean! Are the openly voiced or unvoiced adjustments,

---

to adhere to confessional documents in Switzerland, cf. Barth's own description in "Die kirchliche Zustände in der Schweiz," in *Vu.kl.A. 1922–1925*, 14ff.

18   See the poem by E. Geibel, "Wo still ein Herz von Liebe glüht," in *Gedichte* (Berlin 1840, 277): "O rühret, rühret nicht daran!"

19   Barth means here the "Reformation Alliance" which gathered for the first time for a general assembly in Edinburgh in 1877.

changes, and reinterpretations of the Reformation message that are indicated by such a statement so immaterial that we may spare ourselves from asking by what right, by what calling, and by what authority precisely these things are brought forth in the name of "evangelical Reformed" preaching today? I am not aware of any satisfying settlement of the arguments about this question that took place in the nineteenth century. [208] Is the suggestion to "press on" really so practical with this unsolved question at our backs? Furthermore, we can no longer close our eyes to the fact that the work of overhauling, organizing, and educating, which the people of our churches say they would prefer to be occupied with than theology, only drives closer that fatal moment in which it will be about really having something to offer to those of the east and the west who have noticed all the preparations, or about telling them what is really going on at least — a moment when the congregation, even the most vibrant, active one, will fall silent in order to at last and finally *hear* what the pastor or even professor of the Reformed church has to *say* to them about important and right things, something illuminating about the situation of the human between heaven and earth, something appropriate to the claim that Reformed doctrine is about redeeming truth. Is it prudent to suppress the question about the occurrence of this moment, a question upon which everything else depends for its meaning and value, or to place it at the end of the whole program? Wouldn't it have been better for the entire program to wait until there is clarity, a will, or an urgency about the question on the agenda?

Furthermore, there was also much talk in Zurich about the coming dispute with "*Rome.*"[20] The seriousness and actuality of this task ought not to be doubted. But how can we — and should we — dispute with "Rome" before we have examined ourselves in a completely different way on the issue of what we represent and want as non-Roman Catholic Christians? Do we have [209] a sufficiently urgent, shared concern about

---

20   Keller wrote in "Der Reformierte Weltbund":

> [There were] meaningful statements made in Zurich by Reformed Protestantism about the relation to Roman Catholicism [. . .] As a summary, it can be said that a strengthening of Roman Catholicism has been reported from all sides, an attack that is conscious of its goals. This is to be taken more seriously than other advantages about the present circumstances [. . .] The attitude of the conference toward the entire problem was absolutely worthy. Full attention was given to every true religious power in Catholicism; full trust in the effectiveness within the Roman Catholic church, casual toward the undeniable success of Rome, which is not to be rejected and which is reached with the strongest of means, but also with full awareness to hope in the reaching over; complete decisiveness in the necessary argument from every unevangelical means, a limit to the strengthening of the evangelical position itself, and the production of a better and action-ready Protestant unity.

Half of the article is dedicated to this theme.

Catholicism? If we do *not* have it, or do not know what we should think about this, how ought we then be even a capable negotiating and conversational partner in the coming ecumenical council in 1925,[21] never mind more than that?

One more point along these lines: the friends of a Reformed theology that should be "as untheological as possible" prefer to invoke the practical, union-like tendencies of the old Reformers, especially the active, organized, world-spanning spirit of *Calvin*, but they consistently overlook the fact that Calvin first wrote his *Institutes before* those much-admired literary letters on church politics.[22] In other words, he first had a *theme* and *then* thought about its variations; he first *knew* what he wanted and *then* wanted what he knew. To stand this most highly appropriate order on its head "with resolute decisiveness," to want to begin where Calvin stopped, to want to reap with Calvin without having sown with him [cf. Lk. 19.21] is neither Calvinistic nor beneficial. The Reformation had its beginning for Zwingli in *preaching* and for Calvin in *lecturing*. If what we are talking about today, if the "building up of a more strongly pronounced Reformed consciousness,"[23] is to be genuine, then it *also* has to display a disposition to go only along the way on which Luther *and* Zwingli *and* Calvin went: the way of *reflecting* with seriousness and rigor about its actions. Later, a few years later perhaps, this conscious and "strongly spiritual striving" could still come into its own.

Perhaps one of the few favors performed by the *German* Reformed churches today consists [210] of reminding their confessional relatives in the west (but especially reminding themselves) that there could be something like a Reformed *objectivity*, despite every supposed want and need of the times.

We must now turn to a somewhat more fundamental point of view. Whoever calls himself "Reformed" (not Catholic, not Lutheran, and not even "Evangelical" in nice — much overstated or understated — generality, but rather Evangelical-*Reformed*), a Reformed pastor, a Reformed theologian, or a Reformed churchgoer — and to such individuals I would now like to turn — fulfills, simply and soberly that

---

21   From August 19–31, 1925, the World Church Conference [*Weltkirchenkonferenz*] took place in Stockholm, which was organized by the "For Life and Work" movement. More than 600 delegates from different Christian churches participated (with the exception of Roman Catholics).

22   Calvin had written the first edition of the *Institutes* in 1536 in Basel (*CR* 29 [= *Calvini Opera* I]), before his first work in Geneva. On Calvin's international correspondence, see *CR* 38/2–48 (= *Calvini Opera* 10/2–20).

23   Keller wrote in "Der Reformierte Weltbund": "At this first great convention of the Alliance on the continent, the *building up of a more strongly pronounced Reformed consciousness* has become clear."

which the Zurich report somewhat pathetically called the "turn back to the old and sacred legacy" of the Reformation. This type of individual does not get caught up in the question of whether this legacy is a serious issue for him, or whether he knows what he is doing when he takes this turn. What does "a turn back to the old and sacred legacy" of the Reformation mean, especially to the Reformed Reformation? In short, it is the question of "Reformed doctrine." I mainly hear three answers to it.

The first answer is that of those whose piety is *characteristic* of their own ecclesiastical type, which in this case is Reformed. This friend loves the church like he loves his people, his city, and the household tools of his forefathers. He loves them *more* than others because they are precisely *his* church, just as he loves the valley of his homeland more than other valleys. This pleasure in the distinct uniqueness of the familiar form of his own present brand of Christianity — one may certainly not only call this piety but a genuine *pietas* — recalls for him the sharp profile and contours of the Reformed past with its powerful Christian, churchly self-confidence, its classical literary monuments, and its unique traditions in doctrine and life. The friend of this type holds to the vital or potential fragments and traces of "being" Reformed today, with a well-understood defiance toward the all-leveling and uncreative spirit of the nineteenth and twentieth centuries. Calvin (or in eastern Switzerland, Zwingli) must again come to be honored because he is *our* man. The Heidelberg Catechism, furthermore, must be utilized because it is *our* traditional [211] book. Predestination, the Ten Commandments, and the necessity of church order are truths to be asserted because we read in the history of *our* church that it must be so. Our conversation partners point us to the Reformed confessions, and perhaps are friendly enough to tell us to which of these hardly concordant documents we should dedicate a particular reverence and respect to.

But even if such an answer must finally be invalid, its deep significance should not be doubted. Being Reformed means actually placing oneself into one's historical place as a Christian, that is, placing oneself into a spiritual community characterized by the church of its past, and in particular, defined more sharply by its distant past than by its recent or barely departed present. The open or secret rebellion against the accidental, particular, and historical things of our life circumstances; our desire, at least in the Christian relationship, to take direct flight into the general and absolute; and our impatience to be be a disciple of Jesus from now on instead of a — oh, so banal! — Reformed person has indeed almost become for many of us a self-evident habit of thought. This betrays, however, a perspective that is, to say the least, one-sided. Even as Christians, we all belong somewhere, whether we have long not realized it or not wanted to realize it. To at least recognize and take seriously the primary, significant nature of this matter is an act of simply belonging to a life that can be avoided for a while but surely not forever.

The site where the Absolute *witnesses to itself* is the *relative*, is always the *relative*, which is laid *before our feet* despite later discoveries and advances. The site where the general Christian Church is *believed* is the *particular* church with *its* history and *its* face. The knowledge of the last things cannot be earned by an overly hasty hurrying past the penultimate things, and the peace of Christendom cannot be earned with the inane desire of people to understand or even unite if they have not yet taken themselves seriously for once, never mind their opponent. In itself, the fact that one is Reformed is already a good reason for it to be taken seriously, and [212] thus indeed means *being* under the watchful eye of the particular beginnings of the Reformed tradition, and if nothing urgent gets in the way, *remaining* there. That is what we wanted to deliberately say with our answer.

But the serious thoughts aroused by this answer ought not to be suppressed. The Reformed church will in no way be served by the love of an antiquarian, by the *laudator temporis acti*,[24] by the defenders of the religious homeland, or the friends of the Reformed church who love it because it is Reformed. These friends must be told that the church in this regard as well as in others is very poor soil for the blue flowers of the Romantic age.[25] From the beginning and standing everywhere in our church there is — in a great lack of piety that is different to Lutheranism — a fundamental denial of the entire Christian tradition when it claims to possess religious meaning in itself, when it cannot justify itself before the spirits by the Scriptures which are witnessed to as truth by the Spirit. The "given" things in history that were laid before the feet of our forefathers were not the objects of a loving and devotional reverence but rather the objects of serious and critical examination. The conservative principle with which they, too, naturally operated, was crisscrossed and broken by them precisely through its opposite, such that their beginnings show only a very fragmentary loyalty toward the past, and actually show a broad, smooth, unsparing break with it. Surely the friend of the Old Reformed type will not want to declare this position of the Fathers as antiquated by producing a new, Reformed, and now, finally, sacred tradition, will he?

There is certainly a history of the Reformed church: documents of its faith and characteristic forms of its teaching and its life that are known, respected, and reflected upon by those who want to call themselves

---

24   See Horace, *Ars poetica*, v. 173.
25   The "blue flower," the object of desire of minstrels, goes back to the incomplete novel by Novalis, *Heinrich von Ofterdingen* (1802). It very quickly became a symbol of the romantic feeling for life.

Reformed (and they will not be finished with these too quickly). There is, however, strictly speaking, no Reformed tradition outside the one timeless tradition, namely, that of the appeal to the open Bible and the Spirit which speaks out of the spirits. In a very well-thought-out manner, our Fathers did *not* leave behind for us [213] *any Augustana*[26] which authentically interprets the Word of God, never mind a Formula of Concord. They have not left behind *any* "Symbolic books" which later, like those of the Lutherans, would come to have a whiff of having been "inspired."[27] Instead, they have only left us *confessions*, of which more than one begins or ends with the open caution of better teachings in the future.[28] The Reformed church does *not*, therefore, know of any "dogma" in a strict, sacerdotal sense. The *authority* of doctrine in the Reformed church in no way lies in Christian history but rather in *Scripture* and the *Spirit*, *both* of which (even the Scripture!) stand on the other side of Christian history. Remaining true to the Fathers must mean, then, adhering precisely to history the way they themselves adhered to it: letting history speak but only as an indication beyond itself to revelation, not confusing age with originality, and not confusing the authority that is given to the Church with the authority by which the Church was founded, not recognizing any *invariata* and *invariabilis*[29] besides the

---

26   The preface to the *Augsburg Confession* (1530) reads, "As a result, a short confession was assembled out of the divine, apostolic, and prophetic Scripture . . ." (*BC*, 5, par. 2; *BSLK*, 3, 22–25); and "To this Christian confession, founded upon the witness of the unchangeable truth of the divine Word . . ." (*BC*, 7, par. 7; *BSLK*, 5, 27–29).

27   The locus "Die libris symbolicis" was a standard element of Lutheran dogmatics during the era of Orthodoxy. On the "inspiration" of the confessions, see D. Hollaz in SchmP 79: "Doubtlessly, in a supportive sense the symbolic books are called θεόπνευστοι by quite a few supporters . . . Because we also do not doubt that God in a special assembly has influenced the minds of the faithful teachers, who had written out the symbols of the church."

28   See for example, *Acta Synodi ecclesiarum Belgicarum* (1571), in *Bekenntnisschriften und Kirchenordnungen der nach Gottes Wort reformierten Kirche*, 2nd ed., Wilhelm Niesel, ed. (Zürich: Zollikon, 1938), 284: "These articles are set to be a lawful order of the church, proven in such a mutual agreement that if the use by other churches is proclaimed, they could, or must, be altered, added to, or diminished." See also the *Confessio Scotia* (1560), in ibid., 84; ET *Scottish Confession of Faith, 1560*, trans Arthur C. Cochrane; and *Basler Bekenntnis* (1534), *BSRK*, 100: 14–18; ET, *The First Confession of Basel, 1534*, trans. Arthur C. Cochrane, 96: "Finally we now want to subject our confession to the judgment of the divine, Biblical Scripture, and should we be informed from the same Holy Scripture of a better one, we have thereby expressed our readiness to be willing at any time to obey God and his holy Word with great thanksgiving." See further *Zwinglis Thesen* (1523), *BSRK*, 2, 17f.; ET *Zwingli's Sixty-seven Articles of 1523*, trans. Arthur C. Cochrane, 36; *Confessio tetrapolitana* (1530), *BSRK*, 69: 28–30 (this edition has not been translated into English). See also *The Tetrapolitan Confession of 1530*, trans. Arthur C. Cochrane, 72). The above cited works are found in *Reformed Confessions of the Sixteenth Century*, Arthur C. Cochrane, ed., (Philadelphia: Westminster, 1966); *Böhmischen Bekenntnis* (1609), *BSRK*, 489: 7–10.

29   This is an allusion to the dispute after Luther's death about the standard text of the *Augsburg Confession* (1530). The theologians who were more inclined toward Phillip Melanchthon appealed

one Scripture and Spirit that [214] does not bow down before any hat propped on a stick,[30] even if it is the hat of Calvin himself. It means letting Scripture and Spirit, Spirit and Scripture alike, critically take on the authority — even in the face of the honorable elements of *Reformed* doctrine and ethics, the way it happened back then against the true and *also* honorable Christian tradition of the Middle Ages.

From this perspective, what emerges as *our* knowledge of Reformed doctrine is based on *both* necessities: the respectful *esteem* of the concrete, characteristic greatness of Reformed Christianity in its beginnings, *but also*, precisely on the basis of such beginnings, the unavoidable *critique* of the greatness of these beginnings. Our task *could*, therefore, consist of a careful revision of the theology of the Geneva[31] or the Heidelberg Catechism, or of the *Canons of Dort*,[32] but it *could* also — if we trust ourselves to possess the necessary full power and insight — consist of the setting up of a new confession, a *Helevetica tertia*, just as the founders allowed themselves to replace the prior by a posterior.[33] Both possibilities are equally tenable in the Reformed church.

Let us now consider the second answer to the question of why and in what sense we call ourselves "Reformed." It is the answer of the friends of a certain type of eclecticism when taking up characteristic ideas, tendencies, and institutions for the Reformed past or present. Such a Reformed friend perhaps takes pleasure in anticipating the best of the Reformed "*Soli Deo Gloria!*" with its express rebuff, relativizing, and discrediting of every human justice, and with its exposing of every pietistic and methodistic illusion, and its indication that the One by whom the forgiveness of sins happens is the One we should fear [cf. Ps. 130.4]. Or perhaps it is precisely the opposite side of "being" Reformed that makes sense to him: the strict, direct parallel of the Reformed faith with a sharply pronounced individual and social ethos; the erection of the Law and obedience that is so much more inward and believable than in the

---

to the later text that had been worked over by Melanchthon (the *Variata*). Against this, those oriented toward Luther appealed to the original text (*Invariata*).

30 See Friedrich von Schiller, *Wilhelm Tell*, vv. 1814f., 1819 (Act 3, sc. 3); ET *Wilhelm Tell*, William F. Mainland, trans. and ed. (Chicago: University of Chicago Press, 1972), 77.

31 *Genfer Katechismus* (1545), *BSRK*, 117–153; ET *Treatises on the Sacraments: Catechism of the Church of Geneva, Forms of Prayer, and Confessions of Faith*, Henry Beveridge, trans. (Fearn, Scotland: Christian Heritage, 2002).

32 *Dordrechter Canones* (1619), *BSRK*, 843–861; ET *The Creeds of Christendom*, Vol. I, Philip Schaff, ed. (Grand Rapids, MI: Baker Book House, 1985, 519–523).

33 *Confessio helvetica prior* (1536), *BSRK*, 101–109. This creed was replaced by the *Confessio helvetica posterior* (1562), *BSRK*, 170–221; ET *The First Helvetic Confession of 1536*, trans. Arthur C. Cochrane, 97–112; Schaff, III, 831–909; cf. *The Second Helvetic Confession of 1566*, trans. Arthur C. Cochrane, 221, 224–301.

[215] Lutheran confessions; the "*vita hominis christiani*" laid out by Calvin as a central theme in his *Institutes.*[34]

Perhaps more than these things, however, he senses the humanistic impact on Reformed thought and is pleased by a certain thoroughgoing intellectuality of this strand of Christianity: the struggle against all divinizing of the creature, which Reformed thought in particular has carried out in its doctrine of the sacraments, its *finitum non est capax infiniti*,[35] its affinity to the best traditions of the philosophical project, to Plato and Kant. Perhaps to one from the school of Bengel or Blumhardt, the great spectacle of the coming of the kingdom as seen in Johannes Coccejus[36] has become precious and important. He might praise his Reformed nature because of the fairly healthy "self-negation of our nature" [*abnegatio nostri*][37] which seems so characteristic of the typical Calvinist's inmost heart, and in which there already flickers something of the mysticism of Tersteegen. Perhaps it has become important and precious to him, however, for just the opposite reason, namely, because of his openness to the world that has made this Calvinistic human into an active, exciting, or downright creative person.

From every possible angle, then, he may be able to make a covenant with the spiritual, cultural, and economic movement of modernity, or he may have convinced himself as a churchgoer of the worth and usefulness of Reformed [216] constitutional and cultural forms. He is Reformed in so far that he is a friend of the synodical-presbyterian constitution, based on the ideal of an actively participating congregation of lay people.

The idea of vibrant, independent congregations (in opposition to the pastor-led churches of Lutheranism) is also his ideal, or perhaps the serious sobriety of Reformed worship with its renunciation of all crypto-Catholic things has in fact won his heart. We want to claim all of this

---

34   See J. Calvin, *Institutes of the Christian Religion*, 2 Vols., John T. McNeill, trans. and ed. (Philadelphia: Westminster Press, 1960), Vol. I, book III, chapter 6, 684–689.

35   Against the background of the doctrinal differences between the Reformed church and Lutherans in Christology, this formula became the Reformed counterpart to the Lutheran doctrinal formula "*finitum capax infiniti.*" This form is first seen in T. Kirchner, *Apologie oder Verantwortung des christlichen Concordienbuchs* (Heidelbergae, 1583), 45b: "From the finite to the infinite there is no relation nor communication, the finite is not capable of the infinite." It was taken up again and again in later Reformed theology, for example by L. van Rijssen (HpB, 364; ET 437): "The plenitude is not infinite, because the humanity, which is finite, is not capable of the infinite."

36   Barth's attention was called to the Federal theology of Johannes Coccejus (1603–1669) by G. Schrenk, *Gottesreich und Bund im älteren Protestantismus vornehmlich bei Johannes Coccejus. Zugleich ein Beitrag zur Geschichte des Pietismus und der heilsgeschichtlichen Theologie* (Gütersloh: Der Rufer, 1923). See *Bw. Th.* II, 123 (December 10, 1922). In the days following his lecture, Barth listened to a lecture in Emden by the assistant lecturer from Münster, Karl Bauer, on "Coccejus and his meaning for our times." Cf. *Bw. Th.* II, 186 (September 24, 1923).

37   Calvin, *Institutes*, III, 7, 689: "The Sum of the Christian Life: The Denial of Ourselves."

about ourselves too, and more. Whoever cannot content themselves with just "being" Reformed out of loyalty and obedience (and we all know that this indeed cannot yet be the last word), should pay attention to the true and by far not yet exhausted treasure of truths, orientations, and goals of the Reformed church, which must be learned intimately by those who are lukewarm and uncertain of themselves in matters Reformed, so that they can become a member of their church in their gifts, their thinking, their leading, not by birth but by conviction.

Does not each one of the ideas named above have enough of its own meaning and live potential to give nourishment and momentum to a religious-theological-ecclesiastical, indeed perhaps to a spiritual, move-ment that reaches out beyond this circle? In any case, reasons for why one *can* be Reformed are not lacking.

But exactly this plurality and this *"can"* betray the weakness of my rather diffused way of answering the question. A church does not live from truths, even if they are numerous, profound, and alive. Rather, it lives from *the* one truth which cannot be conceived like any other teaching or conviction. Yet we *must* conceive of it, because this truth has *itself first* grasped the human and therefore has established the church. One can only "be" Reformed for *this* reason and not for any other.

The mutual coexistence of different motives that is characteristic of our modern Reformed tradition *and* of its critics must indeed arouse quite some suspicion, no matter how appropriate this coexistence might be in individual cases, and no matter how visibly it is documented in Zwingli and Calvin themselves, in which one person only wants to know something about the doctrine of sin and grace but in which a second, without even a whiff of heathendom, only wants to declare the Christian understanding of the *lex naturae*, by which a third will pitch his tent on the limits of perfectionism, and a fourth on the limits of antinomianism, and yet a fifth on the limits of a communistic enthusiasm, while a sixth waits for salvation or something close to it in the reestablishment [217] of the Calvinistic ordinances[38] and the singing of psalms, and a seventh, reckoned the boldest of them all, has found his shibboleth for time and eternity in the Reformed concept of God. In any case, the Reformed church did *not* come into being in such a manner. Its beginning was not this pantheon of ideals but rather a site of the worship of the *one* God. Fire from *one* altar was originally the light of them all, in which one thought he saw the light here and then there.

It is unity, not in the form of brackets within a systematic principle, that we would like to affirm here; unity of the teachings, wisdom, and

---

38   See *Les Ordonnances Ecclesiastiques de l'Eglise de Genève* (1561), *BSRK*, 42–64.

trajectories both individually and for themselves, not as they might stand in mid-air as highly misleading, highly dangerous, and highly unchristian (even the commanding "*Deo soli gloria!*" being no exception, for how should even *this* idea not be capable of becoming an idol?) but rather as they stand in the one original truth that subordinates all principles under itself. The Reformed confessions are different from the *Augsburg Confession* of the Lutherans in that they, among other things, keep all doctrine at an appropriate distance from the *one object*. They do not set everything on the card of *one doctrine*, but rather in a theologically less elaborate and impressive manner they content themselves with the relationship of every doctrine to the one object, leaving it to God, not to their *thoughts about* God, but to God's *own* being, God *alone*,[39] in God's proclaimed *Word* through the Scripture and Spirit, to be *the* truth.

Again, if "being" Reformed is to have any authority for us, then all of the above reasons, convincing as they are in themselves, must lead beyond themselves to the revelation that is witnessed to and known in the Scriptures. This revelation is not an idea, not a principle, and not a doctrine. It is the origin of all doctrine and the standard upon which every doctrine is measured, and which must be measured again and again. The expressions and attributes of Reformed Christianity, which are so enlightening, so sympathetic and convincing, [218] now must command our serious attention. But this attention would immediately be interrupted, and have to be interrupted, through the majestic rush of the *source* from which everything flows, rippling so energetically from every side; a rush of the source which might be terribly frightening, terribly unsympathetic, hardly convincing, but in any case is the truth and in no way dependent upon our comprehension or acclaim. It is not the pleasure that *we* have found in certain moments of truth, but rather the knowledge of the *one* truth that is founded in the *object* and exclusively *through* the object.

It is God's Word, which, when necessary, stands *against* all our ideals. It makes us "be" Reformed. *This* being the case, what we would preach would be something like "Reformed doctrine," not as those who are free but as those who are bound; not chosen in a self-governing, one-sided way but under the necessity of an objectivity that is open to us on every side; not as a self-expression but as the expression of those who are subordinated to the overwhelming truth. This would not compel us to necessarily bring forward that which lies upon our own hearts. It might be nothing more than an acknowledgment. Its intention must not be the correctness of individual formulas, nor the systematic order of the

39   On this expression, see Chapter 6, Note 74 in this volume.

whole, but rather the subordination of these things, in detail as well as in their entirety, to the necessity of saying subsequently and humanly the one thing that has first been said to the human; it must be the readiness to be a learning much more than a "teaching," a *didache* [διδαχή] much more than a *doctrina*, even though it does speak within such a conceptual language and does orient itself towards the preferred thoughts of the time or group and its ways.

Let us now hear the third and most modern answer. It is the one given by the friends of the inner movements and personalities that are unique to the Reformed tradition. Their catchphrase is "piety." Such a friend has experienced the Reformed church most profoundly through its Fathers, founders, and heroes. He has been moved by its distinctive features, its life of struggle and profound suffering, its austere accomplishments, and especially the unique coloring and temperature of its religiosity. Compared to the towering and overwhelming figure of Luther, these attributes were only later developed. Although personal piety already, when it comes to Zwingli for instance, had [219] not always played a happy role in the history of the sixteenth-century church.[40] But modernity, with its somewhat weaker, epigenous type of empathy[41] and regard for the past, *has* discovered the distinctive features of the Reformed founders, and has honored them. Words like "Calvinistic" and "Calvinism," which were at one time wrathfully left in the hands of its opponents, have lost their objectionable sound. In fact, "Reformed" now means a good measure of amazement and praise of Calvin, as well episodes of experimental emulations of him. The way to appreciation of this man and these men has become highly trodden and in any case a highly recommended way to appreciate the matter itself.

Who wants to stop here? Historically seen, it is simply true: At the origins of our church there stands everywhere, in an almost frightening

---

40   See the overview (esp. regarding O. Myconius and H. Bullinger) by K. Guggisberg, *Das Zwinglibild des Protestantismus im Wandel der Zeiten*, in *Quellen und Abhandlungen zur schweizerischen Reformationsgeschichte*, II series, Vol. 8 (Leipzig: Heinsius, 1934), 839.

41   "Empathy" [*Einfühlung*], a leading concept of philosophical aesthetics since J.G. von Herder, plays a programmatic role in Georg Wobbermin, *Systematische Theologie nach religionspsychologischer Methode*, Vol. II, *Das Wesen der Religion* (Leipzig: Hinrichs, 1921), 7f. According to Wobbermin, what belongs to the "fundamental characteristic of the religious-psychological method" is "the concept 'religious-psychological circle' and 'productive empathy.'" He continues:

> For, it is about understanding one's own religious experience out of a foreign religious life of the soul, in order to sharpen one's view for the uniqueness of specifically religious things, to turn back with a sharper understanding to the observation of one's own religious consciousness, and to always further expand and always more intensively and inwardly configure this process of alternative promotion by understanding, comprehending, and construing one's own and the foreign forms of expressing religious life.

way, the puzzle of the eminent religious personality. This was a person who took a unique risk with God against half of the world, and whose historical image, by so doing, has received the unique character of a hero, and therefore the honor and adoration of its followers. At this point we should also remember that if it is supposed to be about the adoring imitation of the Protestant individual, then the personality of Luther is not the only possible type of this kind of person. It is true that the images of this great hero, believing, praying and working, are capable of offering encouragement once again to the eon of a small-caliber Christianity that we live in today. [220] They reflect the beginnings and, therefore, perhaps also the origin.

But a strong warning must be given at this point. There is no reason why the confessional writings of our church consistently avoid making *any* use of invoking Zwingli or Calvin, in stark contrast to the invocation of Luther in the Formula of Concord.[42] They even let *these* people entirely disappear behind the matter. The older Reformed dogmatics do *not* even have something analogous to the older Lutheran locus with its "on the calling of Luther" [*De vocatione Lutheri*].[43] There is no good reason why the story of the conversion of Calvin himself and his surroundings was so disappointingly uninteresting to his modern biographers; or why only the two words, "*subita conversione*,"[44] and a number of suppositions, are available to us for the purpose of edification. Nor is there any good reason why there was enough irreverence in the old city of Geneva to let the grave site of the great man fall into oblivion.

Finally, there is no good explanation as to why the Reformed legend of salvation and the Reformed cult of heroes are again being taken seriously at a time when we have become insecure about Reformed *substance*. The question is allowed to be asked what indeed Calvin himself would have wanted to say to the five-volume panegyric of his French admirers.[45] If

42 For the invoking of Luther in the *Formula of Concord*, see *BSLK*, 846: 46; 860: 30; 861: 5; 865: 9, 20; 879: 32; 881: 8; 887: 5, etc.; *BC*, 532: 3; 540: 52, 53; 542: 61; 547: 20ff.; 548: 23; 551: 36.
43 See J. Gerhard, *Loci theologici* (1610–1622), L, 23, sect. 8 (E. Preuss, ed., Lipsiae, 1885, Vol. VI, 83–90): "De vocatione beati Lutheri" [on the calling of the fortunate Luther]. See A. Calov, *Systemata locorum theologicorum* (1655–1677), VIII, art. 3, cap. 2, q. 2 (Wittenbergae, 1677), 303–308: "Can it be that Luther was called legitimately to the service of teaching in the church?"; J.A. Quenstedt, *Theologia didactico-polemica sive systema theologicum* (1685), P, IV, cap. 12, sect.2, q. 3 (4th ed., Wittenbergae, 1710, Vol. IV), 406–409: "Can it be that the calling of Luther to the service of teaching in the church was made as a legitimate and ordained one?"; D. Hollaz, *Examen theologicum acroamaticum* (1707), P, IV, cap. 2, q. 10 (Holmiae/Lipsiae, 1735, Vol. II), 870–872: "Can it be that Luther and the Lutheran ministers are called legitimately, and ordained according to the rites?" Trans. mine.
44 *CR* 59 (= *Calvini Opera* 31), col. 21.
45 The book by E. Doumergue, *Jean Calvin, les Hommes et les Choses de son Temps*, had grown to five volumes by the time it appeared in 1923 (Lausanne, 1899–1917). Two more volumes followed later

he came back, would he rather reach for the angry Kampschulte?[46] [221] Would he consider the alley of Reformed victors which the *new* Geneva has built[47] in his memory and the memory of his grim-faced contemporaries to be simply an atrocity! According to the rather "unhistorical" view of the Fathers themselves, it is precisely the "religious personality" which does *not* belong at the beginning of a church — a *law* does. The question of the Reformation in *old* Geneva does not indicate whether one wants to be inspired, impressed, excited, and carried away by this or that religious thing. Rather, it indicates whether one wants "to live according to the Word of God."[48]

The human does not come into consideration, not even as a prophet, never mind as a Christian hero but rather as a minister, as a *servant* of the divine Word.[49] This servant is called to the proclamation and enforcement of this law, and his "piety" is not considered a work of its own weight and independent significance, but as an anonymous, colorless and undemanding, purely private act of *obedience*. The greatness of the founders consisted precisely in the fact that they saw in the highest concreteness the barrier that lay in the way of all human greatness, especially their own; that they were so *little* occupied with themselves; that their confessions did not want to be presentations of what were nevertheless considerable inner experiences but rather something quite different, namely, "conceptual testimonies of inner faith" [*testificationes conceptae* [222] *intus fidei*].[50] Does

---

(Neuilly, 1926/27).

46   See Friedrich Wilhelm Kampschulte, *Johann Calvin. Seine Kirche und sein Staat in Genf*, Vol. I (Leipzig: Duncker & Humblot, 1869); Vol. II appeared posthumously, edited by W. Goetz (Leipzig, 1899). Barth noted in his lecture "The Theology of Calvin" from the summer semester 1922 that "*Kampschulte* 1869 and 1899, 2 Vols., was written without love; the objections raised against C. come sharply to the fore. It has a redeeming effect according to Henry-Stähelin [author of another, earlier biography on Calvin]. Not to be disregarded but also not to be definitive!" For Barth's first encounter with Kampschulte's book, in 1919, see *Bw. Th.* I, 357–361.

47   For the celebration of Calvin's four-hundredth birthday in 1909, a stone monument to the Reformation, which is over a hundred meters long, was built on the *Promenade des Bastions* in Geneva. In the foreground, it shows the Geneva Reformers, Calvin, Farel, Beza, and the Scot, John Knox. On the sides are more figures which are significant for the history of the Reformation, like the leader of the Huegenots, Gaspard von Coligny, Wilhelm of Nassau-Orange, the great prince of Brandenburg, Roger Williams, Oliver Cromwell, and Prince Stephan Bocskay of Siebenbürgen. The architecture of the monument goes back to the Swiss Eugène Monod, Alphonse Laverrière, Jean Tailens, and Charles Dubois. The French artists Paul Landowski and Henri Bouchard created the sculptures.

48   See *Annales Calviniani 1536, CR* 48 (= *Calvini Opera* 21), where the expression "live according to the Word of God" (col. 201) is also encountered in the variations "live according to the gospel and the Word of God"; (ibid.) "live according to the doctrine of the gospel" (col. 198); and "live according to the gospel of God" (col. 203).

49   "Verbi Divini Minister" (VDM) is until this day the statutory title of a vicar in Switzerland.

50   J. Calvin, *Pro G. farello et collegis eius adversus Petri Caroli calumnies defensio Nicolai Gallasii* (1545),

the fact that the founders were also not fully successful in this, that enough human, personal, and individual things slipped into this testimony, give us the occasion to view it differently than they *wanted* it to be viewed? Is there a better way to venerate and follow Calvin besides placing ourselves where he stood, namely, as those called to be obedient to the law? And if we no longer know the Christian meaning of obedience, calling, and law we ought to continue asking until we know it again, without wasting time or energy in adoring or even imitating Calvin.

Galvanized father-piety is exactly what we do *not* need. What has already happened is not to be brought back and should not be brought back. But the founders, in their seeking, questioning, confusion, and affliction, who stood in the boundless difficulty and need of the human before the Lord, could challenge us to become founders *ourselves*, *also* responding to *our* time. Then they would fulfill the mission which they will always have for us as individuals, as personalities, as heroes. If we were then thrown back onto ourselves from every historical role model, and if we would stand before the same barrier like the founders did — that which we would still risk confessing would then somehow (and here we have a third aspect) be able to be called "Reformed doctrine." Its historical character, its emotional coloring, its mood would have to be absolutely *cura posterior*, indeed an urgent concern, but it could not be the service of humanity or the community but the service of the divine Word [*ministerium verbi divini*] which would be imposed on us today in the same sober but strict manner as it was imposed on the men whose graves we otherwise would have to decorate in vain.

The consideration of the different answers to the question "Why here and now?" [*Dic cur hic?*][51] which we have now laid out, refers from every side to *one* point that characterizes the Reformed doctrine. It is known in [223] Church history under the rubric of the *Scripture principle*. At the origins of the Reformed church stands the knowledge that the truth alone in the Word of God and it alone are contained in the Old and New Testament writings, that every *doctrine* has to admit to the truth and therefore also to its unchanging and highest standard given in the Scriptures. Once a person lets Scripture speak to him — and here I mean the Scripture itself, not the Scripture given through a particular interpreting tradition, not only a part of Scripture but the whole thing, not an enlightened Scripture that is seen through a particular, anticipated

CR 35 (= *Calvini Opera* 7), col. 312: "If the confession of a religion is nothing else but a witnessing of inwardly received faith, so that it be a solid and sincere witnessing, then it is right that it be derived from the pure source of Scripture."

51   See H. Walther, *Lateinische Sprichwörter und Sentenzen des Mittelalters in alphabetischer Anordnung*, Vol. I (Göttingen: Vandenhoeck & Ruprecht, 1963), Nr. 5556: 679.

point of view, but Scripure itself, which is not to be confused with the
voice of pious men from the past or the present, and the Scripture never
without the decisive Word of the Spirit from which it comes — what he
then at best dares to say about God, the world, and the human because he
must say it with fear and trembling [cf. 2 Cor. 7.15 etc.] about things that
sound foolish or like nonsense when they arise from the human alone,
can be called the "Reformed doctrine" that was there at the beginning
of our church. *Doctrina* is the Christian word of the human that has gone
through the crisis, through the merciless refining and purification by the
Word of God witnessed to in the Scripture. It remains a human word.
It does not itself become a divine word [*verbum divinum*]. But it does, if
it has gone along this way, become a legitimate, pure, "predicate of the
divine word" [*praedicatio verbi divini*].⁵² This principle of being *appropriate*
to Scripture has been called the *formal* principle of Reformed theology,
not without a nagging regret over the fact that it primarily has only been
about the form and not, like it is more profoundly in Lutheranism, about
the content.⁵³

Caution in such claims is strongly recommended. One betrays all too
easily how much we are indeed weaker successors and onlookers to the
entire process and not participants. For our Fathers, *God's* witness to
himself in the Holy Scriptures was by no means "only" form — in fact
it was not a "form" at all, but a present, living, complete content. But it
is this, *this* unheard of, fathomless content that cannot in any way arise
in or be exhausted [224] by any other content, and which is therefore
not identical with the content of this or that particular view or experience — not even with the content of the forgiveness of sins! It is also
not so that one such individual view or experience has to first guarantee
the substance of the knowledge that "*God* speaks!" even though every
individual view or experience is founded and guaranteed through the
singular knowledge that *God* speaks. *God* speaks and *he* alone: Even the
highest, the most specific religious relationship of the experience of
grace in which he *also* speaks may not take the place of God himself. *God*
speaks not only in the Gospel but also in the law, not only in the New
but fully in the Old Testament. *God* speaks not only of the forgiveness of
sins and eternal life (in "paradise" and even *about it*!), but also and with
equal seriousness, of the order of our temporal existence, not only as the

---

52 See *Confessio Helvetica posterior* (1562), *BSRK*, 171: 10: "The predicate of the Word of God is the
    Word of God." Cf. Cochrane, *The Second Helvetic Confession of 1566*, 225: "The Preaching of the
    Word of God Is the Word of God."

53 See for example, M. Scheckenburger, *Vergleichende Darstellung des lutherischen und reformierten
    Lehrbegriffs*, whose handwritten papers were put together posthumously, edited, and published by
    E. Güder (Part I: Stuttgart, 1855), 20f.

revealed and friendly One but over and over again as the hidden and terrifying God, demanding not only faith but obedience as well (and this is not entirely the same thing, but it is *also* from God).

This "*God* speaks!" stands facing the Church Fathers in its own truth and urgency, rolling out the ultimate question all along the line and demanding great decisions. This "*God* speaks!" is supremely concrete precisely because of his absoluteness. God releases true streams of "doctrine" exactly because it is commanded that the human must remain silent. If the theses of the *Disputation of Bern* from 1528 begin with the succinct words, "The holy Christian Church, whose one head is Christ, is born out of the Word of God, and in this Word it remains and does not heed the voice of a stranger,"[54] they do not express a second origin but the first, namely, the founding element of the Reformed Reformation. That the "Scripture" [*Gschrift*] must decide about all truth and untruth of doctrine has been strongly self-evident, and not without violation of Catholic conversation partners. This is already seen in the orders of business in that disputation, out of which the oldest confessions grew. It was established even before the first sentence of the confessions themselves was set down on paper, let alone proven or recognized. The Fathers did not want to hear about any previous theoretical foundation for this one, unique foundation. This foundation establishes itself. [225] Spirit is recognized through Spirit; God is only recognized through God.

For this reason, our calling is neither mechanically based and rational nor experience-based and irrational — what do the categories of revelation have to do with *these* categories? Instead, this calling is meant to be a simple bowing down before God's self-proclamation: "The highest proof of Scripture derives in general from the fact that God in person spoke it."[55] With God there is no "Why?" What God wants to say and do has its real ground *and* the ground of its knowledge only *in* God. "You *alone* are it: power, and might are yours!"[56] This is valid also for the question about truth. God *is* not only himself and alone the truth; God himself and God alone *reveals* that he is the truth. How could the statement that the Bible is God's Word somehow be proven in any other way than through the act of the most free pleasure, which God *himself* cites? If it were *God's* Word, how else than through himself would it have to be verified?

This astounding claim has been called an axiomatic proposition.[57] It

54   *Bern Theses* (1528), *BSRK*, 30: 9–11; ET *The Ten Theses of Berne, 1528*, Arthur C. Cochrane, trans., 49.
55   Calvin, *Institutes*, I, 7, 4, 78.
56   The beginning of an 1891 song by V. Fr. von Strauss (*GERS* 29).
57   See Karl Heim, *Das Gewißheitsproblem in der systematischen Theologie bis Schleiermacher* (Leipzig: Hinrichs, 1911), 257–259; Paul Althaus, *Die Prinzipien der deutschen reformierten Dogmatik im Zeitalter der aristotelischen Scholastik* (Leipzig: Deichert, 1914), 203f.

is so, however, only according to its logical form. Based on its content, the certainty that it expresses has nothing to do with the self-evidence of a mathematical axiom. What it expresses is rather the self-evidence of *revelation* that God bestows simultaneously with the biblical witness and to those belonging to it who accept its witness. It expresses obedience to the "inner testimony of the Holy Spirit" [*testimonium spiritus sancti internum*][58] and to the Spirit of God in which the spirit of the human, of the writer and the reader, become one in common worship. The truth of the claim falls together with the reality of this act of lordship that arises from God and is established in God. Precisely this adjusting of doctrine as *un*founded by the perspective of logic was claimed by the Fathers: The authority founded in *God* was the secret of *this* Reformation and *this* church. The mark of the Fathers was not the geniality of a particular insight or piety, but rather their simple understanding about the establishing of that which is founded in nothing else but God. In other words, [226] it was the courage of the Fathers which let such a random, contingent, human greatness like the Bible in all seriousness become a witness of God's revelation; this Scripture, which in itself is profane, become a *holy* Scripture. "Abraham *believed* in the Lord, and the Lord reckoned it to him as righteousness" [Gen. 15.6]. This is how doctrine, message, and preaching come about — and in no other way.

We must be very clear about the fact that today the eyes of every one of us are fixed precisely on that aspect, that our Christian era is a pygmy precisely in this decisive relationship.[59] The days were not long until this simple understanding was lost, until it was forgotten that *God* was being spoken of when the Bible was called the Word of God, until one stepped out of the living circle of Scripture and Spirit in order to quickly not know anything at all about what that statement says. Out of the truth that is grounded in itself and that therefore grounds doctrine, a theorem was developed, which itself was in need of a foundation despite the energy that propelled it. Other reasons were beginning to be set up on the flanks of the witness of Holy Scripture to support the proof that was no longer fully trusted to the witness of the Holy Spirit alone. A vine of human-friendly apologetic began to entwine the solid trunk of the statement, "*God speaks!*," and rob its roots of nourishment. The diminishing spiritual nature of the written page, which was declared holy, became more and

---

58   See Calvin, *Institutes*, I, 7, 4, 78; HpB 21f.; ET 23; SchmP 51f.

59   The pygmies "became a symbol of the insurgency of small spirits against great spirits because they wanted to avenge the death of Anteaus their giant brother against Hercules, and thus they started a war against the demi-god. They climbed all over his arms and legs and occupied his head without being able to do any damage." (Georg Büchmann, *Geflügelte Worte. Der Zitatenschatz des deutschen Volkes*. W. Hofmann, ed., 35th ed. [Frankfurt a.M.: Ullstein, 1981], 51.)

more isolated and more and more dangerous precisely through its arts.

Then when historical criticism set in with its objections against the age, authenticity, and historical reliability of the biblical literature, no one knew any longer how to give the only possible answer, the answer of freedom and of Christian objectivity. One hardened oneself (something like the author of the Formula of the Helvetic Confession from 1675)[60] to the well-intentioned dogmatic assertion, which was like a dried-up branch protruding unbelievably in the air; or he stubbornly, together with stubborn people, got tangled up in an apologetic mini-war whose outcome could be nothing other than [227] what it was. One had lost the wonder of *God* and had to learn, using an assertion about the wonder of the *world*, about the miracles in history and in the inward life (which are both equally dubious), in order to eke out an increasingly miserable, sorrowful existence.

The great misery of modern Protestantism had set in: a hardening of doctrines into *Orthodoxy*, unmoored from their generative origins; a flight into the mistaken Christian experience of *Pietism* that is confused with this origin; a reduction of the doctrine that was no longer understood, and in fact no longer able to be understood, to moralistic-sentimental maxims by the *Enlightenment*; and finally a reduction of the Christian experience to the givenness of the purest appearance of general religious instincts by *Schleiermacher* and his followers on the left *and* the right. These are the four cornerstones of the prison in which we all are stuck (I say deliberately, "we all"!), the one more in this corner, the other more in that corner: "Everyone may choose his heroes!"[61] The roof that these four pillars carry, which binds each of them to one another and which cuts off our, the inmates', view of the heavens, is the latent or open conjuring-away of revelation. Reformed doctrine cannot thrive inside the walls of this prison. Only its surrogate can prosper, which can be described as Reformed theology born of an antiquarian, ideological, or emotional love affair.

In order to be able to come about at all, in order to be born again as a Christian church, Reformed doctrine needs the free, sharp draught of the knowledge of the Word of God from the Scripture and the Spirit, "born" with the natural violence of a volcanic outbreak, from the one-time unity of the Reformed church. Reformed *"through the Word of God"*[62]: This is

---

60   *Helvetisches Konsensus-Formel* (1675), *BSRK*, 861–870.

61   J.W. Goethe, *Iphigenie auf Tauris*, V, 763–765 (Act 2, Entry 1): "Ein jeglicher muß seinen Helden wählen,/Dem er die Wege zum Olymp hinauf/Sich nacharbeitet."

62   This self-characterization of the Reformed church appears to have first surfaced in the seventeenth century (the formulation "reformed *according* to the Word of God" is common earlier, however). Around the middle of the nineteenth century, it appears to have circulated in general use.

the original and proper meaning [228] of the name we carry. What does "a turn back to the old and sacred legacy" of the Reformation mean if in its reflection it does *not* insist on *this* sense of our name? That this reflection has not yet taken place even to this very day (and especially not where one pounds on the Fathers), that our name honestly makes no sense today because it apparently does not carry *this* meaning, is the great dilemma that we mentioned at the beginning of this lecture. It is the *only* serious, *extremely* serious reason why one today circumvents the question of Reformed doctrine with a wide arc.

Thus far, I have only spoken in passing about the specific content of Reformed doctrine. It seems to me, then, that the memory of its presuppositions, of its *genesis*, is the most urgent thing to say about this theme now. With what right and sense can we speak about the Reformed teachings of predestination, confession, or the Lord's Supper when we disagree, and not only disagree programmatically and intellectually but also about the facts and the truth *from where* this all originally comes? Only from *there* could it or something analogous to it again be said with authority today. Talk from somewhere else, and this includes the word-for-word repetition of the *Canons of Dort* and the proclamation of the original Calvinistic ideals of life and church, would *not* be Reformed doctrine but rather archaic boasting. The substance and task of Reformed doctrine is exhausted through the proclamation of that which generates and establishes it, as long as form and content are identical, even down to the details. The question of "Where to?" is finally identical to that of "Where from?"

If the human accepts the doctrine that was born out of the Word of God, then the result ought not to be merely this or that insight, sensation, or resolution, but rather the renewed knowledge of the Word of God — the *God* of majesty. We have already talked about this here, and the reader may have even already learned and experienced it in detail. This God is the One to whom we can *pray*, joyfully or in terror, but only listening for something new, full of expectation, being ready to believe and obey: "Speak Lord, for your servant is listening!" [1 Sam. 3.9]. If we presuppose this alpha and omega of Reformed doctrine, not as a formula but as a living material principle in our churches — let me say it [229] more humbly — if we presuppose this alpha and omega of Reformed doctrine in the study rooms of our parsonages, then we do not need to be afraid of the true Reformed content of our "Dogmatics II." There

See H. Heppe, *Ursprung und Geschichte der Bezeichnungen "reformierte" und "lutherische" Kirche* (Gotha, 1859), 70; E.Fr.K. Müller, *Symbolik Vergleichende Darstellung der christlichen Hauptkirchen nach ihrem Grundzuge und ihren wesentlichen Lebenäußerungen* (Erlangen/Leipzig, 1896), 377f., n. 3.

would then be a relatively easier, greater freedom of the system and the formula, like there was once upon a time. In the future in particular, there will be better, more unified instruction based upon an agreement that is not exclusive but inclusive. Perhaps, if we had reason to not feel ready on our own two feet yet, it could begin as an agreement about the interpretation of the old Reformed doctrinal norms. In this case, I would personally favor the Geneva Catechism of 1545. But perhaps the agreement could even be about the interpretation of a conscious and detailed *new* Reformed confession, one that grows out of *our* situation, that is given in *our* language, and that speaks to *our* time. But first, the question of the *presupposition* of a Christian confession in our church *at all* would have to be awakened very differently! Before this, it would make little sense to bang one's head about the question of the *consequences*.

In my view, the only serious programmatic hope of a Reformed theology for the near future lies in the *preparation* of a new interpretation of the *Scripture principle*, which contains much more than its name says. (I say "preparation" because this interpretation is not to be made and enforced!) To the extent that it can, it would be about a human deed, a rethinking of the category of *revelation*. Under this viewpoint, it would learn anew how to read the Old and New Testaments. Therefore, solely for the sake of *elucidating* the central task — and also our central dilemma — I would like to pose three *questions* as a continuation of the history of the Reformed beginnings. But before that, allow me to briefly go into the so-called *doctrinal* content, a few important individual expressions of the Reformed confessions.

If one reads the writings of Zwingli and Calvin and the oldest Reformed confessions keeping in mind the question of what their authors were actually objecting to in the old *Catholic church*, the same point is clearly bumped up against at every turn. In all the criticisms of the medieval Christian dogmas and rites, the original Reformers accuse the Catholic church of falsifying and perverting the theme of Christian proclamation, indeed the whole of Christianity, in a disastrous way. For the old Catholic church had replaced God with the human, God's history with their traditions, God's [230] rationality with their probabilities, God's good will with their ability to approach grace. In the entirely artistic and hallowed ecclesiastical construction of the medium of salvation, in the profound system of compromises between nature and grace, in the geniality of the attempt of making possible the impossible, which is so characteristic of a perfected medieval Catholicism, the original Reformers saw an offense to God who does not let himself be grasped but who wants to be the sole end and beginning of all things. They wanted to understand, once more and unequivocally, that the subject in the religious relation is God and not the human. That this objection is not simply identical with that of Luther, who said that the old church led poor, terrified consciences to foolishness or doubt,[63] shows itself in an instructive way through a comparison of the doctrine of justification of the *Augsburg Confession* with the contemporaneous *Tetrapolitian Confession* of the highlands.[64]

The Reformed confessions did not lay the emphasis on the fact that the human is justified through *faith* instead of through *works*, but, rather, that it is *God* and not the *human* who completes this justification. The original Reformed thinkers were interested in this primary aspect of the religious relation as well as the ultimate thing, namely, the glorification of God, whom such confessions ought to serve. Much less significant for them, at least in the older, classical age, was the middle aspect, namely, the way of salvation as such. The Reformed argument is innately more comprehensive. With the same dynamic that lies in the faith-versus-works opposition, this argument opens up onto a variety of oppositions that are not exhausted by them: Creator and creature, the truth of God and the inventions of the human, the command of God and the command of the Church. For the original Reformers, not only did the religious relation in a strict sense, namely in the dialectic of sin and forgiveness, become an area to be criticized and rejected from the start, but the *whole* existence of the human as well, corresponding to the breadth of the manner in which Catholicism also claims the *whole* human, and not only the heart and conscience. [231] The Reformed *doctrine of God* with its blunt underscoring of God's uniqueness, lordship, and freedom is simply the positive formulation of this rejection that was directed at the medieval Catholic idea of the person. The doctrine has its emphatic completion in its polemical, core teaching of God's infinite divine providence and election. These points were not so much directed toward the behavior and fortune of humans in and of themselves (in which people later on had an urgent interest) but toward the type of *God's* will and work upon the human.

The relationship of this concept to the positively understood Scripture principle is unmistakable. In this way, as the "jealous" God — in the sense of the Old Testament, who will not let another be honored above himself [cf. Isa. 42.8; 48.11], as the one, unique, singular, sole power, who is Lord alone, who judges and bestows grace upon humans in absolute freedom,

---

63   See for example, the *Apology to the Augsburg Confession* (1530), BSRK, 163f., esp. 164, 13–15; BC, 109ff.

64   See the *Augsburg Confession* (1530), Article IV, "Justification," BSLK, 55: 11–56: 5; BC, 39: 1–40: 3, and the *Tetrapolitan Confession* (1530) Article III: "From where does our justification come?" and Article IV "What does faith add to justification?" BSRK, 57: 1–58, 48; see also Cochrane, *The Tetrapolitan Confession of 1530*, 57–59.

who is absolutely superior and who is commanding without any negoti-
ation — did the old Reformers hear God's voice in the Scriptures. What
was their vehement invoking of the exclusive truth and authority and
salutariness of this *one* book but a confession (precisely *not* a "speculative"
confession but a most highly concrete, contingent, existential one) of *this*
God? The question that has to be raised here is whether we are somehow
united on this battlefront with the Reformed Reformation.

We think indeed about disputing with "Rome," as mentioned. But
today we ought not to answer so quickly with a "Yes." Is such a dispute
necessary for us? Do we *stand* under the overwhelming pressure of that
knowledge of God, so that we *can* do nothing other than protest, and
namely, protest based on *our* reasons, and not like some modern indi-
vidualist and Enlightenment thinker does? Couldn't it still happen that
when a modern Reformed individual is called to accountability he might
bring up, just out of pure oversight, exactly not the Reformed but rather
the Lutheran theses? Or the even greater evil, that his modern Protestant
theses of a semi-Pelagian kind, against which the Reformation fought,
could look similar to the way a bad egg looks like a good one? Is modern
Protestantism on both the left *and* on the right, with its broken relation
to revelation, with its shying away from every "either/or," with its great
fundamental concession to the right and the dignity of the human, anything other [232] than a Catholicism which has been disfigured through
various, relatively untragic heresies? How groundless and shameful might
the planned dispute be! Is it clear to us that this same battlefront, which
Zwingli and Calvin drew up against Catholicism, is the same one that the
Fathers of Dort defended against the Arminians a hundred years later?[65]
However, where is Arminianism not taught today, if you listen carefully? I
will surely not let the "Get out, get out, I dismiss you!" [*Ite, ite, dimittimini!*]
of the grimmest Bogerman[66] pass over my lips. But the question is to be
raised: With what sense and right do we as Reformed Christians want
to fight against the Pope if we honestly feel a closer connection to the

65   On each of the five chapters of the Synod of Dortrecht there is included a "Remonstrance" on the
     address of the Arminian demonstration. See *BSRK*, 846: 22–848: 38; 850: 1–851: 25; 854: 26–856:
     44; 859: 1–861: 9; Schaff I, 516–523.

66   Johannes Bogerman [*sic!*] (1576–1637), pastor of Leeuwarden, was the presiding figure over the
     Dortrecht Synod of 1618/19, to which Episcopus and fifteen other opponents were invited for
     the purpose of justifying themselves. In the fifty-seventh session on January 18, 1619 "it came to
     a hefty argument between Episcopus and Bogerman who was the committee head, concerning
     the eviction of the opponents: Bogerman cried, 'With lies you began and with lies you will stop:
     Get out, get out, you are dismissed! [*dimitt[i]mini, ite, ite!*]. Episcopus and the opponents answered
     with, 'God will judge between us and this Synod,' and then left the hall." (Heinrich Hermelink,
     Reformation und Gegenreformation, in *Handbuch der Kirchengeschichte für Studierende*, Part 3 (Tübingen:
     Mohr, 1911), 265. See also *BSRK*, LXIII, 44–47.

Arminians than to their hard-headed opponents? Could this connection not just as well have been avoided? If we do not want to refrain from having it, then wouldn't the task of careful *self*-reflection about that which we want and do not want have to push the thought of a spiritual tournament with the better-armed opponents into the background for a long time?

Indeed, this is not about Zwingli's doctrine of providence[67] or Calvin's doctrine of election,[68] and again, it is not about the *Canons of Dort*. Rather, it is about the fundamental question as to whether or not the concern that led the founders to make such a sharp break with the old church and construct their own, unprecedented, exclusive doctrine of God is still our concern today, and if it is not, [233] wouldn't we do better to admit openly that this has secretly been the case for quite some time now? Do we still actually see the enemy whom the Fathers thought they must fight against, and the truth that was held out to them? Do we see its urgency clearly enough so that we *have to* speak about it, whether that be in the words of the older theology or in concepts of our contemporary language? In any case, can we speak about it so that it is loud and unequivocal, not eschewing the necessary attack upon on our *own Protestant* Christianity and ecclesial matters? The answer to these questions will decide whether there ought to be a Reformed doctrine of the First Article in the future.

A second important element of the old Reformed literature is devoted to the dispute with *Lutheranism*. I am amazed to find so little attention given in the historical research to the riddle of this dispute, namely, that the controversy between the old Lutherans and the Reformed is not about those opposing sides of the confessions that interest us today, like the contrasting understandings of the relation between religion and ethics, or the different sociological ideas here and there. It is, rather, about something remote and even abstruse to our sensibilities, namely, the Lord's Supper and Christology. Doesn't it seem as if history wants to tease us by remaining silent exactly on the very points where we would like to hear something and by speaking exactly about the very things we do not want to hear? It is true: Despite every genuine Christian love of peace, our Fathers saw themselves reflected in these issues, and yet they were not some small-minded race (despite the deep need of that time, still in the middle of the Thirty Years' War!), separated from those who defined themselves by the name, life, and the teachings of the church established by Luther.

---

67   See esp. H. Zwingli, *Ad illustrissimus Cattorum principem Philoppum sermonis de providential Dei anamnema* (1530), in *Huldrici Zuinglii Opera*, Vol. IV, M. Schuler and J. Schultheß, eds. (Turici, 1841), 79–144.

68   Calvin, *Institutes*, III, 21–24; ET Vol. 2, 920–987.

Based on the confessions, our Fathers saw themselves reflected in the fact that they could not allow a double appropriation to occur in the Lord's Supper. That is, the bread and the wine could not be enjoyed physically and the true body and blood of the Lord enjoyed spiritually,[69] with both being completely [234] united in the "sacramental union" [unio sacramentalis],[70] namely, in the union in a double sense. The other confession was concerned with the same issue, namely, that Christ, the human, the one who was born, was crucified, buried, and raised up, and who then ascended into heaven, is now in another space than we are, in the heavenly glory and not here. Irrespective of his indissoluble "personal union" [unio personalis][71] with the omnipresent divinity, he is still uniquely distinct in the unity, and thus, not participating in the divine omnipresence. Therefore, he is hidden from all of our senses, only accessible to faith and only through the Spirit from above. What does this all mean? Where the humanity of Christ in its relation to us and the way he is present in the Lord's Supper is in question, it clearly becomes the problem of revelation in the strictest sense. It is about God's self-mediation; about the reality of the relationship between God and the human in the world. Can and may this reality become the object of a clear, undialectical expression upon human lips?

Luther and those around him answered "Yes" to this question. Human expression must become an object if the salvation of God that is supposed to be expressed here is not to be turned into a question again. By contrast, the Old Reformers answered "No" to this question. This reality may not under any circumstance become an object of clear human expression, or else it will raise the question as to whether the salvation of God that is expressed[72] here is really the salvation of God. At least two human words are necessary here for God's Word to be truly proclaimed.

---

69   In this section, Barth condensed expressions about the doctrine of the Lord's Supper from a variety of Reformed confessional writings. See for example, Consensus Bremensis (1596), BSRK, 772: 25–30:

> Therefore there is also a double eating and enjoying in the Lord's Supper. The outer and visible thing to eat and to enjoy is the holy bread and holy wine. Such enjoyment occurs with the physical mouth [. . .] The other, inner thing to eat and enjoy is the body and blood of Christ, whose enjoyment happens through faith.

See also Bekenntnis der Casseler Generalysynode (1607), BSRK, 820: 45–821: 3: "Thus, we believe that in the Holy Lord's Supper, next to and with the enjoyment of the Sacraments, we participate in the body of Christ at the same time also the true body and blood of Jesus Christ itself, not imaginary or according to mere thoughts, but true . . ."; and "Aus dem Staffortschen Buche von 1599," BSRK, 813: 46–814: 6.

70   See HpB, 477; ET 597–598; SchmP 345, 360f.

71   See HpB 341–345, 353f.; ET 428–434; SchmP 213f, 218–223.

72   In an earlier manuscript, the word "interpreted" [ausgelegt] stood in the place of "expressed" [ausgesagt]. Barth corrected his copy.

The Reformed Fathers were in agreement with the Lutherans about the fact that Christ was true man and true God in indissoluble unity, and about the presence of this God who has become flesh and blood; that God's revelation in Christ was really the infinite majesty becoming finite, temporal, and contingent; that Christ is present in the Lord's Supper, which means that this sacrament is the concentrated self-portrayal through which Christ witnesses to himself within his Church. But they put a halt to this agreement when the Lutherans, in the affirmation of the [235] unity of God and the human, in the drawing out of the "communication of attributes" [*communicatio idiomatum*],[73] and in that the praising of the fullness of the gift of grace in the sacrament went so far as to tear down the fine but definite *boundary* between God and the world, which is *set* as well as overcome in Christ. They laid aside the hiddenness of the very Lord who became *human*, and for the Reformed, that means, in the words of Heb. 11.1, the miracle of the Spirit and of faith. The Lutherans went so far as to make a *direct*, miraculous, but earthly identity out of the indirect identity between the heavenly and earthly gifts that are only perfected in God himself, between the thing and the sign, between witness and revelation. Thus they made a direct mediation[74] out of revelation, which, if it is real, is always a veiling. They constructed a religious "givenness."

With all these criticisms, the Reformed Fathers picked up what Luther and his followers taught in the Second Article, but the Lutherans were not capable of showing them that it could be meant differently, just as they themselves were not in the position to show the Lutherans that their Reformed theses did not mean a darkening of the reality of revelation or a hidden rejection of the Incarnation and self-revelation of the Revealer. This is my rough outline of the matter.

Again, the relationship to the Scripture principle, which generates everything, is not to be misjudged. What is the strict heavenly distance of the Reformed Christ, the notorious "*extra Calvinisticum*"[75] which brought to expression the divine caution, even in regard to revelation, if it is not

---

73   See HpB 345–352; ET 435–444; SchmP 214–224 and Barth's later discussion in *KD* IV/2, 79–91; *CD* IV/2, 73–77.

74   On this allusion to Kierkegaard, see Chapter 7, Notes 57 and 59 in this volume.

75   This concept, shaped by the Lutheran side (see Chr. E. Luthardt, *Kompendium der Dogmatik*, 8th ed. [Leipzig, 1889], 192), in fact goes back to Calvin (*Institutes* II, 13: 4, 480–481): "The Son of God descended from heaven in such a way that, without leaving heaven, he willed to be borne in the virgin's womb, to go about the earth, and to hand upon the cross; yet he continuously filled the world even as he had done from the beginning!" See also ibid., IV, 17: 30, 1401–1403. The "extra" is discussed by S. Maresius (HpB 335; ET 418): "The Logos so unites the human nature to himself that he totally indwells it and yet is totally transcendent and infinite outside it." See also Barth's discussion on the "*extra Calvinisticum*" exactly one year later in *Unterricht*, 194–197; ET 158–160.

the hiddenness and sublimity which God protects for our salvation and which is never to be overlooked or diminished, [236] *even when* he gives himself as a gift to us in his Word? Doesn't it have to be the *Spirit* poured out in the Lord's Supper (like in the self-giving of God in his Word), done out of his free pleasure, which revelation itself adds to the signs, to the witness of revelation? May the human bring together what God has separated, because he is and remains *God*? [cf. Mt. 19.6]. Due to the circumstances, the church apparently *had to* teach the Second Article in this way. However, what ought *we* say about it? *Must* we also still teach it in this way?

The past disputes about Christ faded out a long time ago, not because the controversy ended with a victory or with an agreement. Rather, despite the protest that a few Lutheran "outsiders" have clung to, it has drifted away. Especially in Germany, it has become the main stage of the old feud, and by the command of the king of Prussia, it has even has been proclaimed dead.[76] Certainly, none of us would wish a return to the days of a Matthias Höe of Höenegg.[77] Nevertheless, the question to be raised here is whether one might be so unreservedly pleased about the prolonged confessional peace in Protestantism, as every responsible individual today undoubtedly is.

Why do we actually have peace? Is it out of power or out of weakness, out of insight, or out of blindness? Is the bustling manner taken by our historical theologians really insufficient to establish that the past disputes were really not barren scholastic exercises or the splitting of hairs, as has been claimed a thousand times, but rather serious and decisive problems with which we actually are in no way finished? Shouldn't they be spoken of, if they are not already the subject of rumor in our churches? Shouldn't we speak of the Word that became flesh [Jn 1.14], [237] and both sides continue to make further claims? Have the things desired and not desired by the Fathers, while certainly incomplete in their rightness and importance, become so completely incomprehensible and indifferent to us? Their insistence on a dialectical, indirect understanding of

---

76 An order of the cabinet of the Prussian king, Friedrich Wilhelm III, from September 27, 1817, which was the beginning of the construction of the later "Evangelical Church of the Union" [EKU], initiated a union between the Lutheran and the Reformed churches, with their doctrinal differences no longer to be regarded as a reason for the rejection of an ecclesiastical communion. See the articles in *RGG* 3rd ed., Vol. IV, by J. Beckmann, "Evangelical Kirche der Union (EKU)," col. 1138; and A. Adam, "Unionen im Protestantismus," col. 1141.

77 As a court preacher to the elected house of the nobility of Saxony in Dresden, Matthias Höe of Höenegg (1580–1645) had a strong influence on the being of the church and politics in elected Saxony during the Thirty Years' War. He lobbied forcefully for the Peace of Prague (1635). However, as a Lutheran he expressed, in literature, a sharp polemic against both the popes and the Calvinists. See the article by F. Lau, "Matthias Höe von Höenegg," in *RGG*, 3rd edition, Vol. III, col. 389f.

revelation and the self-mediation of God; their holding back, which is also an act of the highest community between God and the human, which lets God be *God* and reminds the human that he is dust and ashes [cf. Job 42.6]; their protest against the heaven-storming directness with which Luther, making a fact out of a mystery, asserted the real presence of God who became flesh in the world of objects *without* holding out a "however"!;[78] their memory of how the human will never again be a pilgrim and stranger in faith — indeed in faith to not forget this either; their waiting and haste [cf. 2 Pet. 3.12] — in sum, "Seek the things that are *above*!"[79] [Col. 3.1]?

If we have become indifferent to all this, what then is the talk about a "strengthening of the Reformed consciousness" all about? Why then, are we not all Lutherans? Even among Lutherans, insecurity about their own affairs has gotten out of control and Lutheran theology swarms with crypto-Calvinism and even crypto-Zwinglianism, at least in the question of the Lord's Supper. These facts must not fool us into thinking that even the concerns about the truth which the Lutheran church wants to raise *against us* are in any way finished. Further, we cannot be fooled about the fact that we must wrestle with it (as if with an opponent who also lives in us), even if there were no Lutheran directness, straightforwardness, and overconfidence opposing us today at all. Yet anyone who has ears to hear what his friendly Lutheran neighbor says cannot doubt that they do oppose us. It is not about the continuation of the quarrel; we would be content with the mellowed-out theological ethics. It is about the continuation of the discussion, not about the formulas but about the matter, not necessarily about [238] Christology and the Lord's Supper now, but about the urgent problem of contingent revelation that burns today more than ever. From which pulpit is this *not* spoken of? The possibility, indeed the necessity, to speak about these things, not in a haphazard but in a particular, qualified, Reformed way, could again one day set up a Reformed theology of the Second Article, if old confessions became new in us — but this is a theology that we certainly do not yet have.

In the actual middle point of the Reformed confessional writings — we are coming now to the object of the third and fourth book of Calvin's *Institutes* — there stands finally, unpolemically, and positively a very particular understanding of the existence of a personal, practical

---

78   See Barth's discussion on this in his *Ansatz und Absicht in Luthers Abendmahlslehre* (1923), in *V.u.kl.A. 1922–1925*, 248ff.; ET *T.u.C.*, 74–111.

79   On June 3, 1922, Barth gave a sermon on Col. 3:1f. in Göttingen entitled "Seek the things that are above!" See Karl Barth and Eduard Thurneysen, *Komm Schöpfer Geist! Predigten* (Münich, 1924), 171–179; *Come, Holy Spirit: Sermons*, George W. Richards, *et al.*, trans. (Grand Rapids, MI: William B. Eerdmans Publishing Company, 1978).

Christianity in the world. Nothing would be farther from the truth than the presumption that in the sheer light of the *"gloria Dei"* and *"meditatio futurae vitae"* we do not take seriously the situation of the human as we exist in time. On the contrary: It *has* come to this. The Reformed human, in front of whom the self-proclamation of God is placed like a boulder on the way, stands with both feet unbelievably firm upon the earth. He will praise the dark valley in which we wander not all too loudly and emphatically [cf. Ps. 23.4] as *God's* earthly ground since he knows that the world as the creation of *God* is likewise hidden from us and is revealed only to the Spirit and *his* knowledge, like the true humanity of Christ. But this very humble insight in and of itself, that only in hope can we be blessed in this dark valley [cf. Rom. 8.24], gives the Reformed human the position to take certain steps himself [cf. Heb. 12.13]. Within the entire Reformation, Reformed theology decisively represents the turn from viewing God (who in this temporality can only be *one*, not *everything*) back to viewing *life*, to *humans* and *their* position. Lutheranism also knows of this turn. However, we will not misjudge if we adhere at least to the alleged announcement of the *Augsburg Confession*,[80] which was whole-heartedly approved by Luther himself, that it has its strength somewhere else. It cannot be denied that in Lutheranism the turn to life is still somehow present, but only as something secondary, merely asserted, [239] and not completely necessary.

For the one-time humanists, Zwingli and Cavlin, the knowledge of the divine majesty is the primary but surprisingly heterogeneous answer to the question: "What is the chief end of human life?" [*Quis humanae vitae praecipuus et finis?*][81] The formulation that appeared in Calvin's catechism, where he handed over that overwhelming knowledge, came thoroughly *as an answer to this question*, namely, to know God.[82] That means especially to believe rightly, obey, pray, and give thanks.[83] One would like to say that a program of life presupposed entirely by the decisive activity of the human was established with an almost frightening certainty. The Reformed thinkers unmistakably come directly from this question, and not from the

<hr/>

80 Luther followed the proceedings of the parliament in Augsburg in 1530 from the castle at Coburg because of the imperial ban that was imposed upon him. On May 15, 1530, he wrote to the Prince Johann of Saxon: "I have read over the apology written by Philip Melanchthon, which I almost entirely like, and know nothing in it to improve or change . . ." (WA.B. 5: 319, 5f.; *LW* 49: 297).

81 *Genfer Katechismus* (1545), BSRK, 117: 7; ET *Treatises on the Sacraments*, 37.

82 Ibid., 117: 8; ET 37: "To know God by whom men were created."

83 Ibid., 117: 3–8; ET 38: "What is the method of honoring him duly? — To place our whole confidence in him; to study to serve him during our whole life by obeying his will; to call upon him in all our necessities, seeking salvation and every good thing that can be desired in him; lastly, to acknowledge him both with heart and lips, as the sole Author of all blessings."

specific question of monks about a gracious God.[84] Because of this, the inapproachable God of the Scriptures, who alone is active in the truth and who is strange to the world and to life, must apparently approach humans. In the face of this God, the human finally must find himself in his position on the *lower* stage, in the *creatureliness* that is not to be laid aside and that cannot be overlooked. Now the very knowledge of *this* God must recondition them to take *seriously* the illusion-free objectivity of the human-earthly question of "What ought to happen?" It must recondition them to take Zwingli seriously with *joy* and Calvin with *bitter* seriousness.

Not much depends upon *this* nuance, but the Calvinistic one is incontrovertibly more characteristic. Therefore, they speak of *faith* at the center as strongly as Luther did; and indeed, on this point they unmistakably speak as his grateful students. Yet unlike that of the Lutherans, the core of the Reformed faith does not lay in the fact that it is "*fiducia*,"[85] even though the Reformed Fathers certainly said this along with Luther,[86] but rather [240] in the fact that it is *God's gift*. Therefore *obedience* to the *demand* of this same God can now take its place alongside faith, independently and with no less significance.[87] The laborious considerations of the

---

84   See M. Luther, "Von der heiligen Taufe. Predigten" (1534), WA 37: 661, 20–27; cf. WA 36: 284, 31–33; WA 52: 236, 19–22.

85   See for example, Luther's *Large Catechism* (1529), *BSLK*, 560: 17–22; *BC*, 386: "As I have often said, it is the trust and faith of the heart alone that make both God and an idol. If your faith and trust are right, then your God is the true one." See also his *Genesis Lectures* (1535–1545), WA 42: 564, 5f.; *LW* 3: 22, on Gen. 15.6: "For faith is the firm and sure thought or trust that through Christ God is propitious and that through Christ His thoughts concerning us are thoughts of peace, not of affliction or wrath." See also Philip Melanchthon, *Commentarii in psalmos* (1553–1555), *CR* 13, col. 1340, on Ps. 112.7: "Furthermore, faith assenting to the promise is really trust in mercy alone, not only knowledge of history"; and his *Loci praecipui theologici* (1559), in *Melanchthons Werke*, Vol. II/2, H. Engelland, ed. (Gütersloh, 1953), 378: 21–23: "By faith, that is, by (our) trust in Christ are we justified, that is, because of Christ are we justified"; and ibid., 388: 425, 2–6.

86   See Note 83, p. 230. See also, for example, Calvin, *Institutes* III, 2,15, 561: "For this reason, the apostle derives confidence from faith, and from confidence, in turn, boldness. For such an apostle states: 'through Christ we have boldness and access with confidence which is through him in faith' [Eph. 3.12]." See also the compendium by P. Brunner, *Vom Glauben bei Calvin, antwurten Joannis Ecolampadii und Huldrychen Zuinglis* (1528), *CR* 93/II (= *Zwinglis Werke* 6/II), 194, 5–9: "'faith': therefore trust, that is, the spirit of whom should be a treasure and focusing of human trust [. . .] Faith, which is the firm trust and the highest good." Cf. also the *Confessio Helvetica posterior* (1562), *BSRK*, 193, 3f.; See Cochrane *The Second Helvetic Confession of 1566*, 257, "What is faith? Christian faith is not an opinion or human conviction but a most firm trust . . ."; *Heidelberger Katechismus* (1563), Q. 21, *BSRK*, 687, 28–33; ET Cochrane, *The Heidelberg Catechism, 1563*, 308: "Q. 21. What is true faith! A. It is not only a certain knowledge by which I accept as true all that God has revealed to us in his Word, but also a wholehearted trust which the Holy Spirit creates in me through the gospel . . ."

87   See Barth's related discussion on faith and obedience in *Unterricht*, 207–244 (para. 7, "Faith and Obedience"), esp. 211f.; ET 168–198, esp. 172, where "faith and obedience" are characterized by Barth as "so universal and distinctive that Reformed dogmatics cannot possibly fail to assert

Augsburg Confession as to whether and how far faith and good works do not exclude but include[88] each other [241] comes into play here, because faith in itself does not have the character of a hypothesis that contains the middle between God and the human as it does in Lutheranism, because here Christianity as a whole, including faith, wants to be nothing other than a series of *relationships* of the human to his Creator and Redeemer, because here in fact the talk ought to finally be about *God* and *only* God, the One who bestows *and* demands. But it ought not occur with the poignant clarity of Luther's talk about faith and faith alone. Therefore, there is on the one hand a relativizing of the act of faith as such, and on the other hand a serious, even if relative, validating of *penance*, which is valued not only as a preceding stage to faith but rather as a necessary, although in no way a deserved, act before the face of God.

That the Old Testament with its patriarchs, who never did arrive but continued to wander, has an enduring and positive meaning here, *even* with its Gospel — the Gospel as *law*, proclaimed to Moses; with its prophets who in no way applied themselves merely to the "inwardness" of the individual but to the *community of the people*; with its King David, in whom Calvin recognized more Elijah or himself rather than the model Jesus Christ.[89] What is *not* provided for here is a condition of humanity in which faith becomes capable in love, or in which the law can be suspended because everything happens out of freedom. Here, ethics are not founded upon life at all but upon obedience to the Commandments because they are *God's* Commandments. As something second, something different, the law appears again and again *next to* the Gospel, equally true and authoritative and necessary because the *one* God stands behind *both*, because the *one* Holy Spirit bestows both upon the human: The certainty of the justification of the sinner before God *and* the impulse toward sanctification of this same sinner by the same God. One is not to be confused with the other (not one iota may be changed in the purely imputed righteousness), but neither are they to be separated from one another, as if justification could also only be a moment without sanctification. Rather, both together and running parallel are the work of the Spirit of the Lord, whose very honor is illuminated in that *both* happen:

them." See also para. 19 in *Chr.D.*, 417–434, where Barth speaks of the "principle of the double relation": "We are following a scientific tradition of the Reformed school, in which we describe the relation of the human in revelation as a built-in *double* thing: as *faith and obedience*" (424ff.). On the mutual relationship between faith and obedience (and justification and sanctification) in the Reformed tradition, cf. Calvin *Institutes* III, 11, 6, 732: "Christ cannot be torn into parts, so these two which we perceive in him together and conjointly are inseparable, namely, righteousness and sanctification." See also HpB 448–460; ET 565–580.

88   *Augsburg Confession* (1530), Article XX, "Good Works," *BSLK*, 72: 14–78, 40; *BC*, 235–237.
89   See *CR* 59 (= *Calvini Opera* 31), cols. 19–36.

faith *and* obedience. But both happen as the answer to *God's* call; finally and most importantly, both [242] happen as *God's* work.

It was the victory of a foreign apocryphal interest that the question of the "certainty of salvation" was pushed into the center by the second and third generation (by Beza first, if I see it correctly, and then especially by the English Presbyterians), and thus became characteristic of the entire doctrine.[90] The Reformed Christian of the *first* generation was a fighter who did not have any time or interest in this petulant concern because he knew himself to be very well protected up there in the hand of the Lord. "Their salvation," said Calvin about the elect who build up the true Church, "is supported by such certain and solid beams that even if the entire world machine collapsed, it could not break and fall. For it stands with the election of God, and only in his infinite wisdom could it be changed or fall. Even if they therefore tremble and are torn here and there, or even if they fall, they still could not be destroyed, because the Lord holds them in his hand."[91]

Because of this invisible Church of God, the elect build themselves up with fear and trembling [cf. 2 Cor. 7.15 etc.]. [243] But they are also worldly and capable, and build up the visible human church that is constituted through the proper preaching of the Word of God, through the pure administration of the sacraments ordained by the Lord, but also through the discipline in which it maintains it members. Calvin

---

90 Theodor Beza (1519–1605) belonged to the first Reformed theologians who taught an interpretation of *fiducia* which deviated from that of Calvin. According to A. Walaeus (HpB 426; ET 534):

> The question on which there is disagreement among certain orthodox writers is, whether
> trust in God's mercy is a part of faith, or its form, its consequence and effect. Some think,
> among them Beza and Zanchius, that this trust is rather hope and the result and effect of
> faith rather than the form of faith itself or a part of it. We, however, with all respect to the
> judgment of these gentlemen, feel together with most writers of the Reformed Church
> [. . .] that trust is the very form of faith as justifying and its noblest part, or at least that it is
> included in justifying faith.

See also the description by H. Heppe, *Theodor Beza. Leben und ausgewählte Schriften*, in *Leben und
ausgewählte Schriften der Väter und Begründer der reformierten Kirche*, Part IV (Eberfeld, 1861), 347–359,
"The interest in an unshakable fortification of the evangelical faith and certainty of salvation
appeared in Beza in its full strength and meaning. Indeed, one can say that Beza is characterized
precisely through this" (348). For more on the English Presbyterians, cf. *Die Lambeth-Artikel* (1595),
BSRK, 525, 31–33; Schaff III, 523–525; *Westminster Confession*, chapter XVIII: "On Assurance of
Grace and Salvation," BSRK, 579, 1–581, 11; the *Large Westminster Catechism* (1647), BSRK, 622,
18–34; *Book of Confessions*, Q. 80, 206.

91 Calvin, *Institutio religionis Christianae* (1536), CR 29 (= *Calvini Opera* I), col. 73:

> Nititur enim eorum salus tam certis solidisque fulcris ut, etiamsi tota orbis machina labefacteur,
> concidere ipsa et corruere non possit. Primum, stat cum Dei electione, nec nisi cum aeterna
> illa sapientia, variare aut deficere potest. Titubare ergo et fluctuari, cadere etiam possunt, sed
> non colliduntur, quia Dominus supponit manum suam.

consciously did *not* go along with the all-too-resigned interpretation of the "communion of saints" [*communio sanctorum*] in the *Augsburg Confession*,[92] which does not want to know *anything* of the sanctified *human* except to dream of a church of saints and a community founded upon love.[93] Not to be confused with the holiness of God *above*, there *is* a sanctification of the individual in the congregation *here below*. It is *not* a good work, *not* a bridge to heaven, *not* unification with divinity, *not* an anticipation of the final condition but, indeed, a necessary indication of the idea in the Bible that is not to be explained away. It is an indication of the thousand-year kingdom [cf. Rev. 20.1-6] and a demonstration of the honor of God, which especially in view of the infinite goal of the future life [*vita futura*][94] *must* come despite every fragility of our will and achievement as the wanderers we are.

   The content of the Scripture principle is also the mechanism in the doctrine of the Third Article, namely, from the Holy Spirit and his works. The Fathers meant this to be understood by the human through assigned positions and tasks of the Word of God, so that the human *recognizes God*, as Calvin so finely said. But this particular thing unfolded itself to them with *more* than a question to the Bible, that is, the *entire* Bible, with a plethora of answers that are related to each other like a series of parallel straight lines that can never cross in this finite world: The burning concern is for the human to become and remain a *tree, planted by streams of water*, but another also that *the human yields fruit in his time* [Ps.1.3]. Therefore Paul's Letter to the Romans is urged here, but the *Letter to James* is *not* to be held in suspicion as a mere "straw Epistle."[95] The heart of the human, even the believing human, [244] is only capable of understanding these as one thing only in so far as he recognizes the necessity of *God's* glorification in both: The foundation and the system of that which always appears as a duality of human act and experience rests in *God* and *only* in God, but it *does* rest in God, and therefore this duality, *is valid* for the life of humans. There *is* a duality, indeed, a many-sidedness for Calvin, an obedience *next to* faith, a praying *next to* obedience, a visible congregation giving thanks to God *next to* that of the invisible one of the elect.[96] All this is certainly *one* in God, but it is not therefore to be taken less seriously by us humans,

---

92 See *Augsburg Confession* (1530), Article VII, "The Church," and Article VIII, "What is the Church?" *BSLK*, 59: 15–61, 11; *BC*, 42–43.

93 See *Institutes* IV, 1, 3, 1014.

94 See *Institutes*, III, 9, "Meditation on the future life"; ibid., 9, 4, 716: "But until we leave the world, 'we are away from the Lord' [2 Cor. 5.6]."

95 See Luther, WA.DB 6: 10, 33f; *LW* 35: 362; and *BSRK*, 155: 19–21.

96 See *Institutes* IV, 1, 7, 1021f.

each one of us using our own particular, *earthly* Christian logic. It is enough that we in our contradiction,[97] in the *different* relationships *to God* in which we stand, have *everything*: humiliation and restoration, unrest and peace, comfort and warning, enlightenment and instruction. We have everything in the fact that we thus stand before *God*, truly as creatures of the Creator and as members of the body of Christ. The Fathers meant that the answer to the question of the goal of human life [*vita humana*] in the Old *and* New Covenants must be understood in this way. What ought we say to that? If we are going to grab hold of this and claim an understanding and say a happy "Yes" somewhere, that place is here. But if this is the place for the freedom and sobriety of Reformed doctrine, then here it must be about our becoming mature.

The entire sacredness and power of Reformed doctrine rests in the fundamental *separation* between the heavenly, unified, and the earthly, manifold solutions to the problem of life, between fulfillment and promise — courageously taking the latter seriously when placed in the light of the former — and also in its entire uniqueness (despite, no, because of, the separation!). Its penultimate presupposition is the typical Reformed *wakefulness*, for which the *entire* human life [*vita humana*] has become a real and unresolved problem and question. Reformed doctrtine also encompasses the typical Reformed readiness in a real and unbiased manner, which now lets the *entire* Bible answer the question. In one word, it is the typical Reformed *universalism*, which is less extensive than intensive. It is the risk and the compulsion to go with God through it all. Its *final* presupposition, however, is the [245] majesty of a God who speaks through the Scripture and the Spirit to the race of the *present*, to *ourselves*. To want to *repeat* what has *already been* said to us by the Fathers without reflection upon these presuppositions, and in particular on the last one, would be foolish and dangerous, even if it were to be repeated in such a compelling, empathic, and certain manner.

All this becomes truth and life and therefore the *way* [Jn 14.6] by it being newly generated from the same presuppositions as those of the Fathers. Not only *may* they be said *today*, they *must* be said. These doctrines were constructed not in the brilliant morning, but in the dusky evening of the Reformation, when the shadows had become longer and the insight unavoidable that not every budding dream blossoms.[98] That we find ourselves in *this* situation, in the grim *renunciation* by which it is characterized, that we represent *this* "old sacred inheritance," is not

---

97 See C.F. Meyer, *Huttens letzte Tage. Eine Dichtung*, XXVI, "Homo sum": "Das heißt: ich bin kein ausgeklügelt Buch,/Ich bin ein Mensch mit seinem Widerspruch."

98 See J.W. Goethe's poem "Prometheus" (1785): "Wähntest du etwa,/Ich sollte das Leben hassen,/In Wüsten fliehen,/Weil nicht alle/Blütenträume reiften?"

even as self-evident as today's presenter would like to fool himself into believing. We all come more or less from the small, narrow, "religious" side, from the problematic of real life, from the less mature but undisputedly enthusiastic, profound, theologically satisfying, spiritual thoughts of Lutheranism. They undoubtedly possess the "German mind" but also, in a somewhat more rationalized form, the so-called religious need of the average churchgoing public on this *and* that side of the German border. We theologians will continually feel pulled almost magnetically to the (at least apparent) central orientation of Lutheranism in particular. It is indeed worth making clear what we forfeit with this; indeed some Reformed individuals would be better off giving no more advice than that, namely, to become fundamentally Lutheran, like Zwingli and Calvin were.

The decisive step beyond Lutheranism and the *Augsburg Confession* is risky — I still do not yet see clearly enough whether it actually at the same time is taking a step back to the *young* Luther. It leads to the desert, where not only deprivation but temptation awaits us. For, where [246] the Word of God is clearly understood as an answer to the human question of life, there next to liberating knowledge lurks the worst misunderstandings and abuse. Everything then depends upon an unwavering adherence to the fact that even the human question about life is the question of *God* that is posed to the human. It is actually not easy to hold on to this. Even the words and deeds risked by Zwingli and Calvin themselves in the tendencies visible in their doctrines of the Spirit stand only a hair's breadth away from the boundary of something seriously alarming.

After them in any case, even in the Reformed churches, the glorification of God has become the most objectionable self-glorification of the human. How should the most difficult cases of misfortune, how should the large or small Pharisaical church with all of its abominations be avoided if *we* arm ourselves with spirituality, but not the spirit of the Fathers? For the sake of pure Reformed doctrine — and until we risk picking up the lost trail once again — the word must be, "Please no Calvinistic experiments! They could only bring evil to us!"[99]

With all this being said, now the other thing must be said, namely, that the implications of Reformed doctrine must be drawn out along the lines of this direction. The grim renunciation of an overly one-sided religiosity, of an overly great depth and unity (with a view toward *the* systematic, which God has reserved for himself) is the theological commandment of the hour; the criticism of the Gospel *and* law is the most real message

---

99 On this traditional saying of Greek antiquity, which cannot be traced back to a particular origin, see E.L. von Leutsch and F.G. Schneidewin, *Corpus Paroemiographorum Graecorum*, 2 Vols. (Göttingen, 1839/1851), Vol. 1, 276, 368, and Vol. 2, 528.

of salvation for those of us in the declining West;[100] the constituting of a congregation that stands under the judgment of God, as that which is not only permitted but is a necessary possibility for the Church. A Reformed doctrine of the Holy Spirit would then be our urgent task. It would be at that point where we would once again face the witness of God's revelation from *our* position, with *our* eyes, as the Fathers did from *their* position with *their* eyes. Before this happens, even that task cannot be grasped with full power. Reformed doctrine will therefore have to be what it is now: a torso — less — a silhouette.

As is customary in such lectures, I wish I could now close with a glad blast of the trumpet, but I cannot present the situation in any other way — even by way of conclusion — than what we must see here today. On every side there is a greatly advanced vision of history but little of its own existential, reliable knowledge. It shows the ways, but not many of them are accessible; indeed, there is great hope but barely any power to give birth [cf. Isa. 37.3]. In the middle, where we stand, there is a great weakness. Should we call this fault or fate? "Reformed doctrine" is possible at least on that point where we take our weakness seriously and call it without reserve *fault, not fate*. In the longing, in the crying for the Creator Spirit,[101] which will once again blow across even this field, full of dry bones [cf. Ezek. 37.1, 9], we will meet up with the Fathers, whose legacy we have not yet earned fully enough to own.[102]

100 This is an allusion to Otto Spengler's *Der Untergang des Abendlandes*, 2 Vols. (Munich, 1918/1922; a new edition was published in one volume in Zurich, 1980); ET *The Decline of the West,* Charles Francis Atkinson, trans., (New York: Alfred A. Knopf, 1992).

101 See the beginning of the hymn of Pentecost by Hrabanus Maurus (c. 776–856): "Veni creator spiritus" (*EKG*, 97).

102 See J.W. Goethe, *Faust I*, V, 682f. (Nacht): "Was du ererbt von deinen Vätern hast,/Erwirb es, um es zu besitzen."; ET *Goethe's Faust,* Walter Kaufmann, trans. (New York: Anchor Books, [1961] 1963), 115 (Nighttime scene): "What from your fathers you received as heir,/Acquire if you would possess it."

INDEX